Eagles over the Sea
1943–1945

A History of Luftwaffe Maritime Operations

Lawrence Paterson

Seaforth
PUBLISHING

This book is dedicated to the memory of Philip John Taylor.
The original Animal.

First published in Great Britain in 2020 by
Seaforth Publishing,
A division of Pen & Sword Books Ltd,
47 Church Street,
Barnsley S70 2AS
www.seaforthpublishing.com
British Library Cataloguing in Publication Data
A catalogue record for this book is available from the British Library

ISBN 978 1 5267 7765 2 (HARDBACK)
ISBN 978 1 5267 7767 6 (KINDLE)
ISBN 978 1 5267 7766 9 (EPUB)

Pen & Sword Books Limited incorporates the imprints of Atlas,
Archaeology, Aviation, Discovery, Family History, Fiction, History, Maritime, Military,
Military Classics, Politics, Select, Transport, True Crime, Air World, Frontline Publishing,
Leo Cooper, Remember When, Seaforth Publishing, The Praetorian Press, Wharncliffe
Local History, Wharncliffe Transport, Wharncliffe True Crime and White Owl

Typeset and designed by JCS Publishing Services Ltd

Printed and bound in Great Britain by TJ International Ltd, Padstow

Contents

Acknowledgements

Tʜɪs ɪs ᴛʜᴇ sᴇᴄᴏɴᴅ part of a story that had been designed as a single volume. However, the more I learned, the more I realised the breadth of this topic. Therefore, one book became two. With that in mind there still was no room to fully concentrate attention on many aspects of Luftwaffe maritime operations, such as those of the *Seenotdienst* (air-sea rescue), the shipboard aircraft that travelled as far as New Zealand waters aboard commerce raiders and those seagoing vessels used in support of the Luftwaffe, ranging from recovery ships to Siebel ferries. I have retained a focus on combat operations, and while those of the first volume featured heavily the *Küstenflieger* – the naval air arm – those of the second revolved more around the Luftwaffe's conventional bombing units converted to maritime specialists. There are many threads that lead off into the opportunistic maritime strikes by Junkers Ju 87 dive-bombers and various fighter-bomber units, but unless *specifically* maritime, I have not dealt with these other than in passing. Where fighter-bombers were assigned anti-shipping missions, I have included them. However, this is not a history of the Luftwaffe as a whole, and therefore I have attempted to retain that tight focus on maritime missions. Otherwise one book would have become five!

I would like to thank the following people for their help and support during the researching and writing of these volumes. First, my wife Anna Paterson, who now knows more about the Luftwaffe than she ever expected, my kids James and Megan and my mother, Audrey 'Mumbles' Paterson, and Don 'Mr Mumbles', who are all no doubt wondering what I'm going to do next.

I am also of course indebted to all at Seaforth Publishing for allowing me to turn one book into two. The first volume was brilliantly produced by them and I hope this matching volume fits the bill. I have worked with Rob Gardiner and Julian Mannering since the days when they were at Chatham and have the highest regard for everything that they do and the great books they manage to create out of pages of jumbled manuscript. Thanks to James Payne (Through Their Eyes Military Photo Archive) for access to his photographs and also Leighton DeMicoli for the photos from his family's history.

As I said previously, this is my first foray into the world of the Luftwaffe and it was quite an eye-opener in more ways than expected. As well as pages and pages of original documents available through international archives, there is also a phenomenal amount of knowledge freely shared by people on the Internet, for which I am very grateful. It is easy to sneer at Internet sources, as for every gem there is the equivalent lump of coal (if not more than one), but it can be a very valuable resource for connecting with people who have made the study of certain subjects one of their life's great passions. As with printed books, there is never any replacement for your own independent verification, but it can be a fantastic starting point, if not more. There are myriad forums discussing the Luftwaffe and its role in the Second World War, dealing with everything from strategic operations to the minutiae of uniforms and decorations. Though I am often just a bystander in many of these 'conversations', they have been both informative and enlightening and push your deeper research in directions that may not have seemed so obvious before. I will list some of the most informative in the Bibliography, though the list will by no means be complete.

Likewise, thank you to the many authors who have written fascinating books about the Luftwaffe, without whom I wouldn't have known where to begin.

Glossary

ASV	Air-to-surface-vessel (radar).
ASW	Anti-submarine warfare.
B.d.U.	*Befehlshaber der U-Boote*, Commander-in-Chief, submarines.
B-Dienst	*Beobachtungsdienst des feindlich Funkerverkehrs*, Kriegsmarine radio monitoring and cryptographic intelligence service.
Bordflieger	Shipboard-carried air units, or, alternatively, the pilot of such an aircraft.
CAM ship	Catapult Aircraft Merchant ship; freighter equipped with catapult and fighter, a stopgap measure until the introduction of escort carriers.
Ehrenpokal	An 'honour goblet' awarded by Göring's authority for special achievement.
Fliegerdivison	Early war subdivision of a *Fliegerkorps*. Kept in use for certain specialised formations.
Fliegerführer	Theatre air commander, e.g. *Fliegerführer Atlantik*, *Fliegerführer Tunis*, etc.
Fliegerkorps	Largest operational level subdivision of *Luftflotte*. Numbered consecutively with Roman Numerals, e.g. IX.*Fliegerkorps*.
Flughafenbetrieb-skompanie	(FBK) Company assigned to repair and service aircraft of a specific heavy *Gruppe*; i.e. KG, ZG and StG.
F.d.Luft	*Führer der Seeluftstreitkräfte*, Commander of maritime combat aviation.

F.d.U.	*Führer der U-boote*, early war designation for Commander submarines, later war regional sub-command.
Geschwader	Luftwaffe equivalent to an Allied Air Group.
Gruppe	Luftwaffe equivalent to an Allied 'Wing' (plural *Gruppen*).
IFF	'Identification Friend or Foe'; transponder system installed on aircraft that received a radar signal, amplified it and returned it, making the screen 'blip' appear larger than normal and therefore, theoretically, identifying the aircraft as friendly.
JG	(*Jagdgeschwader*), day fighter single-engine aircraft such as the Bf 109.
Kampfgruppe	Independent bomber formation of *Gruppe* size.
Kette	Flight of three aircraft.
KG	(*Kampfgeschwader*), heavy or medium bombers such as the He 111.
Kommandeur	Commander of a unit, particularly in Luftwaffe use for *Gruppe* commander, not an actual rank.
Kommodore	In the Luftwaffe a *Geschwader* commander, not an actual rank.
Kriegsmarine	German Navy between 1935 and 1945.
Küstenflieger	Luftwaffe equivalent to the Fleet Air Arm.
LG	(*Lehrgeschwader*), advanced training unit often each *Gruppe* of a different aircraft type.
Luftwaffe	German Air Force from 1935 onwards. The term 'operational Luftwaffe' is used here to separate orthodox Luftwaffe units from the *Küstenflieger* and other naval flying units.
Luftflotte	Luftwaffe Air Fleet equivalent to an American numbered Air Force. Numbered consecutively with Arabic numerals, e.g. *Luftflotte* 4.
Luftmine	(LM) Air-dropped mine.

Marinegruppen-kommando	Regional command of Kriegsmarine security forces such as minesweeping, submarine hunters, patrol boats and so on, e.g. *Marinegruppenkommando West*. Abbreviated to '*MGK*'.
MCLOS	Manual command to line of sight weapon guidance system.
OKH	*Oberkommando der Heeres*, Army High Command.
OKL	*Oberkommando der Luftwaffe*, Air Force High Command. Properly established in February 1944, previously designated *Reichsluftfahrtministerium* (*RLM*, Reich Air Ministry).
OKM	*Oberkommando der Kriegsmarine*, Naval High Command.
OKW	Oberkommando der Wehrmacht, Armed Forces High Command.
Pulk	A heavy aircraft combat box, created to provide grouped machine-gun defence.
Radar	An acronym for radio detection and ranging first coined by a US naval officer. Known to the British originally as RDF (radio direction finding).
Reichsmarine	Pre-war German Navy, renamed Kriegsmarine in 1935.
RLM	*Reichsluftfahrtministerium* (Reich Air Ministry).
Staffel	Roughly the Luftwaffe equivalent to an Allied Squadron (plural *Staffeln*).
Staffelkapitän	Squadron Commander, abbreviated to '*Staka*'.
StG	(*Sturzkampfgeschwader*), typically Ju 87 Stukas during the early years of the war.
ZG	(*Zerstörergeschwader*), day fighter twin-engine aircraft such as the Bf 110.

Equivalent Rank Table:

Luftwaffe	Kriegsmarine	Royal Air Force/US Army Air Force
Generalfeldmarschall (GFM)	Grossadmiral	Marshal of the Air Force/General of the Army
Generaloberst (Genobst)	Generaladmiral	Air Chief Marshal/General
General der Flieger (Gen. der Flg)	Admiral	Air Marshal/Lieutenant General
Generalleutnant (Genlt)	Konteradmiral	Air Vice-Marshal/Major General
Generalmajor (Genmaj.)	Vizeadmiral	Air Commodore/Brigadier General
Oberst (Obst.)	Kapitän zur See	Group Captain/Colonel
Oberstleutnant (Obstlt.)	Fregattenkapitän	Wing Commander/Lieutenant Colonel
Major (Maj.)	Korvettenkapitän (K.K.)	Squadron Leader/Major
Hauptmann (Hptm.)	Kapitänleutnant (Kaptlt.)	Flight Lieutenant/Captain
Oberleutnant (Oblt.)	Oberleutnant zur See (Oblt.z.S.)	Flying Officer/First Lieutenant
Leutnant (Lt.)	Leutnant zur See (Lt.z.S.)	Pilot Officer/Second Lieutenant
Stabsfeldwebel (Stabsfw.)	Stabsoberfeldwebel	Warrant Officer/Master Sergeant
Oberfeldwebel (Obfw.)	Stabsfeldwebel	Flight Sergeant/Technical Sergeant
Feldwebel (Fw.)	Feldwebel	Sergeant/Staff Sergeant
Fähnrich (Fhr.)	Fähnrich zur See	Officer Cadet/Flight Cadet

Unterfeldwebel (Ufw.)	Obermaat	Corporal/Sergeant
Unteroffizier (Uffz.)	Maat	Corporal/Corporal
Hauptgefreiter (Hpt. Gefr.)	Matrosenhauptgefreiter	Senior Aircraftman/ Private First Class
Obergefreiter (Ob. Gefr.)	Matrosenobergefreiter	Leading Aircraftman/Private First Class
Gefreiter (Gefr.)	Matrosengefreiter	Aircraftman 1st Class/Private First Class
Flieger (Flg.)	Matrose	Aircraftman 2nd Class/Private

Luftwaffe Operational Organisation:

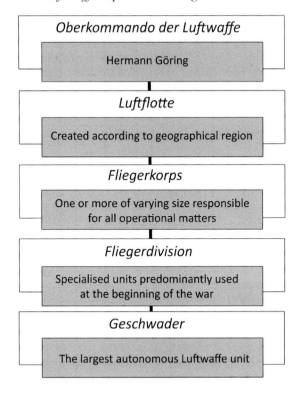

Oberkommando der Luftwaffe

Hermann Göring

Luftflotte

Created according to geographical region

Fliegerkorps

One or more of varying size responsible for all operational matters

Fliegerdivision

Specialised units predominantly used at the beginning of the war

Geschwader

The largest autonomous Luftwaffe unit

Tactical Level Luftwaffe Organisational Notes

Though local circumstances could dictate modification to existing unit structure, the general form of a Luftwaffe *Geschwader* was as follows:

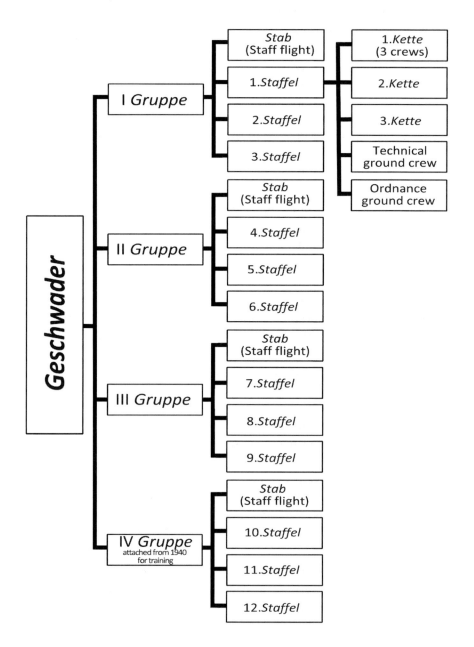

Geschwader: The largest homogeneous Luftwaffe flying unit, roughly the equivalent of an RAF 'Group' or USAAF 'Wing'. Comprising three '*Gruppen*', the *Geschwader* was named according to its purpose and its individual identity suffixed by Arabic numerals, such as KG 26. Amongst the most common identification prefixes within this work are:

Fighters: JG (*Jagdgeschwader*), day fighter single-engine aircraft such as the Bf 109.

Heavy Fighters: ZG (*Zerstörergeschwader*), day fighter twin-engine aircraft such as the Bf 110.

Bombers: KG (*Kampfgeschwader*), heavy or medium bombers such as the He 111.

Dive-bombers: StG (*Sturzkampfgeschwader*), typically Ju 87 Stukas during the early years of the war.

Advanced Training: LG (*Lehrgeschwader*), often each *Gruppe* of a different aircraft type.

The *Geschwader* was commanded by a *Geschwaderkommodore*, typically of rank between *Oberstleutnant* or *Major*. He would have a small staff and a *Stabschwarm* (staff flight) of perhaps four aircraft including one belonging to the *Geschwaderkommodore*.

Gruppe: The basic autonomous Luftwaffe flying unit, roughly equivalent to an RAF 'Wing' and USAAF 'Group'. Typically comprised of a *Stabschwarm* (staff flight) and three *Staffeln* commanded by a *Gruppenkommandeur*, who could be a *Major* or *Hauptmann*. He would have a small staff including administration, operations, medical and technical officers. Each *Gruppe* was identified with a roman numeral (e.g. II.*Gruppe* of 26th Bomber *Geschwader* would be II./ KG 26). The exception to this rule were those *Gruppen* acting in autonomous specialised maritime of reconnaissance roles, such as the *Küstenfliegergruppen* (coastal maritime aircraft) *Aufklärungsgruppen (F)* (long-range reconnaissance), *Bordfliegergruppen* (aircraft carried aboard surface ships), *Seeaufklärungsgruppen* (maritime reconnaissance) and *Trägergruppen* (carrier aircraft), which were designated using Arabic numerals.

Staffel: Roughly the equivalent to an Allied Squadron, comprised of between nine to twelve aircraft and commanded by a *Staffelkapitän* (abbreviated to '*Staka*') generally of a rank between *Hauptmann* and *Leutnant* as the most junior example. The *Staffeln* were numbered consecutively within the *Geschwader* with Arabic numerals (e.g. third *Staffel* of 26th Bomber *Geschwader* would be 3./KG 26) therefore it would always be possible to identify the first three *Staffeln* as belonging to I.*Gruppe*, *Staffeln* 4-6 to II *Gruppe*, and so on. Each *Staffel* generally comprised three *Ketten* of three aircraft each, and associated ground crew.

Numbering of Luftwaffe Aircraft

Luftwaffe aircraft markings are a multifaceted and intricate subject that involves symbols and colour codes each denoting a unit or position within the command structure. The system evolved continuously until 24 October 1939 when a compact four-digit code was introduced. This is simply an introduction to the adopted four-letter numbering system used to identify all aircraft, except for *Jagdgeschwader* who had a separate complex system and are outside the scope of this study. The code is divided with an alphanumeric pair of characters to the left of the *Balkenkreuz* – the famous cross that adorned Luftwaffe aircraft – and two letters to the right. The two characters to the left indicate the parent *Geschwader* (or *Gruppe*) to which the aircraft belonged. To the right of the Balkenkreuz the third letter, usually colour-coded, indicated the individual aircraft number and the last the *Staffel*.

Four-digit *Staffel* letters: *Geschwader* Stab.: A

(I *Gruppe*) Stab.: B	1.*Staffel*: H	2.*Staffel*: K	3.*Staffel*: L
(II *Gruppe*) Stab.: C	4. *Staffel*: M	5.*Staffel*: N	6.*Staffel*: P
(III *Gruppe*) Stab.: D	7. *Staffel*: R	8.*Staffel*: S	9.*Staffel*: T
(IV *Gruppe*) Stab.: E	10.*Staffel*: U	11.*Staffel*: V	12.*Staffel*: W

You will find frequent mentions of such four-digit codes within the text to identify various aircraft, written as so: M2+SL. In this particular case, the numbers denote aircraft 'S' of 3.*Staffel* ('L') belonging to *Küstenfliegergruppe* 106 (M2). Below are relevant unit two-letter coding (used from October 1939) for the units mentioned within this book:

1./BFl.Gr. 196: T3
5./BFl.Gr. 196: 6W
FAGr. 5: 9G
KG 26: 1H
KG 30: 4D
KG 40: F8

KG 54: B3
KG 77: 3Z
KG 100: 6N
KGr. 126: 1T (also used by aircraft of III./KG 26 between January 1942 and February 1943)
Kü.Fl.Gr. 406: K6
Kü.Fl.Gr. 506 and KGr. 506: S4 (originally M7)
Kü.Fl.Gr. 706: 6I
Kü.Fl.Gr. 906: 8L
Küstenfliegerstaffel Krim: 6M
LG 1: L1
Minensuchgruppe der Luftwaffe ('*Mausi*' aircraft): 3K
SAGr. 125: 7R
SAGr. 126: D1
SAGr. 127: 6R
SAGr. 128: 6W
SAGr. 129: X4
SAGr. 130: 6I
SAGr. 131: 8L
2.Seenotstaffel: N7
3.Seenotstaffel: M6
5.Seenotstaffel: P7
6.Seenotstaffel: K3
7.Seenotstaffel: J9
8.Seenotstaffel: M1
10.Seenotstaffel: 5W

The Battlefield

1

Battles Over the Bay

The Atlantic

> To make war on England requires material and mental preparations in peacetime in such a way that it will be possible to knock her out in the first round. For the English have time as their ally in war, whereas we could win only by a blitzkrieg. Since we have emphasized that any war against England is out of the question, and as we did not prepare for it mentally or materially, it is too much to expect that we might defeat her. I can't believe that we will win such a war.[1]

General der Flieger Ulrich Kessler made these remarks to Göring in September 1938 and his opinion had changed little by the time he was appointed *Fliegerführer Atlantik* in February 1942. A veteran naval pilot from the First World War, he had transferred to the Luftwaffe during 1933 and commanded *Küstenfliegergruppe* 106 while simultaneously commandant of the *Seefliegerhorst* Sylt during the heady days when a naval air arm seemed possible under the leadership of *Grossadmiral* Raeder. The years that followed proved the lie to the myth of such an autonomous service branch, steadily absorbed into the all-pervasive realm of the Luftwaffe. By the time Kessler succeeded temporary *Fliegerführer* Wolfgang von Wild in early 1942, the post responsible for reconnaissance and anti-shipping operations over the eastern Atlantic was already a shadow of its former self. Established under the auspices of veteran naval flier Martin Harlinghausen a little over a year previously, *Fliegerführer Atlantik* had been designed to assist Karl Dönitz's U-boats with reconnaissance missions while also posing its own direct threat to precious Allied merchant traffic, but a steady rate of attrition combined with Luftwaffe resources diverted to other sectors of the expanding German war had stripped Kessler's command.

The focus of Luftwaffe maritime operations had changed during the early months of 1942 from the Atlantic to both the Arctic and Mediterranean. From northern Norway, Luftwaffe torpedo

General der Flieger Ulrich Kessler, photographed here aboard *U234* at the time of his surrender in 1945.

aircraft and bombers attempted to destroy the PQ convoys bringing badly needed supplies to an embattled Soviet Union, while in the Mediterranean the siege of Malta and attempted support for Rommel's *Afrika Korps* resulted in attempts to destroy Malta convoys while also protecting crucial Axis supply lines between Italy and Libya. Though both theatres experienced brief moments of triumph, neither would ultimately achieve their purpose. Even the war against the Soviet Navy in the Black Sea had necessitated the transfer of Luftwaffe maritime aircraft to the Eastern Front.

Dönitz's U-boat war had moved west at the end of 1941 after the German declaration of war on the United States of America. His U-boats patrolled the eastern American seaboard, stretching from Canada to Florida, also poised to enter the Gulf of Mexico and mount a concerted assault on Caribbean merchant traffic, including valuable tankers from Venezuela's oil terminals. The battle was fought well beyond the range of *Fliegerführer Atlantik*'s aircraft, thereby freeing them for service deemed more useful. The heavier aircraft, including torpedo bombers, were despatched to the Arctic while the shorter-range aircraft still available to Kessler were only suitable for anti-convoy operations near the British south-west coast. To bolster such meagre strength, bombers of IX.*Fliegerkorps* took responsibility for anti-shipping operations in the North Sea and along the eastern British seaboard. Reconnaissance of the Gibraltar convoy route remained the sole area in which Kessler could hope to cooperate with *B.d.U.*, while escorting of incoming blockade-runners carrying valuable raw materials and technological information from Japan had been undertaken since the previous year and remained fully within Kessler's remit in cooperation with warships of *Marinegruppenkommando West*.

Between April 1941 and February 1942 fifteen Axis ships had departed Japanese ports bound for Europe laden with materials valuable to the war effort, including rubber, metals or metallic ore and edible and industrial oils. The French port of Bordeaux was selected as the main reception terminus and during this first blockade-running 'season' eleven of the fifteen ships traversed the Pacific to round Cape Horn and arrive under naval and Luftwaffe escort during the final run through Biscay. Three ships – MV *Elbe*, *Odenwald* and *Spreewald* – had been sunk en-route and another. MV *Ramses*, turned back, but a total of 74,952 tons of material had been received, including 32,027 tons of raw rubber and 2,747 tons of high-grade metal ores. The last of this initial wave of successful blockade-runners, MV *Portland*, entered Bordeaux on 10 May 1942.

Later, submarines would also be used to transport technological information, key personnel and quantities of raw materials between Europe and the Far East. The Japanese instigated this during 1942 when they despatched *I30* during June on a 'Yanagi' mission to France, escorted into Lorient harbour by a strong minesweeper escort and Ju 88 aircraft on 5 August. Though the cargo capacity of submarines was far below that of the large surface blockade breakers, *I30* carried 1,500kg of mica and 650kg of shellac as its main cargo, also bringing blueprints for the Type 91 aerial torpedo following requests from Harlinghausen as head of the Luftwaffe's torpedo research institute.

The safe arrival of *I30* was both a practical success for the German war effort and of huge propaganda value, presented in newsreel footage as a demonstration that Axis naval forces could safely traverse the world's oceans. The reality was far bleaker. U-boats had been suffering severe depredation at the hands of Allied air forces in the Bay of Biscay, both through minelaying and radar-assisted attacks. The Luftwaffe forces available to *Fliegerführer Atlantik* to counter these had been trimmed to the very bone.

At the beginning of Kessler's tenure in February 1942 the first two *Staffeln* of *Küstenfliegergruppe* 906 had been based around Brest in support of U-boat operations, under the control of Stab/Kü.Fl.Gr. 406 (whose own *Staffeln* were operational in Norway), while 3./Kü.Fl.Gr. 906 lay at readiness under the command of *Oblt.* Wolf-Friedrich Schöne in Tromsø, Norway. *Marinegruppenkommando West* had reported to *SKL* that, following the removal of 1./KG 40 to Norway, *Fliegerführer Atlantik* would be able to muster only an average of five He 111s and four He 115s until further notice, rendering it 'no longer possible to provide adequate reconnaissance for the Group's operations – even of a small area – for more than a few hours before operations are launched'.[2] Matters became worse at the end of March when all of KG 26's Heinkels, the Luftwaffe's primary anti-shipping unit, were relocated to Norway to reinforce attacks on the Arctic convoys and both *Stab* and *Hptm.* Siegfried Kriebel's 2./Kü.Fl.Gr. 906 were withdrawn from active duty. Furthermore, on 14 April 1942:

> The Commander in Chief, Air reports that, effective immediately, orders were given to dissolve [Stab and 2. *Staffel*] *Küstenfliegergruppe* 906. The flying personnel and equipment thus becoming available is to be used by the Luftwaffe General attached to the Commander in Chief, Navy to bring up to strength *Küstenfliegerstaffeln* 1./Kü.Fl.Gr. 406 and 1./Kü.Fl. Gr. 906 (torpedo plane squadrons in Norway) under the command of *Luftflotte* 5. This removes the last He 115 squadron from the West Area. *Marinegruppenkommando West* is notified accordingly and it was pointed out that – apart from these measures – the Naval Staff has submitted a request to the Luftwaffe Operations Staff that reconnaissance forces of *Fliegerführer Atlantik* should be reinforced considerably.[3]

The eight He 115s and seven crews of the disbanded units were distributed between 1./Kü.Fl.Gr. 406 and 1./Kü.Fl.Gr. 906; the former already based in northern Norway, while *Hptm.* Siegfried Kriebel's latter unit moved to Stavanger by April. On 7 April *Fliegerführer Atlantik* was placed under the command of *Generalfeldmarschall* Hugo Sperrle's *Luftflotte* 3, based in France, which in turn had been seriously depleted by the demands of other theatres of operations.

The Kriegsmarine loudly complained in Berlin at the lack of available aerial support and reconnaissance. During June, the ability of the RAF to successfully penetrate Norwegian airspace and reconnoitre German surface fleet dispositions, adjusting their own convoy escort dispositions accordingly, led an exasperated *SKL* to once again

The He 115; an obsolete design by 1942 but still flown by the few *Küstenfliegerstaffeln* that remained operational.

admonish the Luftwaffe for what they considered their lacklustre approach to naval warfare.

> The fundamental importance of continuous air reconnaissance has repeatedly been emphasized to the Luftwaffe Operations Staff by the Naval Staff. So far, however, the shortage of aircraft has made it impossible to permit consideration of this request. As a result, the Luftwaffe will simply have to acknowledge once more that the RAF is numerically better able to cope with the, more or less, self-evident fundamental requirements of any sort of naval warfare. This example shows with striking clarity a discrepancy which can never be sufficiently regretted, namely the absence of a naval air force or even a certain amount of authority of naval commanders over air forces.[4]

Such a lack of available reconnaissance aircraft was later cited as a contributory factor to the success of Operation *Chariot*, the successful British commando raid on Saint-Nazaire that disabled the Normandie dry-dock, the only one capable of servicing the *Tirpitz* on the Atlantic coast. Following the attack during the early morning darkness of 28

5

March, *MGK West* specifically cited the fact that: 'The enemy surprise attack was successful because we lacked continuous air reconnaissance [and] it was impossible to effectively pursue the withdrawing enemy due to a shortage of sufficient fast strong naval forces, sufficient reconnaissance, as well as bombers available for immediate use.'[5] The withdrawing Royal Navy vessels were joined by escorting destroyers and sighted by an He 115 of *Küstenfliegergruppe* 906 which began to shadow while summoning 2./KGr. 106's Ju 88 'M2+MK' to attack. Before *Oblt.* Raymund Scheelke could reach the retreating ships, he was intercepted by a 236 Squadron Beaufighter, both aircraft crashing in flames for the loss of Scheelke and his crew as well as Sergeant Archie William Taylor, RAAF, and his observer Sergeant Hilary Parfitt, RAFVR. Other attempted Luftwaffe attacks were driven off by Coastal Command aircraft arriving to create a protective umbrella over the ships.

On 31 May 1942, following the return of some Fw 200s from Norway, the number of operational aircraft within Kessler's control reached forty-three:

Stab./Kü.Fl.Gr. 406 (Brest *Süd*), one Do 18 (non-operational);
    5./BFl.Gr. 196 (Brest *Süd* and Hourtin), *Hptm.* Werner Techam, twenty-four Ar 196 (fourteen operational);
Stab/KG 6
    KGr. 106 (Dinard), *Maj.* Gerd Roth, nineteen Ju 88 (five operational)
3.(F)/Aufkl.Gr. 123, eighteen Ju 88, Bf 110 and Bf 109 (thirteen operational);
Stab/KG 40 (Bordeaux-Mérignac) *Oberst* Karl Menhert,
    2./KG 40 (Rechilin/Mecklenberg), six Fw 200 (three operational);
    III./KG 40 (minus 7./KG 40), nineteen Fw 200 (eight operational).

However, intensification of RAF Bomber Command raids on Germany from 14 February resulted in German retaliation that reduced yet further the strength of *Fliegerführer Atlantik*. Following the destruction of Lübeck on 28 March by a force of 234 Wellington and Stirling bombers, Hitler demanded retaliation, ordering that the 'air war against England be given a more aggressive stamp'. Thus, began what is now known as the 'Baedeker Blitz' targeting objectives whose bombing was considered to have the greatest potential effect on British civilian life. Beginning with the bombing of Exeter on 23 April, *Luftflotte* 3 was responsible for the campaign and utilised *Maj.* Roth's KGr. 106 transferred away from the Atlantic battle alongside KG 2 and pathfinders of KG 100. However, by 1942 British night fighter technology and operations had improved dramatically since the days of the London Blitz, and though several Baedeker raids inflicted considerable casualties, German bomber losses were disproportionately heavy.

Concurrent with the depletion of Kessler's forces was the rise of Coastal Command's offensive presence over the Bay of Biscay. While the centre point of the U-boat battleground may lie far to the west, all operational U-boats were forced to transit Biscay while headed to and from their French Atlantic bases. These 'choke points' quickly came under increasing Allied aerial pressure, assisted by the decoding of the Luftwaffe and Kriegsmarine's Enigma messages and introduction of new weapons to the Allied aerial onslaught, such as the 'Leigh Light' which, in combination with effective air-to-surface-vessel (ASV) radar, allowed British bombers to attack surfaced U-boats at night. The U-boats were therefore frequently forced to travel submerged through Biscay, lengthening patrol transit times dramatically. Dönitz protested loudly to Göring that the RAF were operating within Biscay with 'absolutely no opposition'. Furthermore, heavily-armed Beaufighters now augmented the Sunderland, Whitley and Hudson aircraft that had originally patrolled Biscay, for which *Fliegerführer Atlantik* had no match. The Bristol Type 156 Beaufighter was a twin-engine, two-seater aircraft of superb performance. Smaller than the Junkers, manoeuvrable and robust, it was capable of a maximum speed that fractionally edged out the Ju 88, carrying a formidable punch of four 20mm nose cannon and six .303 Browning machine guns in the wings.

On 4 March *MGK West* reported that *B.d.U.* and *Fliegerführer Atlantik* had entered into an agreement according to which the air cover would be provided for arriving and departing U-boats whenever there were enough Ar 196 floatplanes and weather conditions permitted their use as it was impossible to assign this task to He 115s due to a sudden acute shortage of them. Though the nimble Arado aircraft were effective in their role as scout planes, and capable of self-defence and limited attack capabilities – shooting down twelve Sunderlands and Wellington and Whitley bombers between April and September 1942 – they were no match for aircraft such as the Beaufighter. Focke-Wulf Fw 190 fighters of *Oblt.* Bruno Stolle's 8./JG 2 were requested by *Fliegerführer Atlantik* to escort the Arado floatplanes, though the matched patrolling between the

The Bristol Type 156 Beaufighter, a highly effective twin-engine fighter that entered action over Biscay in 1942.

slow Arado and faster Focke-Wulf fighter was difficult to master at best. Even the Fw 200s returned from Norway had been tasked with providing air cover for U-boats transiting Biscay, such as on 5 June when *U71* was damaged by air attack and rendered unable to dive, minesweepers arriving to assist while a Condor engaged a Sunderland flying boat in an inconclusive 45-minute battle.

The answer to the Beaufighter was found in the ubiquitous Ju 88, a heavy fighter (*Zerstörer*) version, the Ju 88C-6 being produced from early 1942, an enhanced adaptation of an earlier *Zerstörer* version that had served with the *Zerstörer Staffel* of KG 30 during 1940 before being diverted to night fighting duties. The C-6 boasted a solid metal nose that housed a single 20mm MG FF/M cannon and three 7.92mm MG 17 machine guns.[6] Two further MG FF/M cannons could be mounted in the ventral gondola, and a pair of defensive 7.92mm MG 81 machine guns faced astern from the glazed canopy.

During June four of these Ju 88 *Zerstörer* aircraft arrived at Bordeaux having undergone operational training in Brétigny, south of Paris, as part of IV./KG 6.

The Commander in Chief, Luftwaffe has ordered the first four Ju 88C (twin-engine long-range fighter) planes coming off the assembly line to be allocated to *Luftflotte* 3 in Bordeaux without crews. *Luftflotte* 3 is to employ these planes exclusively for the protection of damaged submarines arriving from the Atlantic and for the escort of blockade-runners.[7]

The business end of
the Junkers Ju 88C-6
heavy fighter (*Zerstörer*)
housing a single 20mm
MG FF/M cannon and
three 7.92mm MG 17
machine guns.

Some confusion exists over the administrative disposition of the four aircraft, with most sources citing them as part of a new *Zerstörer Staffel* to be attached to KGr. 106, the *Kampfgruppe* as a whole having been temporarily removed from *Fliegerführer Atlantik* for the 'Baedeker' raids. At 0900hrs on 24 June, returning U-boat *U753* was escorted by Ju 88 aircraft and minesweepers into La Pallice after being badly damaged in an enemy air attack, although it remains uncertain whether these were existing French-based aircraft or the new *Zerstörer*. Regardless of which unit designation the aircraft carried, four days later the larger Type IX *U105* left El Ferrol, Spain, at dawn and was picked up the escorting Ju 88C-6s at 0745hrs. While outbound from France *Korvettenkapitän* Heinrich Schuch's boat had been attacked by an Australian Sunderland flying boat and damaged, seeking shelter in El Ferrol and requesting fighter protection, which was unavailable at that time. Schuch reached the safety of the neutral port, beginning repairs and awaiting developments. In the pages of his War Diary, Dönitz vented his despair at the inability to protect his U-boats from the growing aerial threat.

The attack on *U105* has shown once more the great dangers to which U-boats are exposed on their passage through Biscay. As there is no defence against Sunderlands and heavy bombers, Biscay has become the playground of English aircraft, where, according to *Fliegerführer Atlantik*, even the most ancient types of Sunderland can be used. As the English aircraft radar set is developed further, the boats will be more and more endangered, damage will be on a larger scale and the result will be total losses of boats. It is sad and very depressing for the U-boat crews that there are no forces whatever available to protect a U-boat unable to dive as a result of aircraft bombs. Therefore a few long-range *Zerstörer* or modern bombers would be sufficient to drive off the [enemy] maritime aircraft, which at present fly right up to the French Biscay coast without fighter escort. Or, at least these aircraft could escort a damaged U-boat until she has reached the area covered by our minesweepers and patrol vessels.[8]

Fortunately, during *U105*'s sixteen days in Spain, the four Ju 88C-6s had finally arrived in Biscay and as Schuch departed its Spanish sanctuary a shadowing Sunderland was driven off by flak from the U-boat as well as its *Zerstörer* screen. By 0230hrs the following morning, minesweepers had taken over the escort in quadrant BF 9817 and the boat reached Lorient without further damage.

The Ju 88s' first operational kill was on 15 July when a Wellington of 311 (Czech) Squadron, only recently transferred to Coastal Command from Bomber Command, was engaged by *Fw.* Henny Passier's aircraft. Sergeant Hugo Dostál and his Wellington crew had already clashed with a Ju 88A-4 of the Luftwaffe's *Wekusta* 51 while on weather reconnaissance four days previously, wounding its gunner *Ob.Gef.* Rudolf Piz. However, this time Dostál was shot down by the heavy Junkers fighter, the bodies of Sergeants František Novák, Vilém Orlík and Rudolf Pancíř and that of Flight Lieutenant Miroslav Cígler later washing up on the Devon coast, while those of Hugo Dostál and Sergeant Josef Holub were never recovered.

On 22 July tragedy overtook KG 40 when during familiarisation flying trials near Bordeaux-Mérignac *Hptm.* Karl-Hans Weymar's Ju 88C-6 collided with a Condor of 9./KG 40 flown by *Fw.* Alfred Praschl, both aircraft crashing and killing all eleven men aboard them. Three extra *Staffeln* (13, 14 and 15) of *Zerstörer* were formed between August and September to create V./KG 40, a cadre of experienced night fighter pilots included within the crew complements to provide further combat instruction. *Hauptmann* Gerhard Korthals, an outstanding bomber pilot who had commanded *Staffeln* in KGr. 100 and KG 51, decorated with both the German Cross in Gold and the Knight's Cross, was placed in command. Kessler had long asked for Dönitz's support in his requests for additional aircraft for *Fliegerführer Atlantik* and, with express permission from *OKM*, Dönitz flew first to Luftwaffe Headquarters and then to Göring's Rominten East Prussian hunting lodge to personally plead for enhanced fighter protection for his U-boats. Despite their often frosty personal relationship, he secured the *Reichsmarschall's* pledge of twenty-four more of the new Ju 88C-6.

The maritime aircraft of KG 40 had received two new commanders by July 1942. *Oberst* Dr. Georg Pasewaldt, provisional *Kommodore* since October 1941, had departed at the year's end to swap places with *Oberst* Karl Mehnert as *Kommodore* of KG 2. Mehnert, a veteran of the Condor Legion, was in turn replaced as *Kommodore* of KG 40 during July 1942 by *Obstlt*. Martin Vetter, an experienced anti-shipping pilot who had been awarded the Knight's Cross for his attacks on British shipping within the North Sea in May 1940 while commander of II./KG 26.

In the interim, the Ju 88s of KGr. 106 had been returned from 'Baedeker' to sporadic maritime operations and during mid-June was engaged against Gibraltar Convoy HG84. The convoy of twenty merchants, protected by an understrength 36th Escort Group, had departed Gibraltar for Britain on 9 June, joined by three extra ships from Lisbon two days later, who unfortunately brought a shadowing Fw 200 with them. A nine U-boat line, codenamed '*Endrass*', was directed to intercept, though only *Kaptlt*. Erich Topp's *U552* was successful, sinking five ships on 15 June in two separate torpedo attacks as aggressive escort tactics drove the remainder away, severely damaging three of the attackers. During the following day, three extra warships arrived to bolster the defence as HG84 came within range of both Coastal Command and KG 40 in the Western Approaches and thirty-three Ju 88s were thrown into the attack, twelve from KGr. 106.

The escort destroyer HMS *Wild Swan* had been detached for refuelling and was passing near to a group of Spanish trawlers as the Junkers approached. Spotting the destroyer and smaller trawlers, the Junkers crews mistook them for the body of the convoy and attacked. Four near misses caused severe damage to the destroyer, one bomb exploding abreast of the boiler room below the waterline, the pressure wave breaking the ship's spine and causing severe flooding, engines stopped, and wheel

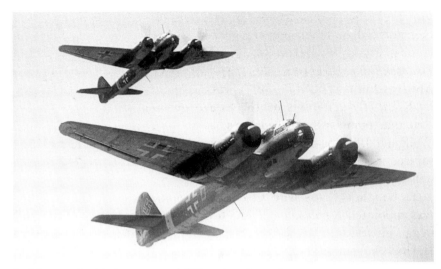

Ju 88s armed with four external SC250 bombs each.

jammed hard to starboard. *Wild Swan* swung violently out of control and collided with one of the trawlers – the 161-ton *Nuevo Con* – sinking her almost immediately although twelve survivors were rescued, some by physically jumping aboard the careering destroyer. Three other trawlers were also sunk, two by bombs and a third by a crashing Junkers that had been hit by anti-aircraft fire before *Wild Swan* finally sank. British gunners claimed six attacking aircraft destroyed – four shot down and two colliding – at least four confirmed as lost by German records, with three complete crews posted as missing in action. The 165 British and Spanish survivors spent fifteen hours in open boats, thirty-one British seamen and a single Spaniard dying of exposure before the remainder were rescued by HMS *Vansittart*.[9]

Losses to *Kampfgruppe* 106 continued past the disastrous engagement with HMS *Wild Swan* as it resumed night operations over British 'Baedeker' targets until August. In the end, by September 1942, the remnants of Roth's KGr. 106 was finally divested of its naval origins when it was taken out of action temporarily and reformed before being redesignated II./KG 6. The formation of this new *Kampfgeschwader* had been ordered on 11 October 1941, created by *Luftflotte* 3 and initially intended to comprise *Küstenfliegergruppe* 106, *Kampfgruppe* 606 and Stab/Kü.Fl.Gr. 406. For its initial months the *Kampfgruppe* comprised only a staff and the replacement and training unit *Ergänzungsstaffel*/KG 6, *Fliegerführer Atlantik* recording KG 6 as being officially established at Dinard on 30 April 1942, though without combat aircraft or aircrews. *Kommodore Obstlt.* Joachim Hahn, former *Gruppenkommandeur* of *Kampfgruppe* 606, was killed on 3 June after the Messerschmitt Bf 108 '*Taifun*' he was flying was shot down near Dieppe by RCAF fighter pilots of 401 Squadron. His place as *Kommodore* – at that point still only administrative – was then filled by *Obstlt.* Wolfgang Bühring for three months during which he was seriously injured in an air crash. Bühring, formerly of *Kustenfliegergruppen* 106, 606 and 806, died in hospital in Paris on 4 June 1944. From September 1942 Knight's Cross with Oak Leaves holder *Obstlt.* Walter Storp was appointed *Kommodore* of KG 6 whereupon formation of the unit began in earnest, I./KG 6 created by the redesignation of I./KG 77, II./KG 6 from *Kampfgruppe* 106, III./KG 6 from III./LG 1 and IV./KG 6 created by the expansion of the Ju 88 replacement and training unit *Ergänzungsstaffel*/KG 6 that had in turn been formed by the amalgamation of *Erg.Kette*/KGr. 606, *Erg.Kette*/KGr. 106 and *Ausb.Staffel*/ *Fliegerführer Atlantik*.

Though obviously of at least partial maritime origin, KG 6 was intended for use against key British industrial targets and was provided with its own pathfinder ability, III./KG 6 almost immediately being posted to the Eastern Front, initially in support of Army Group North until directed to the expanding battle of Stalingrad during October. Not until June 1943 would I./KG 6 turn to anti-shipping operations within the Mediterranean.

As *Fliegerführer Atlantik* had passed over to defensive operations in Biscay, so *Luftflotte* 3's anti-shipping operations diminished considerably. While 94 per cent of the *Luftflotte*'s efforts had been directed against maritime targets in February 1942, by September that percentage had fallen dramatically to just seven, the remainder focussed on 'Baedeker' bombing. On 5 September Kessler sent a seven-page letter to *Generaloberst* Jeschonnek, Luftwaffe Chief of Staff, decrying the miserable state in which his command now languished, describing it as a 'living corpse' and advocating the dissolution of the post. Although the heavy Ju 88 fighters were taking a considerable toll on British anti-submarine aircraft – eight being shot down during September – *Fliegerführer Atlantik*'s reach now barely extended into the Atlantic where U-boat attacks were reaching a crescendo, Kessler's aircraft being unable to bolster the attack on merchant convoys.

Dönitz lobbied for the introduction of the new Heinkel He 177 to the Atlantic battle, but was informed by Air Inspector General, *Generalfeldmarschall* Erhard Milch in charge of aircraft production, that the four-engine bomber was earmarked already by the *Führer* for the Eastern Front. However, in mid-1942, thanks to Dönitz's persuasive power and favoured status with his commander-in chief, several examples of the machine began operational testing in the West, including a pair operated at Bourdeaux-Mérignac by I./KG 40.

In outward appearance, the He 177 was a twin-engined bomber, but this belied the presence of four engines; two coupled within a single nacelle powering the same propeller through a connecting gear train. An installed clutch mechanism also allowed either engine to be shut down while in flight as the Heinkel cruised using the remaining pair, extending the aircraft's endurance. This complicated design had been fraught with trouble. Years before the outbreak of war, initial specifications for the development of a heavy four-engine bomber capable of penetrating beyond the Soviet Ural mountains had been put forward by the Luftwaffe's first Chief of Staff *Generalleutnant* Walther Wever with strong support from Milch. However, following Wever's untimely death in a He 70 flying accident, established design work was scrapped and the parameters altered by Ernst Udet – Head of the Technical Office – to include a dive-bombing capacity, requiring coupled engines in order to reduce drag and prevent weakening of the wing structure.[10]

The troubled Heinkel He 177 heavy bomber; this example aircraft '6N+HK', named 'Helga' and belonging to I./KG 100.

This complex power plant comprised two 12-cylinder, liquid-cooled Daimler Benz DB.601 inverted-V engines such as that used to power the Bf 109, the complete power plant designated 'DB. 606'. Mounted side by side, they drove a single four-bladed propeller. The inner cylinder banks of the two engines were extremely close together, twelve exhaust pipes also wedged into the confined area. Unfortunately, even with the best mechanical care, a certain amount of fuel, grease or oil could be expected to drip free of the engines and come to rest inside the engine nacelle, where the extreme temperature generated by engines and exhausts frequently resulted in fires, leading to crews later nicknaming the aircraft the 'Reich's lighter'. Furthermore, poor lubrication often resulted in engine seizure mid-flight.

The first prototype, He 177V-1 took to the air on 19 November 1939 at the Rechlin Test site (*Erprobungstelle*) piloted by engineer and test pilot *Lt* Carl Francke. The inaugural flight lasted twelve minutes after which engine temperatures rose rapidly past safety limits and though Francke never retracted the undercarriage, the He 177 reached an altitude of over 2,000 metres and aircraft handling was noted as 'adequate'. Several modifications occupied the ensuing eleven days before a second flight was made, this one curtailed due to severe vibration. Such problems dogged the design and by the end of the first round of test flights, three of the initial five prototype He 177s had crashed, killing all men aboard.

Modification continued, including the expansion of the engine cowlings which allowed the cooling system to better fulfil its purpose and reducing the risk of fire. Two airframes (V6 and V7) were transferred to crew training as part of KG 40 during mid-1941, and representatives of the *Geschwader* informed Göring that both crews tasked with the field trials stressed the excellent manoeuvrability of the aircraft, which received unstinting praise. Nonetheless, the process of perfecting the aircraft was catastrophically slow. *Major* Edgar Petersen had been posted during September 1941 from command of KG 40 to control the network of Luftwaffe testing sites (*Kommandeur Kommando der Erprobungsstellen die Luftwaffe*), while concurrently heading the research establishment at Rechlin to bring focus to the Heinkel He 177 development. At the beginning of 1942, Petersen visited the Heinkel factory to investigate the perpetual state of delay in rectifying faults with the He 177 and received direct complaints from senior staff that Ernst Heinkel had been devoting far too little time to the new aircraft, but rather continuing to concentrate of the established He 111 which was nearing obsolescence despite being a commercially successful design. The original production schedule had been slashed to just five per month until faults with the He 177 could be fully eliminated. However, at each stage the aircraft remained dogged by fresh issues; Petersen ordering over 1,300 minor modifications following flight trials which were carried out with what he called 'catastrophic lethargy' by the Heinkel factory.

The relationship between the *RLM* and German aircraft manufacturers was frequently chaotic and openly hostile, designers often at loggerheads due to competing demands from a Ministry in which much work was duplicated, and little open inter-departmental communication took place. The *RLM*, at the mercy of its politically-charged commander-in-chief, was guilty of inflicting sudden and seemingly arbitrary modifications to existing construction projects, infuriating both manufacturers and officers, such as Petersen, charged with development. Often such demands were instigated because of Göring's attempt to curry favour with the *Führer* amidst the fluctuating fortunes of war. Resultant soured relationships between aircraft manufacturers and the Luftwaffe had a further detrimental effect on overtaxed aircraft factories that would have struggled to keep pace with demand even without the additional travails. The *RLM* proved the ineptest ministry of Hitler's Reich, *Reichsführer-SS* Heinrich Himmler even at one point considering taking control of aircraft manufacturing using his army of slave labourers, all the while dreaming of his own SS air force. Ultimately, apart from some component manufacturing, his desire came to nought.

During the troubled development of the He 177, consideration was given by Milch to converting the aircraft to a standard four-engine machine, though he was overruled after being informed that such a change would result in an entirely new aircraft, taking years to complete. On 26 August 1942 Milch was recorded during a conference as saying: 'If one sees how the first He 177 flew on 20 November 1939, and that the aircraft are still not in service, one can only weep.'[11]

The production version that followed, the He 177A-3, incorporated several of the design changes aimed at improving handling and eliminating major causes of engine fires, also introducing an upgraded power plant of two DB605 engines twinned in each nacelle, designated the DB.610 and providing greater horsepower. In May 1942, Göring himself visited the Rechlin testing site and saw, for the first time, his long-awaited four-engine bomber.

Reichsmarschall Hermann Göring.
Though ultimately the wrong man to
head the Luftwaffe, even he could see
the problems with the He 177 design.

> I have never been so furious as when I saw this engine. Surely it must be
> as clear as daylight! How is such an engine to be serviced on the airfields? I
> believe I am right in saying you cannot even take out all the sparking plugs
> without pulling the whole engine apart![12]

During June 1942 the newly established I./FKG. 50 (*Fernkampfgeschwader*,
long-range bomber wing) formed at Brandenburg-Briest from elements
of 10./KG 40 and received the first twenty operational He 177A-3s
straight from the production line, many undergoing modifications
under operational conditions. *Major* Kurt Schede, former *Staffelkapitän*
in KG 40, commanded the unit with valuable assistance from veteran
Hptm. Heinrich Schlosser, previously a flight instructor before becoming
Staffelkapitän of 1./KG 40 and recipient of the Knight's Cross on 18
September 1941 for the sinking of 55,000GRT of enemy shipping. A
small number of the Heinkels came equipped with dual controls allowing
Schlosser to potentially continue training pilots of the *Gruppe* during
active service. However, results were disappointing, new faults being
revealed including weaknesses in the wings that could cause them to
shear off in a shallow dive. The He 177s were soon withdrawn as unfit for
service as Schede refused to take responsibility for sending the aircraft
on operations.

Not until November 1942 was I./FKG 50 placed once again on an operational footing after it was moved to Zaporozh'ye in the Soviet Union, to take part in the emergency supply airlift for the encircled Sixth Army at Stalingrad. Operating from the primitive airfield at Saparoshje-Süd the Heinkels were found patently unsuited for the task, with little empty space available within the fuselage. During twenty supply missions, five He 177s were lost – 26 per cent of the *Gruppe*'s operational strength – none of which were attributed to enemy action. In fact, those that encountered Soviet fighters were found to be robust enough to return to base despite frequent severe damage. Among the *Gruppe*'s casualties was Kurt Schede. His aircraft, 'E8+FH', was lost to mechanical failure during a mission to Gumrak. Crash-landing on 16 January 1943 following an engine fire three kilometres north-west of Talovoy gorge, the crew survived and were rescued by a German truck which was subsequently bombed by Soviet aircraft, killing all aboard. Schlosser took command of I./FKG 50 which began a limited number of bombing sorties over Stalingrad before ordered out of the front line and returned to Brandenburg-Briest from where the He 177s were gradually farmed out to other training units. Lessons learnt in the Russian snow were examined minutely, the He 177 becoming established as a fast, durable heavy bomber, but still plagued with problems. Göring still harboured strong feelings towards Ernst Heinkel for the failure of the He 177, expressed in March 1943 when he summoned him and the designer Willi Messerschmitt to Carinhalle, delivering a violent dressing-down, the result of his own embarrassment at criticism by Hitler after the failure of the Luftwaffe to supply and support the perished Sixth Army. As a stenographer struggled to keep pace with the furious *Reichsmarschall* he turned on Heinkel:

> I was promised a heavy bomber. The Heinkel 177. After calamity upon calamity they tell me, 'If only the plane didn't have to dive, it would be the finest bird in the world – it could go into service at once. At once!' I declare at once, 'It doesn't have to dive!' But now that it's been tried in operations there have been catastrophic losses, none caused by enemy action. So, Mister Heinkel, what do you say today! And how many will go up in flames? Half of them! . . . How amused we all were about the enemy's backwardness, their 'plodding four-engine crates,' and so on. Gentlemen, I'd be delighted if you'd just copy one of their four-engine crates, double-quick! Then at least I'd have a plane to brag about![13]

Nonetheless, the constantly-evolving He 177s were beginning to be distributed to elements of KG 40. In September 1942 *Maj.* Ernst Pflüger's 1./KG 40 relocated to Fassberg from Trondheim and began converting from the Fw 200, a process that took nearly six months to complete. By February 1943, 2./KG 40 also began the conversion process, followed by *Hptm.* Walter Rieder's 8./KG 40 a month later.

While the saga of the troublesome He 177 had been unfolding, *Fliegerführer Atlantik* continued to struggle to meet *B.d.U.*'s expectations. Close inshore to France, the small Arado 196s from Brest were taking heavy losses at the hands of powerful Beaufighters and Kessler requested Fw 190 fighters of *Oblt.* Bruno Stolle's 8./JG 2 'Richthofen' based at Brest-Guipavas airfield to fly as escort for the small floatplanes while engaged on reconnaissance. Stolle doubted the ability of his high-performance fighters to fly close escort for the slower Arados, advocating instead that his fighters rendezvous instead at a given point at sea, though Kessler harboured doubts regarding their navigational ability to do so. Stolle had, however, previously been a blind-flying instructor was successful in mounted escort missions using three Fw 190s for a year beginning in August 1942 while also mounting fighter sweeps against British Coastal Command aircraft in Biscay and the English Channel.

The fighter aircraft of JG 2 had already resumed their own limited maritime operations after both *Jagdfliegerführer* 2 (*Oberst* Joachim-Friedrich Huth) and 3 (*Genmaj.* Max Ibel) had been ordered to each convert a single *Staffel* to fighter-bombers to harass shipping in the English Channel as well as attack coastal installations. During the autumn of 1940 three *Staffeln* of JG 2 had been assigned to anti-shipping missions, though the *Geschwader* as a whole displayed little enthusiasm for the task as the Luftwaffe battled for air supremacy over England, and the enterprise eventually fizzled out. Comprising Bf 109F-4B aircraft fitted with a fuselage rack capable of carrying either a single SC250 bomb or four SC-50 bombs, *Hptm.* Frank Liesendahl's new 13./JG 2 was one of the *Staffeln* selected, *Hptm.* Karl Plunser's 10.(*Jabo*)/JG 26 '*Schlageter*' the other. Plunser's *Staffel* incorporated several pilots deemed 'wildly undisciplined' but was operational by March 1942, claiming twenty ships sunk totalling 63,000GRT within three months.

Liesendahl had already shown a flair for *Jabo* – *Jagdbomber* (fighter-bomber) – missions while part of 6./JG 2 and had actively lobbied for the reinstatement of anti-shipping missions. Shot down and wounded twice thus far, once over Dunkirk in 1940 when he was briefly held as a prisoner of war, the experienced pilot was put in command of the newly-established 13./JG 2 in November 1941 whereupon he began collecting pilots that had shown an aptitude for fighter-bomber missions while developing what became known as the 'Liesendahl Process'. This tactical plan became almost the standard *Jabo* attack method, the aircraft approaching the target at 450km/h at an altitude of only five metres. Once judged to be about 1,800 metres from target, the aircraft would pull into a steep climb to 500 metres, level off and dive at an angle of 3°, increasing speed to 550km/h before pulling up and lobbing the bomb towards the target. On 10 February, Liesendahl was deep in the training of his pilots when he undertook a test mission that badly damaged the 3,167GRT SS *Lieutenant Robert Mory* off the Cornish coast. As two escorting Bf 109s circled the steamer, Liesendahl swooped to the attack and hit the ship in the stokehold, at least one lifeboat manned and abandoning ship before the skipper recalled the crew to reboard their damaged freighter. After being released as operational, 13./JG 2 became 10.(*Jabo*)/JG 2 and their 'tip and run' raids began to claim a substantial toll on shipping and land targets, going so far as to attack Royal Navy warships in Plymouth Sound on 16 May, though *Lt.* Hans-Joachim Schulz was shot down and killed in the attack, later being buried with full military honours by the RAF. The *Staffel* began sporting a new emblem designed by Liesendahl's new bride, a designer at the Messerschmitt aircraft company; a red fox with a ship trapped in its jaws.

The emblem adopted by JG 2's fighter-bomber *Staffeln*, designed by *Hptm.* Frank Liesendahl's wife.

Leutnant Leopold Wenger, Fw 190 fighter-bomber pilot of JG 2 which mounted anti-shipping missions during 1942 and 1943.

Both *Staffeln* remained under *Luftflotte* 3 fighter command which, despite their apparent success, opted to not increase the number of fighter-bombers. Liesendahl was awarded the German Cross in Gold on 5 June 1942 as morale soared within his *Staffel*. *Leutnant* Leopold 'Poldi' Wenger wrote letters home describing some of his operations as part of JG 2.

12 July 1942: This afternoon I flew another mission and sank a watch ship of about 800 tons [minesweeper *MMS 174*] in the harbour of Brixham (Bay of Torquay) with a direct bombing hit to the starboard side of the ship. The other plane damaged a 4,000-ton freighter so severely that I must assume that it sank, too. This time, there were two of us. It wasn't easy to approach the ship, since the harbour was full of barrage balloons and flak and very strongly protected. So, we struck all at once, by surprise, out of a beautiful blue sky, flying through the barrage balloons, firing at the ships with everything we had. My ship sent up jets of flame from the superstructure after being shot at using my guns, that's all. The bombs did the rest.

My ship capsized in half a minute, breaking in half right in the middle, while the other ship began to sink stern first. There was so much flak that we had to give up hope of being able to observe much of anything else. At any rate, I was very happy over this success, since it was the first ship

I ever sank all by myself. Yesterday, my superior officer (*Hauptmann* F. Liesendahl) and another *Leutnant* also sank a destroyer in this area, that is, everybody got one. Unfortunately, the ships aren't always where we'd like to have them.[14]

However, only five days after Wenger's letter home, Liesendahl was killed in action on 17 July, two weeks after the *Staffel* swapped their Messerschmitt fighters for Fw 190A-2s with a resulting partial slackening in the rate of 'tip and run' attacks. Liesendahl was posted as missing after an attack on a tanker two kilometres south-east of Brixham, Devon, his badly-decomposed body washing ashore near Berry Head during September and later buried at sea.[15] Though his accompanying pilots were unsure of what fate had befallen their commander, Admiralty records of the day are quite specific:

At 1245/17 four Fw 190s attacked tanker *Daxhound* escorted by MLs *118* and *157*, course S.E. one mile S.E. of Berry Head. Planes dived from about 500 feet from port bow with cannon fire, rounded Berry Head, and attacked again with bombs. From 50 feet two planes attacking tanker and one plane each ML, *ML118* undoubtedly shot down her attacker the disintegrated in the air. Tanker had two near misses on the port quarter but suffered only minor damage and is ready for sea. *ML157* was hit by a bomb which landed on the bridge, wrecking it, the bomb made a large hole in the armour plating, went into the sea bursting close alongside. She will require extensive repairs. Both MLs put up a determined fire with their Lewis guns. *ML157* had two casualties, the C.O. seriously wounded and the Coxswain less serious. *ML118* had one man slightly wounded. *Daxhound* one D.E.M.S. Gunner seriously wounded.[16]

Command of 10.(*Jabo*)/JG 2 passed to *Oblt.* Fritz Schröter. Meanwhile, Plunser had been replaced as commander of 10.(*Jabo*)/JG 26, on 12 July, his successor temporarily *Oblt.* Joachim-Hans Geburtig, who was shot down into the sea by machine-gun fire and captured after escaping his submerged aircraft following an attempted attack on a collier near Littlehampton on 30 July. Geburtig later claimed that he had not been hit by gunfire but had rather failed to pull out of his bombing dive in time before impacting the sea. *Leutnant* Paul Keller replaced the luckless Geburtig, and he in turn would be killed during December as he strafed petrol trucks near Ashford, Kent, and was hit by anti-aircraft fire. Indeed, the fighter-bombers' target emphasis had by then gradually moved away from shipping strikes, until concentrated once more against land targets, 10.(*Jabo*)/JG 26 moving back to *Luftflotte* 2 command.

Nonetheless, the experienced anti-shipping fighter pilots proved invaluable against the forces of Operation *Jubilee*, the Anglo-Canadian landing at Dieppe on 19 August. The disaster of *Jubilee* has been variously described as a necessary evil for the testing of amphibious assault theory that would later save lives in subsequent Allied landings or a total fiasco from start to finish that wasted thousands of troops, predominantly Canadian, for little real purpose. Regardless of one's interpretation of the raid, an accompanying RAF attempt to lure the Luftwaffe into a crushing battle that would cripple western Luftwaffe strength failed. Though Luftwaffe reaction was initially slow, eventually minelaying bomber elements of IX.*Fliegerkorps* – II./KG 2 (Dornier Do 217s under command of Stab./KG 30), II./KG 54 (Ju 88) and KG 77 (Ju 88) – were committed, alongside some aircraft from 1.(F)/*Aufklärungsgruppe* 33, 1.(F)/*Aufklärungsgruppe* 123 and KGr. 106, as well as fighters and fighter-bombers of JG 2 and JG 26. Coordination of the main bomber attacks mounted against *Jubilee* shipping was largely handled by *Oberst* Friedrich Schily, who still held the post of *Führer der Seeluftstreitkräfte* (commander of maritime combat aviation) after having transferred to *Luftflotte* 3 staff. Based in Chantilly since 17 July, he had been organising bombing attacks against the British Isles while simultaneously tasked with the organisation of Luftwaffe defences in the event of an Allied landing on the French Atlantic coast.

Covered by seventy-four RAF squadrons – sixty-six of them fighters – the Allied supporting fleet remained relatively unscathed, Luftwaffe bombing raids noted as lacking focus and determination. The *Jabo Staffeln*, however, did make some successful attacks and ultimately thirty-three landing craft were destroyed by combined air and ground fire. The destroyer HMS *Berkeley* was also severely damaged by a *Schwarm* from 10.(*Jabo*) JG 2 led by *Oblt.* Fritz Schröter.[17] The destroyer was providing supporting bombardment as well as acting as a platform for embarked aircraft control units before covering the withdrawal of troops from the beach. After stopping to embark Canadian soldiers from a battered landing craft, *Berkeley* was picking up speed when a bomb struck immediately before the bridge, breaking the destroyer's back before a second bomb also hit, forcing it to be abandoned. Thirteen ratings were killed before the wreck was scuttled by torpedoes from HMS *Albrighton*, the after-action British report officially stating that the destroyer had been accidentally hit by a German bomber jettisoning its bombs.

In the air, the RAF had lost sixty-four Spitfires, twenty Hurricanes, six Douglas Bostons and ten Mustang fighters, with sixty-two airmen killed, thirty wounded and seventeen captured. In return, despite dramatic overclaiming by the Allied air forces, the Luftwaffe lost sixteen Fw 190s, one Bf 109, four Ju 88s and seventeen Do 217s destroyed in combat, with another Ju 88 wrecked by accident.

The action at Dieppe marked the swansong of *Oberst* Friedrich Schily's *F.d.Luft* office which was finally abolished on 7 September 1942 after the last of his aircraft formations had transferred to IX.*Fliegerkorps*. However, it did not mark the end of Schily's attachment to maritime related work. Later, from October 1943, Schily served for a period as *Fliegerführer Ausbildung Ostsee* training maritime aircrew in the Baltic before he was made an airfield commander at *Flugplatzkommando* (*Koflug*) 9/XI and later killed in a ground strafing attack in 1945. Years after the end of the war Schily's nephew, Otto Georg Schily, became a practising lawyer before entering West German politics in 1980. Appointed Federal Minister of the Interior in 1980, he later gave a speech that included stories of his family's past, opposed to Hitler and Nazism. He spoke of his uncle:

> My uncle Fritz Schily, a man of loud character, was an *Oberst* of the Luftwaffe. At the end of the war he was commander of an air base near Ulm. In desperation over the crimes committed by Hitler's regime he sought death in a low-flying attack.

The IX.*Fliegerkorps* continued its dedicated minelaying missions throughout 1942, although its operational parameters had widened to shipping attacks along England's eastern seaboard and occasional daylight bombing of land targets. *Generalmajor* Robert von Greim's V.*Fliegerkorps* had been supposed to take over responsibility for minelaying in British waters, moving from the Soviet Union to Brussels in November 1941, but the sudden diversion of Greim and much of his staff to the Crimea had forestalled the effective use of his command to relieve the burden on IX.*Fliegerkorps*. The strength of the forces available to *General der Flieger* Joachim Coeler's IX.*Fliegerkorps* varied considerably dependent on aircraft being withdrawn from the Arctic front against the PQ convoys for either refitting or torpedo conversion training. Those crews that had completed their courses were frequently thrown into anti-shipping missions, alongside many of the training units that comprised IV.*Gruppe* of the *Kampfgeschwader*. With a dearth of available aircraft, such crews were also in action against British land and sea targets as a form of final 'operational training' as, after more than two years of war, a shortage of observers led to their training being dramatically curtailed by the Luftwaffe.

However, with aircraft required elsewhere, the intensity of the minelaying campaign against Britain gradually diminished and only twenty-four ships were lost to Luftwaffe mines throughout 1942, totalling 41,324GRT. By 27 July *Luftflotte* 3's entire bomber strength was contained in Coeler's IX.*Fliegerkorps*:

Stab/KG 2 (Soesterburg), 2 x Do 217
I./KG 2 (Gilze-Rijen) 29 x Do 217 (21 operational)
II./KG 2 (Eindhoven) 26 x Ju 88 (15 operational)
III./KG 2 (Arnhem-Deelen), 35 x Do 217 (29 operational)
I./KG 40 (Bordeaux-Mérignac), 30 x He 177 (16 operational)
II./KG 40 (Soesterburg), 30 x Do 217 (28 operational)
III./KG 40 (Bordeaux-Mérignac) 20 x Fw 200 (11 operational), 4 Ju 88C (1 operational)
KGr. 106 (Dinard), 31 x Ju 88 (23 operational)

Oberstleutnant Georg Pasewaldt's KG 2 '*Holzhammer*' – still in the process of finished conversion to the Do 217 – had been involved primarily in anti-shipping and minelaying operations throughout 1942. The *Kampfgeschwader* had already participated in convoy attacks as part of the '*Kanalkampf*' that presaged the Battle of Britain in 1940, led at the time by *Geschwaderkommodore* Johannes Fink, and again targeted Royal Navy vessels during the invasion of Greece and Crete. Thirty-two bombers of KG 2 had taken part in Operation *Donnerkeil* during February 1942, known as the 'Channel Dash' when the capital ships *Scharnhorst*, *Gneisenau* and *Prinz Eugen* broke out of confinement in the port of Brest to race through the English Channel and return to Germany. Covered by whatever fighter forces could be mustered in the west, Dorniers of KG 2 also flew deception missions while two Heinkels flew over the western Channel with electronic jamming equipment. Ten Do 217s from III./KG 2 attacked Plymouth Harbour and airfield while a further fifteen flew diversionary missions to distract attention from the jamming Heinkels.

Throughout the remainder of 1942 and into 1943 KG 2 shouldered much of the minelaying effort made by Coeler's force but was redirected to take part in the wasteful 'Baedeker Raids'. Between the severe rate of attrition suffered during these conventional bombing raids, and those suffered over Dieppe, by September 1942 KG 2 numbered only twenty-three crews out of an available complement of eighty-eight at the beginning of the year. Increasingly effective British radar-equipped night fighters, and an escalation in intruder attacks on forward airfields used by the *Kampfgeschwader*, eroded both fighting strength and morale.

During March 1942 the first production model of a redesigned Do 217K-1 had flown its inaugural flight and during summer KG 2 began taking receipt of the visibly different aircraft. Gone was the familiar stepped windscreen of the earlier Dornier bomber, replaced by a wrap-around glazed cockpit – a so-called 'stepless cockpit' – that allowed superb visibility. The Do 217K-2, with an expanded wingspan specifically designed to carry the revolutionary FX 1400 glide bomb still undergoing its final design stages, and the outwardly similar Do 217M-1 were soon taken on strength of KG 2. Two ETC 2000/XII racks under the wings outboard of each engine nacelle provided the necessary hardpoint for mounting the weapons, aircraft stability demanding that either two weapons were carried for balance, or one wing instead mounted a 900-litre auxiliary fuel tank in its place.

Dornier Do 217K variant with 'stepless cockpit'.

Germany's Ruhrstahl FX 1400 (also known as the PC 1400 X) guided anti-ship glide bomb was a groundbreaking achievement by armaments specialists of the Third Reich; a world's first and known to both the Allies and Luftwaffe as the 'Fritz-X'. The weapon had begun development by Dr. Max Kramer of the *Deutsche Versuchsanstalt für Luftfahrt* (DVL). Kramer had begun experimenting with remote-controlled free-falling 250kg bombs in 1938 before fitting radio-controlled spoilers to the weapon during the following year; a cheap and simply concealed comb-like metal strip mounted on the trailing edge of a wing or fin and controlled by an electro-magnetic solenoid providing current that moved the spoiler up or down thereby deflecting the airstream and altering the missile's course. The wisdom of controlling the weapon on both axes (up, down, left and right) by the use of spoilers as opposed to conventional hinged surfaces was soon confirmed in wind tunnel tests. The Ruhrstahl AG steel and armaments corporation was invited to join the project in 1940, developing a working model which was essentially a standard PC 1400 armour-piercing bomb, designed to penetrate armour or concrete, with a warhead containing 320kg of Amatol explosive. The bomb was provided with an attached control unit

Test drop of a 'Fritz-X', the *Ruhrstahl* FX 1400 guided anti-ship glide bomb.

housing, and tail assembly complete with spoilers giving pitch and yaw. Four aluminium alloy fins were secured to the missile at approximately the centre of gravity to provide lift enough to enable control surfaces in the tail to exercise adequate influence. The bomb's control unit comprised two gyroscopes for stability (switched on two minutes before launch), radio receiver, power source and a small demolition charge for the destruction of the control unit in the event of malfunction of the main charge. Directional controls were enabled by a FuG-203 *Kehl III* unit (radio control apparatus in the aircraft) and FuG-230b *Strassburg* (receiver in the bomb). This radio-control guidance link (known as '*Kehlgerät*') allowed the weapon's path to be manually adjusted by the bombardier using a joystick controller that moved the spoilers.

The 'Fritz-X' was tracked using the Lofte 7D bomb sight and once dropped, the aircraft throttled back and was put into a gentle climb so as not to overshoot the missile, maintaining an overflight of about 6,000-7,000 metres. At the moment of release, the bombardier started a stopwatch as no control could be exerted over the missile during the first fifteen seconds of its flight. Thereafter the bombardier could track the missile by a flare mounted in its tail, using his remote control to alter its course in the world's first MCLOS (Manual Command to Line Of Sight) weapon system. During trials, the Fritz-X could be guided to within a 50-metre margin of error from target, from an altitude of 7,000 metres that gave a flight time of forty-two seconds. Falling under gravity, the Fritz-X reached a terminal velocity of close to the speed of sound, making it a potentially powerful anti-shipping weapon, designed specifically for use against major warships possessing significant armour plating.

The first test launch was undertaken at Peenemünde using an He 111 carrier aircraft before testing moved to Foggia in Italy during March 1942 to take advantage of better weather conditions. However, although production began at the Rheinmetall factory in 1942 – 1,000 ordered by the *RLM* – output was low and by mid-May 1943 only one hundred had been completed, which did not see operational use until July.

Among those men assessing this new weapon was Heinrich Schmetz, former observer in 7./KG 4, his pilot and *Staffelkapitan*, 'Hajo' Herrmann with whom he transferred to KG 30. During 1942, Schmetz had undergone pilot training and after graduation moved to *Hptm.* Ernst Hetzel's *Lehr und Erprobungskommando 21* at Garz/Usedom tasked with testing the 'Fritz-X'. Hetzel's four *Staffeln* and equipped solely with Do 217K-2s were reorganised at the beginning of 1943 as *Kampfgruppe 21*,

A bombardier uses the FuG-203 *Kehl III* radio control unit to manoeuvre his 'Fritz-X' glide bomb to its target.

until 29 April, when it was redesignated once more, this time as III./KG 100 after the previous incarnation of that *Gruppe* had reverted to its original title of *Seeaufklärungsgruppe* 126 in the Aegean.

The year 1942 also yielded advances in effective Luftwaffe air-to-surface-vessel (ASV) radar that was installed aboard four Fw 200s, assigned to *Luftflotte* 5. German radar development had been bedevilled by inter-service wrangling that had already damaged Wehrmacht progression. As early as September 1935, Raeder and a party of high-ranking naval officers witnessed a demonstration of rudimentary ship locating radar created by physicist Rudolf Kühnold and engineers of his firm GEMA (*Gesellschaft fur Elektroakustische and Mechanische Apparate*) that specialised in radio transmitters and receivers. The successful display clearly illustrated the potential of such technology to the assembled Kriegsmarine observers and GEMA was encouraged to continue development of radar for naval use; no attempt was made to share the technological advance with the Luftwaffe.

Only later, at Göring's insistence, was the Luftwaffe's electronics department fully brought into the quest for effective radar. *Generalmajor* Wolfgang Martini, the Luftwaffe signals chief who had created the Luftwaffe's effective communications network, had been named *General der Luftnachrichtentruppe* (General of Air Force Communications Units) in 1941 and made directly responsible for Luftwaffe radar technology. Martini did his utmost to spur on development of an airborne ASV radar set, tasking the electronics company C. Lorenz AG with the work; a company that held 25 per cent ownership of Focke-Wulf. By the turn of 1941–2 initial service trials were carried out from which would eventually come the '*Rostock*' radar set which was operationally trialled aboard the four Fw 200s. On 2 August 1942 it was reported that one of these KG 40 aircraft, assigned to *Luftflotte* 5 within the Arctic, had detected a target 'for the first time in the fog, at a distance of about 20 kilometres north-east of Iceland, though no visual contact was made.

However, the range of '*Rostock*' was limited. The more advanced '*Hohentwiel*' – named after an extinct volcano in Baden-Württemberg – had begun development as a pre-war ground-based fire-control radar, designated FuMG 40L, but stalled after a design contest for such apparatus organised by the *RLM* was won by competing firm Telefunken with its superior '*Würzburg*' radar. Following a second design contest for an ASV radar, the shelved project was re-engineered as FuG 200 and became the successful candidate for Luftwaffe use. The '*Hohentwiel*' produced 50-kW pulse-power at low-UHF band frequencies (545 MHz), intended for surface search and navigation using land echoes. The radar had three rigid transversely-arranged antenna arrays which meant that, as *RLM* specifications had not dictated the ability to turn the antenna beam relative to the scanning aircraft, a full radar search required the aircraft to fly a full circle, which soon became Luftwaffe operational procedure

During the balmy summer of 1942 '*Sonderkommando Koch*' was established at Athens-Kalamaki from elements of II./KG 100. *Major* Adolf Koch, of the 'Köthen Signals Research Establishment', took command of small groups of specialists operating a mixture of He 111H-6 and Ju 88A-4 aircraft, beneath the umbrella of X.*Fliegerkorps* and based in Kalamaki, Catania and Grosseto. Two of the Heinkels carried captured British ASV sets recovered from downed bombers while the remainder were equipped with '*Rostock*' and '*Lichtenstein S*' sets – the latter an improved variant of one of the Luftwaffe's earliest air-to-air radars – though these were eventually supplanted by FuG 200

Torpedo-carrying Heinkel He 111H-18 with FuG 200 '*Hohentwiel*' ship-search radar.

'*Hohentwiel*' equipment. At least six of the Heinkels were temporarily attached to *Aufklärungsgruppe* 122 in Sardinia and Sicily, using radar jamming equipment against Malta's defences. *Sonderkommando Koch* mounted night radar reconnaissance missions along the North African coast as far west as Philippeville in Algeria. The captured British ASV units were tested thoroughly and highly appreciated due to their effective lateral coverage. By comparison, both the '*Rostock*' and '*Lichtenstein-S*' were considered unreliable and required experienced personnel both to operate and maintain. The introduction of the FuG 200 '*Hohentwiel*' dramatically improved both the technological effectiveness and ease of maintenance.

Initial '*Hohentwiel*' trials had resulted in the successful detection of a large ship at 80 kilometres, a surfaced submarine at 40 kilometres, a submarine periscope at 6 kilometres, aircraft at 10 to 20 kilometres and land features at 120 to 150 kilometres; all within a bearing accuracy of 1 degree, obtained by rapidly switching between two receiver antennas aimed 30 degrees on each side of the transmitter antenna direction. Put into production in 1942, an adapted version for use aboard U-boats was also manufactured the following year as Coastal Command launched a Biscay offensive.

During April and May 1942 RAF Bomber Command had begun to transfer a number of squadrons for service in Coastal Command, mounting increasingly effective anti-shipping strikes off The Netherlands and Norway as well as the Biscay U-boat routes. A number of Whitley and Liberator bombers were transferred from Bomber to Coastal Command in April, despite vociferous protests from Air Vice Marshal Sir Arthur Harris while six of the new four-engine Avro Lancasters of 44 Squadron followed on temporary attachment in June. From July onwards, a Whitley squadron for coastal duties was also maintained by No. 10 (Bomber) O.T.U. to which crews were attached for final training.

Long-range bombers had begun to make their presence felt in Dönitz's Atlantic U-boat battle, for which the Luftwaffe hoped the He 177 would provide a counterweight. Dönitz remained sceptical, on 3 September 1942 the *B.d.U.* War Diary stated:

> . . . the English have succeeded in gaining air control of a large sector of the North Atlantic by increasing the ranges of their shore-based aircraft and have thus considerably reduced the area in which U-boats can operate without danger from the air . . . *B.d.U.* is gravely concerned at the prospect of this same unfavourable air situation extending to almost all parts of the North Atlantic, the main battleground of U-boats; this will undoubtedly be the case if things develop at their present rate. Unless suitable countermeasures can be taken prospects of success of U-boats will be reduced to an unjustifiable extent.
>
> The urgent need of counteracting enemy aircraft protecting convoys must therefore be emphasized once more. Aircraft used for this would have to fulfil the following conditions:
>
> a) Very great range (aircraft must be able to remain over the convoy for some time).
>
> b) Fighting power (must be superior to enemy flying boats and four-engine land-based aircraft in speed and armament).
>
> In my opinion the He 177 does not entirely fulfil these conditions because, as far as I know, the range of this aircraft is only 2,200 km. *B.d.U.* therefore requests that every emphasis be laid on the development of an effective long range aircraft in the interests of continually effective U-boat warfare.

That month, V./KG 40 shot down eight of Coastal Command's anti-submarine aircraft in the Bay of Biscay, six of them claimed by 13./KG 40 whose *Staffelkapitän Hptm.* Paul Heide was in turn shot down and killed by a 77 Squadron Whitley on 9 September. Heide's aircraft, 'F8+KX', was the seventh lost by V./KG 40 since July: four shot down by enemy aircraft, one lost in collision with Fw 200 C-4 'CE+IA' of 9./KG 40, one crash-landing at Mérignac with battle damage and the last destroyed in an accident at the same airfield. In total, fifteen men had been killed. Heide's successor, *Hptm.* Georg Esch, a former Do 17 pilot of KG 77, was also wounded on 16 September in action against Beaufighter 'Y' of 235 Squadron about 275 kilometres south-west of Brest but returned to action soon thereafter.

During October six more RAF Coastal Command aircraft were brought down by the Ju 88s, for the loss of only one of the *Zerstörer* in combat, though introduction of the RAF's Beaufighter aircraft would change the balance of power, their first Condor kill being made in September.

No. 235 Squadron. St. Eval. 18.9.42. Beaufighters N, C, A, H, E, P, J and O. At 1755 hours [on 17 September], aircraft sighted Fw 200 Kurier on easterly course, height 200 ft., over armed trawler of 300 tons. E, P and N attacked Fw 200 from port while O dived from 2,000 feet head on and remainder attacked from starboard. Fw 200 burst into flames, disintegrated, and dived into sea. Three crew were seen in water and one attempting to climb in dinghy. Aircraft H saw 'C' dive into sea from 200 ft., apparently damaged by flak from trawler. 1820, three Ju 88s were sighted flying at 1,000 ft over fishing vessel flying French flag. Aircraft P climbed and attacked while other Beaufighters converged from various directions. Hits were seen on port engine of one Ju 88…[and a second was] attacked by O and E; flames appeared in cockpit and enemy dived into sea enveloped in flames. When Beaufighters left, tail planes of two Ju 88s were protruding from sea. Aircraft A followed third Ju 88 and delivered two successive attacks, but Junkers disappeared into cloud.[18]

Casualties to V./KG 40 through accidents also remained unexpectedly high, including the *Gruppenkommandeur Hptm.* Gerhard Korthals who was killed with his crew at Lorient in a freak occurrence. Apparently, as the aircraft was readied for its training flight, a mechanic lost his cutlery from an overall pocket, the knife, fork and spoon becoming lodged in one of the ailerons and causing a loss of control when the Junkers was airborne, leading directly to the fatal crash. His temporary successor *Hptm.* Alfred Hemm, previously *Staffelkapitän* 4.(F)/Aufkl.Gr. 122, was superseded by *Hptm.* Helmut Dargel, who killed on 30 December when his Ju 88 C-6 'F8+BG' was shot down in combat against P39 Airacobras 350 kilometres south-west of Lorient.

Since the end of 1942, the RAF had come to fully realise the threat posed by the Ju 88C-6 *Zerstörer* of V./KG 40 to its vulnerable bombers over Biscay. In response, Fighter Command moved elements of 264 Squadron of de Havilland Mosquito night-fighters to Cornwall to begin what were codenamed 'Instep' missions aimed at maintaining a heavy British fighter presence over the Bay of Biscay and Western Approaches. The fighting in North Africa had also begun to bring USAAF aircraft over Biscay as they travelled from Britain to the *Torch* battlefront via Gibraltar. Attempting to stay out of range of the Fw 190s of JG 2 flying escort missions for Arado floatplanes, a flight of fifty-one P-38 Lightnings of 82nd Fighter Group, led by an A-20B Boston navigation aircraft of the 47th Bomber Group, was intercepted en-route from St Eval by four Ju 88C-6s of 14./KG 40. The Luftwaffe pilots shot down the A-20B, one P-38 with one other damaged and forced back to Ireland, and two others crash landing in Portugal and Spain. Two Ju 88s were damaged after crash-landing in France having run out of fuel. The Junkers tangled once again with American fighters on 30 December when seventeen P-39 Airacobras led by a B-25 bomber on a similar transit mission were intercepted; a single P-39 shot down for the loss of *Gruppenkommandeur* Dargel.

Kessler and Dönitz had reached a firm footing of cooperation. Contrary to his commander, Dönitz exercised a pragmatic approach to Luftwaffe cooperation. While Raeder and his staff had consistently wrangled over operational jurisdiction of maritime aircraft, Dönitz focussed on the results of such activity, rather than overall control. He requested missions in support of his U-boats and then relinquished responsibility for the carrying-out of such missions, trusting in *Fliegerführer Atlantik* to carry out the necessary task. While some have focussed on this difference between Dönitz and Raeder as providing evidence of the contrariness of Luftwaffe cooperation with the elderly *Grossadmiral*, it would perhaps be unfair to characterise Raeder in such a way. He had consistently fought for complete understanding by the Luftwaffe of naval requirements and had believed strongly since before hostilities began that the only true way of achieving this was at the hands of naval officers themselves.

While those days had since passed, and his dreams of a Fleet Air Arm had been firmly quashed, Raeder continued to lobby for the creation of a de-facto naval aerial presence. The question of completion of the aircraft carrier *Graf Zeppelin* remained on the table at *Führer* Headquarters during 1942. Ironically, given the stops and starts encountered in its construction thus far, serious consideration was given to actually increasing the German aircraft carrier contingent by the conversion of three passenger liners into auxiliary carriers, as, in conference on 13 May 1942 and no doubt informed by the tentative use of capital ships against the Arctic convoys, Hitler declared it 'entirely out of the question for larger surface forces to operate without aircraft protection'.[19] *Oberkommando der Kriegsmarine* declared the *Europa* (56,492GRT), *Gneisenau* (23,129GRT) and *Potsdam* (23,129GRT) of the North German Lloyd Shipping Line all suitable for conversion, the incomplete hull of captured French anti-aircraft cruiser *De Grasse* later also added to the list on 26 August as it lay on a slipway in Lorient. However, the Kriegsmarine General Staff harboured doubts:

> Only the *Europa* has sufficient speed, though insufficient range, for extended operations with the cruisers of the *Scheer* class (25 knots) and the *Tirpitz* or *Hipper* class (30 knots). The two other ships cannot be considered, due to their low speed. Owing to her size and requirements of fuel and operating personnel, the *Europa* would be a liability rather than a help. The above-named three ships can therefore be used as auxiliary aircraft carriers only on a limited scale, for instance:

> a. Under particularly favourable conditions together with naval forces to carry out specific tasks, such as against Murmansk convoys. Primarily they would protect the naval forces against enemy aircraft and secondarily their planes would carry out reconnaissance and bomber missions.
> b. To increase the operational range of planes, for instance in the north area.
> c. To provide an emergency base if aircraft cannot take off from land.
> d. To function as training vessels for carrier planes.

> To fulfil the tasks under a, b, and c, they should be equipped primarily with fighters. To be used as floating airfields they must be equipped with carrier

planes and have specially trained crews. Task 'd' will become an urgent need, because the *Graf Zeppelin* will soon become ready for operations.[20]

Raeder's immediate concern was that any conversion project should not interfere with the established Kriegsmarine construction priority: U-boats (and every vessel pertaining to them, including torpedo recovery ships), light naval forces, naval barges, blockade-runners, merchant vessels and tankers. He sought and received Hitler's assurance of this and the promise of pressure to be applied on the Luftwaffe for the provision of carrier aircraft, the *Führer* reasoning that the mass production of suitable carrier aircraft would be easier to attain with the requirements of four carriers rather than one. However, despite his support of the carrier projects, during a private audience with Hitler on the afternoon of 14 May at the *Wolfsschanze* headquarters near Rastenburg, East Prussia, Raeder was informed that the *Führer* believed it was impossible to build up a naval air force during the course of the current war, though he fully recognised the value of accelerated aircraft carrier construction. In reply, Raeder pointed out bitterly that 'a naval air force with excellent personnel and aircraft existed at the time that the Air Ministry was established'.[21]

Plans for the conversion work on the three liners were drawn up immediately, and the enormity of the task fully dawned by naval designers. They had clearly underestimated the work required and discovered that, built for completely different purposes, the shape, internal subdivisions and weight stability of the ships were insufficient for their new purpose. It was initially believed that stability problems could be mastered by the application of thick belts of heavy cement formed into 'armour plates' and the building of side bulges, but both these tasks also provided complex design problems and, even if successful, would further lower the ships' speed thus negating their ability to operate with other capital ships. During June, the incomplete heavy cruiser *Seydlitz* (*Hipper* class) was added to the auxiliary carrier list. Though 90 per cent complete, the majority of the ship's superstructure would be cut away in preparation for the installation of a flight deck and hangars.

The complement of each auxiliary carrier had, in the meantime, been finalised at forty-six bombers and fifty-four fighters distributed thus: *Europa*, eighteen bombers, twenty-four fighters; *Potsdam*, eight bombers and twelve fighters; *Gneisenau*, eight bombers and twelve fighters and *Seydlitz*, twelve bombers and six fighters. Additionally, the *De Grasse* was later planned to carry eleven fighters and twelve bombers.

However, the addition of *Seydlitz* to the programme led to fresh discussions regarding the shortage of shipyard workers, only to be solved by the allocation of additional manpower. In return, the Minister of Armaments, Albert Speer, indicated that such skilled workers could only be provided by drawing on the Wehrmacht as a whole, including the Kriegsmarine. In the meantime, *OKW* had issued a directive for the transfer of all shipyard workers from the replacement reserves of other Wehrmacht branches to the Kriegsmarine, though confusion arose over whether the Kriegsmarine would therefore be responsible for the replacement of those men. Manpower was not the sole problem to be overcome. The working capacity of all available shipyards was insufficient to meet the demands of the existing urgent work program to supply as many U-boats as possible to Dönitz as the battle of the Atlantic reached fever pitch, let alone handle new conversion work unless 'radical measures' were introduced.

Europa – redesignated 'Auxiliary Aircraft Carrier I' – was to be rebuilt by Hamburg's Blohm & Voss yard, though by November 1942 planning was halted and the order eventually cancelled before any work had begun. The smaller *Potsdam* and *Gneisenau* were to be handled by the Howaldt Werke and Wilhelmshaven naval shipyard respectively, though cancellation of the *Europa* conversion led to *Potsdam* (redesignated *Jade*) being passed to Blohm & Voss. Construction difficulties in solving stability problems in *Gneisenau* (redesignated *Elbe*) led to a cessation of work on 25 November 1942.

Due to the increasing threat of RAF bombing, the transfer of *Graf Zeppelin* to Kiel where work could resume at full pace was delayed until 30 November 1942, when she finally left Gotenhafen under tow by three tugboats and escorted by three minesweepers and six *Vorpostenboote*. She reached Kieler Förde on 3 December and lay at anchor for two days before moving to the Deutsche Werk floating dock. There, work began immediately on building the hull bulges and completing the engine rooms.

Meanwhile the decision was then taken to transform *Potsdam* into a training aircraft carrier, work beginning on dismantling passenger cabins in December. But following the disaster of the 'Battle of the North Cape' and Hitler's subsequent fury at his naval leaders, a '*Führer Befehl*' ordered all work ceased on 30 January 1943; the same order that curtailed work once and for all on *Graf Zeppelin* as the complexion of Germany's naval war, and indeed its command hierarchy, had changed dramatically.

An ignominious end for the *Graf Zeppelin* aircraft carrier, photographed here from a Soviet vessel in the Mönne River, September 1945.

The instruction filtered through to *Graf Zeppelin* by 2 February and the dream of an operational German aircraft carrier was finally and ignominiously over. The projected conversion of *De Grasse* was cancelled with insufficient workmen in Lorient and a problematic propulsion system amongst other design flaws. Work on the final auxiliary carrier – *Seydlitz*, now known as *Weser* – was halted in June 1943, the hulk being towed to Königsberg. The incomplete *Graf Zeppelin* was towed by tugs to Stettin on 23 April 1943 and moored in shallow water in the Mönne River. There she would remain until the end of the war in Europe.

2

Blood and Sand

In Defence of North Africa

O N 6 NOVEMBER 1942 a Heinkel He 111 of *Sonderkommando Koch* operating from Sardinia's Elmas airfield reported an unusually large mass of shipping passing through the Strait of Gibraltar, detected while carrying out a routine radar search off Algeria using a captured British ASV Mk II radar. This corroborated notification from Abwehr agents in both Spain and Spanish Morocco of convoy traffic and a tangible increase in Allied air forces. Nonetheless, in a disastrous German intelligence blunder, any possibility of an attack against the North African coast was dismissed, the movement deemed probably reinforcement for Montgomery's Eighth Army at Tobruk or a fresh resupply for Malta. Regardless of its objective, the accumulated shipping required countermeasures, and the Luftwaffe swiftly moved assets to the Mediterranean.

The Allies' November El Alamein offensive had pushed Rommel's exhausted *Panzergruppe Afrika* (which included the vaunted *Afrika Korps*) away from the Egyptian frontier into a defensive retreat, supply remaining a major Axis problem as maritime convoys were vulnerable to interception from Malta. The Luftwaffe were tasked with convoy escort and had already contributed six large six-engine BV 222 flying boats of *Lufttransportstaffel 222 (See)* to help shuttle supplies between Taranto and Tobruk from the summer of 1942.

The huge Blohm & Voss BV 222 '*Wiking*' aircraft stemmed from pre-war commercial interests. Lufthansa had requested design proposals from Heinkel, Dornier and Blohm & Voss for a non-stop transatlantic passenger flying boat that could accommodate twenty-four day passengers in relative luxury during the crossing, or sixteen by night in sleeping compartments. The contract was ultimately awarded to Blohm & Voss and their Ha (Later BV) 222 on 19 August 1937. The winning model was ambitious, sporting six engines where the competing firms had envisioned four to be sufficient. Final design work began in January

The Blohm & Voss BV 222 '*Wiking*'.

1938 and construction of 'V1' started within six months, 'V2' and 'V3' following weeks later. By the outbreak of war, the aircraft had still not been completed and skilled technicians were drawn away to work on the proven BV 138 flying boats in demand for the *Küstenflieger*. Lufthansa finally approved the final interior mock-up of the BV 222 during early August 1940, knowing that the Luftwaffe were likely to commandeer the aircraft to boost its weak transport capabilities. The 'A series' (V1-6 and V8) were powered by six Bramo 323 R (from 1942 R-2) 9-cylinder petrol engines. As the 'B series' remained a civil project that never materialised, V7 was the first of the 'C-series' which had changed the engines for six Junkers Jumo 207 C diesels.

The maiden flight of 'V1' took place on 7 September 1940, its handling satisfactory during the sixteen-minute test though instability in horizontal flight was noted as was a slight side-to-side movement when taxiing on water. Further remedial testing on the Elbe River was undertaken until December 1940 when the severe winter ice prevented further work.

The Luftwaffe proposed instead that further trials and testing be done in field conditions with 'V1' used for transport missions between Hamburg and Kirkenes in the Arctic. In June 'V1' made its first test supply flight when it flew as part of *Seestaffel der Luftverkehrsgruppe* from Schaalsee in Schleswig-Holstein to Lake Bracciano near Rome, onwards to Augusta, Sicily and returning to Germany over the course of two days. Repainted in Luftwaffe colours and given the code 'CC+EQ', 'V1' completed seven flights between Kirkenes and Hamburg by August 1941, carrying 65 tonnes of supplies to Norway and returning 221 wounded men to Germany. The aircraft was capable of transporting ninety-two fully-equipped troops at one time or seventy-two wounded stretcher cases and was considered fully operational at that point with all design modifications completed, though still operating without armament and requiring fighter escort. Following a complete overhaul, 'V1' was transferred to Athens from where it began regular transport missions to the port city of Derna in eastern Libya in support of the *Afrika Korps*. Between 16 October and 6 November 1941 'V1' had flown 30 tonnes of supplies outbound, returning with 515 wounded men to Greece. Over the winter of 1941 'V1' was fitted with defensive weapons; a nose 7.92mm MG 81, two DL131 turrets equipped with 13mm MG 131s on the upper fuselage and four ventral MG 81s. 'V1' was also redesignated 'X4+AH', with the tail marking 'S1' and was the first aircraft attached to the newly created *Luftransportstaffel* 222. Both 'V2' (re-coded 'X4+BH', tail marking 'S2') and 'V3' ('X4+CH', 'S3') were subsequently attached to the *Staffel* in May 1942 and December 1941 respectively.

By the time Rommel began his retreat from the Alamein battle 'V4' ('X4+DH'), 'V5' ('X4+EH'), 'V6' ('X4+FH') and 'V8' ('X4+HH') had all joined *Luftransportstaffel* 222, 'V3' also undertaking twenty-six supply flights between Constanța and a lake near the Ukrainian town of Woroschilowsk during September and October. On 24 November *Luftransportstaffel* 222 suffered its first BV 222 casualty when 'V6' was intercepted by three Beaufighters of RAF 272 Squadron south of the island of Pantelleria at 1350hrs. *Oberleutnant* Edmund Wilhelm was piloting the aircraft north, returning from Tripoli with forty-one wounded men and nine passengers when Australian Flight Lieutenant Ern Coate opened fire from the flying boat's beam, large pieces of the fuselage being seen to be blasted away and all three port engines and the fuel tank catching fire. The BV 222 rapidly lost height and hit the sea heavily, bouncing 60 feet back into the air before coming down on its left wing, half rolling over and exploding. The body of second wireless operator *Ogef.* Engelbert Theinert was later recovered, though no trace of the remaining eight crew nor any of their passengers were ever found.

Following El Alamein, a stronger air bridge was attempted with Condors of III/KG40 moved from France to Lecce, reinforced shortly thereafter by Ju 90s and Ju 290s to supplement the 150 Ju 52 transport aircraft already in southern Italy. Ironically, limitations on the most

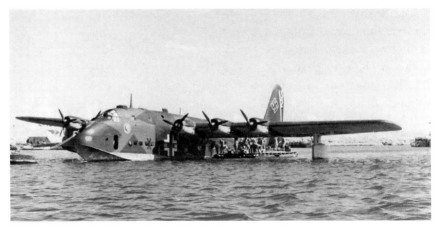

Aircraft 'X4+BH' embarking troops while attached to *Lufttransportstaffel* 222.

crucial cargo – fuel for the panzers – were soon increase by a lack of available barrels for air freight. To counter Allied threats to both aerial and seaborne Mediterranean supply routes, Ju 88s of I. and II./LG 1 were relocated from Greece to Catania. Also, while the Ju 88s of both *Maj.* Ernst-Günther von Scheliha's I.*Gruppe* and *Maj.* Karl Schreiner's II.*Gruppe* of KG 6 had been stationed in France bombing mainland Britain since September 1942, a reinforced *Staffel* was transferred to Foggia during October to join operations in support of Rommel's troops.

Though not clearly understanding the objective of the recently-detected Allied shipping concentration near Gibraltar, the first of five anti-shipping *Gruppen* began moving from northern Norway and Finland – where they had proved devastatingly effective against Arctic convoy traffic – to the Mediterranean between 7 and 14 November. Behind them, winter weather had curtailed operations, their final Norwegian success having been on 5 November when the unescorted 5,445-ton British steamer SS *Chulmleigh* was bombed and damaged by a Ju 88 of II./KG 30, being beached on an isolated part of Spitzbergen 10 miles south-west of South Cape. There she was torpedoed the following day by *U625* before being finished off with shellfire and the smouldering wreck again bombed by KG 30. Of the merchant's complement, only the Master, Daniel Morley Williams, three crew members and nine gunners survived; the remaining thirty-six crewmen and nine gunners died, most due to exposure as they were not rescued by troops from the local garrison at Barentsburg until 4 January.

Of the five anti-shipping *Gruppen* transferred from the northern theatre, four were equipped with Ju 88s – III./KG 26 (*Hptm.* Klaus-Wilhelm Nocken, based at Banak), II./KG 30 (based at Bardufoss, minus 6./KG 30 that remained at Kemi until 13 November 1942), III./KG 30 (from Bardufoss to Comiso) and I./KG 60 (from Banak to Elmas, Sardinia).

The highly experienced dive-bomber and bomber pilot *Maj.* Dietrich Peltz had been placed in command of KG 60, a new unit formed from the training establishment of *Verbandsführerschule für Kampffliegerausbildung* created in Foggia at the beginning of 1942. There, bomber commanders were instructed in the latest operational techniques, Peltz at the forefront of helping develop cutting edge operational doctrine for the Luftwaffe. 'Hajo' Herrmann of KG 30, who made the effort to fly from Bardufoss to Foggia to observe Peltz's training lectures, remembered:

> Dieter Peltz was a year younger than I was and had a record of considerable success as a Stuka pilot on Ju 87s, now converted to standard bombing and the Ju 88. He was the first young man in high authority that I had come across – and, sometimes, into argument with. He was very relaxed, in contrast to our senior officers of the old, imperialist school, who found difficulty in coming to terms with the challenges of technology and the younger generation. Peltz' lectures were graphic, humorous, optimistic, and always thorough as far as detail was concerned. It was a pleasure to be with him.[1]

Peltz, already a holder of the Knight's Cross with Oak Leaves, relocated the bomber school from Foggia to Tours, France, during mid-1942 and it was here at the beginning of August that I./KG 60 was created, comprising only Stab., 1. and 2./KG 60 until three weeks later 3./KG 60 was formed. The former *Staffeln* were posted to Banak in October while the new *Staffel* completed its training. Raised from men of his bomber commander's school, Peltz was appointed *Gruppenkommandeur* on 1 August 1942. Equipped with Ju 88 A-4s, the focus was on developing techniques for the use of the precision guided munitions under development in Germany, such as the 'Fritz-X' and Henschel Hs 293. Three weeks after the operational *Staffeln* had been posted to Norway, they were recalled to Sardinia; on 8 November Peltz moving with 1. and 2./KG 60 to Elmas to reinforce II.*Fliegerkorps*.

Dietrich Peltz, Hermann Göring and Werner Baumbach, photographed in early 1942.

While most incoming Junkers *Gruppen* moved to Sardinia or Sicily, joining those of KG 54 (Catania) and KG 77 (I./KG 77 in Catania, II and III./KG 77 in Gerbini), III./KG 26 flew instead to Grosseto alongside twenty-five Heinkel torpedo bombers of *Maj.* Werner Klümper's I./KG 26 which had transferred from Bardufoss via landings at Aalborg, Lübeck-Blankensee and Munich. The final identification of the *Torch* convoys also brought the remainder of I. and II./KG 6 to the Mediterranean, transferring to Gerbini airfield during November.

The sudden influx of men and aircraft caused considerable confusion at Grosseto, Klümper himself getting lost during the transfer, leading to briefings for I./KG 26's inaugural Mediterranean mission on 12 November being carried out by 3./KG 26 *Staffelkapitän, Hptm.* Bernd Eicke, who had previously deputised for the *Gruppenkommandeur*.

The Ju 88s that flew south to the balmy Mediterranean were crammed to capacity, carrying five men and two torpedoes per aircraft. The Heinkels too had each been loaded with torpedoes and the personnel required for immediate operations, the remaining ground crew following in Ju 52 transport aircraft. Of II./KG 26, both 4. and 5. *Staffel* had been moved to the Don front where they became embroiled in the bombing of Stalingrad, while the torpedo-equipped 6./KG 26 had already been stationed at Heraklion and Catania before moving to Elmas, Sardinia's principle airbase 6.5 kilometres north-west of Cagliari. Only six of these Heinkel crews were trained in night operations with 'assisted take-off'. This latter technique had been introduced during 1942 for aircraft carrying particularly heavy loads, such as twin torpedoes. They were frequently provided with the Walter HWK 109-500 self-contained rocket take-off assist (*Starthilfe*) engine. Capable of producing 500kg of thrust for thirty seconds, the pods were affixed underwing and upon exhaustion of the 'T-Stoff' hydrogen peroxide fuel were jettisoned and floated back to earth by parachute.

The torpedo *Staffel* possessed just seventeen operational torpedoes with a further six undergoing servicing. As KG 26's Staff flight had been removed in June 1941 to form *Fliegerführer Norwegen* under *Oberst* Alexander Holle, the commander of the Grosseto torpedo school, *Oberst* Karl Stockmann was named *Kommodore*.

The efficacy of the F5 aerial torpedo was now firmly accepted within the Luftwaffe after its faltering start, though it was not until a report dated January 1944 by *Oberkommando der Luftwaffe*'s 8. *Abteilung* titled 'The Operational Use of the Luftwaffe in the War at Sea, 1939-1943' in which the different bomb and torpedo operations that had been mounted against convoys PQ16, PQ17 and PQ18 in the Arctic were statistically compared:

For each ship sunk the following sorties were made:
a. In the case of the PQ16 convoy under the best weather conditions for dive-bombing attacks:
9.8 torpedo sorties as compared with 23.6 dive-bomber sorties.
b. In the case of the PQ17 convoy, similarly in the best weather conditions:
7 torpedo sorties as compared with 9.2 dive-bomber sorties.
c. In the case of the PQ18 convoy in unfavourable weather conditions for dive-bomber attacks:
7.3 torpedo sorties as compared with 24.3 dive-bomber sorties.
Of the 340 aerial torpedoes launched, 84 hit the target, i.e. 25 per cent. 32 torpedoes were duds, i.e. 9 per cent.
When the development of long-range bombers makes it possible for heavier loads to be carried, it will also be possible to increase the effectiveness of torpedoes. This could certainly be achieved if their weight

could be increased. In addition to the question of weight, the following developments might be made with regard to torpedoes:

Increase the range and bombing altitude; raising the speed of torpedoes and increasing the distance they can travel; enlarging the warhead; introducing new methods of fusing; using an apparatus that will give a torpedo a zig-zag course on the convoy route; using an apparatus which could enable the torpedo to guide itself to a target; eliminating the effect of high seas and cross winds.

Spread between Italy and Sicily, II.*Fliegerkorps* was commanded by *General der Flieger* Bruno Loerzer, a former First World War flying ace and holder of the *Pour le Mérite*. Between the wars he had fought with various *Freikorps* against Communist forces before becoming head of the National Socialist Flying Corps (NSFK) and rejoining the Luftwaffe in 1935. Awarded the Knight's Cross for his role in the invasion of France in 1940, he had led II.*Fliegerkorps* in Russia before being posted to the Mediterranean in October 1941. Despite his undoubted bravery in the field, Loerzer's close friendship with Göring appears to have permeated through to his professional aptitude and personal behaviour. Quartered in a luxury hotel in the town of Taormina, Sicily, Loerzer accumulated

General der Flieger Bruno Loerzer and Göring. Their close friendship proved detrimental to Loerzer's handling of II.*Fliegerkorps*.

textiles and trinkets from the region, much as Göring had become increasingly distracted with 'acquiring' personal wealth than successfully running his air force. The whiff of corruption began to surround Loerzer and his immediate staff which did little to help operational effectiveness.

Indeed, despite the numerical increase in Luftwaffe strength with the sudden transfer of aircraft to the Mediterranean theatre, conditions upon arrival were far from ideal. Werner Baumbach later complained specifically in a letter to Jeschonnek that:

Although II.*Fliegerkorps* had had at least two days' notice of our coming, no preparations (quarters, headquarters, clothing, feeding, telephone network, bays, motor transport, repair and service staff) had been made to receive us. Our arrival was a complete surprise to the ground staff. The ground staff commandant, *Major* Rose, knew nothing about it before I walked into his room. He is the only bright spot here: (he is a clergyman in civil life). The same thing happened in the case of the other bomber wings. The commanders of the individual units had to do everything, and it was only by willing cooperation among them that we got ourselves into rough and ready order for action. Up to today our own technical personnel (Airfield Maintenance Company) have not arrived. The transport of the most essential key men has proved extremely difficult and would have been impossible without my personal intervention and the efforts of the commanders. In that connection I broke at least ten regulations. It proved impossible to send a few Ju 52/13Ms to Comiso with supplies although a bomber wing flew more than 3,100 miles to a completely new theatre of war inside two days, got 70 per cent of its aircraft in the absence of the most essential ground staff, and carried out sorties of 1,800 operational miles. Neither on arrival nor afterwards was there much sign of preparatory staff work. So far, we have seen nothing of any representative of the *Fliegerkorps*, much less the General. These gentlemen sit far from the firing line in their offices in Catania or, more recently, the comfortable surroundings of the luxury hotel, San Domenico, at Taormina, and in reply to my official reports on the appalling conditions here have informed me by telephone that I may have acquired my experience in the Arctic but conditions here are different and I know nothing about them and must leave everything to them. I have the impression, shared with the other commanders, that there is a lack of overall direction and control.[2]

Despite reinforcement of the Mediterranean Luftwaffe, the Allies knew that the secrets of Operation *Torch* remained secure. Extremely effective intelligence-gathering agencies, spearheaded by the ULTRA Enigma decryption service based at Bletchley Park, betrayed almost every step the Wehrmacht were making. Each *Fliegerkorps* had been given its own Enigma key in January 1942, all of which were quickly broken by Bletchley Park, including that designated 'Locust' by the Allied codebreakers and belonging to II.*Fliegerkorps* in the Western Mediterranean. Through this intelligence source the Allies gleaned information that II.*Fliegerkorps* were transferring aircraft east to X.*Fliegerkorps* in the Aegean as recently as seventy-two hours before the *Torch* landings were due to commence, providing a firm indication that the Germans had no idea of the invasion convoys' true destination. Furthermore, as well as detailed orders of battle of all regional Luftwaffe assets, Enigma decryptions included reconnaissance reports passed along the chain of command, the Allies privy to up-to-date German estimations of their intentions and able to plan accordingly.

The Wehrmacht's *Oberbefehlshaber Süd* (Commander-in-Chief South, held simultaneously with command of *Luftflotte 2*), *Generalfeldmarschall* Albert Kesselring. had already concluded that an Allied landing in the western Mediterranean was likely, although his opinion was ignored by *OKW* who maintained that any likely landing would be near Tripoli. Kesselring reasoned that the bombing of Malta and its relief convoys had adequately demonstrated localised Luftwaffe strength and, combined with the potential Italian naval threat, would dissuade invasion traffic attempting to breach the Strait of Sicily. Furthermore, no major reinforcement of Allied air power on Malta had been detected, which surely would have accompanied any such attempt. Nonetheless, while Göring himself clung to the idea of an Allied landing on southern France, *OKW* remained entrenched in its mistaken prediction.

The Allied shipping concentration belonged to Operation *Torch*, aimed at establishing Allied forces in north-west Africa, launching a campaign against Vichy Tunisia from Algeria. Three amphibious landings were to be undertaken: in the vicinity of Casablanca, Oran and Algiers. Three Allied Task Forces were assigned: the Western Task Force that sailed from the American east coast, carrying 35,000 troops bound for landings near Casablanca at Safi, Rabat and Mehdia under the command of Major General George Patton, and the Central and Eastern Task Forces originating from the United Kingdom; the former commanded

Loerzer in conversation with his superior *Generalfeldmarschall* Albert Kesselring, *Oberbefehlshaber Süd* and commander of *Luftflotte* 2.

by Major General Lloyd Fredendall with 18,500 troops bound for Oran, the latter to land 20,000 troops at Algiers under the command of Major General Charles W. Ryder. With troops established ashore, Allied Supreme Command planned to squeeze Axis forces in Tunisia between an advance from the west and Montgomery's Eighth Army forces from Egypt, Rommel's front line on the eve of Torch resting at Sidi Barrani.

As the *Torch* convoys approached their target landing zones, Allied planners confidently shaped the invasion using Ultra intercepts. The information provided was detailed and accurate and Allied intelligence expected the most significant threats to be Vichy land forces, followed by Axis aircraft from Sardinia and Sicily, though they mistakenly believed that Berlin would despatch no reinforcements for the latter until four days after the initial landings had taken place.[3] They had, however, underestimated Luftwaffe flexibility and Hitler's desire to hold North Africa, despite his previous general neglect of the operational theatre in favour of Operation *Barbarossa*. Somewhat ironically, Kesselring's repeated requests for the allocation of long-range reconnaissance aircraft from Bordeaux and Norway resulted in the redirection of several KG

40 Fw 200s to the south, allowing British convoys destined for the *Torch* landings to sail unobserved through the Atlantic towards Gibraltar.

On 5 November, Kesselring ordered approximately twenty aircraft made ready to attack the convoy within the western Mediterranean, once its location was confirmed by reconnaissance. He stipulated that daylight attacks should only be attempted from cloud cover, while those mounted during the twilight period be undertaken only if weather permitted night landings at Eleusis. However, after multiple intelligence reports of massed shipping, coupled with aerial sightings of dimmed military and merchant vessels moving past Gibraltar during the night of 6 November, Kesselring delayed any other operations against what was clearly more than a Malta resupply mission, in favour of concentrated attacks on the morning of 8 November. Agent sightings of at least three Allied carriers also resulted in all *Kampfgeschwader* being withdrawn from convoy escort duties and prepared for bombing.

Five He III torpedo carriers of 6./KG.26 made that first attack after transferring from Grosseto to Elmas, Sardinia, followed shortly thereafter by eight further He IIIs and three Ju 88s. There they liaised closely with the two Heinkels of *Sonderkommando Koch* which detected the incoming *Torch* convoy KMFI(A) bound for Algiers.[4] As Ju 88s of I.(F)/Aufkl.Gr. 122 kept the convoy under constant observation – despite losing two aircraft – a large force of thirty-seven of KG 26's best trained crews was despatched to attack. Eventually, only six Heinkels of 6./KG 26 made contact with KMFI, the remainder having turned back, and the convoy of nineteen large landing and troop transport ships, was attacked with ten torpedoes, the sixth aircraft unable to locate a target and returning with both torpedoes intact. In early morning darkness as KMFI sailed almost due east on smooth water, the attack troopship USS *Thomas Stone*, sailing in second place of the left-hand column, was hit by a single torpedo. Myriad sources claim that the torpedo was fired by *Korvettenkapitän* Franz-Georg Reschke's *U205* although eyewitness accounts would seem to indicate otherwise, and the U-boat's war diary records an attack mounted in the late evening rather than early morning. Commander C.H. Pike, XO aboard USS *Thomas Stone* described the attack in his official after-action report:

About 0500hrs 7 November 1942, the crew of *Thomas Stone* went to General Quarters. I was at my battle station, Battle II, which is on the after main deck just forward of the five-inch gun almost directly over the propeller. About 0530 while still very dark, a plane was reported coming in from aft on the port side. When I first observed it, the plan was about 800 yards from the ship, altitude about 200 feet. For a short distance it was on a parallel course the bore off to the northward away from the ship climbing rapidly. It was a large twin-engine plane. I observed a black cloud of smoke on the surface of the water over which the plane had passed just abeam of the ship. About the same time there was a warning cry the exact nature of which I do not recall then a tremendous detonation in my immediate vicinity. Practically all personnel on the after deck including myself were thrown to the deck which heaved violently and settled back with a considerable angle of slope from normal . . . My impression at first was that an aerial bomb had struck in the vicinity of number 5 hold, so I went there. I found the repair party at work shoring up the after bulkhead and plugging leaks and it was then that I first realised that the ship had been torpedoed and that the torpedo had exploded directly under me.[5]

The ship carried 1,400 men of the 2nd Battalion, 39th Regiment, 9th US Infantry Division, destined for their landing zone east of Cape Matifou for the British-controlled assault on Algiers. Nine men were killed in the blast, though, despite damage to the stern and losing steerage, the transport was towed by her own disembarked landing craft and then by the destroyers HMS *Wishart* and *Velox* and the tug *St. Day* to Algiers,

USS *Thomas Stone* being emptied after beaching at Algiers, 24 November 1942.

arriving on 11 November. There the disabled ship was later hit again by bombers while in harbour before finally being driven aground by gale-force winds where she was abandoned.

The Luftwaffe contributed to the loss of a second ship of KMF1 on 8 November when the troopship USS *Leedstown* was hit in the stern by one of thirteen attacking Junkers Ju 88s of III./KG 26 while lying at anchor three miles east of Cape Matifou. Hit aft on the starboard side, the explosion destroyed steering gear and flooded the after section. *Leedstown*, which had begun life as the passenger liner *Santa Lucia* in 1933 before commandeered by the US Navy in August 1942, had already landed a detachment of British 1st Commando and the 3rd Battalion of the 39th US Infantry Division during the previous night. The disabled ship was left under the supervision of the corvette HMS *Samphire* while the remainder of the convoy steamed for Algiers, and the following day further air attacks and near misses with Ju 88 bombs increased the damage. *Kapitänleutnant* von Theisenhausen's *U331* also sighted what he believed was a '15,000-ton troopship' lying stationary under destroyer escort and fired a salvo of four angled torpedoes from seaward with only 29 metres of water beneath the submerged U-boat's keel. Three detonations were heard by the German crew, though only two torpedoes had hit amidships on the starboard side, *Leedstown* taking a heavy list to starboard and beginning to settle by the bow. Finally, the order to abandon ship was given and, after yet another bombing attack that afternoon, the ship sank near Cape Matifou, the commander and 103 survivors picked up by HMS *Samphire* and landed at Algiers the next morning.

On 8 November two messages were received almost simultaneously at Kesselring's headquarters; the first from Luftwaffe reconnaissance aircraft and the second from a French radio transmitter in North Africa. Both reported fighting in Oran and Algiers, as the reality of the Allied invasion objective was confirmed. With limited land forces available, and political considerations stopping German occupation of Vichy Tunisia, U-boats were despatched to attack the Allied transport fleet while the Luftwaffe would concentrate on Algiers, Oran beyond the range of available aircraft.

The day following the landings saw an immediate increase in the tempo of Luftwaffe bomber attacks, albeit too far from Sicily for fighter protection to be provided. Emergency provision was also made to bring troops to Tunisia and block the western invasion force. With

Malta restored to a functioning Allied base, sea transport was both time-consuming and risky and *Oberst* Rudolf Starke, *Lufttransportführer Mittelmeer*, gathered together five *Gruppen* of Ju 52 aircraft, including school machines and '*Mausi*' minesweepers pressganged into transport service, beneath two ad-hoc headquarters units, KGr.z.b.V. S (*Sizilien*) and N (*Neapal*). These 514 aircraft began immediately shuttling men and material to Tunisia that same day, by the end of the year having transferred 41,768 men and 10,086 tons of equipment despite a strong Allied air presence attached to the *Torch* forces. Attached to the airlift was 6.*Seenotstaffel* whose Dornier Do 24 aircraft carried personnel to Bizerte, before establishing a *Seenotstaffel* command in Tunis.

During this period 6.*Seenotstaffel* made its 1,000th rescue, commemorated by the mentioning of *Oberstleutnant* Englehorn in the Luftwaffe Roll of Honour. However, the *Staffel* suffered severe losses in the days following the *Torch* landings. On 13 November 1942, *Stafflekapitän Oberleutnant* Fritz Wölke, one of the most experienced air-sea rescue pilots and holder of the German Cross in Gold, and his crew were killed on a return flight from Tunis to Syracuse with ten people aboard when their Do 24 was attacked by a Beaufighter VIC of RAF 227 Squadron. The following day Do 24N 'KK+UP' was shot down by a 72 Squadron Spitfire off Marsaxlokk Bay. Later during December two more Dorniers were lost; one to an accident while taking off with a cargo of fuel bound for North Africa and the other to a mine while landing off the Sicilian coast.

It is worth noting that in the early days of deployment of *Seenotsdiesnt* aircraft to the North African theatre, a slightly higher level of respect had been accorded the German aircraft from British forces as they quickly discerned that Allied airmen were benefiting from the Axis air-sea rescue forces as much as their enemy. For example, *Lt.* Wolfgang Kretschmar, operating with 6.*Seenotstaffel* in Benghazi during June 1941, responded to a Ju 88 report of a life raft containing three occupants, mid-way between Tobruk and Crete. As Kretschmar arrived at the location a British twin-engined seaplane was circling, unable to land in the relatively rough sea conditions. Demonstrating the robustness of the Dornier, Kretschmar landed on his second attempt, recovering the three British occupants of the raft and returning to base accompanied by the British aircraft, both crews exchanging waves as they parted company near Benghazi.[6]

However, by the time of Operation *Torch* such chivalry appears to have diminished to the same level experienced in Northern Europe. The

Italian air-sea rescue equivalent used commercial civilian seaplanes for the purpose, generally crewed by their original civilian crews and marked with the Red Cross, though they too found that this no longer afforded the expected protection from enemy attack.

At noon on 9 November *Oberst* Martin Harlinghausen arrived by He 111 from Sicily at El Aouina airport in Tunis. There, while German security troops began landing along with the forward elements of JG 53's and StG 3's ground personnel, he entered immediate discussions with Vichy commanders and established the office of *Fliegerführer Tunis* to provide tactical air support to ground operations with the begrudging permission of ranking Vichy commander Admiral Jean Pierre Esteva. Relations between Vichy and Italian forces had always been severely strained and at first Harlinghausen was obliged to promise that no Italian troops would be stationed in Tunisia. However, within days this promise was rescinded as the need for fighting manpower outweighed such diplomatic concerns. By the month's end three German and two Italian divisions had been successfully shipped to Tunisia, *Generalmajor* Walther Nehring placed in command of this newly formed XC Corps on 12 November

Vichy forces had put up unexpectedly stiff resistance around Casablanca and Oran, although Algiers was firmly in Allied hands, and three fighter squadrons – RAF 43 Squadron (Hurricane IIs), 81 Squadron (Spitfire Vcs) and 242 Squadron (Spitfire Vbs) – swiftly established at Maison Blanche airfield which had surrendered to an American assault group almost immediately. Furthermore, the carriers HMS *Formidable* and *Victorious* added the weight of their aircraft to the defence of shipping around Algiers, and the airfield at Elida was hastily occupied by four naval Martlet aircraft.[7] By the day's end British fighters had claimed the shooting down of fifteen bombers attempting to attack shipping near Algiers, navy gunners claiming five others. In total, on 9 November, sixteen Ju 88s and two He 111s had been lost. Among the casualties were the *Gruppenkommandeur* of II./KG 6, *Maj.* Gerhard von Roth, killed with his crew in aircraft '3E+CC' shot down over Bougie and *Gruppenkommandeur* of II./KG 26, *Hptm.* Karl Barth, his He 111 H-6, '3E+CC', crashing off the Algerian coast, all men listed as missing in action. Knight's Cross holder *Hptm.* Klaus-Wilhelm Nocken, *Staka* of 7./KG 26, was also brought down, north of Bougie, *Lt.* Ernst Georg Lampe and *Uffz.* Johannes Rompel killed as the Ju 88 '1T+AR' hit the sea. Both Nocken and *Uffz.* Horst Muller were able to take to their life raft, the officer having been wounded during the action. They were finally rescued by *Oblt.z.S.* Otto Hartmann's *U77* on 14 November and returned to La Spezia in early December.

Italian SM 79 torpedo aircraft of 130° Gruppo sank the *Black Swan* class sloop HMS *Ibis* near Algiers on 10 November, the same day that a convoy departed for Operation *Perpetual* and the planned occupation of Bougie, 115 miles to the east, and Jijel another 30 miles distant and hosting a strategically valuable airfield. The latter landing and airfield seizure was thwarted by heavy seas and dangerous surf, the troopship HMT *Awatea* instead returning to Bougie to unload its troops and supplies, which included a large number of RAF personnel and fuel intended to bring the airfield into operational use as quickly as possible. However, as the carrier HMS *Argus* which had been providing fighter cover was withdrawn westwards, this left the convoy without local air protection and although RAF fighters from the more distant Maison Blanche airfield attempted to fill the vacuum, the ships were attacked by nearly thirty Ju 88s and torpedo-carrying He 111s of KG 26 on 11 November. The monitor HMS *Roberts* was damaged by two 500kg bombs and two of the large transport ships also hit; the 15,225GRT P&O liner SS *Cathay* and the 13,482GRT HMT *Awatea*. The New Zealand liner *Awatea* was bombed and strafed, returning fire with every possible weapon until two torpedoes hit the port side. Fires broke out immediately and a dud bomb that smashed through the deck was ignited by the flames, and soon the entire ship was ablaze. Several had near-misses blasted apart most of the first-class accommodation and the crew abandoned ship, the beached hulk later destroyed by further bombing attacks. The liner *Cathay* suffered severe flooding after being attacked in deep water while still unloading troops into lighters and was also abandoned, one man being killed during the initial raid. A single Ju 88 of 5./KG 6, was lost, two wounded crewmen later being recovered by a Do 24 flying boat.

Bougie itself was taken without fighting by men of 6th Battalion, Royal West Kent Regiment, and an assault unit was sent overland to capture Jijel airfield. British paratroopers of 3rd Battalion, 1st Parachute Regiment were hurriedly dropped by American transport aircraft on Duzerville airfield six miles south-east of Bône barely pre-empting a *Fallschirmjäger* landing to capture the same airfield that had been betrayed by ULTRA decrypts. Luftwaffe bombers returned to Bougie the following day and damaged the 9,891GRT Landing Ship Infantry HMS *Karanja*, which sank some hours later. Ammunition stored aboard the burning abandoned hulk of SS *Cathay* also finally exploded and blew off the stern, the ship capsizing and sinking on her starboard side. On 14 November the 16,632GRT impressed P&O liner SS *Narkunda* was also hit by Ju 88 bombs and sunk in the Gulf of Bougie after having disembarked her load of ground troops. Attacking out of strong cloud cover, the Junkers hit the ship astern to port, the liner sinking with thirty-one crew killed, the remaining 211 men being rescued by the minesweeper HMS *Cadmus* before *Narkunda* heeled over and sank, her whistle, jammed open by the force of the explosions, silenced only as the bridge submerged.

Though the destruction of the large troopships and damage to other cargo transports was an undoubted victory for the Luftwaffe, by the time that *Narkunda* was attacked, Spitfires of 154 Squadron were operating in a limited capacity from Jijel airfield though the sporadic fuel supply proved a hindrance. On 12 November fuel trucks arrived from Bougie and that day KG 60 lost two Ju 88s and KG 26 two He 111H-6s, 154 Squadron soon joined by RAF 242 Squadron and other fighters arriving at Duzerville airfield. Though the Allied pilots and maintenance crews servicing the aircraft while squadron groundcrews travelled from Gibraltar existed in the most primitive and difficult conditions, their presence accelerated German bomber losses. Fighter aircraft of Harlinghausen's *Fliegerführer Tunis* were in almost constant action attempting to shield them, but their losses outpaced replacements, numbers outpaced by the steady Allied build-up. Furthermore, in Tunisia a severe shortage of spare parts, infrastructure and supplies lowered serviceability while airfields and communication centres came under direct attack.

The Luftwaffe despatched reinforcing fighters and dive-bombers to the Mediterranean from all fronts including Stalingrad where the imperilled Sixth Army battled Soviet forces on the River Volga. Hitler, almost unexpectedly, signalled his firm intent to hold the 'North African bridgehead in Tunisia' against the Allied invasion. On 11 November he had also triggered 'Case Anton' and the long-prepared emergency occupation of Vichy France after Admiral Darlan directed all French forces in North Africa to cease resistance. The Luftwaffe's unopposed part in the occupation was code-named '*Unternehmen Stockdorf*' which provided southern French airfields for anti-shipping units of *Generalmajor* Johannes Fink's 2. *Fliegerdivision*, transferred from the eastern front to Montfrin in the Occitanie region during November and placed under the command of *Luftflotte* 2. Headquartered in the Château de Montfrin, Fink would eventually accumulate five torpedo bomber and two air-to-surface guided weapon *Gruppen* under his immediate command. However, alongside missions to disrupt Allied supply shipments to the *Torch* beach heads, he also prepared operational plans to intercept every detected eastbound convoy, bringing him into direct conflict with KG 26 *Kommodore Oberst* Karl Stockmann and his successor from February, the veteran *Obstlt.* Werner Klümper. The KG 26 officers advocated selected attacks to maximise bomber effectiveness, the opposing positions becoming so intractable that Klümper took his case directly to Jeschonnek at the *RLM*. There he risked the charge of insubordination as he threatened to resign lest his opinion prevail, successfully swaying Jeschonnek to his point of view.

Regional *Seenotbereichskommando* XIII was established at the seaplane base on Etang de Berre 24 miles north-west of Marseilles following 'Stockdorf', placed under the control of *Luftflotte* 3, while 3.*Seenotstaffel* was transferred from Amsterdam equipped with He 59 and Do 24 flying boats and augmented by eleven captured Vichy Bréguet Bizertes. An air traffic control boat was stationed at Port de Bouc, west of Marseilles, another with two accompanying He 59s at St Raphael, south-west of Cannes, and a third at Port Vandre near the Franco-Spanish border.

By the middle of November, seventy-four Luftwaffe torpedo bombers were present in the Mediterranean; fifty-four in Italy and Sicily with a further twenty stationed in Greece. British convoy traffic sailing in the

A captured French Bréguet Bizerte, used to bolster aircraft numbers of the *Seenotdienst*.

eastern Mediterranean came under attack by the latter, a mixed force of He 111s and Ju 88s attacking the Malta-bound Convoy MW13 of four heavily escorted merchant ships codenamed Operation *Stoneage*. After failed daylight attacks, six He 111H-6 torpedo bombers of I./KG 26 and one Ju 88 of III./KG 26 struck at twilight, hitting the cruiser HMS *Arethusa* with simultaneous approaches from port and starboard. A single torpedo impacted to port abreast 'B' turret, blowing a 53-foot-long by 35-foot-high hole in the ship's side. The explosion penetrated four decks, spraying oil throughout the bridge and starting fires as the ship began flooding, communications being lost throughout the ship which took a list to port. One officer and 155 men were killed, forty-two injured and the captain badly burned. *Arethusa* limped towards Alexandria, manoeuvred by auxiliary wheel with the ship's Quartermaster steering by compass and relaying directions by a chain of men. Taken in tow as the hull began buckling, the cruiser struggled into port, subsequently being under repair for more than a year after transfer to a United States' shipyard. The remainder of the convoy reached Malta as bad weather thwarted further torpedo attacks, effectively ending the island's siege once and for all. Two KG 26 crews were lost, a third ditching south of Syracuse but recovered. Among those that failed to return was *Maj.* Horst Kayser, acting *Gruppenkommandeur* of III./KG 26, missing in action.

Heinkel He 111 of KG 26 loaded with torpedoes.

Also present in Greece at that time was the original incarnation of III./KG 100 that had been formed on 20 September 1942 from the former *Aufklärungsgruppe* 126 (*See*). Under the command of *Maj.* Hans Schulz (former *Staffelkapitän* of 4./KG 4) and based first at Athens-Kalamaki and then Athens-Eleusis, the *Gruppe* was subordinated to X.*Fliegerkorps* and operated predominantly He 111H-6 bombers alongside a number of Arado Ar 196s and a single Blohm & Voss BV 138. Schulz's *Gruppe* was engaged in attacks on enemy troop concentrations and harbours but also ASW missions and convoy escort within the Aegean Sea. It formed part of the escort for the Italian 5,322-ton freighter MV *Delphin* when it was torpedoed and sunk on 14 December by British submarine HMS *Taku* 5nm north of Macrosini island. Though an Arado attacked the submerged submarine with a 50kg bomb and recorded sighting an underwater explosion and oil slick, HMS *Taku* escaped both the airborne attack and subsequent depth-charge hunt by *U-Bootsjäger UJ2102*.

In late November III./KG 100 was relocated to Catania in Sicily, chiefly engaged in attacking ports along the Tunisian and Algerian coastlines until on 10 February Schulz received orders for his unit to revert to its original identity, becoming *Seeaufklärungsgruppe* 126 and returning to Skaramanga, Greece, re-equipping with Ar 196 aircraft

Junkers Ju 88 of KG 30 photographed in Sicily.

under the new command of the highly experienced naval aviator and former *Fliegerführer Nord* (*West*), *Obstlt*. Hermann Busch. In the Aegean, the small nimble Arados continued their patrol and escort duties, successfully defending a *Pulk* of Junkers Ju 52 transport aircraft from Beaufighter attack on 29 May 1943, but losing two of their own Arados and a single transport.

A new III./KG 100 formed from on 29 April 1943 at Hessental airfield, Schwäbisch Hall in southern Germany, from Ernst Hetzel's *Lehr und Erprobungskommando* 21, continuing its 'Fritz-X' training, incorporating handling characteristics of the Dornier while carrying two glide bombs or a single bomb counterbalanced with a 900-litre auxiliary fuel tank under the other wing. Attendance at a blind-flying school established in Belgrade was mandatory, as was night flying, astral navigation and specialist instruction for the observers in control of the glide bombs. This latter training began on the ground using tabletop 'flight simulation' before graduating to launching practice glide bombs in the air (without warheads) and cement bombs against a mock battleship built from wooden planking on the Einkorn, a hill spur in the northern Limpurg Hills near Hessental. The simulator was later described to British intelligence officers by a captured airman:

Though popular with their crews, the Arado Ar 196, used extensively for reconnaissance in the Mediterranean, proved vulnerable to increasing numbers of newly-arrived enemy fighters.

An upright post with a horizontal area on top was mounted on a four-wheeled trolley. A white ball representing the bomb was suspended on an endless wire which ran around two pulleys, one of which was attached to the horizontal arm and one to the trolley. The trolley, which was fitted with an electric motor, travelled at a constant speed and by means of remote control could be turned to left or right as desired . . . The movements of the bomb, which normally travelled on the endless wire in a downward direction at a constant speed, could also be regulated by means of this remote control. . . . The trolley was steered in the direction of a model ship on wheels, which was about six metres away. . . . The combined result of the motions of the bomb and the trolley is similar to that of a Fritz-X bomb when controlled in flight. Informant found that this apparatus was surprisingly easy to control, and he obtained a direct hit on the ship with his first attempt.[8]

Simultaneously to Hetzel's *Gruppe, Maj.* Fritz Auffhammer's II./KG 100 underwent an almost identical training regime while stationed at Garz on the island of Rugen, however, their weapon was the Henschel Hs 293 powered glide bomb, for which bombing practice they were able to use an actual target ship moored near Peenemünde. An interesting distinction in the tactical application of the two weapons was that aircraft using the 'Fritz-X' operated in a *Kette* of three aircraft, while those using the Hs 293 either flew as individual aircraft or in two-aircraft *Schwarm* instead, the defensive capabilities of merchant-ship targets being deemed likely to be less than those possessed by warships. Kriegsmarine officers instructed crews in the essential tactics of naval warfare as they were transformed into a maritime strike force, with daily lectures in ship identification and the characteristics of major warships aimed to minimise the risk of target misidentification.

Doctor Herbert Wagner, a former Junkers aeronautical engineer, had been employed by Henschel in 1940 to develop a functioning glide bomb, based on conceptual work already completed by the Gustav Schwartz Propellerwerke in 1937. While the 'Fritz-X' was an unpowered glide bomb, the Henschel Hs 293 was propelled by a Walter HWK 109-507 rocket engine slung underneath, providing 590kg of thrust for ten seconds. This allowed the bomb to be used from a lower altitude and at an increased range to the 'Fritz-X', also providing the necessary power and punch to penetrate armour plating; the first three prototypes having been unpowered and lacking effectiveness. However, warhead size – a standard 500kg SC 500 'general purpose' bomb – limited optimum target choice to freighters, or warships up to a maximum size of a light cruiser and without significant deck armour plating. The unpowered 'Fritz-X' remained the iron fist for use against capital ships and aircraft carriers. Initial Hs 293 test launches were made at Karlshagen in February 1940 from an He 111H-12, the weapon reaching a maximum speed of 260 metres per second. The Hs 293A-0 entered production in November 1941, followed by the more refined Hs 293A-1 in January 1942. Trials were also conducted during 1941 using a prototype Heinkel He 177A-0, followed by a pair of He 177A-1 aircraft, though they entered action with II./KG 100's Dornier Do 217 bombers.

Like the 'Fritz-X', two of the weapons could be carried outboard of the wing's engine nacelles, mounted aboard the Do 217E-5 aircraft on ETC 500/XII racks, supplied with warm air from hoses inbuilt into the aircraft wings to keep the weapon at a constant temperature and offset the effect of icing or changes in relative humidity. Equipped with a pair of aileron-fitted wings but no rudder on the ventral tailfin, commands were sent by the FuG-203 *Kehl III* unit aboard the carrier aircraft and received by the FuG 230 component of the Kehl-Straßburg MCLOS guidance and control system, identical to that utilised by the 'Fritz -X' glide bomb. Coloured flares mounted in the tail allowing the operator to maintain visual contact; replaced by flashing lights during missions undertaken during the hours of darkness. Once the Hs 293 was launched, the bomber was compelled to fly a straight and level path, at a set altitude and speed, parallel to the target so as to be able to maintain the line of sight required by the operator, rendering the bomber unable to evade enemy aircraft without aborting the attack. The monopropellant booster rocket provided for only a short burst of speed, making the missile's range dependent on the height of launch. From a launch height of 8,000 metres the Hs 293 had an estimated range of about 12 kilometres.

Auffhammer's II.*Gruppe* absorbed the remains of the testing *Erprobungsstaffel*/KG 30 to bolster its strength and was declared operational in July 1943 when it deployed to Istres in France, by this time the *Gruppenkommandeur* having changed to *Maj.* Franz Hollweg as Auffhammer was appointed *Kommodore* of KG 100 on 4 May replacing *Oberst* Heinz von Holleben who was hospitalised due to a plane crash.

Werner Baumbach in his later role as *General der Kampfflieger* became responsible for the ongoing development of the guided weapons, enthusiastically supporting their use:

The rocket-powered Henschel Hs 293 anti-shipping bomb.

Operations on the grand scale with guided missiles were hampered by a shortage of suitable aircraft. The selected bomber, the He 177, never appeared in quantity at the front. Previously, some of the test planes of the He 111 type had been used and lost in carrying supplies to Stalingrad. So, in 1943, as a last resort, the last Do 217 aircraft, the serial production of which had ended, were transformed to equip an FX group. But their range was so limited that it was no longer possible to use them effectively in the Battle of the Atlantic. The enemy convoys simply kept out of range. But in the Mediterranean, off the Portuguese coast and during the invasion the great possibilities of this weapon were clearly revealed on the few occasions it was employed. At a demonstration of the V-l and guided missiles at Peenemünde Admiral Dönitz drew me aside and asked me whether the ship which had been the target for some guided bombs had really been hit. When I assured him of the fact he invited me to a conference in Berlin. On this occasion the critical position at sea was very frankly discussed. It was August, 1943. After I had presented my proposals Dönitz simply remarked: 'Why don't you say all that to your own C.-in-C?' When I replied that for the time being I was unable to get in touch with him as his personal staff were keeping me away, the head of the navy remarked with a sigh of resignation: 'Where's the Reichsmarschall stag-hunting now? I haven't seen him for weeks.'[9]

While Loerzer's II.*Fliegerkorps* carried the main burden of the anti-shipping thrust in the western Mediterranean, the results he announced to Berlin far outstripped achievements. During the first week of operations against *Torch* shipping, Loerzer claimed 183,000GRT of shipping sunk and 234,000GRT damaged. In reality five ships totalling 55,305GRT had been destroyed. Luftwaffe maritime bomber strength was steadily disintegrating in the face of fierce, effectively handled and growing Allied resistance. Though the Luftwaffe experienced occasional success – including the armed merchant cruiser HMS *Scythia* hit and damaged near Algiers on 23 November – during November KG 26 lost twenty-two crews in action: eleven from I./KG 26, two from 6./KG 26 and nine from III./KG 26. Indeed, in a combat return from mid-December KG 26 reported that from an expected establishment of 120 aircraft, only sixty-one were on strength and of those only eighteen were operational, with twenty-six of an available seventy-nine crews also considered operationally ready.

During December only two ships were confirmed sunk by German torpedo bombers, HMS *Quentin* on 2 December and the French steamer SS *Mascot* off Bougie seven days later. The 'Q' class destroyer had just taken part in what became known as the battle of Skerki Bank in which four transport ships under Italian escort were attacked, all transports being sunk with over 2,000 casualties, including 1,766 troops, 698 tons of cargo (mainly ammunition), four tanks, thirty-two vehicles and twelve artillery pieces all destined for Tunisia. As the British cruisers and destroyers withdrew they were attacked first by Italian SM 79 torpedo bombers and then by Junkers Ju 88s, *Quentin* hit and going down with twenty men killed, the remainder rescued by HMS *Quiberon*.

The Mediterranean air war against the Allies dwindled to virtually nothing, as bad weather set in over Christmas. Furthermore, Loerzer, a long-time crony of Göring's and ardent National Socialist, had lost the confidence of his subordinates. Werner Baumbach, the highly-experienced *Gruppenkommandeur* of I./KG 30, recorded his despair within the pages of his diary after only a week in action off Algeria.

'Lasciate ogni speranza, voi che entrate!' The angel of death cast its shadow over us immediately on our arrival. Dante's Hell is a reality here.

Roth's crew gone, Lieutenant Grigoleit shot down, little Quisdorf missing, Stoffregen down and mortally wounded, Metzenthin's and Lieutenant Harmel's Ju 88s shot down in flames over Algiers.

Yesterday evening I had the jumbled-up crews lined up before me once again. Briefing; target same as yesterday. With everything we have. Same as yesterday. Always same as yesterday. And early next morning, when we assemble after the sortie, two, three or four crews will be missing once more. Have not returned from the sortie! Who will be the next? What cruel fate has already decided on the next batch? All of us have got together our few belongings and tied them up as 'casualty pack' by the time the lorry arrives to take us off to the airfield.

I often lie on my bed in a sort of paralysis, dripping sweat and yet feeling frozen to the bone while gazing at blood-red oranges hanging in the leafy trees. It is worry, heart-rending worry, which shakes me to the core and is growing to a horrible, nerve-racking fever. Since we have been here, I have stopped talking to the men. I could not find anything to say which would lessen the feeling of hopelessness. They understand me. No one is quicker in the uptake than the man in the ranks.

Two weeks later:

I have had a long struggle to make up my mind. It is our last chance. I shall write to Jeschonnek. He shall at any rate know what is going on here. I sat at my typewriter until after midnight getting out my report. The courier leaves for H.Q. in East Prussia in the early hours. I believe I have recovered my old self-confidence. I had nearly lost it altogether in the last few weeks, but I shall need it more than ever now.[10]

Baumbach's letter to Jeschonnek, circumventing all accepted military channels, was a damning indictment of Loerzer's mishandling of operations. Baumbach baldly stated baldly that 'Loerzer . . . has shown that he has no understanding of our situation'. The response was swift. Only days after the letter had been received and following promises of assistance from both Jeschonnek and Kesselring, Baumbach was promptly reassigned to Berlin and the staff position of Chief Inspector of Bombers (*Inspizient der Kampfflieger*). Loerzer would not be far behind, promoted to *Generaloberst* in February 1943 and transferred to Berlin as Chief of the Luftwaffe Personnel Office, Personnel Armament and National Socialist Leadership of the Luftwaffe/Air Ministry (*Chef des*

Hermann Göring, Hans Jeschonnek and Erhard Milch at an air display. Jeschonnek, Luftwaffe Chief of Staff, would later become his master's scapegoat following Luftwaffe campaign failures.

Lw.-Personalamt und Chef der personalen Rüstung und der NS-Führung d.Lw./RLM). In his place came the reliable *Generalleutnant* Martin Harlinghausen, though the complexion of the Mediterranean theatre had changed by that time. The post of *Fliegerführer Tunis* was dissolved on 12 February, replaced by *Generalmajor* Walter Hagen's *Fliegerführer Afrika*, that had been tasked since 1941 in the main with tactical air support of the *Deutsche Afrika Korps* and *Panzergruppe/Panzerarmee Afrika*. Renamed *Fliegerkorps Tunis*, it now encompassed not only the aircraft disposed within Tunisia but also those in Tripolitania to the east.

Seaborne Axis supply and reinforcement convoys to North Africa collapsed following *Torch* due to rising Allied naval and air supremacy, guided by ULTRA codebreaking. The onus instead fell upon the Luftwaffe to assume the mantle of supplying beleaguered forces in Tunisia. The 5.*Panzerarmee* (previously XC *Korps*) had been created on 8 December 1942 as a command formation for units forming to defend Tunisia, placed under the command of *Generaloberst* Hans-Jürgen von Arnim, who, fortuitously for the Allies, held a strong personal enmity for Erwin Rommel, the two men barely able to cooperate in operational matters. Although Allied troops in Bône were only 185 miles from Tunis, Luftwaffe fighter-bomber attacks combined with supply and transport problems and torrential winter rains significantly slowed their advance, allowing German forces to become firmly established in Tunisia. Despite ULTRA decrypts revealing Wehrmacht intentions to fight for Tunisia, the Allied response to such priceless information was sluggish at best. However, in terms of grand strategy, Hitler's decision to concentrate considerable air and ground forces to hold Tunisia – of little strategic value to Germany now that Rommel's threat to the Suez Canal was but a distant memory – while the entire Sixth Army in Stalingrad was threatened with annihilation, was a major blunder. Additionally, despite the Luftwaffe's best efforts against *Torch* there were too few aircraft available, fragmented between too many smaller theatre commands to effectively interfere with either the landings or subsequent Allied advances. Nonetheless, Göring bitterly passed the buck after the war:

'Why didn't you attempt to cut us off in Africa and send the Luftwaffe, which was then superior in the air, against our shipping and the concentration of our airplanes at Gibraltar?'

'We had too few long-range airplanes and then, later, when you got to Algiers, the airfields in Italy were inadequate. You have no idea what a bad time we had in Italy. If they had only been our enemies instead of our allies, we might have won the war.'[11]

The decision to hold what remained of Axis-controlled North Africa as a buttress to Europe must have caused some measure of resentment within the grandly renamed *Panzerarmee Afrika* which could have used such concentrated effort when Rommel had stood with the Suez Canal almost within his grasp. Instead, Hitler reinforced failure now that he could least afford to, despatching men and material in a forlorn hope on the African continent. Italian fears that the loss of Tunisia could mean the end of support the population's already wavering for Mussolini's war proved the final nail in the coffin.

As the Luftwaffe air bridge persevered, a second BV 222 of *Lufttransportstaffel* 222 was lost on 10 December when aircraft 'V8' ('X4+HH') was shot down by a Beaufighter flown by Flight Lieutenant Rae of RAF 227 Squadron. The huge flying boat was in company with 'V1' and 'V4' headed for Libya at extremely low altitude when attacked 180 kilometres north of Misurata. Loaded with twenty-eight barrels of gasoline, *Oblt.z.S.* Heinz Mrochen's aircraft went down in flames and exploded on impact with the sea, killing all nine crewmen and the three passengers which included Knight's Cross holder *Hptm.* Wolf-Dietrich Peitzmayer who was travelling to take up his new appointment as *Gruppenkommandeur* of the ground-attack unit I./*Schlachtgeschwader* 2. Only 'V1' escaped damage from the Beaufighter attack which was eventually driven off by overlapping fire from the remaining flying boats' defensive gunners.

Luftwaffe aerial resupply of both North Africa and Stalingrad resulted in a shocking loss of Junkers Ju 52 aircraft and bombers impressed into transport services for which they were patently unsuitable. The concentration of such aircraft, many crewed by highly experienced instructors, virtually shut down Luftwaffe bomber and instrument schools – immediately cutting the supply of highly-trained bomber crews – and by the end of January 1943, 56 per cent of Luftwaffe transport strength had been lost in action. Furthermore, poor coordination between transport units and the *Seenotsdienst* resulted in an unnecessarily heavy loss of life amongst crews and transported men forced down into the Mediterranean Sea. The lack of maritime training of the hastily-assembled transport crews resulted in frequent navigation errors reporting crash locations, so much so that Do 24 aircraft of the *Seenotdienst* began flying escort to transport groups bound for North Africa whenever possible. Alongside the transport crews, combat units within the area were frequently found to have been inadequately prepared for potentially bailing out over the sea, fighter pilots of at least one *Staffel* not even carrying lifejackets or basic survival equipment until significant loss of life and appeals from the *Seenotdienst* convinced them of their error. Conversely, cooperation between Klümper's experienced torpedo *Staffeln* and *Seenotbereichskommando* XIII at Etang de Berre remained exceptional, resulting in the successful rescue of many of Klümper's ditched men. The rescue crews had also instigated training for night operations, eventually allowing recovery missions to be undertaken perilously close to enemy-held coastlines under cover of darkness.

Deftly-handled Allied fighter strength now established in Algeria and Tunisia forced Luftwaffe fighters on to the defensive, while the bombers were gradually directed away from naval targets to bombing missions over land, though to little effect. Between November 1942 and May 1943, the Luftwaffe lost 2,422 aircraft within the Mediterranean theatre, including 734 bombers, representing 58.3 per cent of the Luftwaffe's total bombing strength as recorded on 10 November 1942. Luftwaffe power had been frittered away in the hopeless defence of a position on the African continent, at a time when air, ground and even naval forces could have been judiciously withdrawn to Italy or the vulnerable Eastern Front. The rippling effect of Luftwaffe missions against *Torch* and the simultaneous attempted air-bridges to Tunisia and Stalingrad was disastrous. In the Atlantic, Condor missions were drastically cut as aircraft were misused elsewhere and RAF Coastal Command did not encounter a single Focke-Wulf between 22 November 1942 and 26 February 1943.

Göring himself had steadily retreated from the reality of the Luftwaffe's struggles on all fronts into a cosseted life of luxury and confiscated art within the walls of his various villas and lodges. As head of the Luftwaffe, Göring could barely have performed more poorly. While a man of considerable personal bravery in his younger years, highly intelligent and possessed of an undeniable charisma during his rise to power, by the outbreak of war he had grown corpulent and self-indulgent, traits that worsened as the war progressed. His political acumen reigned paramount, gradually eroding and riding roughshod over military demands required of a rational leader for the Luftwaffe. Indecisive regarding the best use of his jealously guarded aerial strength, he was malleable to whomever had time to massage his inflated ego. While Hitler steadfastly refused to allow ground yielded in strategic withdrawals, Göring could be persuaded of its wisdom as was the case during a two-day journey in the company of Erwin Rommel between Berlin and Rome aboard his personal train 'Asia' during late November. By humouring the Luftwaffe commander, who prattled endlessly about jewellery and his latest art acquisitions, Rommel was able to gain tacit agreement to defy Hitler's orders and pull his retreating *Panzergruppe Afrika* back to a new line at Gabès in Tunisia, where he proposed to fight a completely new campaign. By the time the train arrived in Rome, he had secured Göring's enthusiastic agreement, immediately reversed after the Luftwaffe commander met with *Feldmarschall* Kesselring who opposed such a move, believing the best way to defeat the Allied forces approaching from the west was to keep Montgomery's Eighth Army as far from the Tunisian border as possible. Rommel wept with frustration at his inability to exercise tactical control of his own forces. Ultimately, Kesselring's decision was rendered moot by 4 February when Rommel had been pushed back to the Tunisian border anyway.

On the very last day of 1942, KG 40 launched an audacious but ill-fated attack against expected merchant shipping of Convoy UGS3 reported by intelligence sources to be in Casablanca harbour. Twelve aircraft of III./KG 40 would mount the biggest single strike by Condor aircraft of the war thus far, though almost immediately the number was whittled down to eleven after one aircraft failed to take off. Three others returned to Bordeaux-Mérignac with instrument failure, control and engine problems over the Bay of Biscay. Of the remaining eight Condors, seven attacked the harbour between 0303hrs and 0442hrs, reporting several bomb hits, although the Allies recorded no significant damage. Though aware of the presence of at least eight Fw 200s operating within the Gibraltar area, the Allies did not seem to connect them with the raid on Casablanca. Eisenhower issued a report to the British Admiralty that US intelligence estimated it to be a 'token raid by planes with auxiliary tanks and small bombs, from southern France'.[12]

Though they had faced no effective defence or enemy aircraft, the tribulations of the Condors were not yet over as during the return flight *Hptm.* Fritz Hoppe was forced to land his aircraft of 8./KG 40 at San Pablo airport near Seville due to lack of fuel, the aircraft and crew both being interned. *Oberleutnant* Günter Graeber, *Staffelkapitän* of 7./KG 40, also experienced problems south of Huelva aboard 'F8+FR', a radio message at 0805hrs reporting failure of two engines and forced landing being attempted in Spain. Nothing was seen of the aircraft again though the body of Flight Engineer *Uffz.* Rudi Sureck washed ashore on 26 May at Puerto de las Nieves, Gran Canaria.[13]

During January, the area of responsibility allocated to Kesselring's *Luftflotte* 2 was subdivided; his existing command henceforth responsible for Italy and the central Mediterranean Sea, while *Gen.d.Fl.* Otto Hoffmann von Waldau was appointed chief of *Luftwaffenkommando Südost* responsible for Greece, Crete and, from 1 September the Balkans, and beneath which X.*Fliegerkorps* was placed.[14] While Loerzer remained in charge of II.*Fliegerkorps*, the strength of available Luftwaffe torpedo aircraft and crews reached intolerably low levels. By the third quarter of the month, KG 26 was reporting only fourteen operational aircraft and crews. An influx of forty young crews from the *Geschwader* training IV.*Gruppe* replenished some of that strength, although they were inexperienced and their training had been hastily completed to allow commitment to action as soon as possible. Nevertheless, the Luftwaffe continued to make its presence felt against the *Torch* convoys.

Propaganda photograph of a Heinkel He 111 cockpit from below, showing the Lofte-7D bombsight.

In Berlin, *OKW* claimed the destruction of 16,000GRT of enemy shipping off Bougie by torpedo bomber attack at dusk on 7 January. Although the figure of two ships sunk was correct, the size of the targets had been overestimated by the crews of the seventeen I./KG 26 Heinkels. From Convoy KMS6, travelling from Algiers to Bône, the British 7,150GRT SS *Benalbanach* and the Norwegian 1,520GRT SS *Akabahra* were both sunk and American Liberty Ship SS *William Wirt*, carrying aviation fuel, damaged, the Heinkels returning without loss and only two men injured by anti-aircraft fire. The minesweeper HMS *Acute*'s propeller was also damaged by a torpedo forcing a return to Gibraltar for repair.

While SS *Akabahra* suffered no casualties from its 25-man crew, she took to the bottom a cargo of railway tracks and crossties and assorted foodstuffs destined for Allied forces. Hit in the port side abreast of the boiler room by a single torpedo, the ship sank immediately while HMS *Bicester* rescued the crew. Aboard SS *Benalbanach* there was pandemonium as two torpedoes from a single Heinkel impacted the passenger/cargo ship's hull in Number 3 and 5 holds. This was their second voyage to the landing area, having landed assault troops at Mersa Bu Zejar during the initial landings. Returning to Britain and reloading with 800 tons of ammunition, 300 tons of military equipment, 136 motor vehicles, 68 tons of fuel and 389 men of the Motor Transport Corps, the ship returned in KMS6. Master David Kilpatrick Coutts MacGregor barely had time to order his ship abandoned before part of the stored cargo exploded, blowing the stern off and sinking *Benalbanach* in less than two minutes. Three hundred and fifty-three of the embarked army personnel were killed along with fifty-seven of the seventy-four crew. MacGregor was among the casualties, dying of exhaustion after three hours spent in the water while escort vessels located survivors.

Luftwaffe torpedo aircraft only managed to damage three more vessels during January as their strength ebbed away; two freighters and the destroyer HMS *Avon Vale*, the latter being beached with its entire bow section wrecked on 29 January. The Heinkels of I./KG 26 had combined with Italian SM 79 torpedo bombers of *Gruppos* 105, 130 and 132 for the attack, the Italian tri-motor aircraft severely damaging anti-aircraft cruiser HMS *Pozarica* with hits to the stern, taking shelter in Bougie harbour where she capsized on 13 February.

In January the western Mediterranean Luftwaffe was devoted to convoy escort, reconnaissance, weather reporting (to facilitate land operations) and conventional bombing or ports and ground forces, Bône coming under Luftwaffe attack eight times during January alone, and most aircraft of the Ju 88 *Staffeln* diverted from maritime operations to conventional bombing. The transporting to German reinforcements to North Africa assumed ever increasing importance; *Gen.Maj* Ulrich Buchholz replacing *Oberst* Starke as *Lufttransportführer Mittelmeer* during January with some 400 Ju 52s, twenty Me 323 'Gigants', fifteen Fw 200 Condors and three six-engine Blohm & Voss BV 222 flying boats at his disposal. During January they transported 15,816 men, 4,742 tons of weapons and ammunition, 5,155 cubic feet of fuel, 8.5 tons of food as well as two 105mm field guns and their halftrack prime movers. Inversely proportional was the decline of Italian supply shipping capability, reduced dramatically through loss and damage and a lack of skilled dockyard workers in the repair yards at Genoa and Trieste.

During December 1942, *Oberst* Wolfgang von Wild had been appointed to the new post of *Fliegerführer Sardinien* and the following month set about securing permission for the Luftwaffe to upgrade the grass surface of the Sardinian airfields at Decimomanu and Villacidro, north-west of Cagliari. Though the soft surface hampered operations during periods of heavy rainfall, Italian torpedo bombers maintained a base and Luftwaffe torpedo bombers staged through the airfield after stockpiling LT F5b torpedoes and the installation of runway floodlights. Men of the 7.*Flughafenbetriebskompanie* KG 26 which had been responsible for the repair and service of III./KG 26 Ju 88 aircraft, were still travelling from Norway to the Mediterranean, at Rennes when diverted towards Civitavecchia north of Rome before embarking for Sardinia. By the middle of the month, although no progress had been made on concreting the airfield, the servicing company had established functional mobile workshops at Villacidro, Grosseto used for heavier work beyond their means.

In January I./KG 26 was rebased to *Fliegerführer Sardinien* control at Decimomanu, its personnel billeted in surrounding villages with no suitable accommodation at the airfield itself, only a small cluster of administration buildings and an officers' mess. While fuel, water, ammunition, communications and other essential amenities were available, there were few aircraft shelters and only one small hangar, bombers parked instead around the airfield perimeter. By March 1943 the final component – two officers and twelve torpedo mechanics (from *LufttorpedoBetr.Kp.* 8) – had established themselves at the airfield.

By contrast, in Villacidro Italian authorities agreed to immediate German construction of runway lighting and accommodation, evacuating their own men and handing it entirely over to German control during

Nose of the He 111 photographed from over the pilot's shoulder.

February. The Wehrmacht brought in enough tents to accommodate approximately 500 men although during mid–March, while the grass runway was frequently unserviceable due to heavy rain, a severe outbreak of influenza affected many of the nearly 1,500 men of II./KG 26 and I./KG 60 who had arrived during recent weeks.

By this time the Luftwaffe had already failed in its maritime interdiction mission within the western Mediterranean. Misdirection of bombers for convoy escort duties and employment of Ju 88s for night bombing of ground targets released pressure on both Allied shipping and disembarkation ports. The Luftwaffe maintained a thin line that stretched to the Aegean, rather than a more potentially decisive concentration against the Atlantic supply lines to *Torch* forces, though regardless of this, a lack of experienced maritime strike crews lowered efficacy. When Harlinghausen took command of II.*Fliegerkorps* in Sicily he reported the sorry state of his command on 23 January 1943.

> Here I found a sad inheritance. I took over the combat ready remains of five bomber *Geschwader*. Each *Geschwader* had a planned strength of 120 aircraft and crews. My bomber *Geschwader* had a combined strength of only forty-five operationally ready crews, including *Kommodore*, *Gruppenkommandeur* and *Staffelkapitäne*. The torpedo squadron KG 26 had only fourteen crews.
>
> The crews themselves looked pitiful; the old hands had fallen, been wounded or were sick. The new replacements showed a level of education that could not be described as ready for action. The pilots were only just able to take off and land the planes at night and blind flight training is limited to only the simplest instrument flying in good weather. Neither observers nor pilots understand anything of navigation, relying on target approach by transmission from a *flaksender* [flak direction station]. The crews are barely trained in bombing and they will only learn air gunnery in action against the enemy.[15]

During February, both torpedo training *Gruppen* of *Kampfschulgeschwader* 2 at Grosseto were placed on a combat footing, redesignated *Kampfgeschwader* 102. Officers of KG 26 were reshuffled, *Oberst* Karl Stockmann overseeing the training unit transition, his place as *Kommodore* of KG 26 taken by Werner Klümper, in turn replaced as *Gruppenkommandeur* by *Hptm.* Herbert Vater, a former He 115 pilot and *Staffelkapitän* of 1./Kü.Fl.Gr. 406. Stockmann did not remain with KG 102 for long, being transferred at the beginning of March as *Bevollmächtigter für die Lufttorpedowaffe/RLM* (Commissioner for the Aerial Torpedo Service), a post previously held by Harlinghausen, charged with overseeing Luftwaffe torpedo development, supply, training and operations.

There was a small interchange of personnel between KG 102 and KG 26, *Hptm.* Georg Teske, *Gruppenkommandeur* of I./KSG 2 was moved to command II./KG 26 and promoted to *Major* while *Maj.* Karl-Ferdinand Hielscher, former *Gruppenkommandeur* of III./KG 26 became the new commander of I./KG 102. *Oberst* Wilhelm Edmonds, recently promoted, retained command of II./KG 102 while the new *Kommodore* was *Oberst* Horst Beyling, a former Kriegsmarine officer that had been pre-war *Staffelkapitän* of 3./Kü.Fl.Gr. 406 before taking command of II./KG 26 in May 1941.

Despite the paucity available torpedo aircraft, *Oblt.* Rudolf Schmidt, *Staffelkapitän* of 4./KG 26, led seven He 111 and seven Ju 88 bombers from Sardinia against Convoy KMS8 headed to Algiers on 6 February. The convoy comprised thirty merchant ships under strong escort by Catapult Aircraft Merchant (CAM) ships, destroyers and corvettes. The attack commenced with high-level bombing runs eight miles from the North African coast and as Allied escorts opened fire, three He 111H-6 aircraft swept in below mast height from landward with the setting sun at their backs. Torpedoes were released at point blank range as defending gunners were unable to depress their guns below the ships' guardrails. One torpedo hit the Canadian corvette HMCS *Louisberg* in the engine room, the ship sinking rapidly by the stern, her exploding boilers killing many survivors struggling though a thick layer of diesel oil coating the sea. Fifty of the 109 crew were saved from what was the only Canadian warship sunk by aircraft in the Mediterranean. The 7,135GRT British freighter SS *Fort Babine* was also hit but survived its damage and was towed by HMS *Stornoway* to Oran.[16] Two Heinkels were brought down, the crew of one rescued by Spanish fishermen and later landed on Mallorca, while KMS8 lost two more ships the following day to torpedoes from *U77*.

With sufficient Allied bomber strength now accumulated in North Africa, a retaliatory strike was made the next day against Elmas airfield and seaplane base by thirty-one B-17 and twenty B-26 bombers of the USAAF 12th Air Force under heavy fighter escort. The Americans claimed twenty-five aircraft destroyed on the ground, although only two He 111s were completely written off. Eighteen more were damaged, including four He 111s of I./KG 26, two He 111s of II./KG 26, five Ju 88

A-4s of III./KG 26 and two He 111H-6s of Stab/KG 26. Furthermore, the runway was badly cratered, communications knocked out and several Luftwaffe personnel and Italians killed. Adjacent to Elmas airfield, the seaplane base on the lake suffered four Italian Cant Z506Bs destroyed by the bombing. The airfield was out of action for three days before declared partially serviceable despite several unexploded bombs remaining.

There was precious little achieved by Luftwaffe maritime aircraft during the remainder of the month. An early-morning attack against KMS9 off Algiers on 18 February brought reports of torpedo hits on an enemy cruiser, but the Allies suffered no casualties and the weak attacks fended off. On 22 February *Oblt*. Werner Franken, Technical Officer of I./KG 26, was brought down by naval anti-aircraft fire south of Sardinia, his Heinkel He 111H-6 '1H+AB' crashing into the sea and the entire crew officially declared missing in action. Franken – a KG 26 veteran – was credited with sinking an accumulated 46,000GRT of enemy shipping and severely damaging a further 44,000GRT and was posthumously awarded the Knight's Cross.

February's final success was the destruction of the American Liberty ship SS *Nathanael Greene*. The ship had already survived Convoy PQ18 during the previous September, but at 1354hrs on 24 February while in Convoy MKS8, she was hit by two torpedoes from *U565* about 40 miles north-east of Oran. Severely damaged and with engines disabled, Luftwaffe torpedo bombers subsequently attacked, and *Nathanael Greene* was hit amidships by a single torpedo. All but four of the crew were rescued, most from two lifeboats, while some managed to jump on board the minesweeper HMS *Brixham* which came alongside. The wrecked ship was taken under tow and beached at Salamanda, later being declared a total loss.

Aircraft of II./KG30, III./KG77 and I./KG54 raided Tripoli harbour and its approaches on 19 March in the first use of the LT350 circling torpedo. The weapon was a derivative of the Italian parachute-torpedo '*Motobomba FFF*'. Ellipsoid in shape rather than the familiar 'cigar' of the LTF5, the LT350 was fractionally greater in diameter than the F5 (50cm rather than 44.96cm) but less than half its length at only 2.6 metres. Its three-bladed propeller was streamlined flush with the torpedo body, powered by a 250-volt electric motor. Held by a ring bolt attachment, the LT350 was designed to be dropped from an altitude of 150 metres or less at speeds up to 300km/h, a parachute deployed that then broke loose on impact with the water. Its nose slightly more buoyant than the rest of the weapon, the torpedo would rise towards the surface, activating a mercury switch and starting the motor after which the LT350 executed an irregular course. With no depth or lateral control, although designed to run near the surface, they frequently broached, leaving a visible wake as it travelled for approximately one hour, the initial speed of 14 knots gradually decreasing. Carrying a 120-kilogram warhead, it contained three separate pistols; the direct-action exploder designated 'sea' (*Seepistole*) with a small propeller not activated until striking the water and situated to the lower right of the warhead centre if viewed from the front, the inertia exploder designated 'land' (*Landpistole*) working the same way but with a larger propeller and situated dead centre of the warhead, and the scuttling 'destroyer' (*Zerstörpistole*) of a large propeller and long body, situated to the lower left of the warhead centre.

The *Seepistole* was secured against rotation while in flight by a rubber disc attached by chord to the aircraft's rack, which was pulled out as the weapon was released. A thin pin was then shorn once the torpedo impacted the water surface and the torpedo became live. If the LT350 then impacted a ship's hull, pier wall or any other solid target, the *Seepistole* would detonate the warhead.

The *Landpistole* was secured while in flight by an identical method, once dropped, the rubber disc pulled free and the propeller beginning to turn. After thirty turns the bolt securing the propeller would be completely unscrewed and fall off the weapon taking the propeller with it. A thin shear plate prevented the trigger activating upon impact with the sea but hitting a ship or land would detonate the warhead. Therefore, while jettisoning the weapon at sea was not possible, it could be dumped over land from a minimum height of thirty-five metres lest the propeller thread not fully unscrew.

The blades of the final scuttling trigger, the *Zerstörpistole*, was also prevented from turning in flight by the same method as the others, released upon dropping and beginning to turn. After impact with the sea, the pistol's trigger was held in place by a soluble salt crystal plug. As the torpedo made its run the salt would gradually dissolve, lasting for an estimated seventy minutes. Once exhausted, a locking pin released and firing pin thrown forward, detonating the explosive charge and destroying the torpedo.

Though it is difficult to ascertain exactly who achieved success during the attack, three ships were hit by torpedoes and bombs. The incoming aircraft were not detected by RDF and therefore no warning of the

Ju 88 raid was given. Initially, panicked reports ashore asserted that all telephone wires had been cut immediately before the attack, leading to fears of a commando raid, though it was later ascertained that heavy rains had rendered all bar one landline unusable.

The 7,200GRT SS *Ocean Voyager* carrying a cargo of petrol drums and ammunition was lying at anchor when it was struck and began burning fiercely. The ship's Master, Duncan MacKelar, and four others were killed in the initial explosion, leaving Scottish Chief Officer, George Preston Stronach, to take charge. Briefly knocked unconscious, Stronach rescued several men from below decks over the course of the next hour and twenty minutes as the ship burned. He was subsequently awarded the George Cross, one of only three given to a member of the Merchant Navy, while Second Engineer Officer H. Hotham and Boatswain Ewart Alfred Gardner were also decorated for gallantry. *Ocean Voyager* finally exploded at 0100hrs the following morning.

A second steamer, the 1,474GRT Greek SS *Varvara* carrying munitions was also bombed near the entrance to Tripoli harbour, two men killed and the ship sinking after being completely burnt out at 0400hrs the following morning; a combined cargo of 6,400 tons of petrol and ammunition was lost from both ships. The British destroyer HMS *Derwent* was hit by a circling torpedo on the port side whilst getting under way, suffering substantial damage, with six men killed, flooding amidships and fierce fires. The magazines were flooded to prevent explosion; *Derwent* was beached to prevent her sinking. Later the destroyer was towed to England by HMS *Allegiance*, but scrapped in 1947.

Nearly all ships, boats, lighters and tugs in Tripoli suffered at least superficial damage from the attack and waves thrown up by the subsequent explosion of *Ocean Voyager*. All Royal Navy ships and four merchants left harbour, many steaming through burning oil to reach the open sea. In return British anti-aircraft gunners claimed five aircraft shot down, heavy rains and low cloud cover resulting in no night fighters sent up in opposition.

The He 111s of KG26 attacked inbound Convoy KMF11 at 0202hrs on 23 March about sixty miles north-west of Algiers and 19,140GRT SS *Windsor Castle*, carrying 2,500 troops, was torpedoed. A hole was blown in the hull as the entire engine-room crew, with the exception of one man, Junior Engineering Officer William Ogilvie Mann, were washed through the bulkhead door to safety by the inrush of water. Almost miraculously given the number of men aboard the ship, Mann was the sole casualty.

The remainder were evacuated by accompanying Royal Navy destroyers as fighter protection arrived overhead, the troopship finally sinking at 1120hrs. A second torpedo also hit the Norwegian MT *Garonne* which had detached from the convoy and waited outside Oran for orders to enter harbour. The tanker carried P-38 aircraft on her decks in addition to a cargo of diesel and fuel oil from New York and was hit in the middle of the after-side tank, tearing a 45-foot long hole in the hull side, blowing portions of the decking away and destroying two of the aircraft. The ship listed to starboard although 'gravity trimming' of cargo into empty tanks returned *Garonne* to an even keel. Temporary repairs enabled a move to a more secure anchorage from where intact cargo was transferred to other vessels and the empty ship later entering Oran for further repair.

The following night, a similar mission by KG 26 sank the 1,525-GRT Dutch MV *Prins Willem III* between Cap Tenés and Algiers despite bad weather. The merchant ship was en-route from the Solway Firth to Algiers and of the crew of thirty-five men and one gunner aboard, the gunner and ten of the crew were killed. Badly damaged, the ship remained afloat and was taken in tow by British tug *Hengist* but capsized and sank early the next day.

For the third night in a row a single merchant was sunk when the 9,550GRT MV *Empire Rowan* was hit by Axis aircraft while travelling as part of a convoy designated 'Untrue' attacked by Heinkels of II./KG 26, alongside Italian torpedo bombers and two Ju 88 pathfinders from II./KG 54. The merchant ship was attacked while in convoy north-west of Philipville before Allied fighters drove the attackers away. Three SM 79s were shot down as well as two He 111s and a Ju 88, both Heinkels being brought down by Hurricanes as they flew at wave-top height towards the convoy. *Leutnant* Hubertus Kordgien of 5./KG 26 was shot down with himself and his crew killed, while *Lt.* Gerhard Campe of 6./KG 26 survived, he and his three crew recovered from the sea and taken prisoner.

The balance of losses to the Luftwaffe maritime units and results achieved had reached a critical level, no longer justifying continual commitment to action. Casualties were also suffered among technical personnel as airfields in Sardinia and Grosseto came under sustained attack from American aircraft during April. As early as February as the German renovation of the Sardinian airfields of Decimomanu and Villacidro began to improve Luftwaffe operations, the Allies considered bombing them. On 16 February, ULTRA decryption betrayed the arrival of F5 aerial torpedoes for KG 30 in Villacidro and a raid was scheduled for the following day to hit several main Sardinian targets. Over forty B-17s bombed Elmas Airfield, although heavy cloud cover prevented a particularly effective strike and Cagliari itself was badly hit. Two American formations of B-25 and B-26 medium bombers were despatched to Villacidro, one of them, the B-26-equipped 17th Bombardment Group, personally led by Major General James Doolittle, who had become famous for the USAAF's first raid on Tokyo during April 1942. Though they successfully reached their target the cloud cover prevented them from bombing. The other unit involved, the B-25s of 310th Bombing Group, mistakenly flew into another valley and bombed the built-up area of Gonnosfanadiga, killing ninety-six civilians with their fragmentation bombs.[17]

With the issues of coordination and cooperation between the USAAF, RAF, and Allied naval and ground forces of major concern to Allied leaders, their Mediterranean air force hierarchical structure was reorganised to greater integrate American and British units. The Mediterranean Air Command (MAC) was established on 18 February with RAF Air Chief Marshall Arthur Tedder at its head, providing flexible direction of operations and unit distribution.

Observer aboard an He 115 signalling the presence of enemy vessels to ships below.

The resultant increased coordination between the Allied air forces wreaked havoc on the Luftwaffe's Mediterranean presence. On 26 February Elmas was again bombed by B-17s, with buildings and workshops being destroyed, and numerous casualties caused, the airfield not fully serviceable again until 12 March. Construction began at Elmas in early April of fourteen blast pens and improved taxiways, a number of prefabricated barrack huts swiftly erected which raised the station's personnel capacity. However, within days B-17s attacked once more, destroying several aircraft, damaging others and severely cratering both the runway and taxiways such that they were never restored to full serviceability by the Luftwaffe.

Sardinian airfields remained under regular bombardment, as did Grosseto which was attacked by B-17 Flying Fortresses on 26 April; one He 111 was destroyed and three He 111s and two Ju 88s badly damaged. The runway was badly cratered, a hangar severely damaged and four barrack buildings destroyed, sixteen men killed and another forty wounded. Among the aircraft damaged was one of *Sonderkommando Koch*'s radar-equipped models that had been mounting anti-shipping night patrols off the Tunisian east coast. Though the main body of the *Sonderkommando* had returned from Italy to Köthen, a small group of specialists remained in Grosseto where maintenance of the FuG 200 installations was carried out within the airfield's workshops.

On 20 May, Grosseto and the Sardinian airfields were again severely attacked causing widespread damage and destroying numerous KG 26 aircraft among others. The Heinkels of *Sonderkommando Koch* were almost annihilated, *Oblt.* (posthumously promoted to *Hauptmann*) Josef Schwaighart and two ground crew killed and *Oblt.* Helge Markert and four men badly wounded in the attack and the unit was disbanded later that month.[18] Grosseto was rendered temporarily unserviceable and KG 102 transferred to Riga-Spilve in Latvia where it was re-established with an initial strength of five Ju 88s.

The maritime units had been decimated both in the air and on the ground. Between 1 January 1943 and 20 May, KG 26 had lost forty-one aircrew and twenty technical personnel killed, and another forty-three technical and ground crew injured, to enemy bombing alone. In the air, repeated torpedo attacks had been aborted due to increasingly strong and effective fighter defence of Allied shipping. Only at the beginning of May was Convoy MW 27 – code-named 'Liquid' – bound from Alexandria to Malta successfully attacked by available KG 26 aircraft of two *Gruppen*.

Hauptmann Klaus Nocken led III./KG 26 while *Maj.* Werner Klümper coordinated the attack while leading II./KG 26. Alternating between torpedo and bomb attacks, KG 26 achieved their best result for weeks.

A single aircraft approached the convoy out of the sun during the late afternoon, flying only 15 metres above sea level and passing between the starboard line of escorts and the six columns of the convoy body. Only two escort ships were able to engage with gunfire, though scoring no hits. Reports differ as to whether the aircraft released a torpedo or jettisoned something, but no ship was hit and it was pursued by shore-based fighters of RAF 33 Squadron who claimed to have destroyed it. This was probably Ju 88A-4 'IH+DT' of 9./KG 26, two men being killed by machine-gun fire and three others escaping their ditched aircraft to spend ten days in a life raft before being recovered as prisoners of war. Shortly after 1910hrs another plane attempted to repeat the same tactic, but it was driven off by fire from the escorts. Retreating to the north-west, Hurricanes of 33 Squadron gave chase and claimed it shot down.

These two probing efforts presaged the main attack on 'Liquid' that commenced at 1950hrs 30nm north-north-west of Benghazi with synchronised bomb and torpedo runs. As the convoy twisted in evasive manoeuvres to evade medium-level bombing, a Heinkel 111 dropped a torpedo about a mile from the convoy flank, 8,366GRT tanker MV *British Trust* hit on its port side, opening the hull for a third of its length, the cargo of heavy fuel oil catching fire. The tanker listed heavily and sank within three minutes with the loss of ten of the crew. The same attack sank troopship SS *Erinpura*, struck by a bomb launched by a KG 26 aircraft in its forward hatch twelve minutes after *British Trust* had sunk.

Aboard *Erinpura* all embarked troops had been ordered below in order to minimise potential casualties from machine-gun fire or bomb splinters. The bomb that struck the troopship passed through the forward hatch-cover and exploded below, the ship heeling to starboard and going down rapidly by the head, sinking within four minutes and turning over as the stern jutted at a 45-degree angle from the sea. Two junior engineers, fifty-four Indian seamen, three gunners, 140 Palestinian Jewish soldiers serving in 462 Transport Company of the British Army, and 600 Basuto troops of the African Auxiliary Pioneer Corps were lost with *Erinpura*. Of the ship's total complement of 1,215, only 273 survived.

As further RAF fighters were scrambled to intercept the German attackers over 'Liquid', they were joined by Hurricanes of 3 SAAF Squadron, one further Ju 88 and two He 111s claimed destroyed by the Allied fighters, though only He 111H-1 '1H+CP' of 6./KG 26 is recorded by the Luftwaffe as lost with all crew killed.

On 13 May the inevitable happened and the last German troops in Tunisia surrendered. Allied dominance of the entire North African coastline now provided continuous fighter cover for convoys routed via the Suez Canal. With the tempo of air raids against airfields used predominantly by KG 26 increasing, *Kommodore* Klümper was summoned to a conference with Kesselring at *Luftflotte* 2 headquarters in the magnificent Villa Falconieri at Frascati near Rome. Present also was Harlinghausen as commander of II.*Fliegerkorps*. Between them they decided to withdraw KG 26 from its Italian bases. Six existing crews and aircraft belonging to II.*Gruppe* would be handed over to I./KG 26, with the exception of *Staffelkapitäne* and their own crews. They and the ground staff would return by rail to Grossenbrode in Holstein for reinforcement with fresh crews and conversion from He 111 to Ju 88 bombers. Meanwhile, both I. and III. *Gruppen* would relocate to southern France and await reinforcements from the training IV.*Gruppe*; the former along with Klümper's *Stab.*/KG 26 to Salon de Provence, forty-four kilometres north-west of Marseilles, and the latter to Montpellier, further west.

Salon de Provence's grass airfield had been a pre-war French Air Force base and subsequent site of the primary Vichy training schools and fighter base until 'Case Anton' in November 1942. During April the He 111Hs of *Maj* Paul Claas' I./KG 100 had been the first Luftwaffe unit to briefly base there for three weeks training on the Lotfe 7D bombsight before returning to the Eastern Front. Arriving KG 26 flight crews and Klümper's staff were billeted in nearby towns and villages, while the groundcrew occupied barracks within the airfield perimeter itself. Montpelier boasted both a partially-completed concrete runway and grass surface, units of the Reich Labour Service being brought in to complete required construction work for III./KG 26, while, in the meantime, crews and ground personnel lodged near the airfield in requisitioned houses. Previously, only two Luftwaffe *Staffeln* had based sporadically in Montpelier; the Ju 88-equipped 1. And 3.(F)/Aufkl.Gr. 33. Reinforcements for I. and III./KG 26 began arriving during June, each *Staffel* gradually brought up to a strength of twelve crews and machines, many of the new aircraft being He 111H-11s.

During the summer of 1942, Heinkel and the *RLM* had decided to reduce He 111 production in favour of newer aircraft designs. The H-6 variant was to be scaled back and one third future production dedicated to the improved H-11 model. The H-11 carried more powerful engines (1,340hp Junkers Jumo 211F-2), heavier armour plating around crew spaces and revised defensive armament. The drum-fed 7.92mm MG 15 was replaced with a belt-fed 13mm MG 131 in the now fully-enclosed dorsal gunner position protected by armoured glass. The single MG 15 in the ventral gunner position was also replaced, a belt-fed 7.92mm MG 81Z with much higher rate of fire installed in its place. The beam gunner positions originally retained the single MG 15s, but the H-11/R1 replaced these with twin MG 81Z which became standard in November 1942. Some of the additional armour plating was fitted to the lower fuselage and could be jettisoned in an emergency.

Three KG 26 aircraft were lost during June, two in action over the Mediterranean and *Lt.* Heinz Hirschfeld's 'IH+ML' of 3./KG 26 crashing during an exercise flight south-south-west of Marseilles, Hirschfeld and his crew being listed as missing in action. Though both He 111 and Ju 88 formations mounted sporadic raids against sighted convoys in the eastern Mediterranean as well as against shipping concentrations in and around the North African ports, there was little by way of success. Overly zealous claims related several hits and damage inflicted on several ships both merchant and military, though they remain largely unsubstantiated.

Harlinghausen strongly recommended withdrawal of his battered bomber units for rest and rebuilding but was overruled on the matter by Göring himself. After the commander of II.*Fliegerkorps* remonstrated once again via Kesselring that night operations lasting a month from mid-May had been compromised by faulty navigation due to the lack of specialist training, it proved one truth too far and Harlinghausen was relieved of his command. Kesselring had made his last major decision as head of *Luftflotte 2*, replaced by Wolfram von Richthofen as Kesselring concentrated on his post of *Oberbefehlshaber Süd*.[19] The mercurial new broom made immediate changes in command. Harlinghausen's replacement was *Generalleutnant* Alfred Bülowius, a First World War infantry and *Fliegertruppe* veteran who had been awarded the Knight's Cross while *Kommodore* of LG 1. Shot down and captured by the French on 18 June 1940 near Brest, the French capitulation had freed him. Richthofen also brought in the recently promoted *General der Kampfflieger* Dietrich Peltz, fresh from coordinating bombing raids over England and appointed the head of a new office responsible for the entire Mediterranean bomber force; *Kampffliegerführer Mittelmeer*, simultaneously *Fernkampführer* responsible for all long-distance reconnaissance aircraft allocated to *Luftflotte* 2. This required the transfer of the highly efficient air traffic control centre situated on the north-eastern tip of Sicily to the barracks of the radio operating centre in Frascati where Peltz was situated.

Luftwaffe communications had proved somewhat problematic in Italy. During 1943, in anticipation of more frequent Allied bombing, a specially-equipped train had laid a command cable between the armed forces' signals centre in Rome and *Luftflotte* 2/*OB Süd* headquarters at Frascati, by-passing roads and airfields south of Rome which were vulnerable targets. The shortage of telecommunication lines in Italy stemmed from the fact that a single trunk cable ran along both east and west coasts, attempts at installing Wehrmacht overhead long-distance lines hampered by bad terrain and a sensitivity of Italians to their olive groves. All landlines were augmented by *Luftflotte* 2's dedicated line-of-sight radio communications systems wherever possible, though these were obviously vulnerable to enemy listening stations and therefore unsuitable for higher-level communications, even in oral code.

In Sardinia Wolfgang von Wild, with whom Richthofen had clashed repeatedly during the Crimean campaign, was relieved as *Fliegerführer Sardinien* and transferred to the staff of *Luftflotte* 2 as *Geleitzugführer Mittelmeer*. In his place came ground-attack specialist *Oberstlt* Hubertus Hitschold, holder of the Knight's Cross with Oak Leaves and pioneering Stuka pilot who had sunk the destroyers HMS *Greyhound*, *Kelly* and *Kashmir* during the 1941 battle for Crete.

Extra fighter-bomber units from France were soon earmarked for the Mediterranean theatre with an eye to augmenting anti-shipping capabilities. Within the maelstrom of retributory raids on the United Kingdom from northern French airbases, the Focke-Wulf Fw 190A-4 fighter-bombers of 10.(Jabo)/JG 2 that had distinguished themselves over Dieppe had been redesignated 13./*Schnellkampfgeschwader* 10 during April 1943. Concurrently, 10.(Jabo)/JG 26, which had become initially part of JG 54 for a period of two months, was also redesignated as 14./SKG 10 during April. *Major* Günther Tonne had been given command of the new *Schnellkampfgeschwader* 10 upon its creation in December 1942, formed from three *Gruppen* at Saint-André-de-l'Eure airfield, before the addition of IV.*Gruppe* on 10 April.

The *Schnellkampfgeschwader* operated by both day and night and across the Channel coast, its target emphasis shifting from shipping and industrial objectives to more arbitrary reprisal missions targeting civilian gatherings and even British livestock as Hitler's wrath was piqued by increasingly devastating Allied air raids on German cities. By the end of April 1943, no less than fourteen British coastal towns had been hit by these nuisance raids. The unit had been provided with many experienced pilots, built around a cadre of flying instructors, but improved British anti-aircraft and fighter defences had caused heavy casualties to Tonne's *Geschwader*. During the month ending 6 June 1943, anti-aircraft batteries destroyed twenty-five fighter-bombers and damaged thirteen, while the RAF shot down seventeen and damaged another four. The Focke-Wulfs were reduced to night bombing raids on Britain for which the aircraft were unsuited and crews untrained, before most of the *Geschwader* moved to the Mediterranean.

On 4 June 1943, *Lt.* Leopold 'Poldi' Wenger, *Staka* of 13./SKG 10 flew his final combat flight over the Channel coast, being lightly wounded in the leg by accurate anti-aircraft fire. Eleven days later he and his *Staffel* took off from Cognac bound for Gerbini. The Focke-Wulfs began departing at 1353hrs, making stopovers in Bourges, Istres and Albenga and Pratica di Mare near Rome the following day. After refuelling the aircraft passed via Capodichino, near Naples, and onwards to Gerbini-West. Throughout the entire journey, Poldi's first maintenance engineer Thielen had been accommodated in the rear fuselage baggage compartment. While I./SKG 10 remained in northern Europe, continuing its futile nocturnal nuisance raids against London and the south coast, and Stab., II. and IV.*Gruppen* departed for Gerbini, *Hptm.* Fritz Schröter's III./SKG 10 already in Sicily, having been formed at the Tunisian Sidi Ahmed airfield from III./*Zerstörergeschwader* 2 during December and retreating to San Pietro with the Axis surrender of North Africa.

> The advanced landing ground that I had chosen was called San Pietro. Actually, it was only a field on a kind of high plateau, surrounded by a bush area called the Macchia. It was situated approximately twenty kilometres north-east of the small harbour of Gela on the south-eastern coast of Sicily. ... Our new advanced landing ground ... on this flat upland area, framed by the Macchia and surrounded by a hilly landscape, lowering towards the sea in the south, was exactly the right place for us. The landscape would have been so idyllic, but we had no leisure time to enjoy it. It was important to camouflage the aircraft in a way that the enemy reconnaissance aircraft

could not, or at least not immediately, discover that we were occupying the field. My men were given the task of building taxiways into the Macchia. Where there were not enough bushes, camouflage nets had to be used. The hard work in the extreme heat made them swear from time to time, but the labour paid off. For a few weeks everything was quiet, and there were no mission orders. Possible targets were beyond our range. I had a primitive but reasonably well-protected *Gefechtsstand* dug, where we also positioned our telephone exchange. For our accommodation, I had someone explore a cork oak grove to the north of our airfield. It was quickly reachable on quite a decent road. Beneath those cork oaks, tents could easily be set up. With the warm Mediterranean climate, you could sleep very well there during the nighttime.[20]

To add strength to the Mediterranean fighter-bomber presence, the ground attack unit *Schlachtgeschwader 2* had been formed in late 1942 from elements of *Jabogruppe Afrika* combined with fresh units, predominantly equipped with Bf 109 and Fw 190 fighter-bombers. In Brindisi, Bf 109Fs and Fw 190As of II./*Schlachtgeschwader 2* had arrived during April accompanied by *Geschwaderkommodore* Maj. Wolfgang 'Bombo' Schenck and his Staff flight, I./SchG. 2 transferring to Gerbini. Schenck, a pre-war coffee farmer in Tanganyika before returning to Germany in 1936 to enlist in the Luftwaffe, already held the Knight's Cross with Oak Leaves and had been involved in the testing of the Me 210 at Rechlin as head of the *Eprobungsstaffel* before a period on the *RLM* staff ended with his transfer to command *Schlachtgeschwader 2*. As well as the fighter-bombers, the *Geschwader* also hosted two *Staffeln* of Hs 129 ground-attack aircraft, which had been in action in Tunisia before withdrawing to Italy; 4./SchG. 2 being briefly based at Bari before relocated to the Eastern Front as a tank-destroying unit, while 8./SchG. 2 was based at Decimomanu between May and June until it also moved east.

Meanwhile, the Allies began preparation for Operation *Corkscrew*, the invasion of the Italian island of Pantelleria between Tunisia and Sicily, administratively a part of the Sicilian Trapani Province. The Italian bastion posed a threat to Allied shipping within the area, various caves and grottoes along its shores having been used as shelter and refuelling points for MAS boats and its airfield used for fighter and bomber refuelling. While landed on the island, such aircraft could be sheltered in a steel and concrete shelter built into a rocky hillside and protected by a thick blanket of lava and earth, which withstood a number of direct hits during

Major Wolfgang 'Bombo' Schenck of ground-attack unit *Schlachtgeschwader* 2.

the subsequent bombardment without significant damage. Even before the close of the war in North Africa the Allies had initiated heavy air attacks on Pantelleria, the most severe taking place on 8 May when over one hundred bombers pounded the aerodrome, hitting administrative buildings, fuel storage depots, and grounded aircraft. The garrison of 12,000 Italian troops were heavily entrenched, but the bombing intensified at the end of May to be joined by naval bombardment as the Allies planned to send the first wave of assault troops ashore on 11 June. By the time of the actual invasion, it was estimated that the defending Italians' combat effectiveness had been reduced to less than 50 per cent with heavy casualties and a severe shortage of drinking water.

While Luftwaffe bomber units regrouped during early June, the fighter-bombers of SchG. 2 and SKG 10 mounted continual harassing attacks against Allied shipping both off the North African coast and around Pantelleria, though with little success. The Focke-Wulf *Jabos* were suffering frequent tyre damage from uneven airstrips, many cratered from frequent bombing and littered with bomb splinters. Undercarriage problems and a lack of spare parts plagued the fighter-bombers. Furthermore, there was a shortage of ground crew spread between the eastern Sicilian airfields around Catania that prevented the fighter-bomber *Geschwader* operating united at any given time. Instead, the aircraft were mechanically prepared at their home airfields and travelled to a forward jumping-off airfield at Chinisia on Sicily's west coast. Each Fw 190 flew to the staging point with a mechanic stowed within the rear fuselage compartment, accessed by a small hatch and allowing a single man to lie prostrate. Upon landing they required only refuelling, loading with ammunition and a single 500kg bomb before they were ready for action without the necessary addition of drop tanks for extra fuel.

Several operations against enemy shipping near Pantelleria were foiled by bad weather and mechanical problems before Schenck's *Schlachtgeschwader* 2 scrambled twenty Fw 190As of *Hptm.* Werner Dörnbrack's II./SchG 2 on 3 June, escorted by twenty-one Bf 109s for an evening attack on ships south-east of Cape Bon. During the raid they claimed one ship hit and sinking and a second damaged by a bomb hit on the bow before Spitfires drove the attackers away. Royal Navy reports record no damage. An attempted interception of Allied shipping south of Pantelleria on 6 June was foiled by Spitfires that forced bombs to be jettisoned and the mission aborted. The next day II./SchG. 2 and III./SKG 10 attacked Korba North airfield at Cape Bon instead of attempting an anti-shipping strike.

Almost as the first British commandos stormed on to Pantelleria during the morning of 11 June the Italian military governor, Admiral Gino Pavesi, surrendered with permission from Rome. Three days later as the Allies evacuated Italian prisoners and stockpiled supplies on Pantellaria, Luftwaffe fighter-bombers attacked again. Thirty-three Fw 190s targeted shipping targets near the island during late morning, scoring hits on landing craft and transports, sinking *MGB 648* and the 813-ton water tanker *Empire Maiden*.

The capture of Pantelleria with little serious Luftwaffe interference was instructive to the Allies. At no point was any serious challenge made to the Allied bomber forces battering the island and, despite myriad excellent targets being available, anti-shipping missions were limited to little more than small fighter-bomber attacks of negligible effect and some desultory Ju 88 night raids. Minor Italian garrisons on nearby islands Lampedusa and Linosa were similarly captured as the Allies cleared those that stood between North Africa and the Sicilian mainland. The stage was now set for the expected Allied invasion of Sicily, Operation *Husky*.

3

North and South

The Arctic and Eastern Fronts

THE LAST MAJOR TORPEDO operation by the Luftwaffe in the Black Sea had taken place on the night of 2 August 1942 when a number of II./KG 26 Heinkels attacked the Soviet cruiser *Molotov*. The attack was unsuccessful, but the cruiser was damaged by a nearly simultaneous attack by Italian MAS torpedo boats, two torpedoes hitting the port side and blowing nearly twenty metres off the stern.

At that point in time *Fliegerführer Süd* controlled only III./LG 1 (thirty-two Ju 88s), II./KG 26 (twenty He 111H-6 torpedo bombers, ten of 6./KG 26 having moved to Grosseto), Stab. and 2./Aufkl.Gr. 125 and, briefly, *Oblt.* Hans-Ulrich Rudel's training *Ergänzungsgruppe*/StG 2 (twenty Ju 87s). Maritime reconnaissance in the region was reinforced by eight aircraft in June 1942, as well as forty Heinkel He 114s that were assigned to the Romanian Air Force.

As *Fliegerführer Süd Oberst* Wolfgang von Wild had managed to achieve relative success in the Black Sea despite constant whittling away of his available aircraft for either Mediterranean service or reallocation to area bombing and army ground-attack support. He had also firmly established effective inter-service cooperation with regional Kriegsmarine units, a feat not often repeated elsewhere. By using the meagre forces at his disposal von Wild had kept a steady surveillance and attacking presence over the Soviet Black Sea Fleet, resulting in their eventual withdrawal to Poti and Batumi where they were protected by anti-aircraft guns ashore. The direct benefit to Wehrmacht land forces was the cessation of major shore bombardment by Soviet warships.

However, von Wild's immediate superior, *Generalfeldmarschall* Wolfram Freiherr von Richthofen, who had risen to command of *Luftflotte* 4 on 20 July 1942, had frequently disparaged the achievements of *Fliegerführer Süd* and though a gifted tactician, failed to show any interest in anti-shipping operations. Due to a noticeable lack of heavy weapons and with no specific strategic mission of its own, the Luftwaffe in the East had been largely relegated to the role of flying artillery for ground troops. In Berlin Göring supported such a use for the Luftwaffe in the East and as a result disregarding the threat posed by Soviet naval units in the Black Sea. Richthofen reasoned that the maritime strike assets available to *Fliegerführer Süd* would be better used if repurposed for land operations and during August 1942 the post of *Fliegerführer Süd* was abolished and its aircraft transferred to *General der Flieger* Kurt Pflugbeil's IV.*Fliegerkorps* headquartered in recently-captured Maikop. The abolition of his post coincided with von Wild's hospitalisation due to illness and he did not return to active service until November 1942, as *Lufttransportführer* I (*Südost*), Athens.

Hitler's decision to launch '*Fall Blau*' on 28 June 1942 marks the turning point of the war in the east. Army Group South was ordered to advance on Stalingrad and the Volga simultaneous to a ninety-degree divergent course into the Caucasus towards the Soviet oil fields at Maikop, Grozny and Baku. To this end Army Group South was subdivided into two smaller constituent Army Groups A (Caucasus) and B (Volga). Ultimately both offensives would fail, and the junction between the two Army Groups would provide Soviet forces with a perfect weak spot in which to strike.

On 15 October, *Fliegerführer Krim* was established in Kerch, given responsibility for air operations in support of '*Fall Blau*' and headed by the return of *General der Flieger* Konrad Zander from his staff position in *Luftflotte* 4. Despite Zander's best efforts, he was unable to maintain more than sporadic anti-shipping missions and, emboldened once more, by early 1943 the Black Sea Fleet was again mounting shore bombardment missions against targets in the Crimea, Ukraine and Romania as Axis forces reeled from the unfolding disaster of Stalingrad.

As Luftwaffe operations stretched over the Caucasus, an unusual ad-hoc unit was formed during the second part of 1942. *Oberleutnant* Hans Klimmer was appointed *Staffelkapitän* of *Küstenfliegerstaffel Krim* created from twenty-four crews in training using Focke-Wulf Fw 58 *Weihe* aircraft and nominally under command of IV.*Fliegerkorps*. Based at Bagerovo airbase on the Kerch Peninsula, this small unit helped augment the ranks of a severely overtaxed Luftwaffe, patrolling the Crimean coastline, mounting armed reconnaissance and ASW missions over the Black Sea as well as providing aerial escort for transport convoys from Odessa to the Crimea. Over time the unit would shift away from nautical missions, being tasked with nocturnal bombing of Soviet troop concentrations near Tuapse from October onwards.

Focke-Wulf Fw 58 *Weihe* of *Küstenfliegerstaffel Krim*.

Elements of *Oberst* Gerhard Kolbe's *Aufklärungsgruppe* 125 (*See*) remained in the Black Sea for reconnaissance duties. Stab (He 114, Ar 196 and BV 138s) and 3./Aufkl.Gr. 125 (Ar 95 and BV 138s) were stationed in Constanza and Mamaia/Varna respectively, while the BV 138s of 1./Aufkl.Gr. 125 were based in Norway and Ar 196s of 2./Aufkl. Gr. 125 remained between in Scaramanga and Suda Bay, Crete.

The air-sea rescue headquarters of *Maj.* Julius Hansing's *Seenotbereichskommando XII* had come into being in June 1942, formed from *Seenotzentrale (L) Schwarzes Meer*, and stationed from August in Eupatoria, taking over a sanatorium in Frunze Park.

Hauptmann Hannibal Gude's 8.*Seenotstaffel* continued to operate search and rescue flights throughout 1942, flying elderly He 59, Fw 58 and Do 24 seaplanes. Gude had received training only on the He 59 and had been surprised at the ad-hoc nature of his *Staffel* and its lack of pilots, frequently flying missions himself but only able to act as observer aboard the more sophisticated Do 24s. On 8 August five temporarily non-operational Do 24s were at the seaplane base near Constanța along with a single He 59, one Do 24 at Kasantyp on the Sea of Asov, an Fw 58 in Odessa and another in Kerch. The seaplane station was situated less than seven kilometres north-north-west of the port city, on the southern shore of the lagoon Lake Siutghiol. Constructed by the Romanian air force during 1933, the station included underground fuel tanks and bunkered ammunition storage, and three hangars connected by tracks to slipways with piers and jetties for further moorings. Air traffic control boats of *Hptm.* Strecker's 12.*Seenotflottille*; Fl.B 404 (Constanza), 426 (Feodosia), 415 (Sevastopol) and 408 (Odessa), bolstered by the arrival of *Heinrich Tjarks* (Sevastopol) and *Ferdinand Laisz* (Kerch) on 16 August offered seaborne support.

On 25 August, Zander ordered 8.*Seenotstaffel* to establish a forward base near Novorossiysk harbour, possession of the port on the eastern Black Sea coast still being contested by German and Soviet ground forces until the night of 9 September when Novorossiysk harbour fell to the Germans, only a tiny Soviet enclave at Mount Myskhako remaining which proved a running sore in the Wehrmacht's Black Sea flank. A relatively primitive forward base at Lake Tobechikskoye, near the village of Ortaeli south of Kerch, had already been established, though initially under heavy Soviet shellfire until German troops captured the Taman Peninsula. Unfortunately, fighter escorts were unavailable for the *Seenotstaffel*, so rescue missions were frequently aborted as Soviet fighters tenaciously contested Crimean airspace.

Further to their air-sea rescue purpose, Zander earmarked the Kuban Dorniers for use as convoy escort and reconnaissance aircraft over the south-eastern stretches of the Black Sea, drawing strong but futile protest from Gude. In fact, 8.*Seenotstaffel* had already undertaken such missions during the early days of Barbarossa while under the command of *Oblt.* Fritz Freiherr von Buchholz. In conjunction with the Kriegsmarine Training Detachment in Constanţa, Buchholz had mounted reconnaissance missions over the western half of the Black Sea, given tactical control over two Romanian seaplane squadrons at Mamaia and three land-based Bulgarian squadrons from Varna.[1] The small aircraft of *Küstenstaffel Krim* were also attached to Gude's unit for the purpose, and when despatched on such missions, they and aircraft of 8.*Seenotstaffel* came under the temporary operational control of 3./Aufkl.Gr. 125.

Hauptmann Walter Gladigau, previously of 8.*Seenotstaffel*, was promoted to head *Seenotkommando* 18, one of two regional sub-commands subordinate to *Seenotbereichskommando* XII and based in Varna before moving to Ak Mechet in the Crimea in May 1942. Gladigau had accompanied the aircraft and men based at Lake Tobechikskoye and later recounted the activities and difficulties faced by the air-sea rescue flying boats during this period.

The ceaseless German air attacks called for the maintenance of constant air-sea rescue patrols, in which a number of rescue planes kept the approach and return routes as well as the areas of main effort constantly under observation. Although accompanied by escort fighters when on particularly dangerous missions, rescue planes were struck frequently by anti-aircraft shellfire or Soviet fighter weapons while on their rescue patrols. In this way one rescue aircraft was forced to surface within the Turkish three-mile zone. In an on-the-spot inspection, I convinced myself of the impossibility of salvaging the aircraft and then had it destroyed by weapons fire after the crew had been picked up. In the case of another Do 24 lost off the coast of Turkey owing to enemy action, the crew reached Turkish territory.[2]

During 1942, the 8.*Seenotstaffel* rescued sixty men, German, Romanian and Russian, with every aircraft crew receiving at least one Iron Cross First Class, and three the German Cross in Gold.

Fearing the isolation of Army Group A within the Caucasus – its advance stalled before Grozny – Axis forces throughout the entire region were thrown onto the defensive, expecting a strong Soviet attack expected against the Taman Peninsula. On 16 December 1942, the Red Army had launched Operation *Little Saturn* in the Ukraine, pushing the First Panzer Army steadily back towards Rostov on Don and sealing the fate of the Sixth Army when weak flanking units were shattered by a Soviet counterattack timed to coincide with the onset of winter. In the Caucasus, the Seventeenth Army retreated towards the Taman Peninsula, establishing a defensive line along the Kuban River Delta after Hitler had uncharacteristically authorised a withdrawal to protect the eastern approaches to the Crimea and provide a potential launching point for renewed offensive operations against the Caucasus during 1943.

By the end of the year the Wehrmacht's Sixth Army had been surrounded at Stalingrad for over a month and Hitler had summoned Jeschonnek to the Berghof on 19 November and asked whether the Sixth Army could be supplied by air in the event of 'temporary encirclement'. Understanding the situation was likely to be brief, Jeschonnek assured him that provided both transport aircraft and bombers were used, and if adequate airfields were maintained both inside and outside of the pocket, then the resupply could be successfully undertaken, using the Luftwaffe resupply of the II Army Corps in the Demyansk pocket near Leningrad as an example. The comparison was, however, specious. In

Demyansk, 100,000 men had required 100 tonnes of supplies daily, and the Luftwaffe had barely managed, losing 265 aircraft and 387 aviators, the cost in aircraft alone equalling over half a year's production of transport aircraft. In Stalingrad, however, there were approximately 300,000 men trapped, requiring in the region of 750 tonnes of supplies daily (the number reduced to 500 after hours of stressful phone calls between Army and Luftwaffe commanders), far beyond the abilities of the Luftwaffe which at that moment was spread thinly on every front and already heavily engaged in supplying the Tunisian bridgehead. Upon further consideration Jeschonnek appears to have almost immediately regretted his assurance to Hitler and attempted to withdraw support for the idea, only to be informed by the *Führer* that Göring himself had given his endorsement.

The result was calamitous. *General der Flieger* Martin Fiebig's VIII. *Fliegerkorps* was made responsible for the Stalingrad airlift, requisitioning all available Ju 52 aircraft and gathering assorted bombers press-ganged into transport duties, including one *Gruppe* of He 177s and one of mixed Fw 200s, Junkers Ju 90s and Junkers Ju 290s (forming KGzbV 200, commanded by *Maj.* Hans-Jürgen Willers of 11./KG 40).

The Junkers Ju 290 was a direct descendant of the Ju 90 airliner which had been originally considered by *Hptm.* Edgar Petersen as a long-distance maritime reconnaissance aircraft in September 1939 before being passed over in favour of the Fw 200.[3] The first test flight of the civilian Ju 90S (*Schwer*) 'V1' took place on 28 August 1937, although engine specifications were changed for a second prototype as the original Daimler Benz 601 fuel-injected engines were reserved for Bf 109 production. Instead, BMW 132 H engines were mounted in the 'V2' and 'V3' aircraft. During long range tropical test flying, 'V2' crashed near Bathurst, Africa, shortly after take-off when both port engines failed. The aircraft, named 'Preussen' stalled, hit a palm tree and exploded after hitting the ground, killing twelve occupants including all three crew.

Nevertheless, the aircraft was finally cleared for use and Lufthansa ordered eight of the production type A-1s, to operate alongside prototypes that they put into passenger service. Only seven were received, the final production model – and two ordered by South African Airways – going directly to the Luftwaffe. During April 1939 the *RLM* requested a military version of the Ju 90 for transport usage, given an altered fuselage shape, new wings and control surfaces and a loading ramp in the fuselage floor capable of accommodating reconnaissance vehicles or

A late-war photo of a Junkers Ju 290, first disastrously employed around Stalingrad.

artillery pieces. The Ju 90 'V7' was fitted with a DL131 turret above and behind the cockpit, a glazed rear MG 15 position, a gondola-mounted MG 81Z underneath and ventral machine-gun positions, becoming the first proper testbed of what was soon redesignated the Ju 290 and seeing action in the Mediterranean and then during the Stalingrad airlift.

Around Stalingrad, hastily created ground support units and poor airfield infrastructure led to excruciating serviceability problems. Between 26 and 30 November a daily average of only 75 tons of supply was successfully delivered, rising to 117 tons per day over the following nine days, but still spectacularly short of requirements. With aircraft continually lost to heavy Soviet anti-aircraft fire, accidents and mechanical breakdowns, more He 111s from III./KG 4, two *Gruppen* of KG 27, II. and III./KG 55 and I./KG 100 were thrown into the ad-hoc transport units, along with several Fw 200s of 1. and 3./KG 40 and the troubled He 177s of I./KG 50.

Through the ten weeks leading to 2 February 1943 when the last of Paulus' men surrendered, the Luftwaffe carried or dropped 8,350 tons of fuel and ammunition, a daily average of 115 tons. They had also evacuated nearly 30,000 wounded. However, in return they had

lost 488 aircraft, including 165 Heinkel He 111 bombers and five KG
40 Condors, with nearly 1,000 men killed or missing in action, many
of them experienced instructors from training establishments. In
Stalingrad, 91,000 men shuffled into Soviet captivity from which only
4,000 or so would ever return.

In the meantime Luftwaffe reconnaissance flights noted a steady
build-up of Soviet forces in Black Sea ports and a fresh storm finally
broke on 4 February 1943, when elements of three Soviet infantry
brigades landed at the tiny Red Army enclave at Cape Myskhako that
had defied attempts to remove it and were soon firmly lodged ashore
inside an expanding beachhead.

Fiebig's VIII.*Fliegerkorps* was given tactical control over the seaplanes
of *Obstlt.* Hansing's *Seenotbereichskommando* XII, part of his task being
the maintenance of supply transport from the Crimea into the Kuban
Bridgehead. As winter gave way to spring, thaw and mud threatened
the successful use of wheeled aircraft in the area, Hansing was made
Lufttransportführer (*See*) Sevastopol, with instructions to organise a unit
of seaplanes for transporting supplies into the Kuban. Hansing swiftly
assembled a three-man staff comprising *Oblt.* Karl Wind – formerly of
KG.z.b.V. 172 which had run supply missions into both Demjansk and
Stalingrad – *Lt.* Stephany and *Stabsfw.* Geiger and amassed a force of
eighteen Do 24 flying boats, seven from 8.*Seenotstaffel*, the remainder
transferred from various other *Seenotstaffeln*. The Dorniers were
gathered at Sevastopol and divided into two *Staffeln*. While *Oblt.* Hans
Tretter (*Staffelkapitän* of 7.*Seenotstaffel* and promoted to *Hauptmann* at
the beginning of April) took command of 1.*Seetransportstaffel* and was
the man made primarily responsible for the Dornier contribution to the
airlift, *Hptm.* Gude, promoted to *Major*, was given command of the new
2.*Seetransportstaffel*. Tretter flew from his Mediterranean station to the
Crimea in a Do 24T-3 during late February and did not return to Athens
until 3 April, while Gude had recently recovered from injuries after his Do
24 collided in darkness with a cement obstruction in Sevastopol harbour
at the end of December. Meanwhile, the fall of Stalingrad had freed many
remaining Ju 52s of their transport duties and twenty-five were flown to
Sevastopol where their wheeled undercarriages were replaced with floats
in 8.*Seenotstaffel* workshops.

Hansing instructed Gude to reconnoitre a lake between the Taman
Peninsula and the front lines of the Kuban Bridgehead as a potential
landing site. His pilot for the mission, *Lt.* Werner Lange, remembered:

97

That lake had to be used for floatplanes of diverse types and had to be well sited giving the opportunity to unload the planes quickly and without problems. On 21 February 1943 I started from Sevastopol at 0903hrs in Do 24 'CM+IV'. *Major* Gude acted as observer and we landed at 1120hrs on the Vityazevski Limar Lake. That stretch of water had been chosen for its depth and proximity to the bridgehead. It was risky to land there, as we were not certain of its depth. It was widely known that many Russian lakes are too shallow, and if so, our Dornier could hit rocks. After two hours in the air, we were over the lake and tried some practice landing approaches. Finally, we decided to land near the village of Gostagayka as we thought it was the best place, judging from the air. The landing and the taxiing on the lake went smoothly and the people were very friendly. They welcomed us and gave us Kuban wine. After verifying lake depths, bank composition etc, we returned to Sevastopol that same day. On the 28th we returned to Vityazevski and began preparing the site for seaplane operations. On 7 March I took the command of the *Aussenkommando Ortasli* (SK 18).[4]

Army engineers were drafted in to construct a log landing stage complete with loading ramp. Seaplanes moored to makeshift rubber anchor buoys and engineers transferred cargo to rafts which were towed to the landing stage by army assault boats. The entire area was reinforced with a heavy anti-aircraft presence to protect the supply missions, each aircraft returning to the Crimea with wounded evacuated from the bridgehead.

Between 5 and 25 March, the seaplanes delivered 1,910 tons of supplies into the Kuban, losing two aircraft in the process. On 9 March two Do 24s were flying in thick fog near Feodosia when a sheer cliff face loomed

The Dornier Do 24 performed well for the *Seenotdienst* in the Black Sea and as a transport aircraft for the resupply of the Kuban bridgehead.

up unexpectedly before them. While one managed to narrowly miss the cliff, aircraft 'DI+ZO' on loan from 6.*Seenotstaffel*, crashed, killing five men and leaving only second engineer *Ogfr.* Otto Ulmer injured. The second casualty occurred on 23 March when the damaged Ju 52(M) of 2.*Transportstaffel* 'CM+IV' was found on the surface of the Black Sea by a Do 24, its three-man crew being rescued before the aircraft sank. On 1 April, VIII.*Fliegerkorps* ended the resupply missions by maritime aircraft, disbanding the *Transportstaffeln* and all of their Ju 52s and Do 24s returned to their original units.

Air-sea rescue work continued apace and during spring and summer 1943, 8.*Seenotstaffel* Dorniers, in conjunction with boats of 12.*Seenotflottille*, rescued sixty-nine German, Romanian and Russian airmen and sailors from the Black Sea in twenty-one separate missions.

At the beginning of 1943 *Obstlt.* Hellmut Schalke, former Kriegsmarine officer, *Gruppenkommandeur* of III./KG 26 and I./KG1, had been attached to the staff of *Führer der Luft Tunis* before being appointed *Seefliegerführer Schwarzes Meer*, a new post that replaced the defunct office of *Fliegerführer Süd*. On 28 April he was made provisional commander of Aufkl.Gr. 125 in Constanța and the post of *Aufklärungsführer Schwarzes Meer West* created. Amongst the staff of Schalke's reconnaissance headquarters was the naval officer *Oblt.z.S.* Ralf Jurs who after service aboard the battleship *Gneisenau* in 1939 had transferred as an observer to Aufkl.Gr. 125, earning the German Cross in Gold and *Ehrenpokal* for his service. During 1943 he transferred to *Stab/Aufklärungsführer Schwarzes Meer – West* and was promoted to *Hauptmann* before being recalled to the Kriegsmarine for U-boat training in July, becoming the commander of *U778* at the rank of *Kapitänleutnant*.[5]

Norway

In the Northern theatre the three existing *Küstenfliegergruppen* maintained a presence after the dramatic reduction of maritime bomber strength following Allied landings in North Africa. *Major* Rupprecht Heyn had departed command of *Küstenfliegergruppe* 406 on 14 June 1942, transferred as Operations Officer to the staff of X.*Fliegerkorps* before promotion to *Oberstleutnant* and appointment as *Kommodore* of KG 40. At the end of 1942, Stab/Kü.Fl.Gr. 406 was disbanded, though the three combat *Staffeln* remained operational: 1./Kü.Fl.Gr. 406 equipped with twelve He 115 torpedo aircraft spread between Tromsø and Kirkenes;

A pilot of *Küstenfliegergruppe* 406 celebrates completion of his 100th mission.

and both 2. and 3./Kü.Fl.Gr. 406 operating BV 138s from Trondheim and Tromsø respectively.

The BV 138s were a constant reconnaissance presence around northern Norway in the search for PQ convoy traffic. Before the successful attacks against Convoy PQ18 in September 1942, aircraft of *Küstenfliegergruppe* 406 took part in Operation *Wunderland*, a sortie by the 'pocket battleship' *Admiral Scheer* which sailed from Narvik on 16 August bound for the Kara Sea to attack Soviet vessels sheltering from pack ice while transiting to the United Kingdom. *Admiral Scheer* was accompanied during the first leg of her voyage by three destroyers and *U601* and *U251* were attached once the ships neared their target area

Two days before the cruiser slipped from Narvik, the U-boat group *Nebelkönig* had begun to disperse. Ten boats had lain in wait for the expected – though delayed – PQ18 between Iceland and Jan Mayen Island. *Kapitänleutnant* Reinhart Reche's *U255* was among those boats, having been at sea for ten days, working in conjunction with BV 138 'K6+HL' of 3./Kü.Fl.Gr. 406 that had been allocated to support the U-boats in the lead-up to *Wunderland*. Powered by diesel engines, the BV 138 was perfect for operating in remote areas in conjunction with a U-boat able to supply both crew accommodation when not airborne, and fuel from the boat's own bunkers.

On 11 August, Reche supplied *Oblt.z.S.* Karl Dierschke's aircraft 'K6+HL' with a cubic metre of fuel near Spitzbergen while the crew were accommodated below decks for a brief period of rest. Taking off once more, two of the aircraft engines stopped not long after becoming airborne and the BV 138 made an emergency landing, Reche taking the seaplane in tow as some of his diesel engineers assisted in establishing the cause of the engine failure. It soon transpired that a small quantity of seawater had been pumped into the aircraft tanks by accident. With drainage impossible where they were, Reche and Dierschke agreed to tow the aircraft to a more sheltered place, but two towing attempts failed as the steel hawser broke, a stabilising wing float then tangling in the severed cable and cause the aircraft to capsize. With no real alternative, the crew were kept aboard *U255* and the flying boat sunk with gunfire at 1710hrs on 17 August in the Storfjorden.

With weather conditions a primary concern for *Admiral Scheer*'s impending operation, five BV 138s, able to stay in the air for twelve hours without refuelling, were detailed to cover large swathes of sea along the predicted shipping routes, adding meteorological information to that from U-boats and a network of weather stations, stretching from Spitzbergen to Novaya Zemlia. Ultimately, though the flying boats sighted convoy traffic outbound from Archangelsk, *Wunderland* was only moderately successful, *Scheer* prevented by heavy pack ice from reaching its objective the Wilkitsky Strait. The ship's Arado crewed by pilot *Ofw.* Wilhelm Elke and observer *Oblt.z.S.* Karl-Adolf Schlitt landed so heavily after returning from a scouting mission on 21 August that one float was damaged, requiring extensive repair. However, the second Arado aircraft, 'T3+EK' was written off four days later after crash-landing near *Scheer*, though both crewmen were rescued. During *Wunderland*, *Scheer*'s two Ar 196A-3 aircraft had mounted twelve sorties, spending twenty-two hours and thirteen minutes aloft. Though the supporting U-boats experienced some success, *Scheer* herself sank only a Soviet icebreaker and bombarded Port Dikson. Despite badly damaging two ships and wrecking several buildings ashore, the impact of the attack was fleeting and ultimately *Wunderland* achieved little as *Scheer* returned to Narvik.

After Convoy PQ18 and the diversion of considerable aircraft strength to the Mediterranean, *Luftflotte* 5 reported no major convoys sighted between October and December 1942. The severe losses accrued by both PQ17 and PQ18 combined, coupled with demands elsewhere for Allied naval craft such as supporting Operation *Torch*, led to the suspension of the Arctic convoys until December 1942. Instead, independently sailing merchantmen would be despatched in what was known as Operation *FB*.

In response, *Luftflotte* 5 employed armed reconnaissance (*bewaffnete Aufklärung*) tactics in which pairs or entire flights of aircraft fully loaded with bombs or torpedoes were despatched on reconnaissance missions, ready to engage any ships sighted, though the vastness of the search area effectively neutered such tactics.

Between 29 October and 2 November, thirteen ships sailed at approximately 12-hour intervals from Scotland to Murmansk. Although unescorted, there were ASW trawlers stationed at intervals along the route and local escorts available from Murmansk. Of the ships that sailed, three were forced to abort their voyages and five were sunk, the remaining five reaching the Soviet Union. Of the ship's sunk, 7,708GRT Soviet freighter SS *Dekabrist* was bombed by Ju 88 aircraft of I./KG30 on 4 November. Defensive fire hit one Junkers, forcing it to break off the attack with engine damage and make a forced landing on Bear Island. Escorted by a weather reconnaissance aircraft that had received their distress call, the Junkers successfully crash-landed and the following day a Do 24 flying boat of 10.*Seenotstaffel* retrieved the crew, able to partially destroy their aircraft before departing.[6]

A second attack later that night was more successful, the steamer hit in the bow tearing a large hole in the ship's hull and despite damage control efforts, *Dekabrist* was abandoned at midnight and sank the following day. The entire crew of eighty safely abandoned ship in four lifeboats, though only one containing nineteen crew members and the ship's cat reached land. Fourteen of them later died from hunger, cold and sickness before July 1943 when an He 115 investigating possible Allied weather stations sighted one of the survivors near a small hut used infrequently by seal hunters and dropped a parcel containing bread, butter, cigarettes, bandages, aspirin and antiseptic. They were later recovered by *U703* in early October.

The only other *FB* ship that the Luftwaffe could claim any success against was the 5,445-ton British steamer SS *Chulmleigh*, bombed again by II./KG 30 Ju 88s on 5 November and beached on Spitsbergen's South Cape where *Kptlt.* Hans Benker's *U625* torpedoed the stranded wreck and finished it off with gunfire the following day.

The Soviet authorities demanded the resumption of supply convoys which recommenced in what the Royal Navy hoped would be the

A Heinkel He 115 of *Küstenfliegergruppe* 406 in Norway.

advantageous environment of Arctic night, now code-named 'JW' for outbound and 'RA' for those returning to the United Kingdom. Convoy JW51A departed Loch Ewe on 15 December and all fifteen merchants arrived at the Kola inlet on Christmas Day, undetected by an increased Luftwaffe reconnaissance presence. On 22 December, fourteen merchant ships of Convoy JW51B departed Scotland but these were found by Luftwaffe aircraft on Christmas Eve, briefly identified as inbound before contact was lost in stormy weather. On 30 December *U354* regained contact and began to shadow, as the Kriegsmarine decided finally to use their heavy ships again. Operation *Regenbogen* was launched with the 'pocket battleship' *Lützow*, the cruiser *Admiral Hipper* and six destroyers. The debacle that followed became known as the Battle of the Barents Sea in which the cruisers were driven off by Royal Navy destroyers in the darkness of the long polar night, damaging *Admiral Hipper* (destroying one Arado aircraft and damaging the second) and sinking the destroyer *Friederich Eckoldt* for the loss of the destroyer HMS *Achates* and the radar-equipped minesweeper HMS *Bramble*.

Fortunately for the Luftwaffe, they had played no combat role in *Regenbogen*, the atmospheric conditions making identification of enemy and friendly ships difficult even during the brief hours of daylight. Plans by *Luftflotte* 5 to launch a torpedo attack against JW51B were thwarted by fog and driving snow squalls and a single Condor piloted by *Oblt.* Dietrich Weber of 2./ KG 40 failed to return from shadowing the convoy.

The convoy suffered no damage, resulting in a fit of apoplectic rage from Adolf Hitler when he learned of the failure; sporadic communications throughout the unfolding battle already having led him to believe that the Kriegsmarine were in the process of eliminating the convoy. The navy's failure was in no small part due to contradictory orders from *OKM* and the *Führer*, issuing strict instructions not to risk capital ships unless success was assured. Nonetheless, with the military situation dire in all land theatres, Hitler had clung to his premature positive conclusions and the consequences of his disappointment were far reaching. Hitler ranted uncontrollably and demanded Germany's surface fleet be scrapped and the guns used ashore. Within days, *Grossadmiral* Raeder had become aware that whatever influence he once had with the German dictator was at an end and he resigned.

Germany's naval chief since 1928, Erich Raeder had comprehensively failed to establish a working 'Fleet Air Arm', the *Küstenflieger* now but a shadow of their previous establishment and, though a harassing presence to coastal convoys and trawler fleets, never a serious threat to the Royal Navy. Raeder's desire to establish a maritime strike force had been vehemently opposed by Göring, a typical situation in the upper echelons of the Third Reich as inter-departmental rivalry frequently obstructed military necessity. Hitler's method of 'divide and rule' between his subordinates is no more obvious than here. While Göring was possessed of a wily political acumen, Raeder was the direct opposite. A conservative Christian aristocratic officer of the Imperial Navy, he was the antithesis of both Göring and his master, never able to challenge Göring's control over his chosen domain of the air service.

The vacant position of naval commander-in-chief was filled by Karl Dönitz. Unlike Raeder, Dönitz had retained Hitler's favour once he had risen to prominence. Somewhat overawed by the *Führer* – once stating that being in his presence made him feel like a 'little sausage' – his apparent willingness to align more closely to National Socialist principles than Raeder would ever have done had no doubt helped secure his own position. By the time he rose to command the Kriegsmarine in 1943, Göring was unable to refuse Dönitz's demands in the same way that he had refused Raeder's, his own star having waned for good following the

Raeder in conversation with Hitler and Keitel. Raeder never enjoyed Hitler's complete confidence, his resignation in January 1943 finally ending dreams of a German Fleet Air Arm.

debacle of the Tunisian and, particularly, Stalingrad airlifts. However, by that point in the war, it was too late for Göring's acquiescence to naval demands to have any real effect.

During 1942 the Wehrmacht had been unable to close the Murmansk supply route from Great Britain, either by land offensive, naval blockade or air power, which was in steady decline. Though inter-service cooperation was generally very good regionally in northern Norway, the testiness between the heads of the Luftwaffe and Kriegsmarine remained as entrenched as ever, as shown by the entry in the *SKL* War Diary from 29 April 1942:

> The Commander in Chief, Luftwaffe sent the following telegram in reply to the Naval Staff's request for reinforcement of the Trondheim fighter defence:
>
> 'The Commander in Chief, Luftwaffe knows it is desirable to have a stronger fighter defence in Trondheim. However, reinforcements cannot be made available at present. Conditions in the Luftwaffe are like those faced by the Kriegsmarine with respect to scarcity of forces at its disposal.

The Commander in Chief, Luftwaffe would like the Navy to transfer more destroyers to the Norwegian area so that they could combat effectively and successfully enemy convoy traffic passing the coast of northern Norway, in close cooperation with the Luftwaffe.'

The Naval Liaison Officer attached to the Commander in Chief, Luftwaffe was instructed by telephone to inform the Operations Staff of the Commander in Chief, Luftwaffe verbally, in a comradely way, that the Naval Staff must consider this telegram in very bad taste, and that it requests the Luftwaffe to use more civil language. Otherwise no action is to be taken.[7]

Nevertheless, away from Berlin's corridors of power, a satisfactory level of mutual support was achieved. But lack of a genuine joint command structure no doubt hampered attempts to isolate Murmansk. With bad weather a frequent challenge, Luftwaffe units were instead used for ground support, though *Luftflotte* 5 attempted to rest maritime aircrews wherever possible rather than waste such experienced men, or specialised aircraft, in operations over land.

As far as the few *Küstenflieger* units that remained, the severely downsized *Küstenfliegergruppe* 706 had maintained a presence in the Norwegian theatre since 1940, comprising at the end of 1942 and into early 1943 just *Stab* and 1./Kü.Fl.Gr. 706 stationed in Tromsø/Søreisa and Stavanger respectively, under the command of *Maj.* Hans-Joachim Tantzen. The elderly He 115s of 1./Kü.Fl.Gr. 706 had gradually been replaced by BV 138s, though the number available was low as aircraft were frequently poached by other units and crew conversion to the new type was correspondingly slow. A few Ar 196s were maintained to fly short-range patrols over the North Sea at the behest of *Fliegerführer Nord* (*West*). Additionally, the catapult ships *Friesenland* and *SP22* 'Falke' were used as motherships for BV138 aircraft of 1.*Staffel*.

Küstenfliegergruppe 906 had also lost its Staff flight, disbanded in April 1942 at the same time as 2./Kü.Fl.Gr. 906 which had by that time been reduced to just three aircraft.[8] By the end of 1942 this left the seven He 115s of 1./Kü.Fl.Gr. 906 in Billefjord and nine BV 138Cs of 3./Kü.Fl.Gr. 906 in Tromsø. On 22 October a single He 115 of 1./Kü.Fl.Gr. 906 was detached for a special mission and temporarily assigned to 2./ *Versuchsverband* Ob.d.L., commanded by *Hptm.* Edmund Gartenfeld, responsible for the clandestine dropping of sabotage groups behind enemy lines. For this operation, the *Küstenflieger* were despatched

He 115 '8L+IH' of 1./Kü.Fl.Gr. 906, captured by Soviet forces after attempting to recover thirteen Estonian commandos.

by the Abwehr to recover thirteen Estonian commandos, operating as part of the Finnish Army, stranded behind enemy lines. Unfortunately, the Estonians had been captured by the NKVD and their radio operator was obeying Soviet orders when he requested the aircraft land on Lake Jungozero to recover the commandos. Ambushed, the entire crew were killed and their aircraft captured.

The *Staffel*'s last casualty of 1942 occurred on 28 December, He 115 '8L+FH' of 1./Ku.Fl.Gr. 906 being lost during a hard landing on the water after escorting a convoy to Hafrsfjord. The port float was torn off and the Heinkel sank, though all three crew survived. In 2012 the wreck of the aircraft was raised and is now in the Sola aviation museum, the only surviving example of its kind.

Harassing bombing raids on shipping in Murmansk were carried out wherever possible, and by mid-January 1. and 3./KG 30 were stationed at Kemi, while 2.*Staffel* had moved from its previous base at Nautsi to Petsamo. They comprised the only real bomber strength remaining above the Arctic Circle by the end of 1942, the remainder of the *Kampfgeschwader* transferred to the Mediterranean in response to the crisis in North Africa.

On 24 January five He 115s of 1./Kü.Fl.Gr. 406 attacked fifteen heavily-escorted merchant ships of Convoy JW52 at 1230hrs as they sailed east-south-east of Bear Island. The convoy was being trailed by U-boats and was sighted and shadowed by a BV 138 reconnaissance aircraft of 1./Kü.Fl.Gr. 706; mistakenly reported by HMS *Onslaught* to the Admiralty as a Condor. The torpedo-carrying Heinkels made contact and attacked in the middle of the short winter day, two of them – aircraft 'K6+EH' and 'K6+MH' – shot down with all six crewmen never recovered. Both had been brought down by intense anti-aircraft fire, gunners aboard SS *Cornelius Harnett* claiming the first. In return the convoy suffered no damage. The following day a single Ju 88D-1 appeared over the convoy, belonging to *Aufklarüngsstaffel* 124, having taken off from Kirkenes to shadow JW52. It too received significant flak damage, forced to break away and return prematurely.

The returning Convoy RA52 of eleven ships departed the Kola Inlet under heavy escort on 29 January and would suffer a single casualty, the American SS *Greylock* torpedoed by Reche's *U255*. The following inbound convoy, JW53, was spotted by a BV 138 reconnaissance aircraft on 23 February sixty miles south-south west of Bear Island during the early afternoon. The twenty-eight merchant ships had already experienced problems since departing Loch Ewe eight days previously, heavy winds damaging six which were diverted to Iceland. Perhaps more serious, the carrier HMS *Dasher* suffered engine trouble during the storm forcing it to return to the Firth of Clyde and leaving the convoy bereft of

Maintenance work carried out on a Norwegian-based BV 138 flying boat.

air cover. Third Radio Officer David B. Craig was aboard the 5,818GRT steamer SS *Dover Hill* when she departed the United Kingdom.

We were heavily loaded with fighter aircraft, tanks, guns, lorries and a large tonnage of shells and high explosives. Our deck cargo was made up of lorries in cases, Matilda tanks and drums of lubricating oil covered with a layer of sandbags, presumably to protect them from tracer bullets. Needless to say we were not very happy about this last item . . . The escort was made up of three cruisers, one anti-aircraft cruiser, one escort carrier, sixteen destroyers, two minesweepers, three corvettes and two trawlers which was a very good escort and as the daylight hours were getting longer, trouble was obviously expected.

As we sailed North the gale developed into a hurricane and ships began to get damaged . . . On our ship the deck cargo began to break adrift and we were not sorry to see the oil drums going over the side but when the lorries in wooden cases were smashed up and eventually went overboard things were not so good. But we managed to save the tanks and kept on battering our way northwards. I remember trying to use an Aldis lamp from our bridge to signal to a corvette and found it very difficult since one minute she would be in sight, then she would go down the trough of the wave and all I could see would be her top masts; then up she would come and our ship would go down and all that would be seen was water, but eventually we got the message through. At one stage the convoy was well scattered but as the weather moderated the Navy rounded us all up and got us into some semblance of order once again.

The loss of our escort carrier meant that we had no air cover and, as expected, a few days later a German spotter plane arrived which flew round the convoy all the daylight hours to keep an eye on us. The next day we had a heavy attack by Ju 88 bombers in which our ship was damaged and our gunlayer was wounded by bomb splinters, but we still kept plodding on towards North Russia. At this part of the voyage we were steaming through pancake ice floes which protected us from the U-boats which could not operate in these conditions. The blizzards when they came were always welcome as they hid us from the enemy.[9]

Fourteen Ju 88s of II./KG 30 had attacked with level bombing at 0800hrs in the morning and again around midday on 25 February, *Dover Hill* suffering the only minor damage inflicted by the raids. Convoy JW53 arrived off the entrance to the Kola Inlet on 27 February, fifteen of the merchants bound for Murmansk and the remaining seven to the White Sea ports near Archangel. While the merchants would remain in Soviet waters until November, escort ships then prepared to shepherd the previous JW convoy back to the United Kingdom as RA53, reported leaving port by German *Gebirgsjäger* ashore and again attacked by KG 30 bombers, but with no effect as dense anti-aircraft fire thwarted accurate bombing. The convoy did, however, suffer at the hands of U-boats of the 11th U-flotilla; *U255* and *U586* sinking three ships.

At that stage of the war the most effective operations against Arctic convoy ships took place as part of the continuous harassment attacks against the ports of the Murmansk coast. Alongside Bf 109 fighter-bombers of JG 5 that mounted sharp 'hit and run' raids against port installations and moored ships, Ju 87 dive-bombers of *Maj.* Horst Kaubisch's I./StG 5 were a frequent presence over the moored ships and harbours. They were the sole *Stukagruppe* based in Norway, though its strength of thirty-two aircraft divided its time between attacks on the Murmansk railway and maritime targets of opportunity. During late January it broadened its targets to the area around Leningrad. During early June 1943 I./StG 5 was redesignated I./StG 1 and transferred to the central Russian front while a new I./StG 5 was formed in Bodø under the command of Knight's Cross holder *Maj.* Martin Möbus.

The Ju 88s of KG 30 also mounted regular attacks against Murmansk, sinking the 7,173GRT SS *Ocean Freedom* at pier number 6 on 13 March, the ship catching fire and illuminating the harbour for other bombers. On 4 April KG 30 hit *Dover Hill* with a 500kg bomb as the ship lay anchored in Misukovo, a few miles north of Murmansk. Two Junkers approached from astern hitting the ship despite anti-aircraft fire. The bomb penetrated the main and tween decks before coming to rest in the ship's coal bunker, failing to explode.

We informed the Senior British Naval Officer Murmansk of the situation and were advised that there were no British Bomb Disposal people in North Russia. We then realised that we would have to dig the bomb out ourselves in order to save our ship. The minesweeper HMS *Jason* was ordered to anchor astern of us and to come alongside to render assistance if the bomb should explode, although I doubt if there would have been much to pick up . . . You must understand that though the *Dover Hill* was only a battered old merchantman she was our home and no German was going to make us leave her while she was still afloat. The Captain lined the whole crew up on the after deck and asked for volunteers, and nineteen of us including our Captain formed our own Bomb Disposal Squad. We had no bomb disposal equipment, in fact we only had a few shovels borrowed from our stokehold and nineteen stout hearts when we started digging back the coal, trying to find the bomb. The bunker was full of good British steaming coal which we were saving for the homeward run so we used a derrick to bring it up on deck, hoping to replace it when we got the bomb out. When the Russian authorities heard what we were doing, although they had many unexploded bombs to deal with in the town, they kindly offered to send one of their Bomb Disposal officers [named Panin] to remove the detonator if we could get the bomb up on deck. When we dug about ten feet down into the coal we found the tail fins and, by their size, decided our bomb must be a 1000 lb one. Unfortunately, the Germans also discovered what we were up to and came back and bombed us again, hoping to set off the bomb we were digging for. Between bomb explosions and the concussion of our own guns the coal used to fall back into where we were digging and things got difficult at times. We had to dig down approximately 22 feet before we got to the bomb, but after two days and two nights hard work we finally got it up on deck.

I was standing beside the bomb with two of my fellow officers as our Russian friend started to unscrew the detonator when after a few turns it stuck. He then took a small hammer and a punch and tapped it to get it moving. I can honestly say that every time he hit it I could feel the hairs on the back of my neck standing against my duffle coat hood. After removing the detonator and primer we dumped the bomb into the Kola Inlet where it probably lies to this day. We then moved back to Murmansk for repairs.[10]

The aircraft of I./KG 30 were also regularly assigned land operations either in support of the static land battle or, more commonly, against the Murmansk railway to frustrate the onwards transport of successfully landed supplies. They remained thus engaged until 19 July 1943 when a fresh crisis in the Mediterranean prompted their hasty transfer south to be reunited with the remainder of the *Kampfgeschwader* already in action there. Apart from a scattering of meteorological and reconnaissance aircraft within the Arctic, that marked the end of a Ju 88 bomber presence in *Luftflotte* 5 until the autumn of 1944.

While the U-boat battle against Convoy RA53 had been taking place, Dönitz had exercised his influence on Hitler as commander of the Kriegsmarine and initiated Operation *Paderborn* that returned the battleship *Scharnhorst* to the Arctic, arriving with a destroyer escort on 9 March in Bogen Bay and anchoring near the 'pocket battleship' *Lützow*. Dönitz had decided to form a powerful surface group comprising *Tirpitz*, *Scharnhorst* and *Lützow* with attached destroyers to defend Norway from potential invasion, while also threatening Russian convoys. The cruiser *Nürnberg* was also present in northern Norway until April 1943 when she returned to Germany, never to leave the Baltic again along with the Kriegsmarine's remaining capital ships.

Despite Hitler's reluctance, Dönitz had even attained a certain measure of autonomy and tactical freedom for the *Scharnhorst*, removing Hitler's severe operational restrictions. British intelligence had noted the ship's arrival and – fearing a more aggressive stance from Dönitz – advised against further Arctic convoys as the lengthy days of summer approached, favouring the Luftwaffe. With Admiralty agreement, JW convoys were suspended during March, Soviet authorities surprisingly

Tirpitz prepares her crane to recover an Arado Ar 196 aircraft. The battleship would remain a threat to Arctic convoys until 1944. (James Payne)

making little protest. Indeed, the strategic situation on the Eastern Front had changed beyond recognition by March 1943, the Sixth Army having surrendered and plentiful supplies flowing into southern Russia via the Persian Gulf. In North Africa the Wehrmacht was in full retreat and Royal Navy forces hitherto engaged in Arctic convoys were redeployed in the Mediterranean and Western Approaches, throwing their weight against the U-boat presence in both theatres.

There remained in Norway the aircraft of the *Küstenflieger* to reconnoitre the Arctic sea and northern stretches of the North Sea as British Atlantic presence increased following the suspension of Russian convoys. The aircraft of *Küstenfliegergruppe* 906 were also frequently used as escort for the coastal transportation of men and material inshore to Norway, the bulk of supply for *Generaloberst* Eduard Dietl's 20.*Gebirgsarmee* in the north transported by sea as Norwegian road and rail infrastructure was both inadequate and vulnerable to sabotage. By the beginning of 1943 *Küstenfliegergruppe* 906 comprised a strength of seven He 115 torpedo aircraft of 1./Kü.Fl.Gr. 906 and nine BV 138Cs of 3./Kü.Fl.Gr. 906. During February, crews of 1./Kü.Fl.Gr. 906 began a slow conversion programme over to operating Heinkel He 111 bombers, subsequently changed to the Junkers Ju 88 and not completed before September 1943 whereupon 1./Kü.Fl.Gr. 906 was officially disbanded; renamed 8./KG 26 and based at Montpellier to face the onslaught of the Allied Mediterranean campaign.

Alongside British air power from carriers or long-range Mosquito and Beaufighter attack, the Soviet air force had significantly reinforced its northern presence. With only a limited supply of additional anti-aircraft guns, those that were provided to Norwegian and Finnish-based Luftwaffe batteries tended to be concentrated around valuable nickel mines around Petsamo, airfields or ports. The German supply convoys that typically trailed close inshore with up to eight or ten ships at a time receiving scant cover other than the *Küstenflieger*. Heavily-armed Soviet IL-2 'Sturmovik' aircraft, torpedo and fighter-bombers began regular interception of the German supply convoys, German ground troops on the Finnmark front frequently able to observe the aircraft taking off and provide early warning. The flying boats and floatplanes of the *Küstenflieger* provided valuable ASW capability but were outmatched by Soviet fighters and *Luftflotte* 5 established new coastal fighter airfields for JG 5 which, on 26 August alone, shot down twenty-five Soviet aircraft near Kirkenes and another ten at Petsamo.

Both the strength and role of the *Küstenflieger* was steadily diminishing and Kriegsmarine control over the last few *Seeflieger* units progressively removed by Luftwaffe reorganisation. The units previously known as *Aufklärungsgruppe* (*See*) were subtly redesignated *Seeaufklärungsgruppe* (SAGr.) and either brought up to strength or formed from scratch by an influx of men and machines from the *Küstenflieger* during July 1943, removing them from any vestiges of naval control. Thousands of miles to the south, as part of this general reorganisation of maritime units, *Aufklärungsgruppe* 125 (*See*) in the Black Sea was disbanded, its constituent units either transferred or renamed, the latter remaining under the command of *Oberst* Hellmut Schalke:

Stab/Aufkl.Gr. 125 (He 114, Ar 196, BV 138) redesignated Stab/SAGr. 125 in Constanţa;

1./Aufkl.Gr. 125 (BV 138) was used to form 2./Kü.Fl.Gr. 706, while a new 1./SAGr. 125 was formed in Sevastopol;

2./Aufkl.Gr. 125 (Ar 196) redesignated 2./SAGr. 125 in Suda Bay, Crete;

3./Aufkl.Gr. 125 (BV 138) redesignated 3./SAGr. 125 in Varna, Bulgaria.

A small *Küstenflieger* infusion of BV 138 aircraft from the disbanded 1./Aufkl.Gr. 125 took allowed the formation of 2./Kü.Fl.Gr. 706 in Tromsø. However, it was short lived as the last vestige of Kriegsmarine control over the unit was removed within a month July after the Luftwaffe redesignated it *Seeaufklärungsgruppe* 130, remaining under the command of *Maj.* Hans-Joachim Tantzen. The final casualty recorded by *Küstenfliegergruppe* 706 was on 2 July when BV 138 aircraft 'BC+TW' of 1./Kü.Fl.Gr. 706 was being prepared for an operational flight at List, and the on-board starter unit exploded, burning out the central engine and control surfaces and virtually destroying the aircraft. The explosion was later attributed to sabotage, a dismal postscript to *Küstenfliegergruppe* 706's existence. The units redesignated during the July reshuffle were:

Stab/SAGr. 130 (Ar 196, BV 222), formed in Tromsø from Stab/Kü.Fl. Gr. 706;

1./SAGr. 130 (Ar 196), formed in Tromsø from 1./Kü.Fl.Gr. 706 and relocated to Stavanger;

2./SAGr. 130 (BV 138), formed in Trondheim from 2./Kü.Fl.Gr. 706 with catapult ship *Bussard* attached;

3./SAGr. 130 (BV 138), formed in Billefjord from 2./Kü.Fl.Gr. 406.

Indeed, *Küstenfliegergruppe* 406 had been so reduced in strength during operations in the North Sea that it too was largely redesignated with the formation of a second Luftwaffe maritime reconnaissance unit, *Seeaufklärungsgruppe* 131 commanded by *Maj.* Wolfgang von Zezschwitz, also on 13 July:

Stab./SAGr. 131 (no aircraft until a single Ar 196 taken on strength in October 1943) formed in Stavanger;
1./SAGr. 131 (BV 138) formed in Tromsø from 3./Kü.Fl.Gr. 406;
2./SAGr. 131 (BV 138 and Ar 196) formed in Tromsø from 3./Kü.Fl. Gr. 906.[11]

Though already officially redesignated, BV 138s listed as still belonging to 2./Kü.Fl.Gr. 406 took to the air on 28 July to search for a strong Allied task force reportedly near the Shetland Islands. The Allied formation was engaged in Operation *Governor* to both divert attention away from landings in Sicily that were well underway and perhaps draw Dönitz's capital ships into action from their Norwegian harbours by persuading the Germans that a major landing was about to be made in Norway. Primarily British, *Governor* comprised five groups in the form of Force A (the battleships HMS *Anson* and USS *Alabama*, the fleet carrier HMS *Illustrious*, and the destroyers HMS *Milne*, *Mahratta*, *Meteor*, *Musketeer* and USS *Emmons*, *Fitch*, *Macomb* and *Rodman*); Force B (the battleships HMS *Duke of York* and USS *South Dakota*, the light carrier HMS *Unicorn*, the light cruiser HMS *Bermuda*, and the destroyers HMS *Onslow*, *Grenville*, *Impulsive*, *Matchless*, *Obdurate*, *Obedient*, *Saumarez*, *Scorpion* and *Ulster*); Force C simulating an invasion convoy (the destroyers HMS *Savage* and *Ripley*, the trawlers HMT *Cedar*, *Hawthorne*, *Larch*, *Lilac*, *Oak*, *Sky*, *Switha* and *Willow*, *LCI[L]-167*, and the motor launches *ML252*, *ML286*, *ML442*, *ML473* and *ML445*); Force D (the light cruiser HMS *Belfast* and the destroyers HMS *Oribi* and *Orwell*); and Force E (the heavy cruisers HMS *Kent*, *London* and *Norfolk*).

Having departed Scapa Flow on 26 July, BV 138s of *Küstenfliegergruppe* 406 found the Allied ships as expected during the early morning two days later and began to shadow.

Our air reconnaissance reported at 0605hrs three cruisers in AF7475 on course 90°. The Group thinks that they may have been misidentified destroyers. At 1102, one light cruiser, fifteen smaller ships, of which six were destroyers and the other corvettes or guard boats, on a south-easterly course in AF7810; at 1105, three light cruisers sailing south-east in AF7550, at 1145 one (apparently) cruiser, two destroyers, on course 110° at high speed in AF7820. The ships were shadowed until 1440. Three aircraft were sighted north of the formation at 1135. At 1503 one cruiser, two destroyers on a northerly course in EF7610. At 1750 one battlecruiser, one aircraft carrier, one heavy cruiser in AF7350 and small vessels in AF7350. No details could be made out because of defending fighters . . .

Marinegruppenkommando Nord believes that the report of 1750 may indicate:

a. A carrier attack on a base which it has not been possible to reach by land-based aircraft, probably Narvik. Less probably Alta.
b. Flank protection for a landing operation or an approaching enemy.
c. A demonstration like the movements on 8 and 9 July . . .

At 2108, Group North placed the battle group on three hours readiness and called attention to the possibility of an attack by carrier-based planes. The Group also requested Luftflotte 5, in spite of its expressed objections;

a. to reconnoitre from Stadtlandet a sector between 290° and 0° for other enemy forces, and
b. to maintain a continuous patrol for a radius of 250 miles around the Narvik and Alta areas as protection against possible carrier operations.[12]

The difficult job of maintaining effective reconnaissance in the face of enemy aircraft was evident from the loss of five of the BV 138s despatched by *Küstenfliegergruppe* 406. Martlet fighters from HMS *Illustrious'* 890 Naval Air Squadron shot down aircraft 'K6+KK' that carried an increased crew of six, all listed as missing in action, while four others were also brought down by four Beaufighters of 404 Squadron RCAF and two shot down near Force D during the early morning. Flying Officer Ernest James Keefe and his navigator Beecham Steed brought down one confirmed Blohm & Voss flying boat and believed that they had merely damaged a second, though defensive fire knocked out the Beaufighter's port engine, the Canadians crash-landing at their base without injury.[13] The damaged BV 138 subsequently went down in the sea while attempting to return to Norway; pilot *Fw.* Klaus Kopatzki

An SC250 fragmentation bomb load being prepared for an Fw 200 Condor of KG 40.

and flight engineer *Ofw.* Werner Heinrich were both killed when the centre engine broke free during the hard landing and collapsed into the cockpit. The remaining three survivors – navigator *Lt.z.S.* Hans Knittel, wireless operator *Uffz.* Heinrich Hengst and gunner *Uffz.* Werner Mohlau – escaped in the aircraft's life raft, their distress signal answered by the Type XIV '*Milch Kuh*' *U489* sailing from Kiel towards the North Atlantic and directed towards the airmen's location by *B.d.U.* The three survivors became additional crew as the U-boat continued on its patrol, frequently being forced to dive as the British launched a concerted offensive against the refuelling U-boats. *U489* was sunk on 4 August by Sunderland depth charges, the RCAF 423 Squadron flying boat itself brought down by flak from the large U-boat and crashing with five of its eleven crew killed. The heavily damaged U-boat sank by the stern, Chief Engineer, *Oblt.* (*Ing.*) Nude dying of wounds received while activating scuttling charges, and the remaining U-boat crew and their three *Küstenflieger* passengers captured by the destroyers HMS *Castletown* and *Orwell*.

Meanwhile Operation *Governor* had been judged a success by the British Admiralty despite being unable to draw the German battle group into action, and the ships withdrew successfully to Scapa Flow. During the day in which the potential threat had been identified, *MGK Nord* had already surmised that it was likely a feint designed to cause unnecessary alarm to the Norwegian coastal commands. With exhaustive air reconnaissance on 29 July finding nothing, their assumption was proved correct. Two Fw 200 aircraft were despatched to search off Trondheim for any signs of enemy activity, deciding not to reconnoitre further to the north as the carrier group was judged unlikely to be there and the loss of the BV 138s had reduced available reconnaissance forces to an inadequate level.

With the end of *Küstenfliegergruppe 706* and the conversion process of 1./Kü.F.Gr. 906 ongoing, the only fully operational units the Kriegsmarine retained control over were the *Bordflieger* and He 115s of 1./Kü.Fl.Gr. 406; the latter continuing to patrol the North Sea and Arctic Ocean throughout the remainder of 1943. *Staffelkapitän Hptm.* Christian Fischer was shot down and killed during a reconnaissance flight ordered by *Fliegerführer* Lofoten on 4 October in response to Operation *Leader*, a successful air attack conducted by aircraft from USS *Ranger* as the United States Navy attacked moored German shipping near Bodø and north and southbound convoys. After sinking six German ships and damaged seven, the American force withdrew with two pairs of Wildcats flying combat air patrol over the fleet. They were guided to intercept shadowing Luftwaffe aircraft by *Ranger*'s fighter director and a Junkers Ju 88 was brought down 35 kilometres from the carrier while a second pair of Wildcats intercepted Fischer's He 115 at a distance of 21 kilometres from USS *Ranger* and shot him down with all three crewmen missing in action. These were the first German aircraft to have been shot down by US Navy fighters.

By July 1943 plans were also under way to attempt a repeat of the *Admiral Scheer*'s Operation *Wunderland*, codenamed Operation *Husar*. Three U-boats were once again to be sent into the Kara Sea, this time in support of the *Lützow*, acting as advance reconnaissance for the cruiser and potentially driving enemy merchant ships to seek the protective coastline where they could then be destroyed by *Lützow*'s guns; the U-boats were initially forbidden to attack and instructed to maintain radio silence until *Lützow* was in position north of Novaya Zemlya. A BV 138 flying boat from 2./SAGr. 130 was dedicated for the operation, with further BV 138s made available for extended reconnaissance dependent on fuelling stations to be established by U-boat. Though controlled by the *Lützow*, the flying boat was to be refuelled by *U255* and *U601*, both equipped with fuelling gear tested previously in exercises with *U601* in Altafjord. The aircraft would penetrate to the Wilkitsky Strait, beyond which the Kara Sea becomes the Laptev Sea, searching for Soviet shipping while also reporting ice conditions.

Aboard *Oblt.z.S.* Erich Harms' *U255* – designated primary refuelling boat – a number of extra personnel were carried: a Luftwaffe officer, in charge of operations pertaining to the aircraft, an auxiliary flight crew which would allow the BV 138 to maintain almost continuous flights with only minimal refuelling stops, a Luftwaffe meteorologist and an extra radio operator (for coordination with *Lützow*). A second boat, *Oblt.z.S.* Peter Ottmar Grau's *U601*, was tasked with a separate minelaying mission before also cleared for refuelling duties in support of the BV 138 and carrying a third aircrew alongside more technical personnel and seven extra sailors. *U255* established its base on the north-east coast of Novaya Zemlya, near Sporyj Navolok on 1 August.

Harms carried enough fuel for the refuelling of two flying boats; a second being held in readiness for when *Lützow* approached the Kara Sea. During Operation *Husar* (also variously named *Südwind* and *Dudelsack*) continuous reconnaissance by BV 138 would be possible along the West Siberian Sea route and the first BV 138 took off from the Lofoten Islands on 3 August, landing successfully next to *U255* at 1615hrs the following day. Harms refuelled the aircraft and subsequently between 5 and 11 August reconnaissance flights were made as far as the Wilkitsky Strait.

However, bad weather overtook *Husar*, *U255* suffering damage when severe winds tore the cover from the deck torpedo container that was being used as temporary fuel storage spoiling the boat's stock of aviation spirit that was used for the initial ignition of the BV 138's diesel engines. To make matters worse on 20 August the BV 138 in the Kara Sea despatched an urgent SOS, having crash landed and taxied toward the lee of the coast near Pankrateva Island. U-boats were rushed to assist in heavy seas, and it was *U601* that chanced upon the aircraft, aircraft commander *Oblt.* Hans-Karl Stieler coming aboard to confer on options with Grau.

U601 attempting to recover a disabled BV 138 during Operation *Husar*.

Short signal 050/789 received from *U601* (Grau): 'Have found seaplane in AT 2521.'

1605hrs. Radio message 0321/705 received from *U601* (Grau): 'BV unserviceable for flying. Crew and instruments saved. Wreck sunk. Naval grid square 2513. Air patrol.'

'1830hrs. In answer to the request for the reason he added in radio message (concerning the BV): 'Engine jammed. Boat leaking.'

A BV 138 *Feldwebel* shares a cigarette with *U601*'s *Oberbootsmann*.

That evening the stand-by BV 138 took off from Lofoten, but *U255* reported weather conditions deteriorating and the flying boat soon returned to base. With that, *Husar* was at an end, enemy convoy traffic being shadowed by a single U-boat until lost in fog. The BV 138 had spotted nothing worthy of *Lützow*'s attention and so the operation was scrubbed, Kara Sea U-boats continuing to hunt individually with minor success and *Lützow* never leaving port.

However, this did not mark the end of U-boat cooperation with SAGr. 130 as at 2010hrs on 12 September Harms' *U255* rescued the crew of BV 138C-1 'BC+TH' of 1./SAGr. 130 in the Barents Sea about 100 miles south of Franz Josef Land. The U-boat had set up its refuelling station – named 'Base One' – on Novaya Zemlya while engaged on Operation *Husar* and fully expected a reserve aircraft to continue operations after Stieler's disaster. However, the new flying boat got lost due to a compass error and was forced to land when fuel was exhausted in the late afternoon of 11 September. The drifting BV 138 was found by *U307* and taken in tow, attempting to reach Fridtjof Nansen Land and refuel. *U307* was relieved by *U255*, which was eventually forced to remove the crew and scuttle the aircraft in worsening weather on 13 September.

The loss of another flying boat convinced *Luftflotte* 5 that BV 138s were unsuited to extended operations given the prevailing polar weather conditions and they therefore declined to provide further aircraft for such operations. In Berlin, the Naval Staff notified the Luftwaffe of the operation's curtailment while lamenting the fact that they believed the decision to remove all aircraft from the action was premature given the few actually lost, the rescue of all crew and saving of valuable equipment before they sank. They strenuously requested that *Luftflotte* 5 not only reconsider cooperation missions between BV 138s and U-boats, but also criticised the cessation of daily air reconnaissance flights over the Denmark Strait, cut due to fuel shortages. In its place, *Luftflotte* 5 proposed aerial reconnaissance of the ports and airfields off Iceland, the Scottish east coast and the Shetlands, while also keeping a watch over German minefields. No *Luftflotte* aircraft were required for Operation *Zitronella* in September (also known as *Sizilien*), the only offensive action undertaken by *Tirpitz* when she sailed with *Scharnhorst*, nine destroyers and an infantry regiment in a raid on Spitsbergen. Arados of both battleships' *Bordflieger* provided reconnaissance in their place. Though the raid was successful, a subsequent retaliatory midget submarine attack on *Tirpitz* after returning to Norway disabled the battleship temporarily.

The sole remaining *Küstenflieger* units, 1./Kü.Fl.Gr. 406, continued to patrol the Arctic area though they and other aircraft failed to locate the Allied task force assigned to Operation *Leader* that approached Bodø on 4 October. Centred on the American carrier USS *Ranger*, temporarily attached to the Home Fleet, a strong battle group sailed in support of *Ranger*'s three squadrons of Grumman F4F Wildcat fighters, Douglas SBD Dauntless dive-bombers and Grumman TBF Avenger torpedo-bombers. The American aircraft successfully attacked both north and southbound convoys as well as shipping in Bodø harbour, sinking six steamers totalling approximately 22,300GRT and damaging another four including tanker *Schleswig* carrying fuel oil and the troop transport *Skramstad* with 834 troops aboard; though only one man was killed, 27 missing and 40 seriously wounded.

Fliegerführer Lofoten immediately ordered two Ju 88s and an He 115 on reconnaissance flights searching for the presumed aircraft carrier, one of the two Junkers, Ju 88D-1 '4N+EH' of 1.(F)/Aufkl.Gr. 22 piloted by *Lt.* Johannes Hoss, sighting the carrier and sending a short-range message that was only picked up at sea and aboard the second Junkers. Hoss was intercepted south-west of Rost Island, 125nm west of Bodø and twenty-two miles from USS *Ranger*, by two covering USN Wildcats – flown by Lt (jg.)s D. Laird and B.N. Mayhew – the Junkers returning fire before disappearing into a cloud bank. When next seen by the Americans, it had just crashed, water still cascading around a ring of fire surrounding the wreckage. No survivors were seen and the signal *Ob.Gefr.* Friedrich Krieger, Hoss' wireless operator, had sent regarding the sighting of USS *Ranger* did not reach naval headquarters until after the second Junkers had landed.

Only fifteen minutes after the battle with Hoss' Junkers, Laird and Mayhew were among four pilots that also attacked the He 115 flown by *Hptm.* Christian Fischer, *Staffelkapitän* of 1./Kü.Fl.Gr. 406 as it approached to within thirteen miles of USS *Ranger* at only 200 feet, dodging in and out of rain squalls. Fischer's observer, *Ofw.* Friedhelm Schulz, was also a *Küstenflieger* pilot, flying as observer on this mission for unknown reasons. The floatplane's port engine was seen by the attacking Americans to begin smoking following the four beam attacks, as Fischer made a 180-degree left turn, bursting into flames just after rear gunner *Fw.* Heinz Geyer opened fire. Moments later the Heinkel crashed into the sea under fresh Wildcat attacks, the aircraft disintegrating on impact. Although three survivors were seen in the water, one of whom

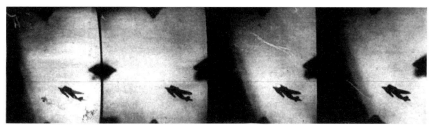

Gun camera footage showing the destruction of the He 115 flown by *Hptm.* Christian Fischer, *Staffelkapitän* of 1./Kü.Fl.Gr. 406, by Wildcat fighters from USS *Ranger*, October 1943.

appeared surrounded by a pool of blood. Lieutenant E.N. Seiler, leader of the Wildcat group circling above the scene, was unable to radio their location due to a defective transmitter and could not make his wingman understand his hand signals to radio the Germans' location. Fischer and his men were never seen again.

On 20 October 1943 *Luftflotte* 5 listed the following maritime aircraft under its command in Norway:

1./SAGr. 130 (BV 138), nine aircraft, four operational;
2./SAGr. 130 (BV 138), nine aircraft, seven operational;
1./SAGr. 131 (BV 138), nine aircraft, all operational;
2./SAGr. 131 (BV 138), five aircraft, four operational (Ar 196) five
    aircraft, all operational;
1./BFl.Gr. 196 (Ar 196), twenty-nine aircraft, twenty-three operational;
1./Kü.Fl.Gr. 406 (He 115), twelve aircraft, nine operational;
Arado *Kette* (Ar 196) two aircraft, both operational.

The Allies resumed their JW convoys in November 1943, JW54A arriving at the Kola Inlet from Loch Ewe on 24 November without having been sighted by Luftwaffe reconnaissance or U-boats; JW54B arriving on 2 December, the polar night negating virtually all useful activity by *Luftflotte* 5. German determination to intercept the expected return Convoy RA55A as well as the incoming JW55B led to establishment of the eight U-boat '*Eisenbart*' patrol line, and commitment of *Scharnhorst* and five destroyers into action. On 22 December, a Do 217 meteorological aircraft sighted eastbound JW55B; reporting '40 transports and escorts vessels'. Aircraft of *Fliegerführer Lofoten* then detected the convoy in the

Heinkel He 115C-1 'K6+GH' of *Küstenfliegergruppe* 406 over the Norwegian coastline.

early afternoon of Christmas Day when a single BV 138 reported RA55A – though its composition could not be ascertained – with no covering force sighted within eighty kilometres. At 0945hrs on 26 December *U277* and aircraft made contact, two Ju 88s and three BV 138s having taken off on diverging search patrols. However, the Luftwaffe message was vague, course and composition of the enemy forces not included. In worsening weather and the darkness of the long polar night, aircraft were unable to assist with further reconnaissance or torpedo missions as *Scharnhorst* raced into action. In the darkness, the resulting Battle of North Cape ended with the separation of *Scharnhorst* from her destroyer screen and her destruction by superior British radar directed gunfire, leaving only thirty-six survivors. Among the dead were all six aircrew and eight ground staff responsible for the operation of the ship's three Arado Ar 196 float planes.

The Black Sea

Since early 1942 I./KG 100 had been stationed on the Eastern Front, primarily bombing ground targets in support of the army's advance, but also occasionally directed to reconnoitre the Black Sea and attack shipping on the Volga River and as far east as the Caspian Sea. After the debacle of the Stalingrad air bridge and subsequent heavy losses, the *Gruppe* had withdrawn to France to train with the new Lofte 7D bombsight and planning to re-equip with Dornier Do 217K bombers. However, the latter decision was reversed and instead I./KG 100 received upgraded He 111H-11 and H-16s, training until strong Mistral winds interfered and *Maj*. Paul Claas and his *Gruppe* returned east in April 1943, moving via Munich, Lviv and Zaporozhye to Stalino at the southern section of the Eastern Front under the control of IV.*Fliegerkorps*, *Luftflotte* 4.

Their first mission was flown on the night of 29 April, mining the Volga River with BM 1000 *Luftminen*; an operation repeated over the nights that followed, *Oblt*. Hans Meuer's aircraft hit and disabled by flak on 7 May during its return flight from the Volga. The pilot, *Uffz*. Gerhard Ponto, made a successful emergency landing, although deep behind enemy lines. After days of marching west, the entire crew of four were captured by Red Army troops. Theirs was part of a steady trickle of losses suffered as Claas' *Gruppe* maintained its mining missions throughout May, combined with occasional anti-shipping strikes against targets on the Volga.

Before long I./KG 100 was again primarily targeting ground units and tank manufacturing plants until 18 June when elements of the *Gruppe* were directed to attack shipping in the Caspian Sea, led by Claas in aircraft '6N+MH'. One aircraft, that led by observer *Obltn*. Klein, claimed a freighter of between 3,000 and 4,000GRT damaged, though return fire wounded wireless operator *Uffz*. Otto Kus and gunner *Ob.Gefr*. Walter Robing. Identical anti-shipping missions were repeated over the following two nights, with a further 8,000GRT freighter claimed damaged. However, on the night of 19 June, Claas' bomber was shot down, pilot *Fw*. Franz Dittrich successfully making an emergency landing on the water and all four crewmen – including wireless operator *Fw*. Klaus Fritsche and gunner *Ob.Gefr*. Hubert Both – escaping before the aircraft sank. Discovered soon thereafter by a Soviet ship, Claas refused to surrender some of his personal possessions to his captors and was shot while still sitting in the life raft.[14]

Major Hansgeorg Bätcher – the Knight's Cross-holding *Staffelkapitän* of 1./KG 100 and first bomber pilot to reach 400 combat missions (in October 1942) – was promoted to *Gruppenkommandeur* as I./KG 100 prepared to fly in support of the German offensive at Kursk, engaged in the bombing of ground targets from that point onwards.

In Sevastopol, the BV 138-equipped 1./SAGr. 125 had been created as part of the Luftwaffe drive to remove any direct Kriegsmarine control over remaining *Seeflieger* units, those previously known as *Aufklärungsgruppe* (*See*) now deftly redesignated *Seeaufklärungsgruppe*. *Oberst* Hellmut Schalke's Stab/SAGr. 125 had also been created from its forerunning Aufkl.Gr (*See*) in Constanţa, remaining equipped with Ar 196 and BV 138 aircraft. While the Ar 196s of 2.*Staffel* stayed in Suda Bay, Crete, until December 1943 before moving to Sevastopol, the BV 138s of 3.*Staffel* were based in Varna, Bulgaria, using Sevastopol as an operational forward staging area.

Maritime aircraft operating within the Black Sea until September 1943 were predominantly involved in reconnaissance or air sea rescue activity, with no offensive operations recorded. Regular ASW flights were made, particularly in waters near the primary German and Romanian ports. *Major* Hannibal Gude departed for Norway and command of 10.*Seenotstaffel*. In his place came *Hptm.* Hermann Hülsmann, formerly *Staka* of 2.*See Transportstaffel*. During this period onboard medical orderlies of the rescue aircraft received additional training as air gunners, enabling them to play a dual role during flights that were becoming increasingly dangerous as the Red Air Force gradually grew in strength and confidence. By September 1943 the Eastern Front was rapidly failing. During July and August the ambitious German offensive against the Kursk salient had been fought to a standstill and then forced backwards by a Soviet summer counter-offensive and by 7 September the Wehrmacht's battered Seventeenth Army finally began evacuating the Taman Peninsula. Anapa was abandoned on 21 September, constricting the German defensive pocket, and six days later Temryuk fell to the Soviets. By 9 October the German Kuban bridgehead had been destroyed, Wehrmacht forces pushed back in southern Ukraine and land access to the Crimea severed by November 1943. The Dornier flying boats of 8.*Seenotstaffel* withdrew from the Ortasli-See, operating from a lake near Odessa until January temperatures iced it over and they relocated to Varna. The air-sea rescue service would be hard-pressed during the impending evacuation of the Crimea, fulfilling their original purpose while simultaneously assisting in the removal of besieged troops.

4

Losing Control

The Struggle for Biscay

D URING LATE 1942 *FLIEGERFÜHRER Atlantik* was used not only for escorting U-boats from their Biscay bases, but also a second wave of blockade-runners sailing between the Far East and the Gironde. On 2 November the first of them reached Bordeaux from Japan; the 7,840GRT *Tannenfels* docked after a difficult voyage from Yokohama that had lasted for eighty-six days. The need for the transport missions had become acute as Germany's available stocks of such raw materials as tin, quinine, opium and natural rubber diminished. Since the end of the First World War, Germany had forged ahead in the creation of synthetic rubber, known as Buna, but despite these advances, synthetic compounds were unable to completely replace the natural product and a significant quantity of raw rubber was still required in Germany. An increasingly tight Royal Navy blockade combined with political pressure soon cut off supplies from South America. Instead, Hitler looked to the East for his source of rubber, metals, ore and edible oils. Before June 1941 the Trans-Siberian railway had been available for the shipment of some supplies from Japan, but this route was closed by Hitler's attack on Russia. By then, twenty-four large German merchant ships lay in several scattered Far Eastern harbours, caught by the outbreak of war and unable, or unwilling, to put to sea. Twelve of them were diesel powered and highly suitable for requisition by the Kriegsmarine for blockade-running supply missions to Europe. Augmented by four motor ships chartered from the Japanese government and two prize vessels captured by raiders, seventeen ships were available by April 1941. Italian naval command added four of their own freighters in the East and between April 1941 and February 1942 the first fifteen ships – including three Italians – initiated the first 'season' of blockade-running. Timed to pass areas of greatest risk during the winter months, all ships were routed across the Pacific and around Cape Horn. Despite the loss of three vessels at sea and the recall to Japan of a fourth, eleven freighters carrying 74,960 tons of goods (including 32,000 tons of rubber) out of a total of 104,233 tons loaded in Japan reached occupied Bordeaux which the Germans had designated to be the European terminus. In turn, five ships carrying 32,540 tons of mainly technological cargo reached Japan from Europe, fulfilling the Japanese demand for 'quid-pro-quo' from the Germans. Alongside material bound for the Japanese, these five ships also carried equipment and supplies for German assets in the East.

The success of this first season prompted an escalation of the entire project. With Japanese entry into the war in December 1941 and their swift subjugation of Malaysia and Indonesia, German ships benefitted from the shorter passage through the Sunda Strait, refuelling in Batavia and proceeding via the Cape of Good Hope to Europe. However, the second wave of blockade-runners was affected by a combination of heightened Allied strength in the Atlantic as well as penetration of German naval codes. Once again, the final approach to France and the relatively confined space of the Bay of Biscay proved especially perilous. By 16 December 1942 things had deteriorated to the point that *MGK West* postponed further departures until greater protection could be provided by sea and air through Biscay. Ultimately the originally planned schedule was reduced by half and only eight of thirteen blockade-runners despatched between September 1942 and April 1943 from France reached Japan. Worse for Germany, of sixteen ships that departed Japan carrying vital raw materials, only four reached France intact, including *Tannenfels*.[1] The import of edible oils by tanker from Japan had also proved a dismal failure, only two out of nine fleet supply tankers reaching Europe. This crippling blow to the blockade-runner project led to a delay in fresh attempts until October 1943.

In a conference on 13 February with the Kriegsmarine's new commander, *Grossadmiral* Dönitz, Hitler emphasised the vital importance of maintaining the importation of raw rubber. He ordered *Fliegerführer Atlantik* to assign Fw 200 aircraft for reconnaissance duties on behalf of the incoming ships, instructing the Luftwaffe in the West that support of the blockade breaker service become the focal point (*Schwerpunkt*) of operations. In turn, Dönitz suggested that such trade missions could potentially be carried out by U-boat, a concept that dated from the First World War and the U-cruisers *Deutschland* and *Bremen*. A week previous to Dönitz's proposal, Kriegsmarine command had discussed the possibility of converting a number of Type VIIC U-boats into transport submarines, although the idea was soon dismissed on the

Tannenfels; part of the German '*Etappendienst*' service of blockade-runners from Japan.

grounds that although the potential cargo space reached a maximum of 250 tons, combat boats could not be spared for adaptation to unarmed vessels. From this was spawned the '*Monsun*' missions that saw U-boats traversing the Indian Ocean to operate from Penang, Malaya and Singapore, most acting as combined attack and transport missions.

The resultant creation of a U-boat presence in Penang led to the formation during October 1943 of *Fliegerkommando beim Marinesonder-dienst Ostasien*, a tiny unit of two Arado Ar 196 aircraft based in the former Imperial Airways station. One of two observers that had been aboard the raider *Schiff 28 'Michel'*, Oblt.z.S. Ulrich Horn, became the commander of the small outpost, he and his men being accommodated in the Elysee Hotel at the junction of Farquhar and Leith St in downtown Penang. The other observer aboard *Michel* had been Kaptlt. Konrad Hoppe who had transferred to the Marine Attaché office in Tokyo during April and later return to Penang as the first commander of its U-boat base, before taking the post of IWO aboard *U168* for the first six months of 1944. He would end the war as commander of the U-boat station at Surabaya.

Horn and his pilot, *Uffz.* Rehnen, operated the two Arado Ar 196A-3s that had been part of the complement of aircraft carried by the raider before USS *Tarpon* torpedoed and sank her on 20 October 1943 as

Michel was returning to Yokohama. From Penang, Horn and Rehnen flew regular reconnaissance and ASW missions over the port approaches for the benefit of transiting U-boats and submarines of the Imperial Japanese Navy. Where Arados carried by raiders had been unmarked and painted light blue overall, from Penang they flew in standard Japanese camouflage colours, carrying the Japanese rising sun national marking in order to eliminate the possibility of mistaken identity by Japanese pilots or anti-aircraft gunners.

Horn also took part in the rescue of men from *UIT23* sunk by the British submarine HMS *Tallyho* on 2 February 1944. Fourteen men, including the captain *Oblt.z.S.* Werner Striegler were found clustered together in oily water as the Arado circled low overhead, landing nearby when Horn and Rehnen determined to shuttle the men back to safety. Five men at a time lashed themselves securely to the aircraft's floats and all fourteen were returned to Penang.

The Arados suffered occasional problems with ammunition and spare parts supply, either cannibalising and adapted from local sources or using parts included in U-boat cargoes from France. For replacement or maintenance of floats, Horn and Rehnen flew to the Japanese seaplane base in Singapore. There Japanese pilot Hiroshi Yasunaga, who operated a three-seater E13A Aichi reconnaissance floatplane, remembered an encounter with the Germans.

> It touched down gently on the sea about 200 metres off the command post. It was a beautiful touchdown . . . a surprise for me who firmly believed that we Japanese are much superior than the white people at such delicate operations as bringing a float plane down . . . The two German Navy officers appeared at the command post. The pilot was a tough looking man, at least ten years older than I was. He put out his big clumsy looking hand to our commander, and I wondered how that hand could make such a delicate and gentle landing manoeuvre. They said they were here to change the floats, so moved the German plane to the hanger and our maintenance crew brought out the pair of floats, struts, and the wires. The floats were smaller than those of our Type O, and I felt a bit superior since they looked stubbier and less refined than the floats on my mount. However, the feeling didn't last long as the big handed pilot started giving instructions to our ground crew who held up the floats.
>
> 'Choi ue, mou choi ue (up, a bit more up)' the pilot instructed in Japanese. But that was as far as his Japanese went. The instructions to

left and right were given in German and gestures. When the fittings on the end of the struts and the fittings on the bottom of the fuselage were matched, our crew swiftly inserted the bolts . . . and in no time, the pair of brand new floats were mounted on the airframe.

The maintenance crew at Singapore were used to this and performed all this matter-of-factly, but the fleet crew, pilots, and officers were all very much surprised. The time it took to change the floats was about a tenth of the time it would take to do the same for our Type O. And the German officer did this by commanding a band of our crew mostly by gestures only!

Curiosity took the better of me. I stepped forward to the workbench between the two floats, took the spanner from the maintenance man's hand, and touched the brand new bolt that he was tightening. My guess was, there was considerable 'play' between the bolt and the bolt hole for it to go in that smoothly. However, the bolt was securely inserted without any play. There was not even a tenth of a millimetre nor even a hundredth of a millimetre of space between the hole and the bolt. It was amazingly precise. Utterly unthinkable from experience. And the material of the bolt was high-grade steel with a beautiful gleam. I was no expert on steel, but the difference of material was obvious.

When we changed floats, it was a much more of a major operation . . . The holes on the three fittings do not match, so the bolts do not go in. The fittings are filed, and the bolts are sometimes hammered in. The banging of the hammer kills my nerves. If all that hammering creates unseen cracks on the fittings, maybe the floats will collapse when landing on rough sea. The filing was also depressing to the pilot as each second of filing lowered the strength of the fittings and consequently, the safety margin on emergencies. Sometimes the bolts go through really smooth, but then I have to worry that the bolt is loose.

The sad fact was there was a world of difference in the precision of our products, as well as in the quality of material.[2]

Hitler's insistence on *Fliegerführer Atlantik* giving priority to protecting blockade-runners was challenged by Dönitz. During a second February conference, this time at the Ukrainian *Werwolf Führerbunker* in Vinnitsa, he forcefully argued once again for the allocation of aircraft for U-boat reconnaissance work. During the previous fourteen days, no enemy shipping had been sighted which the naval commander in chief attributed to poor visibility, possible Allied location tracking of U-boats at sea, but, above all, a complete absence of airborne reconnaissance.

Kessler's aircraft strength by mid-January 1943 was lamentable for a *Fliegerführer* command responsible for all Atlantic operations, reporting the following available aircraft to *OKW*:

Reconnaissance:
III./KG 40 (Fw 200), ten aircraft (five serviceable);
3.(F)/ Aufkl.Gr. 123 (Ju 88), eleven aircraft (eight serviceable);
Heavy fighters:
V./KG 40 (Ju 88C), thirty-five aircraft (nineteen serviceable);
ASW/coastal reconnaissance:
5./BFl.Gr. 196 (Ar 196), twenty aircraft (nineteen serviceable).

Kessler had lost the Condors of I./KG 40 at the beginning of 1943 as *Maj.* Karl Henkelmann's *Gruppe* began a confusing series of transfers and conversions. During early January 1. and 3./KG 40 had moved to Stalino as KGr.z.b.V. 200 to participate in the Stalingrad air bridge, while new 1. and 3./KG 40 began forming in Fassberg with He 177 bombers. Survivors of both original *Staffeln* were later reunited as a new 8./KG 40. In the meantime, 2./KG 40 remained in Trondheim-Vaernes with its Fw 200Cs until moved to Germany and disbanded during November 1943, replaced by a new 2./KG 40, formed from the original 8./KG 40 which converted to the He 177 bomber.

Painfully aware of Kessler's aircraft starvation, Dönitz repeated direct requests to the Luftwaffe and *Führer* for aircraft to be allocated for U-boat reconnaissance, armed with the knowledge that the previous day, 25 February, *SKL* Chief of Staff, *Admiral* Wilhelm Meisel, had already conducted talks with Göring in which the *Reichsmarschall* offered a weak pledge of support.

The *Reichsmarschall* declared that, in his opinion, U-boat warfare was the only possible means of successfully attacking England and America. He promised to give all possible backing to the U-boat campaign by provision of long-range reconnaissance aircraft. However, he warned against over-optimism regarding the aircraft's readiness for action. Developments took a long time and the industries usually did not keep their promises. However, he hoped that the He 177 type might be suitable as a reconnaissance plane by the fall of this year. He did not believe that the Me 264 would ever be ready for action. These planes had their gasoline supply in the wings and could not be flown against current defences. He agreed that the three BV 222 planes, at present employed on supply service in the east, should be used instead for U-boat reconnaissance. He could not issue orders to this effect, however, because the *Führer* had assigned these aircraft to carry supplies. The request of Commander-in-Chief, Navy that long-range reconnaissance be flown twice a day, each time with six planes, was not considered exaggerated by the *Reichsmarschall*, who believed that it could be done by one wing.[3]

Though obviously swayed to agree with his naval commander, Hitler nonetheless remained sharply critical of previous promises regarding projected capabilities of new maritime reconnaissance aircraft, particularly the He 177. Neither he, nor Dönitz, believed much good would come of redesigning the He 177 as a genuinely four-engined machine and Dönitz persuaded Hitler to intervene directly and at least order three of the large BV 222 flying boats be made immediately available for U-boat reconnaissance in the west.

The large flying boats had already proved their worth as transport aircraft and their long-distance capability was beyond doubt. However, they were a poor third choice behind two other aircraft which would have proved preferable to the Kriegsmarine; the Messerschmitt Me 264 and its back-up design, Focke-Wulf's Ta 400. The four-engine Me 264 had been born due to Willi Messerschmitt's desire to produce a sophisticated, long-range transport aircraft capable of shipping fresh luxury produce from tropical regions to Germany. Its potential as an intercontinental bomber were immediately obvious to the *RLM* and development as such began in 1940, nicknamed the 'Amerika bomber' due to its maximum projected range of 15,000 kilometres. The first prototype was flown in December 1942, showing great promise but obviously not likely to be operational before 1944 at the absolute earliest. The Ta 400, a six-engine machine running as a potential secondary candidate for the same role, never graduated beyond a wind-tunnel airframe, and would not have been anywhere near production-ready before 1946. Furthermore, Heinkel submitted the He 277 to the 'Amerika bomber' competition; a reworked He 177 with four separate engines, of which not a single entire prototype was built. Instead, for long-range missions into the Atlantic Dönitz would be forced to rely on the provision of Fw 200 aircraft – which had already shown their structural weaknesses and which suffered several combat losses and accidents during the first three months of 1943 – the ill-fated He 177, the Ju 290, available in only small numbers, and the BV 222 which also numbered only a handful of machines.

A BV 222 loading troops. This large-capacity flying boat began Biscay operations from Lac de Biscarrosse during early 1943.

In response to Dönitz's plea, the BV 222s of *Lufttransportstaffel* 222 (*See*) began returning to Travemünde where they were equipped with FuG 200 '*Hohentwiel*' radar. The *Staffel* was renamed *Aufklärungsfliegerstaffel* 222 (*See*), under the command of *Oblt.* Fritz Führer, a former BV 222 pilot and *Staka* of *Luftransportstaffel* 222 (*See*) since May 1942. The *Staffel* was subordinated to *Fliegerführer Atlantik*, flying to France and located at Lac de Biscarrosse, a lake-based seaplane station south-west of Bordeaux, separated from the sea by a five-kilometre strip of land. The station had initially been constructed by the French airline Aéropostale and its successor Air France as a transatlantic air base, the arrival of the new reconnaissance *Staffel* its first use by the Luftwaffe. A single large slipway and multiple hangars were already constructed, the Luftwaffe installing five light flak positions, augmented by coastal batteries of the Atlantic Wall. During May six BV 138C-1s (including aircraft 'NA+PS' from 3./Kü.Fl.Gr. 406) were also attached to *Aufklärungsfliegerstaffel* 222 (*See*). Dönitz cherished the notion of using the large six-engine BV 222 flying boats for 24-hour deep-penetration Atlantic missions, refuelling from U-boat tankers near the Azores. Trials were conducted in the Baltic for such purposes but, though feasible, the plan never reached fruition for the strengthening of the reconnaissance *Staffel* was too little too late, as May 1943 unexpectedly marked the nadir of Dönitz's Atlantic U-boat war.

For the heavy fighters of V./KG 40, 1943 had begun badly. Following a period of bad weather that limited flying, the first reported combat was on 3 January when two crew members were hit by defensive machine-gun fire from a B-17 Flying Fortress of the USAAF Eighth Air Force engaged on a daylight bombing raid against Saint-Nazaire. Not until 29 January was a second combat recorded, *Ofw*. Johannes Kriedel's '4D+GB' and *Uffz*. Paul Paschoff's 'F8+HZ' (15./KG 40) being shot down by four Beaufighters of 248 Squadron Coastal Command for the loss of both crews. The following day three of the same squadron's Beaufighters intercepted four Ju 88s from 14./KG 40, being led by *Staffelkapitän Hptm*. Hans-William Reicke. The Beaufighters attacked from astern, *Ofw*. Georg Heuer being shot down and killed, while Reicke's 'F8+HY' collided with one of the British aircraft, both crashing into the sea with no survivors. A single Beaufighter was shot down by *Uffz*. Jürgen Heicke before the engagement was broken off. The loss of Reicke, a popular officer and a highly experienced maritime pilot having been part of *Küstenfliegergruppe* 606 before piloting an Fw 200 of I./KG 40, was acutely felt within the *Gruppe*. His place as *Staffelkapitän* was taken by 22-year-old *Oblt*. Kurt Necesany who had enlisted in the Luftwaffe in October 1939.[4]

A third disastrous battle against 248 Squadron took place on 9 February between four Ju 88Cs of 15./KG 40 and four opposing fighters. Although two Beaufighters were claimed shot down by *Lt*. Dieter Meister, no British aircraft were posted as missing from the sortie, while both *Oblt*. Franz Isslinger's 'F8+BZ' and *Ofw*. Heinrich Dettmar's 'F8+FZ' were shot down with both crews lost.

The purpose of the *Zerstörer* over Biscay had been to tackle large anti-submarine bombers and the depredations of the heavily armed and manoeuvrable Beaufighters were unsustainable. Pilots of V./KG 40 were instructed to avoid combat with Beaufighters unless, at the very least, present in equal numbers, preferably with a two-to-one advantage. If engaged, the German pilots were taught to attack from astern, although the higher speed and agility of the Beaufighter made this unlikely in all but situations in which total surprise was achieved. Though Mosquitoes

The de Havilland Mosquito, introduced by the RAF to the battle over Biscay in 1943 where it proved highly effective.

had not yet been encountered on their 'Instep' patrols, the Junkers pilots were strictly advised to avoid combat with them altogether. As a twin-engined fighter the de Havilland Mosquito was superior in every respect to the versatile yet outdated Ju 88. It possessed a top speed of 391km/h and its primarily wooden construction offered extremely high manoeuvrability and the capacity to absorb enormous punishment in combat as well as dish it out with four 20mm Hispano cannon in the fuselage belly and four .303 Browning nose-mounted machine guns.

In a meeting between Dönitz and Kessler on 2 March, Kessler stated in no uncertain terms that the situation regarding the Junkers Ju 88C-6 heavy fighters over Biscay had noticeably deteriorated against superior enemy aircraft and that V./KG 40 was no longer able to provide effective protection for incoming and outgoing U-boats. For Dönitz this news could not have come at a worse time as he and his staff had begun to think that the FuMB 1 Metox 600A radar detector installed upon U-boats since the previous August was no longer capable of detecting enemy radar, later believing that its own radiations were being used to by enemy aircraft to locate U-boats by night. The use of the Leigh Light in conjunction with ASV II sea-search radar had robbed U-boats of the cloak of darkness, Metox was initially believed the answer to this threat, although inexplicable attacks on U-boats during December 1942 appeared to point at its fallibility. Furthermore, a captured British bomber pilot planted the misinformation that Metox gave off its own faint trace signal which could be tracked by Allied aircraft. Once German technicians confirmed that this was indeed a possibility, Metox was incorrectly viewed as the potential source of the Allies' success against U-boats travelling surfaced at night. Unbeknownst to the Kriegsmarine, the U-boats' four-rotor Enigma code had been broken that December after an intelligence blackout that had nearly lasted a full year.

Meanwhile Allied technological developments continued apace and on 1 March 1943 the centimetric ASV Mk III radar was first employed in a test installation aboard two RAF bombers. Metox was unable to detect centimetric wavelengths, rendering U-boats vulnerable yet again as the Mk III radar sets were in regular use over Biscay within weeks, U-boat losses rising alarmingly.

Nevertheless, *Fliegerführer Atlantik* achieved some measure of success during March in both reconnaissance and combat. Between 9 and 31 March, KG 40 Fw 200s flew 146 daylight missions on behalf of *MGK West* in support of blockade-running missions, mainly off the west coast of Portugal and outer Bay of Biscay. In general, the westerly limit of these reconnaissance flight was 19°W, sometimes extended to 25°W, stopping at the 45°N latitude except on *grosse Aufklärung* when it was extended to 50°N. During those accumulated flights, twenty large enemy convoys were sighted as well as myriad smaller groups or unaccompanied vessels. For the *Zerstörer* of V./KG 40, four bombers were shot down: a 10 OUT Whitley, an RAF 59 Squadron Flying Fortress, a 511 Squadron (Ferry Command) Liberator and a 58 Squadron Halifax. However, in return RAF 264 Squadron Mosquitos finally announced their presence by shooting down two Junkers of 14./KG 40 on 22 March, while another pair crashed accidentally during the following two days and *Gefr.* Florian Stabenheiner's 'F8+HY' force landed at La Alberica airfield near Santander and was briefly interned. The most painful casualty to the *Gruppe* was *Hptm.* Georg Esch, *Staffelkapitän* of 13./KG 40, who crashed into the sea near the Spanish coast while engaged in a search for *U665*, missing since 22 March and ultimately never found. The aircraft 'F8+LB' went into the sea twenty-five miles from La Coruna for unknown reasons while engaged in what was recorded as 'combat practice'. Though the crew were seen to escape the aircraft and successfully take to their life raft, attempts to recover them failed. *Leutnant* Dieter Meister went as far as flying to the

Spanish mainland where one of his crew bailed out with the attention of guiding Spanish authorities to the site of the crash, but the bold attempt failed. The bodies of Esch, *Uffz.* Karl Friederich Winkelmann (observer), and *Ofw.* Fritz Mayerhofer (wireless operator) later washed ashore and were buried at Cocus de Yuste. Esch was another highly experienced officer lost to V./KG 40, his place as *Staffelkapitän* taken by *Oblt.* Hermann Horstmann. Command of the *Gruppe* was then passed to *Hptm.* Alfred Hemm, previously *Staffelkapitän* of 4.(F)/Aufkl.Gr. 122, promoted to *Major* when his new appointment was made permanent.

On 10 March *Konteradmiral* Wilhelm Mössel, *Marine-Verbindungs-offizier beim RLM/Oberbefehlshaber der Luftwaffe* (Naval Liaison Officer to the Commander-in-Chief Luftwaffe), wrote:

> The protection of U-boats by the Ju 88 *Zerstörer* has become quite illusory. The U-boats are caught at night and, recently, by use of the enemy's ship search device which works on a wavelength that we do not know yet. Furthermore, during the day, the aircraft appearing over Biscay have outgrown the Ju 88 *Zerstörer*, so that the initial combat successes have diminished considerably. A quick remedy is not possible here. Only when the He 177 comes into service, perhaps it can be used as a long-distance *Zerstörer*. Until then, the U-boats cannot be assisted during the day while protection against the night attacks has not yet been found.[5]

As an interim solution, *Fliegerführer Atlantik* requested Fw 190s equipped with drop tanks make combat patrols towards the Cornish coast to combat the escalating 'Instep' campaign. To that end, rather than reliance on JG 2, a pair of Fw 190A-5s were attached directly from the factory to 5./BFl.Gr. 196 alongside its Arado 196 coastal reconnaissance aircraft. By April six Focke-Wulf fighters were on strength, each equipped with a pair of 300-litre drop tanks under each wing enabled them to reach Cornwall. Kessler's plans for combatting 'Instep' missions were articulated on 9 April 1943:

1. Missions by Fw 190 with drop-tanks and Me 210 against the in- and-outbound aircraft from south-west Cornwall.
2. Day and night attacks to be mounted on airfields in south-east England by fighter-bombers and bombers.
3. Bombing missions against shipping around England thereby tying up long-range fighters.

The Messerschmitt Me 410, seen here in its reconnaissance variant. This aircraft belonged to 2.(F)/Aufkl.Gr. 122 and was captured intact in Sicily and shipped to the United States in 1944.

Meanwhile, Dönitz continued to lobby for the most suitable aircraft to be provided to *Fliegerführer Atlantik* with which to combat heavy RAF fighters. Both Ju 88C-6 and the Bf 110 *Zerstörer* aircraft were becoming more commonly attached to night fighter units to counter powerful bomber streams battering the Reich. Production of the outdated Bf 110 had all but ceased in late 1941 and with it the existence of most *Zerstörergruppen*. However, its planned successor – the Me 210 – had been a complete design failure with poor in-flight handling and severe undercarriage problems. Bf 110 production resumed in February 1942, alongside a redesigned successor to the Me 210, the Me 410 '*Hornisse*'. Possessing an improved wing form, longer fuselage and more powerful engines, the Me 410 began to enter service during January 1943. Though intended to counter the Beaufighter or Mosquito, it proved inferior to both and the majority were used either against bombers or as fast fighter-bombers for harassing raids against the United Kingdom. Several experimental models were also developed, the Me 410B-5 having a PVC rack slung under the fuselage to accommodate an F5 *Lufttorpedo*, with the MG 131 nose armament removed to make room for '*Hohentwiel*' radar equipment and the bomb bay used for an additional 650-litre fuel tank. The Me 410B-6 was a similar anti-shipping conversion but bereft of torpedoes and intended to for coastal strike missions. Viewed by both Kessler and Dönitz as a great hope to establish equilibrium in the battle against the 'Instep' aircraft, the first such aircraft of III./ZG1 arriving during July at Brest-Lanvéoc airfield, across the bay from the port city itself and previously home to *Kampfgruppe* 606, among other units. Under the command of *Hptm*. Hans-Georg Drescher, previously *Kommandeur Jabo Gruppe Afrika*, the *Gruppe* had initially been equipped with the near-useless Me 210 while in Bir el Abd, Egypt, the site of a desert airstrip abandoned by the retreating RAF in July 1942. The Me 410 had first flown operationally on 18 June, when aircraft of V./KG 2 mounted a bombing raid on Portsmouth and on 28 July, six Me 410s made their baptismal appearance over Biscay, though encountering no enemy aircraft. The presence of the Me 410s in Brittany was to be brief, however, moved to Vörden in Lower Saxony during September and the unit subsequently renamed II./ZG 26 on 11 October, dedicated to anti-bomber missions in defence of the Reich. Somewhat ironically, their place in Brittany would be briefly taken by Bf 110G-2s of II./ZG 1 transferring from Italy until November when they too relocated to Austria.

Meanwhile Coastal Command's No 19 Group, which the Junkers had been introduced to combat, began the eight-day Operation *Enclose* on 20 March in which 115 aircraft – many equipped with centimetric radar and Leigh Lights – flew anti-U-boat patrols in a box area of Biscay between 7° and 10° west. Of the forty-one U-boats that crossed the patrol box, twenty-six were sighted, fifteen attacked and *U665* sunk with *U332* damaged. Operation *Enclose II* followed in April with *U376* sunk and *U465* damaged, in turn followed by Operation *Derange* with a wider search area in which *U332* was sunk and *U566* and *U437* badly damaged.

Darkness no longer sheltered the U-boats and, mistakenly blaming Metox, with effect from 1 May Dönitz ordered cessation of night transit through eastern Biscay, but rather travelling in daylight with anti-aircraft guns manned. This played directly into the hands of Coastal Command. Dönitz's order remained in effect for ninety-seven days during which twenty-six U-boats were lost to combined air and naval attack, and seventeen damaged. U-boats were unable to dive once engaged by enemy aircraft – defenceless and vulnerable during the time it took for gun crews to abandon their weapons and the boat to submerge – and Royal Navy ships were vectored to the surfaced U-boat as the RAF circled above. Though U-boats shot down at least twenty-eight aircraft and damaged many others, it was an attritional war that Coastal Command could not lose.

Allied air power had become
one of the dominant factors
in defeating Dönitz's
U-boats within the Atlantic.
Crews crossed Biscay on
high alert with steel helmets
to protect against potential
gunfire or splinter injury.

The U-boat war had finally reached its crescendo in the first half of
1943. During March four major convoy battles, including the largest
single engagement of the war between nearly 100 merchant ships and their
escorts and thirty-eight U-boats around Convoys HSX229 and SC122,
were fought in the North Atlantic. The Allies considered it a crisis point,
losing 120 merchant ships during the month in all European theatres of
action while only twelve U-boats were sunk. Though April saw a decline
in merchant losses, due to many U-boats withdrawing from the Atlantic to
replenish, sixty-four ships were still sunk including four tankers from the
South Atlantic Convoy TS37, in return for fifteen U-boats.

However, by May, Allied strategic and tactical improvements rapidly
took hold. The battle for Convoy ONS5 resulted in thirteen ships sunk
for seven U-boats, an unsustainable exchange rate for Dönitz's forces.
Worse followed through May and although combat U-boats were at
their peak operational strength, casualties for the month amounted to
thirty-four U-boats destroyed in the Atlantic – one for every merchant
ship sunk that month within the same area – and nine elsewhere. With
such crippling losses, Dönitz withdrew his U-boats to the waters near
Gibraltar, never regaining the initiative in the Atlantic.

On 5 June Dönitz met with Hitler at the Berghof to explain his
decision and outline requirements for a successful resumption of his
U-boat campaign. These included efficient ship-location radar, enemy
radar countermeasures, acoustic torpedoes and powerful U-boat flak
weaponry as a central theme remained the aerial threat as recorded in the
meeting's minutes:

The substantial increase of the enemy Air Force has caused the present crisis in U-boat warfare . . . It is necessary to concentrate aerial attacks on the Bay of Biscay, where enemy aircraft are attacking our U-boats on departure and return without interference. Support from the Luftwaffe is completely inadequate there at the present time. The Ju 88 can fly only in formation, since otherwise it would, in turn, become the victim. Only when flying in formation are the Ju 88s occasionally able to shoot down an enemy aircraft. In my opinion it is essential that the Me 410 be brought to the Bay of Biscay as soon as possible. In this I concur with the request of *Luftflotte* 3 and *Fliegerführer Atlantik*.

The *Führer* is doubtful whether the Me 410 is suitable for this purpose but will look into the matter. He then criticises the faulty production schedule of combat aircraft.[6]

Hitler then proceeded to rail against the decision to favour Stuka and medium bomber production over four-engined strategic bombers, though also betraying his fixation with revenge attacks against Great Britain by stating that should such machines become available in quantity, he would still have to decide between naval cooperation or the bombing of England. Dönitz retrospectively complained that suitable maritime aircraft should have been built concurrent with the expansion of the U-boat service, Hitler agreeing without appearing to remember the continual struggles Raeder had undertaken against Göring against subjugation of his proposed naval air arm.

Clearly impervious to the irony of the moment, Hitler then fully endorsed Dönitz's request for the opening of a new school for naval aviators in Danzig. Operated in direct conjunction with Baltic U-boat training flotillas, the aviators would receive the same systematic maritime instruction as U-boat crews. The naval fliers would learn nautical navigation, drift computation, convoy contact techniques, DF cooperation with U-boats and effective communication with other maritime aircraft. By training alongside U-boat personnel, Dönitz reasoned that they would effectively speak the same language, eliminating fundamental errors that could lead to 'the false generalisation that cooperation is useless'.[7] Hitler concurred, and during further discussions during the following month, pledged to push for the completion of Messerschmitt's 'Amerika Bomber' to fulfil long-range U-boat reconnaissance requirements.

The Kriegsmarine tabled proposals for the Luftwaffe to direct all air units not directly engaged in defending European airspace to the destruction of Anglo-American sea power. Now that the U-boats had been 'temporarily' bested, Dönitz asked the Luftwaffe to fill the void and provide future support for a renewed U-boat offensive. He re-emphasised the need for improved aircraft cover in Biscay, better reconnaissance, increased torpedo-bomber attacks against convoys, bombing of British harbours, yards and docks and heightened minelaying around the British Isles.

Jeschonnek transmitted to *OKM* 'Excerpts of a Luftwaffe proposal to which the *Reichsmarschall* had agreed in principle'. Within its pages the Luftwaffe omitted Dönitz's U-boat focus but pledged to increase *Fliegerführer Atlantik*, to become a new III.*Fliegerkorps*:

> The focal point for the assignment of the Luftwaffe must be shifted to enemy shipping. Henceforth, the Luftwaffe must always be assigned with all means at its disposal to operations against enemy supply lines; that is against shipyards, docks, harbours and ships in harbour and at sea . . .
>
> All operations against British sea power will be carried out by *Luftflotte* 3. Under *Luftflotte* 3 will operate: III.*Fliegerkorps* (*Fliegerführer Atlantik*) and IX.*Fliegerkorps* (*Angriff-Führer England*).
>
> Strength requirements to be fulfilled by the summer of 1944 are as follows: III.*Fliegerkorps* to be composed of one long-distance reconnaissance *Gruppe*, two long-distance maritime reconnaissance *Staffeln*, one maritime patrol *Staffel*, two and one-third long-distance heavy fighters *Staffeln*, one fighter-bomber *Staffel*, one fighter *Staffel*. The IX.*Fliegerkorps* is to be composed of three combat *Staffeln*, two fighter *Gruppen* (He 177) [vastly overestimating the versatility of the He 177 by intending to use it as a 'heavy fighter'], two fast fighter *Staffeln*.

While the struggle to protect U-boats in Biscay continued, *Luftflotte* 3 was instructed to provide adequate aircraft for rescuing survivors of any U-boat sunk. Initially encouraged by the *RLM* to provide a BV 222 for air-sea rescue at the expense of reconnaissance duties, officers of the *Luftflotte* pointed out that such aircraft could only really be employed for rescue purposes as an 'additional measure', since the large flying boats were only seaworthy in the relatively calm sea state 2. *Seenotdienstführer* 3 remained responsible for the Dutch, Belgian and French coastlines, divided into five separate *Seenotbereichskommandos* using as many aircraft as they could muster, including Do 24s and captured French Bizerte flying boats as well as obsolete aircraft such as the He 59.

The Arado Ar 196 featured as one of thirteen stamps issued on issued on 'Armed Forces Heroes Day' 1944.

In June Kessler's combat reconnaissance forces were reorganised, *Luftflotte* 3 creating *Seeaufklärungsgruppe* 128 from 5./BFl.Gr. 196 (becoming 1./SAGr. 128) which would continue to be based in Brest and forming 2./SAGr. 128 stationed at Étang de Berre, a lagoon on the Mediterranean coast north-west of Marseille, from nine Arado Ar 196A-3 aircraft that did not arrive until July. At its inception the strength of 1./SAGr. 128 stood at seventeen Ar 196A-3s, three Fw 190A-4s and three Fw 190A-5s; all of the Focke-Wulf fighters soon being converted to the A-5/U8 model that was equipped with SC-250 centreline-mounted bombs, underwing 300-litre drop tanks and only two MG 151s.

Though the U-boats had withdrawn from the North Atlantic in May, they continued to sail from the Atlantic bases on long-distance missions or against convoy traffic near Gibraltar, the Junkers of V./KG 40 escorting them to and from Biscay. On the first day of the month, twenty-three aircraft were despatched to search for the crew of *U563*, sunk the previous afternoon in the North Atlantic north-west of Cape Ortegal, Spain, by repeated depth-charging from British and Australian aircraft. Badly damaged in an initial attack though still able to dive, *Oblt.z.S.* Gustav Borchardt requested urgent air cover, though bad weather prevented its despatch. Further attacks crippled *U563* and Borchardt transmitted a final distress message as the boat was abandoned, the crew seen by attacking bombers swimming away from the sinking boat. Nearby *U621* began searching for survivors and was also bombed. With limited diving capability and low fuel, the boat was forced to break off and head for France.

As the weather moderated the first formation of eight Junkers took off at 0700hrs on 1 June, carrying rubber rafts which could be dropped if necessary, though in rough seas and long heavy swells, no trace was found of the U-boat crew. Nonetheless, the Junkers notched up a considerable tally of aircraft that day, shooting down two Wellingtons of RAF 420 Squadron, a 58 Squadron Halifax and a civilian KLM DC3 airliner. There were no survivors from any of the aircraft.

The Douglas DC-3 was on the regular transport route between the United Kingdom and Portugal, chartered by BOAC and designated Flight 777, a service operated up to four times per week, flying from Whitchurch to Lisbon. By June 1943 it had carried 4,000 passengers on over 500 flights. The four aircraft chartered by BOAC had their bright orange KLM livery oversprayed with camouflage and British civil markings, and were left unmolested until 1942 when intensification of the air war over Biscay led to the first attack on one of the scheduled flights by a single Messerschmitt Bf 110 fighter, though the DC-3 escaped and reached Lisbon for repair. On 19 April 1943, the same aircraft was again attacked, this time by six Bf 110 fighters, Captain Koene Dirk Parmentier evading the German fighters by dropping to an altitude of only 50 feet before climbing steeply into cloud cover. It was this aircraft engaged as Flight 777 on 1 June that was sighted at 1000hrs by aircraft of 14./KG 40 engaged of the search for *U563*. *Oberleutnant* Herbert Hintze later recalled:

> The DC-3 was flying on a reciprocal course towards us. I first saw her as a grey silhouette from the range of 2–3,000 metres . . . Bellstedt and Wittmer who had been flying as the lookout *Rotte* above the rest of us, attacked from above; the rest of us intended attacking from below. By the time we got within range of the aircraft, Bellstedt had attacked and set fire to the port engine and wing, and as we closed up I saw the aircraft was a DC-3 and had civil markings. I immediately ordered cease fire.[8]

The transport aircraft was already doomed, three people seen to bail out with parachutes, though they failed to open, appearing to the German pilot to be on fire. The aircraft entered a flat spin and hit the sea, the Spanish destroyer *Melilla* leaving El Ferrol the following day to search for survivors or wreckage but finding nothing.

The DC-3 had carried seventeen people in total, a crew of four headed by the highly experienced Dutch pilot Captain Quirinus Tepas, and thirteen passengers, the youngest eighteen-month-old Carolina Hutcheon travelling with her mother and sister, and the most famous passenger being the stage and film actor Leslie Howard.

The story of the shooting-down of Flight 777 continues to elicit conspiracy theories that German pilots had been ordered to destroy the civilian aircraft. While all subsequent BOAC flights from Lisbon were re-routed and took place during the hours of darkness, no more were attacked by German aircraft. Theories range from the highly unlikely scenario that Abwehr intelligence presumed Winston Churchill to be aboard, to the deliberate targeting of the actor Leslie Howard either as a perceived enemy agent due to his well-publicised opposition to Nazism, or due to a personal hatred fostered by Joseph Goebbels after the actor's successful string of anti-Nazi propaganda films. British and German civilian aircraft operated from the same facilities at Portela airport, Lisbon, where Allied and Axis spies carefully watched both the aircraft and their occupants. There would be little doubt that German agents would have been aware of the flight and the people aboard the aircraft, though whether that had any bearing on its destruction is doubtful.

German historian and author Sönke Neitzel included a brief passage related to the incident in his book detailing wartime experiences of captured German servicemen via transcripts of casual conversations secretly recorded by hidden microphones in Trent Park, Enfield. Among the prisoners caught on tape was *Obergefreiter* Heinz Dock, wireless operator aboard 'F8+NZ' of 15./KG 40 when he was shot down and captured after combat with a Whitley on 12 June 1943:

> DOCK: I usually took two photos of the same object; the ops. people always kept one. My best pictures were of a Whitley, the first enemy aircraft shot down by the *Staffel*. How we celebrated our first victory! Until half-past five the next morning; and we had a sortie at seven. We all got into the aircraft as tight as lords! The Whitley was the first our *Staffel* shot down, then came nothing but four-engine aircraft, Liberators, Hellfires, Stirlings, Sunderlands. Then came Lockheed-Hudsons and so on. We shot down four civil aircraft.
>
> HEIL: Were they armed?
>
> DOCK: No.
>
> HEIL: Why did you shoot them down?

DOCK: Whatever crossed our path was shot down. One we shot down
– there were all sorts of bigwigs in it: seventeen people, a crew of four
and fourteen passengers; they came from London. There was a famous
English film-star in it too, Howard. The English radio announced it in the
evening. Those civil aircraft pilots know something about flying! We stood
the aircraft on its head, with the fourteen passengers. They must all have
hung on the ceiling! (Laughs.) It flew at about 3200 m. Such a silly dog,
instead of flying straight ahead when he saw us, he started to take evasive
action. Then we got him. Then we let him have it all right! He wanted to
get away from us by putting on speed. Then he started to bank. Then first
one of us was after him, and then another. All we had to do was to press the
button, quietly and calmly. (Laughs.)
HEIL: Did it crash?
DOCK: Of course it did.
HEIL: And did any of them get out?
DOCK: No. They were all dead. Those fools don't try to make a forced
landing, even if they can see that it's all up with them.[9]

However, despite the somewhat callous recollection and the myriad
conspiracy theories – some of which are more plausible than others –
the likelihood is that the DC-3 was a victim of circumstances, being
in the wrong place at the wrong time. Post-war interviews with several
Luftwaffe airmen involved in the attack back up the original account
offered by *Oberleutnant* Hintze, who recalled all of the crews being rather
angry that they had not been informed of the possibility of encountering
a civilian aircraft during their patrol.

After the downing of the BOAC flight, during the following day Short
Sunderland 'N/461' of the RAAF's 461 Squadron was vectored over the
last reported position of the DC-3, scouring the area for thirty minutes
as part of its assigned ASW patrol but finding nothing. They too then
encountered Junkers of V./KG 40.

At 1855 hours, whilst flying at 3000' an unidentified aircraft was sighted
six miles on our starboard beam and almost immediately afterwards a total
of eight aircraft were reported in the same position; four in formation in
the lead followed by two lots of two. The Captain [F/Lt. Colin Braidwood
Walker] took control and turned away making for the nearest cloud . . . The
aircraft had now sighted us and as they were closing rapidly on us, were
identified as eight Ju 88s and our depth charges and bombs were therefore

run out and jettisoned. The enemy formed up for the attack with three aircraft on each beam 1500' above us and 1500 yds away with one aircraft on each quarter at the same height and range. The first attack was made at 1900 hours from the port beam and hits were scored simultaneously on our port outer engine, which immediately caught fire, and the P4 compass alongside the Captain's left knee. The engine immediately lost power and white smoke poured from it for about twenty-five minutes when the engine seized and the propeller flew off, fortunately without damaging the aircraft. The compass was apparently hit by an incendiary bullet and was completely shattered, showering glass all over the cockpit. This was followed by extensive fire with flames 2½ to 3 feet high in the cockpit extending from alongside the Captain forwards down into the 'George' compartment. The Captain's clothing also caught fire but all fires in the cockpit were extinguished by hand fire extinguishers. It was later agreed that this fire was caused by the incendiary igniting the alcohol from the compass. Until the fire was extinguished, the 1st pilot [F/O. Wilbur James Dowling] took over the controls and carried out the evasive action indicated by the navigator who was fire controller in the astrodome . . . Within the first fifteen minutes of the action two Ju 88s were seen by him to crash into the sea, both in flames – the first, which was shot down by the mid-upper gunner after passing over him at 100' dived straight in and disintegrated and the second, shot down by the tail gunner and possibly aided by the mid upper gunner, checked his dive at the last minute, hit the sea, bounced, stalled and dived in, also disintegrating.

The 88s which had formed up on quarters came in climbing attacks but these were checked by our port and starboard galley gunners, and must have come as a nasty surprise to them as our aircraft was the second to be fitted with these guns which were used in action for the first time on this occasion. By this time the wireless operator had changed from H/F to M/F and the Captain had the following message sent out 'Being attacked eight Ju 88s, aircraft on fire.' The base of the rear turret now received a direct hit by a cannon shell and became jammed, the hydraulics being shot away. At the same instant violent evasive action was taken and the tail gunner [Fl/Sgt. Ray Marston Goode] was knocked unconscious for about five minutes. Shortly after another hit by a cannon shell freed the turret which was operated by hand from now on with only two guns serviceable, the gunner extracting the securing pins, elevating and depressing the gun, rotating the turret and depressing the sears by hand. These same shells severed both elevator and rudder trimming controls and with the port engine lost, it took both the Captain and the 1st pilot their combined strengths to control the aircraft in the violent evasive action taken – greater than rate 4 turns towards the dead engine losing 3000' per minute were by no means uncommon.

At 1925 hours the Captain asked that the following message be transmitted: 'Two 88s shot down.' At 1930 the wireless received a direct hit from a cannon shell and both transmitter and receiver became U/S . . . Shrapnel from the cannon shell which wrecked the wireless also wounded the navigator [F/Lt. Kenneth McDonald Simpson] in the leg, passing right through his calf, caused cuts from the broken glass about the face of the wireless operator, punctured one of our dinghies and caused a small cut under the eye of one of our pigeons which had its head stuck out inquisitively from its container. About this time the starboard galley gunner [1st Fl/Eng: P/O. Edward (Ted) Charles Ernest Miles, RAF] was fatally wounded, became unconscious and died approximately twenty minutes later: his gun being manned by the other engineer [Sgt. Philip Kelvin Turner]. The navigator did not mention his wound until towards the end of the action when it was attended to while he continued his job in the dome, by which time he had lost a considerable amount of blood. Despite his wounds he carried on as fire controller in a magnificent way and was never flurried in spite of the complexity and number of attacks. A third 88 was now seen to crash in flames by the navigator and tail gunner; this one being shot down by the nose and mid-upper gunner. The engagement now became completely chaotic, the continuous evasive action and the firing being controlled by the navigator. The aircraft was hit repeatedly and became filled with the smell of cordite, bursting cannon shells, fire extinguisher chemicals and the strong odour of de-icing fluid from the tank which had been hit. The 88s continued to attack from the beam and bow, reforming for another attack immediately after breaking away from the previous one.

At about 1935 the intercom received a direct hit and the gunners, realising their fire control had gone, fired independently as the opportunity offered. The navigator continued to give his evasive actions by hand signals passed to the 2nd pilot P/O. James (Jim) Collier Amiss] and thence to the Captain. With his hand signals, the navigator looked more like an orchestra conductor than a fire controller. At about 1940 the nose gunner fired a short burst at an 88 attacking from 70' on the starboard bow and his port engine immediately burst into a mass of flames with smoke pouring from the cockpit. This one was not seen to crash . . . At 1945 there were only two 88s left and although one came in to attack on the starboard beam, he broke off at 1500 yds, and they were not seen again. We continued our evasive action, making use of what little cloud there was, until 2000 hours when we set course 030°C. The action lasted 45 minutes and was fought out between 1500' and 2500', the cloud being of almost no use, during which time it is estimated we were attacked at least 40 times. Having formed up on both beams the 88s attacked alternately from port and starboard, the attacks being continuous for 45 minutes and the aircraft never being straight and level for more than 15 seconds.

The weakness of the 88s lay in their poor range estimation and very weak break away. Several times they opened fire (with 20 mm or 37 mm cannon) at 200 yds. often at 1,500 yds. and endeavoured to correct their aim by hose-piping. They pressed home their attacks to 200 yds. and the mid-upper gunner held his fire until they were about 250 yds. away then let them have it point blank. His coolness and straight shooting were remarkable and the 88s couldn't attack often enough for him. He was singing 'Praise the Lord and pass the ammunition' and shouting 'Come on you bastards, come and get it'. He must have a charmed life as the hull round his turret received dozens of hits. The nose gunner also did excellent work and it is considered every 88 which attacked received hits as it was almost impossible to miss at the close range. It is estimated that N/461 had at least 400 holes in her after the action and had been hit about 12 times by cannon shells. After the action it was found that owing to the extremely coarse use of controls necessary for evasion, the whole airframe was so twisted; doors which were shut couldn't be opened and vice versa. After an hour's hectic weaving round the sky with our main compass in bits and the directional gyre useless owing to precision and toppling, we had only the vaguest idea of our position. Until things got sorted out we therefore set course at 20.00 hours on 030°, with no airspeed, only 3 engines, and using the P 8 compass which we didn't trust, and the navigator took a sun shot.[10]

The Sunderland crew jettisoned everything that they could to lighten the load of their battered aircraft, reaching The Lizard on England's south coast at 2228hrs, flying along the coast before successfully putting down on the sea and grounding the flying boat on Praa Sands, Cornwall. Three of the surviving crew had been wounded and Flight Lieutenant C.B. Walker was subsequently awarded the Distinguished Service Order.

The Junkers Ju 188.

As U-boats suffered further attacks during darkness by aircraft using centimetric radar, Fw 200 and Heinkel He 111 aircraft equipped with *'Hohentwiel'* began mounting night sorties, attempting to intercept enemy aircraft at the behest of *MGK West*. Use of the new Dornier Do 217 in this role was proposed, but the Luftwaffe deemed the aircraft unsuitable for such maritime operations, three of the new Junkers Ju 188 ordered re-equipped for that purpose instead.

The Ju 188 was a direct result of the 'Bomber-B' design competition begun before the war for the development of a second generation of *Schnellbomber*, potentially replacing the Dornier Do 17 and Junkers Ju 88. Larger, faster and of greater range, 'Bomber B' was intended to form the backbone of the Luftwaffe's bombing fleet and came down to the competing Focke-Wulf Fw 191 and Junkers Ju 288, prototype airframes for both completed by mid-1940. The high-performance 24-cylinder Junkers Jumo 222, liquid-cooled six-bank inline engines – also in development and a requirement for the aircraft's expected performance – were, however, not available until October 1941, and then only as testbeds themselves. The Jumo 222 possessed a take-off power of 2,000hp, as opposed to the Jumo 213's 1,500hp, itself in turn the successor to the Jumo 211 powering existing Junkers Ju 88s. Instead, designers closed their eyes to the reality of the potential problem unfolding and underpowered BMW and Daimler Benz engines were used instead, the project floundering as wartime shortages began to plague the Luftwaffe. The result was a disaster of the highest magnitude. By June 1943 the entire development programme for 'Bomber B' had failed to produce an operational aircraft and the Jumo 222 engines themselves requiring high-temperature alloys in increasingly short supply. Meanwhile, existing combat aircraft were swiftly becoming obsolete.

With the Ju 288 no closer to completion by 1942, the *RLM* quickly ordered an improved version of the Junkers Ju 88, to be designated Ju 188. An existing stop-gap Ju 88B-0 that had been under modification and development as the delay of the Ju 288 appeared inevitable was adopted, a second airframe constructed, known as the Ju 188V-1. Equipped with existing Jumo 213A engines, the Ju 188 possessed a longer more streamlined wing than the Ju 88, with rounded wingtips for better high-altitude performance. The changes to the airframe moved the aircraft's centre of gravity slightly and so the Ju 188 was balanced by a slightly extended glazed Plexiglas cockpit which afforded excellent visibility for the crew. The first three production Ju 188E-1 machines were delivered with the more readily available BMW 801D-2 14-cylinder air-cooled radial piston engines in February 1943. A modified version mounting a FuG 200 'Hohentwiel' sea-search radar set under the nose and PVC 1006 torpedo rack was then delivered as the Ju 188E-2, still equipped with BMW engines. Finally, those that mounted the planned Jumo 213 were designated Ju 188A-2, though they did not enter service until July 1944 with KG 26.

Meanwhile other new weapons were approaching combat use. During June, *Maj.* Martin Kästner's II./KG 40, stationed in The Netherlands, converted from Do 217 bombers to Me 410 *Zerstörer* and were subsequently redesignated V./KG 2 and relocated to Merville airfield near Lille for bomber interception and fighter-bomber attacks on England. A new II.*Gruppe* would not be created for KG 40 until October at Burg-Magdeburg, formed from the remains of I./KG 50 which had suffered heavy losses of its He 177 bombers during the Stalingrad airlift. *Major* Heinrich Schlosser had returned his battered *Gruppe* to Germany where his depleted crews were reinforced and began training in the use of the Hs 293 missile. With its redesignation to II./KG 40 on 25 October, the anti-shipping unit would relocate to Bordeaux-Mérignac.

The original plan envisaged Do 217-equipped missile units assuming responsibility for Mediterranean operations, and those equipped with long-range He 177s to operate in the Atlantic. That remained, however, some months in the future as *Fliegerführer Atlantik* struggled to answer the immediate problems facing its command. Deployment of the additional BV 222 aircraft to the Atlantic coast had incurred some delay, Mössel offering the explanation to *SKL* that technical difficulties were causing interruptions in supplying aircraft. In return, *Vizeadmiral* Meisel asked Jeschonnek whether Mössel could be granted authority to 'exercise influence' on the progress of making these long-range reconnaissance aircraft operationally ready. However, Jeschonnek's reply ended any such arrangement, the Luftwaffe Operations Chief of Staff stating that: 'the statements transmitted by Naval Staff concerning the delay in making the BV 222A available for *Fliegerführer Atlantik* were incorrect'. There was no special delay and Kessler was expected to have four BV 222s at his disposal by the end of June. Jeschonnek also curtly reminded the naval high command that inter-service co-operation concerning operational questions 'would be best effected in direct agreement and he would continue to inform Naval Staff about plans influencing naval warfare'.[11] Furthermore, he did not intend to follow up proposals to provide Mössel greater authority to influence progress regarding the BV 222s, as that was an affair only of the Luftwaffe's Quartermaster General.

The Dornier Do 217P.

However, within two days Göring himself had interceded and countermanded Jeschonnek's decision. Aware perhaps that his star had faded considerably following the disasters of Stalingrad and Tunisia, and no doubt conscious of Dönitz's popularity with the *Führer* unlike his previous sparring partner Erich Raeder, he ordered Mössel given full responsibility for the speedy conversion of the BV 222 A aircraft, a second due to be operationally ready that same day, assigned to *Aufklärungsfliegerstaffel* 222 (*See*) at Biscarosse.

Over Biscay the 'Instep' patrols had started to truly bite, *Luftflotte* 3 reporting that pilots of V./KG 40 were finding it impossible to evade the fast Mosquitos during cloudless days and relied on safety in numbers or fighter escort from Fw 190s, though the latter possessed limited range even with drop tanks. Fortunately for departing U-boats sailing in groups for collective anti-aircraft defence, engagements between Junkers and Mosquitoes frequently diverted attention from them. Flight Sergeant Harry Reed was one of the pilots of 264 Squadron assigned the 'Instep' patrols:

> Flying from Predannack placed two extra hazards on crews. The airfield had been built on a bog and runways and taxi-track were elevated above the soggy land. Runways etc. had to be built 18 inches or more above the land, so a swing on take-off could be disastrous. The other Predannack hazard was a sea fog which could creep in very quickly. It was called 'The Wizard' and an R/T call saying 'The Wizard's About' was used to give us warning. Our primary work was on 'Instep' patrols in the Bay of Biscay. These were of three or four Mosquitoes and were of up to five hours duration. Our patrols really started once we had flown over the Scillies and reached Bishop Rock Light House 58 Km.S.W from Land's End. We were briefed to fly as low as possible over the sea to give us more opportunity to surprise. This was a good ploy but demanded a lot of concentration. Of the 20 'Insteps' I flew, most were uneventful, but I managed to damage a Ju 88 one day before it reached cloud cover. One of our aircraft flown by Pilot Officer Bill Bailey flew his Mossie 150 miles low over the sea on one engine. He made it back but opted to land at Exeter as he did not expect to be able to climb to land at cliff height Predannack. Wing Commander Allington led a small formation made up of the more experienced crews on daylight raid on the seaplane base at Biscarosse.[12]

At 2015hrs on 20 June four 264 Squadron Mosquitoes lifted off, the squadron flying daily 'Instep' patrols that month thus far. This time the four aircraft were being led by Wing Commander William James Allington, squadron commander since March.

Sixty kilometres from the coast at Biscarosse, the BV 138 'NA+PS' of Aufkl.St. 222 (*See*) was spotted and shot down in flames with the crew never recovered.[13] Heading east from the site of the downed aircraft, the four fighter-bombers crossed the coast at 2230hrs and spotted several flying boats moored on the lake at Biscarosse, immediately diving to strafe. Allington and his three accompanying pilots – F/O E.E. Pudsey, S/L L.T. Bryant-Fenn and F/O L. H. Hayden – claimed a collective total of four BV 138s set on fire and destroyed and one BV 222 damaged despite heavy, accurate flak. One Mosquito was hit but not seriously damaged, a large explosion being seen from the lakeside as they flew towards Ouessant. Four auxiliary minesweepers were also attacked by the RAF aircraft near Brest, three claimed sunk and the last damaged although only casualties aboard *M444* were recorded by the Kriegsmarine.

At Biscarosse the BV 138C-1 'NA+PS', and BV 222s 'X4+CH' (S3) recently arrived from Travemünde, and 'X4+EH' (S5) were burnt-out wrecks. The loss of the two large flying boats was particularly keenly felt as high hopes had been pinned on their potential rejuvenating effect on U-boat warfare. In Berlin, the *SKL* War Diary recorded the blow as 'a heavy one, equivalent in naval terms to the destruction of two cruisers'.[14] Camouflage and protection of these valuable aircraft was urgently undertaken and three short 'inlets' soon under construction by the Organisation Todt on the forested western shore a kilometre to the south of the station itself. The first was completed on 10 October and by the end of the year they were being used as large open shelters for the BV 222 flying boats.

Six days after the Bisacrosse attack, discussions took place between leading officials of the Reich Air Ministry in Berlin, chaired by Göring, regarding the continued air war over the Atlantic and against Great Britain. Looking as far ahead as the summer of 1944, *Generalleutnant* Rudolf Meister (*Chef d.Führungsstab d.Lw*) presented his case for Luftwaffe requirements based on a Kriegsmarine study. In total he listed:

1 Reconnaissance Group (*Fernaufklärungsgruppe* 5) equipped with Ju 290, He 177 and Ju 88H-1 aircraft;
2 *Seeaufklärungssteffeln* with six BV 222s;
2 ⅓ *Fernkampfgeschwader* with He 177s (half with torpedoes, half with remotely-guided missiles);

1 *Zerstörergeschwader* equipped with Me 410 and Ju 88G-1 aircraft (for
    U-boat security in Biscay);
1 *Jagdgeschwader* (both fighters and fighter-bombers).

Jeschonnek in turn pointed out that due to the loss of the two BV 222s
at Bisacrosse, and through delays in adaptation of the next two aircraft,
completing the first *Staffel* equipped solely with such machines would
necessarily be postponed until the end of the year. Two aircraft were to
be expected in August, with an ambitious – and unrealised – production
schedule of one per month from September.

In the interim – in line with Meister's approved request to Göring
– and during the course of a general reorganisation of the *Seeflieger-
verbände*, *Seeaufklärungsgruppe* 129 was created on 13 July from two
already operational BV 222s, bolstered by BV 138s of *Aufklärungsstaffel*
222 (*See*):

'X4+BH' S2 (previously briefly assigned to the *Seenotdienst* and arriving
    in Bisacrosse on 16 September first reconnaissance mission nine
    days later with its new coding 'X4 + EH');
'X4+DH' S4 (also after brief *Seenot* service, arriving in Bisacrosse on 16
    September and first mission made eleven days later).[15]

Thanks to continual petitioning by Dönitz, the troubled He 177
aircraft was finally becoming available to *Fliegerführer Atlantik* although
the anticipated triumphant entry of the new design into the war over
Biscay never fully materialised. Werner Baumbach later wrote in his
memoirs:

It had already become out of date. As a result of the eternal modifications
its performance had fallen so low that there were many objections to its
employment as a long-range aircraft in the jobs for which it was intended.
In June, 1943, *Grossadmiral* Dönitz made a report to Hitler: 'The
declining figures of sinkings in the U-boat war can only be made good by
making more use of the Luftwaffe.' On an order at top level, the He 177
was immediately put into service as escort for our submarines far out into
the Atlantic. Though Milch knew well enough that the outstanding defect
of this aircraft, the coupled engines, had not been remedied, he reported
that the He 177 could be employed at any time for high-level attack and
would be equally useful for submarine escort duties. This report was in

direct conflict with the views of the *Fliegerführer Atlantik* based on actual experience of the usefulness of the He 177 for the sea war: 'With a tactical range of only 930 miles the He 177 certainly cannot be used in all areas open to long-range reconnaissance. Its useful range does not extend beyond the area west and north-west of the Bay of Biscay.' Thereupon the Air Force Staff issued an order: 'In the light of first experience with the He 177, modifications of this aircraft must be taken in hand at once. The value of this class for dealing with ships in distant waters will be greatly enhanced by the use of guided missiles. The most urgent task is to extend its range beyond the existing limit.' The German aircraft industry was no longer in a position to carry out that order. Quite the reverse. Further modification of the He 177 reduced its range and made it unsuitable for the mounting demands of the Battle of the Atlantic.

On the 3rd July 1944, Saur was able to persuade Göring to order the production of the newly modified He 177B with four separate engines. When Hitler approved this decision, he added that all the old He 177s should be scrapped. And so the most tragic chapter in the history of German air armament came to a close.[16]

Dönitz's continued vexation at the inability to protect U-boats transiting Biscay remained unabated. During early July he asked for fresh suggestions from both *MGK West* and *Luftflotte* 3. In its reply, *MGK West* proposed that U-boats be grouped into companies of between four to six, escorted by minesweepers or *Vorposteboote* alongside destroyers or torpedo boats to the outer limits of Biscay, and thereupon for a further 100 miles by destroyers or torpedo boats and a close escort of Ju 88 aircraft. Theoretically, the same escort ships could then bring in U-boats returning from combat. Five more destroyers were needed to enable the continuous shuttling of such convoy traffic, although *B.d.U.* was not encouraged by the idea, given the risks of U-boats sailing in such large groups.

Acting in parallel, *Luftflotte* 3 requested immediate reinforcement of *Fliegerführer Atlantik*, its current strength clearly insufficient. Dönitz added his own weight to the request by opining that unless the bomber, heavy fighter and fighter formations of *Fliegerführer Atlantik* were soon reinforced, a further increase in U-boat losses in the Bay of Biscay would be inevitable.

Enacting urgent measures, *Luftflotte* 3 requested that V./KG 40 immediately be expanded into a *Zerstörer Geschwader* of three *Gruppen* and that a fourth *Staffel* be established at once. Furthermore, they called for two *Staffeln* be added to III./ZG 1 and the limited number of Fw 190 aircraft of 1./SAGr. 128 be brought up to the establishment of a long-range fighter *Staffel* with additional seagoing crews transferred by Luftwaffe Air Force General Staff and *OKM*; the *Staffel* continuing to be expanded until it reached *Gruppe* establishment. Long-range bombers of KG 40 were also to be assigned anti-surface force operations off Cape Finisterre, Spain.

It was an ambitious – though realistic – appeal and could potentially have rectified the increasing imbalance between diminishing German and growing Allied air forces over Biscay. However, aircraft production was unable to keep pace with Luftwaffe requirements in its entirety, the poor state into which the Luftwaffe had declined not aided by extremely inefficient manufacturing practices. There remained frequent confusion and misplaced priorities stemming from the very top, Hitler himself frequently issuing impulsive requests to produce aircraft types resulting from battlefield reversals. For example, following the Stalingrad disaster he demanded transport aircraft produced in quantity, changed in February 1943 to Ju 52 floatplanes and then to He 177 bombers. The failure to employ women in factories replacing men transferred to the front was a direct result of the Nazi Party's inherent chauvinism, Hitler himself being opposed to women in the workplace or in direct support of combat units. While in Britain automobile manufacturers were converted to aircraft production, the same was not true in Germany and factories devoted to producing military aircraft were increasingly identified and targeted by Allied bombing, though Albert Speer did his utmost to negate its effect by dispersal of production lines.

However, despite Speer's genius for restructuring and reorganising Germany's beleaguered industrial sector he also allowed the diversion of valuable resources to the demands of the Army's complicated V2 rocket during 1943, further draining limited raw materials from Luftwaffe construction and costing one hundred times as much as the Luftwaffe's V1 flying bomb. Furthermore, the cheap V1 reprisal weapon tied up a certain amount of British defensive aircraft and artillery, while there was no defence against the V2. Though German aircraft production peaked in July 1943 with 1,263 fighters, 743 bombers, 191 transports and 190 training aircraft manufactured, it declined thereafter.

As the Luftwaffe declined, both the RAF and USAAF grew in strength, confidence, and ability. Demonstrating their new power, on 24 July the Allies launched Operation *Gomorrah*, an eight-day and seven-night bombing of Hamburg that killed 42,600 civilians, wounded 37,000 more and virtually destroyed the city and its myriad industrial plants. The *RLM* reacted automatically with a building programme of fighters above all else. Speer had candidly stated that just six more such bombing attacks would end Germany's war, while Milch publicly declared to Goebbels that the war was lost. Bombers were now fourth priority, behind fighters, *Zerstörer* and V1 missiles, the bomber types to continue production being the Ju 88, Ju 188, He 177, Ju 87 and Ju 288 with the next priority being the long-range Ju 290 reconnaissance aircraft.

Nevertheless, the attempted reinforcement of *Fliegerführer Atlantik* began. From August, further elements of ZG 1 had begun to arrive on the Atlantic coast to join Kessler's command; Stab/ZG 1, equipped with Bf 110 and Ju 88 aircraft, was based at Lorient's Kerlin-Bastard airfield six and a half kilometres west-north-west of the town itself. One of the largest Luftwaffe airfields in occupied France, the inhabitants of surrounding farms had been expelled from their homes and relocated, their land and buildings subsumed into the airfield infrastructure alongside new construction.

On 5 August 1943 *Maj.* Heinz Nacke's II./ZG 1 of Bf 110 aircraft were withdrawn from Salerno in Italy where they had been used to counter enemy bomber missions and transferred first to Lorient's Kerlin-Bastard airfield and then on to Lanveoc-Poulmic and under Kessler's control. However, they too did not stay long, achieving little in Biscay. On 2 August Nacke had been badly injured in Bf 110 G-2 after a forced landing at Thalfangen near Trier during a delivery flight. His place as *Gruppenkommandeur* was taken by *Hptm.* Karl-Heinrich Matern, a highly experienced *Zerstörer* pilot, who was shot down and killed aboard aircraft 'S9+RP' by RAF Spitfires 200 kilometres north-west of Brest on 8 October. A group of eight of the twin engine fighters were intercepted by single engine aircraft of Fighter Command, all but two of the Bf 110s lost during the running battle.[17] That night, Lanveoc-Poulmic was bombed by RAF Bostons as part of attacks against three French airfields, Spitfires strafing during the day and accounting for three more Bf 110s destroyed and another damaged. Over twenty-four hours, eleven aircraft had been destroyed, with eight crews killed in action.

On 25 October, the battered *Gruppe* was withdrawn and relocated to Wels, Austria, where they fought American bomber streams inbound from Italy, their brief Biscay attachment having cost twenty machines and twelve crews.

Messerschmitt Bf 110 *Zerstörer* of ZG 1 were briefly deployed over Biscay but withdrawn after heavy losses.

Condors of KG 40 experienced at least some small measure of success in the first six months of 1943. In total, five vessels were sunk between March and June, beginning with the 6,009GRT SS *City of Christchurch* sunk west of Lisbon from Convoy KMS 11 on 21 March by 7./KG 40 and ending with the 1,846GRT SS *Shetland* and the 3,423GRT SS *Volturno* west-north-west of Cape Saint Vincent, Portugal, on 23 June by 1./KG 40. The latter attack was made by three Condors against a convoy of five merchant ships escorted by FFS *Renoncule* and HMT *Sapper* during the early evening. SS *Shetland* received direct hits and sank quickly, four men being killed and thirty taken aboard the trawler while *Volturno* was hit and severely damaged, three men killed, and survivors evacuated before uncontrollable flooding sank the ship.

Two Condors of 7./KG 40 attacked an RAF 295 Squadron Halifax acting as tug for a Horsa glider of the British Glider Pilot Regiment that was being ferried to North Africa. While the Halifax was shot down, the Horsa cast off its tow rope and ditched one hundred miles from Spain's north-west coast, all three army crew later being rescued by a Spanish fishing boat. The men from the Halifax were seen by *Hptm.* Georg Schobert's crew to take to their dinghies, but there was no trace of them ever found.

Despite these victories, during the first quarter of 1943 KG 40 Condors had contributed to the shadowing of only six convoys due to a lack of available machines and allocation of many to *MGK West* in support of blockade-running missions. In June no convoys were either seen or attacked, ULTRA aiding the British Admiralty in rerouting its convoy traffic beyond Condor range as often as possible. However, during the month that followed, Condors achieved an almost unexpected triumph with far-reaching benefit to the Japanese war in Burma.

The British Army had decided to transport the 91st (West African) Division from West Africa to Burma, requiring an unusually large quantity of troopships due to the number of porters that the division required. After successful transfer of advance units and 6th (West African) Brigade, the 12,000 men of the 5th (West African) Brigade were scheduled to depart Freetown at the end of July with Convoy WS 32. The liners *Britannic*, *Largs Bay* and *Tamaroa* were already available in Freetown, the additional troopship 16,792GRT SS *California* sailing from the Clyde to increase available capacity. The passenger liner, which had spent time as an armed merchant cruiser before conversion to a troopship, carried 470 personnel bound for West Africa. It sailed in company with the 20,021GRT SS *Duchess of York* carrying 600 RAF personnel and civilians destined for Freetown and the store ship MV *Port Fairy*, bound ultimately for Australia and New Zealand. The convoy, known as 'Faith', was escorted by the destroyer HMS *Douglas* and frigate HMS *Moyola*, joined when under way by Canadian destroyer HMCS *Iroquois*.

During early evening on 11 July a Condor was reported by radio intelligence to be within the vicinity, all ships going to action stations and the aircraft finally being sighted by lookouts aboard *California* at 1930hrs. The reconnaissance aircraft approached from the south and began to circle the convoy, all three merchants sailing in line abreast to counter the more likely threat from U-boat attack. Three Fw 200s from 7./ KG 40 were immediately despatched, commanded by *Hptm.* Helmut Liman, *Hptm.* Ludwig Progner and *Oblt.* Egon Scherret, guided to the 'Faith' ships by beacon transmission from the shadowing aircraft. At 2010hrs, the Condors began attacking in medium altitude bombing runs, beyond the range of defending anti-aircraft fire; the 250kg bombs being dropped with extreme accuracy thanks to the Lofte 7D bomb sights.

The first aircraft scored two direct hits on *Duchess of York*, crippling the ship's engines, and starting fierce fires running from amidships to stern. The second aircraft tore a long hole in the starboard side of the *California*, a second bombing run striking the ship with two bombs, one landing in the Number 2 hold and the other exploding between bridge and funnel. This ship was also soon ablaze and began sinking by the bow, the engines undamaged but the steering gear disabled. Subsequent attacks narrowly missed *Port Fairy* and the ailing *Duchess of York*. After completing six separate bombing runs in which a total of fourteen bombs were dropped, the Condors departed leaving as first *California* and then *Duchess of York* lowered boats to abandon ship. Official British figures record eighty-nine people killed on board *Duchess of York* and twenty-six from *California*, both blazing hulks subsequently torpedoed by escort ships once evacuated.[18]

The frigate HMS *Swale* was despatched from Gibraltar to rendezvous, arriving at the convoy as the attacks were underway, and narrowly missed by bombs itself. After conducting an anti-submarine sweep, *Swale* was ordered to escort MV *Port Fairy* to Casablanca. The two ships were attacked by a pair of Condors of III./KG 40, *Port Fairy* hit on its port side by *Oblt.* Joachim Ohm, the *Gruppe*'s Operations Officer. The ship was holed, and her steering gear disabled, though fires were soon brought under control with assistance from the escorting frigate and the store ship steered by engine once all but the minimum crew had been evacuated, eventually making successful landfall at Casablanca on 14 July.

The loss of the two troopships came as a complete shock to the British Admiralty who had almost dismissed the threat of Condor attack following the success of 'Instep'. Mindful that the new method of accurate medium-altitude bombing attack enabled by the Lofte 7 bombsight had apparently emboldened the Luftwaffe – unaware that demands placed on KG 40 Condors for blockade-running escort had been suspended releasing more aircraft – the Admiralty re-routed further west beyond easy Condor range. This, in turn, made the convoys more susceptible to U-boat interception but strengthened escorts and improved ASW tactics had largely got the measure of Dönitz's boats active on the Gibraltar convoy route.

Later that month Condors attacked Convoy OS52 which had departed Liverpool bound for the South Atlantic collection point of Freetown, Sierra Leone, from where the vessels would separate for other destinations. The convoy was large; sixty-six merchant ships escorted by eight warships including a *Dido* class anti-aircraft light cruiser. On 26 July, while OS52 passed west of Lisbon, a pair of III./KG 40 Condors attacked during the early evening, three bombs hitting the 9,501GRT MV *El Argentino* travelling in ballast from Glasgow to Montevideo, the ship sinking with four men killed. The steamer *Empire Brutus* was also hit by a single bomb which impacted the port side dividing bulkhead between engine and boiler rooms, causing severe flooding. The crew hastily abandoned ship until it became apparent that the steamer was in no immediate danger of sinking and returned aboard. Once flooding had been brought under relative control, although there was no power to pumps or steering, the rescue tug *Empire Samson* took the ship in tow taking off all but essential crew. In deteriorating weather and accompanied by the corvette HMS *Jonquil* the tug dragged the wallowing ship to Lisbon, fighting off one further Focke-Wulf attack during the following day but eventually evacuating the skeleton crew as the engine room bulkhead appeared on the point of collapse. Nevertheless, the tug's Master, Lt A.S. Pike RNR, refused to abandon the tow and finally reached Lisbon with *Empire Brutus* still afloat.

On 27 July, five Fw 200s returned for a second level bombing attack from an altitude of 3,000 metres and impervious to anti-aircraft fire. They damaged SS *Empire Highway* and narrowly missed 5,298GRT SS *Halizones*, shock from the four explosions rupturing the hull and causing uncontrollable flooding. Escort vessels evacuated the crew as their ship listed to starboard and all ninety people aboard were saved although two were later hospitalised in Casablanca with severe burns, and another with a minor back injury. Taken under tow, the abandoned ship later sank.

The following day, 28 July, Convoy SL133 was attacked over four hours by six Condors while on the final leg of its voyage from Freetown to the United Kingdom, two salvos of bombs landing in the vicinity of the convoy but without hitting anything. The last two CAM ships in service, SS *Empire Tide* and *Empire Darwin*, were part of SL133, the latter's Hurricat first to launch and P/O John Stewart managing to damage one of the attackers before his guns jammed as a likely result of accumulated sea spray on the exposed aircraft. Pilot Officer Patrick Flynn launched to intercept a second Focke-Wulf, opening fire as the Condor relied on its defensive gunnery to keep the fighter at bay, rather than undertaking evasive manoeuvres. Flynn nearly collided with a bomb dropped by the German aircraft as he sustained punishing damage from the Luftwaffe gunners before driving the attacking aircraft away with one engine trailing smoke, claiming the aircraft as a 'probable'. Both CAM fighter pilots were successfully recovered after ditching their 'single-use' aircraft.

Seven Condors returned the next day to try again, only managing three near misses from five attacks but damaging CAM ship *Empire Darwin*. This time an RAF 59 Squadron Liberator engaged the attacking Condors amidst thick anti-aircraft fire from the ships below, scoring no hits but helping drive the attackers away. *Oberfeldwebel* Alfred Bolfrass' 2./KG 40 Condor was intercepted by 248 Squadron Beaufighters during its return flight to Bordeaux and shot down in flames about 300 miles west of Cape Finisterre, Bolfrass being killed and the remaining crew able to escape after the aircraft ditched. The survivors languished in a rubber dinghy, two days later hearing the sound of distant battle in which a group of three outbound U-boats – *U461*, *U462* (both Type XIV tankers) and *U504* – were sunk by combined air and sea attack as part of British Operations *Musketry* and *Seaslug*. Not long thereafter, the surviving Condor crew were rescued by one of the British warships involved, HMS *Woodpecker*. The dual *Musketry* and *Seaslug* operations had opened in mid-July, mounted the former by No 19 Group RAF Coastal Command acting in concert with the *Seaslug* naval component to find and destroy Dönitz's U-boats adopting the tactic of running surfaced in groups through Biscay.

Despite heavy Condor losses III./KG 40 mustered a total of twenty-one aircraft to attack Convoy OS 53/KMS 23 north-west of Lisbon on 15 August. Led by the highly experienced *Gruppenkommandeure Maj.* Robert Kowalewski, the Condors' massed attack of eighteen bomb salvoes dropped from a height of between 2,500 and 3,000 metres sank only the 6,060GRT steamer SS *Warfield* on passage from Glasgow for Alexandria; ninety-four crewmen were rescued and two killed. Two other steamers, SS *Baron Fairlie* and *Ocean Faith*, were damaged and temporarily disabled, though both subsequently made Gibraltar. In return, *Oblt.* Bernhard Kunisch's Fw 200C-4 from 7./KG 40 was hit by anti-aircraft fire from the escorting HMS *Stork* and force landed at Lavacolla, Spain, where Kunisch and his crew were briefly interned before repatriation. This full-scale effort against OS 53/KMS 23 was the last of that magnitude that III./KG 40 could manage as attritional losses in aerial combat and accidents drew the teeth of the anti-shipping unit. During the remainder of 1943, the Condors of III./KG 40 would only manage to damage HMS *Winchelsea* in a nine-aircraft attack on Convoy OG 93/KMS 26 on 12 September and sink the 7,135GRT SS *Fort Babine* the following day as three aircraft bombed from an altitude of 4,000 metres while the ship was being towed from the Mediterranean for repairs in the United Kingdom.

A previous assignment of American air forces to the eastern Atlantic battle had taken place in November 1942 and been unsuccessful short-lived. However, to compound *Fliegerführer Atlantik*'s woes, in June 1943 a fresh American initiative began. The USAAF's 480th Antisubmarine Group, comprising two squadrons of B-24D Liberators, was created at the US Naval Air Station Port Lyautey, French Morocco, on 19 June, tasked with patrolling north and west of Morocco along the Atlantic approaches to the Strait of Gibraltar. Shortly thereafter, on 8 July, the USAAF 479th Antisubmarine Group was formed at RAF St Eval primarily for patrolling the Bay of Biscay under the operational control of No. 19 Group, Coastal Command. With St Eval already at capacity with British units, the USAAF group moved to RAF Station Dunkeswell, 100 miles away in Devonshire during August.

Additional American forces entered the Atlantic battle when the US Navy deployed PBY-5 Catalina aircraft of VP-63 to Pembroke Dock, South Wales. Equipped with magnetic anomaly detectors (MAD gear) the Catalinas could detect U-boats even while running shallowly submerged. On 1 July, VP-63 lost its first aircraft to the Ju 88s of V./KG 40 when Lt. Bill Tanner's aircraft was shot down with two crewmen killed and the remainder eventually rescued by the Royal Navy. Return fire from the Catalina had damaged the Ju 88 flown by *Lt.* Knud Gmelin, which was subsequently ditched while attempting to return to its French airfield, the crew later picked up by a Bizerte aircraft of 1.*Seenotstaffel*.

Between March and October 1943, USAAF Liberator aircraft shot down nine German aircraft, including five Condors, three Dornier flying boats and one Junkers Ju 88, for the loss of three Liberators of the 480th Antisubmarine Group and four from the 479th. Most American aircraft shot down were tackled by Ju 88s of V./KG 40, but the large bombers also occasionally encountered Fw 200s over Biscay and generally proved themselves to be the superior machine.

The B-24D was a formidable aircraft, crewed by eleven men, armed with ten .50 calibre M2 Browning machine guns in four turrets and two waist positions and capable of a maximum speed of 297 mph (478km/h). However, it was not without its own problems. The Liberator utilised a wing design created by David R. Davis, a freelance aeronautical engineer, who had approached the Consolidated Aircraft Company with a new and revolutionary low-drag, high aspect-ratio wing design for their Model 31 flying boat, providing a 20 per cent increase in range and speed performance when compared with contemporary aircraft. The trade-off for the greater fuel efficiency provided by the wing design to the B-24 was diminished durability when compare to the B-17 which could withstand greater battle damage and continue to fly.

For the crews, the B-24 was considerably less comfortable than the B-17. Gunners not at action stations had nowhere to sit other than the floor of the fuselage which was cold and draughty. Moving around the B-24 interior was awkward in full battle gear due to a considerable amount of additionally installed equipment, as opposed to the B-17 where it had been built into the design. The accident rate for B-24s was considerably higher; 850 Second Air Force crewmen being killed in 298 B-24 accidents during 1943 alone. However, the B-17 had been designed during peacetime when quality could triumph over quantity, whereas the Liberator was a wartime development requiring numbers above all else.

On 13 August *Oblt.* Günther Seide's Fw 200C-5 'F8+IT' of 9./KG 40, clashed with a Consolidated B-24D Liberator of the 1st Squadron, 480th Antisubmarine Group, over the Bay of Biscay. Second radio operator *Uffz.* Werner Zerrahn recalling the battle that followed:

> . . . We had been briefed to fly an armed reconnaissance sortie over the Bay of Biscay as far as the Azores. Flights like this had a duration of about ten to twelve hours and our aircraft carried four 250kg bombs and later two Henschel Hs 293A radio-controlled missiles. During our approach, we were able to make out a convoy and reported its position to Bordeaux by sending a coded radio message. Only a few minutes later, a B-24 Liberator appeared which caused a lot of trouble.
>
> The enemy's speed was considerably higher than ours and we received many hits. Our gunner, *Obergefreiter* Heinz Wagner, was wounded and holes in the fuel tanks caused the loss of quite an amount of fuel. Fortunately, we reached a layer of cloud and with the last drop of fuel we were able to make a good belly-landing in a harvested field of maize near La Coruna in Spain.[19]

Gunners aboard the Liberator, piloted by Lt. Fred W. McKinnon, expended no less than 1,790 rounds of .50-calibre ammunition to bring Seide's aircraft down, the German crew being briefly interned before travelling to Madrid and repatriation onwards to Bordeaux within a fortnight.

Another such battle took place on 17 August when a Liberator flown by Lt. Hugh Maxwell Jr. clashed with two Condors while on patrol from Port Lyautey, tasked with covering convoy traffic bound for North Africa. Warned by radio of the German presence, Maxwell's radar operator reported two contacts at a range of fifteen miles; all three aircraft were likely to arrive over the expected convoy position simultaneously. Maxwell attempted to close on the tail of the first Condor piloted by *Obfw*. Karl Bauer of 2./KG 40 but started taking damage from its defensive gunners.

> I shoved the throttles and prop pitch forward and closed as fast as I could, and I opened fire. They never came out of their diving turn and went in on fire. But boy, they had done us damage.[20]

Oberleutnant Heinz Küchenmeister's aircraft had managed to latch on to the Liberator's tail and accurate machine-gun fire disabled the American's number three and four engines, holing the right wing which began to burn. Maxwell ordered the aircraft's depth charges jettisoned.

> All of us got hit by shrapnel and our hydraulic system was knocked out, our intercom radio system was knocked out, the whole instrument panel was knocked out . . . As I realized that our right wing would no longer fly and I couldn't raise it, and was trying to hold left rudder and aileron, my left foot kept slipping off the rudder pedal. I looked down and said, 'Oh my God.' My whole left leg and foot were covered with blood, and there was a pool of blood and it was all over that rudder pedal. And I knew I'd been hit in the left side with shrapnel. But then I realized: It ain't blood, it's hydraulic fluid.
>
> Hell, I was scared. I didn't want to die, but I had to do whatever I needed to do. The thing that sticks out in my mind the most was when I realized we were going to be crashing into the Atlantic Ocean, and I thought we were goners. But in a last-minute desperate effort to avoid catastrophe, I kicked in full right rudder and threw the plane into a skid, and sure enough, instead of our plane cartwheeling and breaking up and exploding, the water put the fire out, and the airplane broke in three pieces, but it didn't explode or burn.[21]

Seven of the ten American crew members survived the ditching into the sea as Küchenmeister's Condor made its way back to France with one engine disabled by return fire from the Liberator. The convoy escort HMS *Highlander* rescued the surviving members of Maxwell's crew as

Lieutenant Hugh Maxwell Jr, forced to ditch his B-24 Liberator after combat with two KG 40 Condors on 17 August 1943.

well as four from Bauer's Condor, two of whom were severely burned and later died.

With its resumption of convoy attacks, III./KG 40 had lost eleven Condors during June and July 1943, an operational strength of only nine aircraft remaining by the beginning of August. Six further Condors were lost in combat during the month that followed – two making forced landings in Spain – and another aircraft was lost after ditching as the result of an accident, eleven aircrew listed as killed, eleven captured and one injured. In September and October two more were lost to enemy action and five to accidents for minimal result. On 1 October, III./KG 40 committed all of its eighteen operational Condors to an attack on convoy MKS 25 off the Spanish coast. However, in bad weather only three of the aircraft found the convoy, and none managed to score any success with their level bombing attacks.

The effectiveness of the Fw 200 was rapidly nearing its end. In Norway at the end of November, 1. and 2./KG 40 had moved from Trondheim to begin conversion to the He 177, leaving only *Hptm.* Robert Maly's

3./KG 40 behind. Somewhat confusingly, *Hptm*. Kurt Herzog's 2./KG 40 was made subordinate to III./KG 40 of which Robert Kowalewski had yielded command to *Hptm*. Walter Rieder as he moved to the post of *Kommodore* of KG 30. Not until 24 November did the Condor-equipped 2./KG 40 swap designation with *Maj*. Fritz Hoppe's He 177-equipped 8./KG 40, returning III./KG 40 to a *Gruppe* equipped only with Fw 200s, I./KG 40 operating mainly He 177s with a small number of Fw 200s flying predominantly from occupied Norway, and II./KG 40 solely He 177s after conversion from Do 217s and Me 410s.

Three Condors of I./KG 40 – now listed officially on the strength of III./KG 40 as I.*Gruppe* had converted to He 177s – mounted a rare offensive sweep over Iceland during February 1944, sinking the 7,264GRT British tanker *El Grillo* lying at anchor in Seidisfjord with a cargo of 9,000 tons of fuel oil. On a fine day with good visibility, the three attacking aircraft released five bombs from a height estimated at 300 metres, three falling only twenty feet from the tanker's port side and one the same distance to starboard, the last exploding wide to starboard. All detonated underwater, the pressure wave rupturing the hull and flooding the forward hold. As all fuel storage tanks were full, the only reserve buoyancy was the fore hold and engine room and *El Grillo* settled rapidly by the head, distress signals being transmitted as the starboard Oerlikon cannon fired ineffectually at the retreating Condors. Within fifteen minutes the foredeck was awash, and ten minutes later the entire bow submerged, all forty-eight crew abandoning ship and picked up by a Norwegian drifter before the tanker sank in twenty-five fathoms of water.

With the eclipse of the Condor, *Fliegerführer Atlantik* had already begun to rely more heavily on the Heinkel He 177 and Dornier Do 217 to shoulder the burden of its anti-shipping war. On 22 August Dönitz urged *Fliegerführer Atlantik* to provide Do 217 aircraft equipped with 'Kehlgerät' to support a scheduled departure the next day of several U-boats from Western France. Göring had previously issued a directive that the 'Kehlgerät' was to receive its baptism of fire against a large convoy target for maximum damage, and *Luftflotte* 4 appealed for a decision on Dönitz's request from the *Reichsmarshall*. However, Allied patrol forces had been detected in increasing numbers once more within the Bay of Biscay and in Berlin, *SKL* advised Luftwaffe Operations Staff of the urgent necessity of sending the requested Do 217s to *Fliegerführer Atlantik*, emphasising that such a deployment 'must have priority over actions against convoys which, in any case, had begun to evade in an area beyond the range of the Do 217'.[22] Within twenty-four hours Göring ordered compliance with Dönitz's wishes, and the Dornier aircraft were instructed to attack British warships cruising off the north-west corner of Spain in cooperation with aircraft to intercept U-boats on the 'Piening' U-boat route that hugged the Spanish coast and its promised protection of neutral waters.

Fink's *2.Fliegerdivision* – under the command of Richthofen's *Luftflotte* 2 headquartered in Frascati, Rome – controlled the Dornier Do 217K-2s of *Hptm*. Bernhard Jope's III./KG 100, Jope having succeeded Ernst Hetzel in late July after the *Gruppe* had trained in the use of the 'Fritz-X'. The *Gruppe* had then deployed to Istres in southern France, some sixty kilometres north-west of Marseille, while a single *Kette* was based in Foggia, southern Italy. Likewise *Maj*. Franz Hollweg's II./KG 100 equipped with Do 217E-5s and but armed instead with Hs 293 glide bombs had moved to Istres also under Fink's command before being transferred to Cognac, only fifty kilometres from Royan, and placed under the control of *Fliegerführer Atlantik* (*Luftflotte* 3) for a period of two months, awaiting the opportunity to demonstrate the capability of the new weapon.

5

Fractured Axis

Defending Sicily and Italy

IN THE MONTHS FOLLOWING the collapse of Axis North Africa, intense Allied bombing of Sicilian and southern Italian airfields continued, claiming casualties as the Luftwaffe was reduced to flying little more than reconnaissance missions over the western Mediterranean. Kriegsmarine and Luftwaffe staffs already recognised that such systematic bombing heralded a probable Anglo-American seaborne landing but in Berlin, Hitler's attention remained focussed elsewhere as the ambitious Operation *Zitadelle* had begun near Kursk, absorbing large numbers of ground-attack aircraft in support of what remained the cream of Germany's armoured forces.

Strong winds swept across Sicily on the night of 9/10 July, lulling defenders into a false sense of security. An Allied deception operation codenamed *Barclay* also contributed greatly to a widely-held belief in Berlin that any potential invasion mounted from North Africa would be directed at the Balkans, not, as Mussolini feared, Sicily. Correspondingly, available Luftwaffe strength was spread thinly from southern France to Crete; the number of aircraft, of all types, based in the eastern Mediterranean more than doubling between May and July from 125 machines to 305, the majority fighters or Ju 87 dive-bombers.

On Sicily, heavy air attacks presaged the actual day of the invasion. The seaplane base at Syracuse was among those targets attacked, nine Wellington bombers of RAF 205 Group successfully bombing the harbour which accommodated 6.*Seenotstaffel* and 10.*Seenotflotilla*. The *Staffel* was compelled to move first to Taranto, then Vigna di Valle (near Rome), Portofino, La Spezia-Cadimare and, finally, to German-occupied Venice in October and was thereafter confined to Adriatic operations.

During 9 July, Bülowius' II.*Fliegerkorps'* forward headquarters at Taormina was attacked three times, destroying the central regional Luftwaffe telephone exchange.[1] In the air, Luftwaffe aircraft sighted what they reported to be strong landing formations approaching from

Malta–Pantelleria, five convoys detected north of Malta totalling approximately 150 to 180 vessels, including what were identified as two probable battleships sailing a north-north-westerly course. Fears of a landing operation against Sicily getting underway appeared confirmed by repeated reconnaissance details provided by *Luftflotte* 2 that night; heavy formations sighted heading towards the Sicilian coast, although naval staff indicated that 'the exactitude of these reports is still uncertain. In many cases, the observations were made by fighter pilots inexperienced in reconnaissance.'[2] Destruction of both the telephone connections and the II.*Fliegerkorps* headquarters complicated matters, hampering the ability to form a full immediate picture of an obviously developing situation. Nonetheless, Bülowius' staff issued clearly worded reports of an imminent extensive invasion of Sicily to Kesselring as *Oberbefehlshaber Südost*, via Kriegsmarine command in Italy. As Kesselring remained frustrated by the fog of war, despite inclement blustery weather Allied paratroopers began landing a little before midnight, heralding the opening of Operation *Husky* and the Allied invasion of Sicily.

In early morning darkness, landing craft were loaded with men of the US Seventh Army bound for beaches in the south-western Gulf of Gela, while the British Eighth Army landed to the south-east in the Gulf of Noto. Despite a strong offshore wind, the landings were successful in the face of demoralised Italian defenders in disarray after intense bombardment. Not until the half-light before dawn did the Luftwaffe and *Regia Aeronautica* respond, their strongest attacks against the western American landing areas. There, US Navy ships were sometimes as far as six miles offshore, covering USAAF fighters stretched to provide protection for both they and the smaller craft shuttling from ship to shore. Off Licata – designated sector 'Joss' – where the American 3rd Division was landing, minesweeper USS *Sentinel* of Naval Task Group 86.3 was on anti-submarine patrol, flares dropping inshore of *Sentinel* illuminated the ship for Ju 88 dive-bombers, a single bomb exploding near the ship's starboard quarter, followed by a flurry of other near misses that slashed a hole one foot wide and eight feet long in the aft engine room. At no point were the Junkers seen, though the sound of their engines pulling out of the dive was clearly audible despite thunderous anti-aircraft fire. The forward magazine, wardroom and crew compartments were holed, and the after engine room wrecked and flooding quickly as auxiliary engines were started despite lubricating oil lines being ruptured by the blast. Casualties had depleted damage control and engine room personnel.

With the radio room wrecked, ship-wide interior communications, except for one sound-powered telephone circuit, were disabled. Four further attacks followed, two being repulsed without bombs being dropped before a third at 0525hrs managed to disable the forward 3in gun, with two men killed, another blown overboard and the gun's recoil mechanism shot away. The port-side 20mm anti-aircraft gun was also put out of action with men killed by strafing that caused casualties on the bridge as well. One further bomb sealed the ship's fate, holing the forward engine room; surviving gunners claiming definite hits on two Me 210s before the badly listing minesweeper was ordered abandoned. Fresh waves of bombers were now visible in the dawn light as patrol and landing craft came to the crew's assistance. USS *Sentinel* finally capsized at 1030hrs, the hull sinking within fifteen minutes. Nine of the crew had been killed and fifty-one wounded, twenty-five later hospitalised in Bizerte. A single man, the gunner blown overboard, was listed as missing.

USS *Sentinel* listing off Licata after a Luftwaffe attack, soon capsizing thereafter. (Naval History and Heritage Command NH 89208)

Thirty kilometres east, in the central American invasion sector code-named 'Dime' centred on the fishing town of Gela, bombs and flares had also begun falling in the pre-dawn darkness, as the first Italian and German air attacks began. Within a little over thirty minutes, the destroyer USS *Maddox* was hit in the forward magazine by an Italian Ju 87 Stuka about sixteen miles offshore and sank within two minutes taking 212 of her crew to the bottom. As the bombing continued, *LST-345* and the submarine chaser *PC-621* were damaged in collision while undertaking evasive manoeuvres, the light cruiser USS *Savannah* claiming one Ju 88 shot down at 0514hrs. Axis fighters and fighter-bombers made low-level approaches from Catania, flying beneath the Allies' radar screen by following the contours of the Acate River canyon at the eastern edge of the Gela beachhead. Meanwhile, Allied fighters patrolling at altitude intent on engaging bombers were frequently misidentified and fired on by naval gunners, several being lost as proximity-fused anti-aircraft ammunition was employed for the first time in the European theatre.

Focke-Wulf Fw 109 and Bf 110 fighter-bombers attacked the Gela beachhead during the early afternoon in support of a ground assault

Luftwaffe bombs fall on shipping off Gela as LCIs manoeuvre towards shore.

made by armoured units of the Hermann Göring Division, though this counterattack stalled in the face of intense naval bombardment. As the panzers withdrew, the reserve force of the US 2nd Armored Division and 18th Infantry Regiment began landing to reinforce the beachhead. The 1,490GRT *LST-313* began offloading anti-tank artillery via a swiftly erected pontoon causeway when a *Kette* of Fw 190s attacked with bombs and machine-gun fire, one bomb striking *LST-313*'s port main deck at an oblique angle, penetrating the main and tank decks and detonating in the void to starboard. The force of the explosion ignited ammunition and land mines loaded aboard trucks awaiting disembarkation, blowing the elevator upwards onto the forecastle guns. Twenty-one men were killed, and a fierce blaze swept through stored vehicles, gasoline and ammunition. Though the structural damage caused by the bomb had been relatively minor, fires accelerated rapidly, fed by subsequent explosions and causing mayhem among the men aboard, unable to fight the blaze with hoses due to a fractured fire main. Equipment and bodies were hurled skyward by the force of some explosions, the LST was soon in flames from stem to stern. Lieutenant Samuel Hugh Alexander ordered her abandoned, he being the last to leave after ensuring survivors had been evacuated, and later awarded the Navy Cross for his actions. The LST was left to burn, later recorded by the US Navy was 'the worst LST fire on record . . . It is improbable that any firefighting facilities would have been adequate in such a situation where the cargo is so inflammable that any fire, once started, is apt to spread with uncontrollable rapidity.'[3] Continuing explosions aboard the burning hulk scattered the pontoon causeway, causing nearby *LST-312* to broach and preventing any other immediate offloading of supplies. Over the course of the following days, the fires gradually burnt themselves out. *LST-313* was deemed too badly damaged for repair and was towed offshore and scuttled by the US Navy in fifty metres of water.

Above the British landings sectors there was little Axis air activity. A half-hearted bombing attack on the anchorage off Canadian beachhead 'Bark West' dropped a stick of bombs near HMS *Hambeldon* and *Wallace* but to no effect. Though flares were again dropped illuminating the target area, the anchorage was heavily protected by smokescreens. Two LCTs were damaged off 'Bark East' sector during raids by Ju 88s and Fw 190s as well as near misses on SS *Bergensfjord* and *LST-407*, though once again of no appreciable consequence.

LST 313 in flames off Gela following a Focke-Wulf fighter-bomber attack, killing twenty-one men.

During the first twenty-four hours of Operation *Husky*, *Luftflotte 2* had managed approximately three hundred sorties of all types against the invasion beachheads, as opposed to the Allies whose Desert Air Force alone flew more than 3,000. Though the Luftwaffe claimed one cruiser and four transports hit, as well as damage to landing craft, their attacks had no impact on Operation *Husky*, the Allies having braced themselves for considerably greater loss amongst the invasion shipping; expecting at worst the destruction of three hundred craft but losing only twelve from all causes. Nevertheless, though the attackers may not have had the operational strength or value of bygone years, their effect on the invading force was profound, as related in the pages of the US Navy's Armed Guard official history:

> Other Armed Guard voyage reports testify to the severity of the battle for the eastern beachhead on Sicily during the first few days. Practically every merchant ship off the beaches had one or more close calls. All fired continually at the enemy and thereby kept his bombing from being much more accurate and deadly. In truth, there was probably no action in the European theatre in which merchant ships participated which was more dangerous and more bitterly fought than that for eastern Sicily.[4]

German and Italian fighter and fighter-bomber aircraft were based mainly in Sicily, Sardinia and southern Italy, while the Luftwaffe twin-engine *Zerstörer*, which numbered about seventy-five aircraft, were divided between Sicilian and northern Italian airfields. In central Italy the Luftwaffe maintained its Ju 88 night-fighter force, most bombers and long-range reconnaissance units having relocated from Sicily to either southern France or northern Italy. While the potential threat against the Balkans remained foremost in German planning, some 180 Italian and 265 German aircraft – including 130 bombers, dive-bombers, and reconnaissance aircraft – remained in the Aegean area.

Air raids against the *Husky* beaches intensified during the second day as merchant ships arrived carrying reinforcements and supplies for the men fighting ashore. Within the American sector, three ships hove to off Gela including the Liberty ship SS *Robert Rowan* carrying ammunition and over 400 men; its crew, naval gunners and soldiers from the US Seventh Army. Artillery fire from ashore straddled the ship, wounding one embarked soldier, before the cruiser USS *Boise*'s counterbattery fire silenced the guns. Then, during the afternoon, Ju 88s of KG 6 and KG 54 mounted a high-level raid missing *Boise* with bombs but squarely hitting *Robert Rowan*. Flames swiftly overwhelmed the heavily laden vessel and, fearing a sympathetic explosion of stored ammunition, the crew and passengers were ordered to abandon ship, which remarkably they did without loss, thanks in large part to the bravery of neighbouring vessels that mounted a swift evacuation. Six minutes after the last man had left the ship, at 1635hrs, the stored ammunition in No 2 hold exploded, followed within twenty minutes by a final terrifying blast that blew the ship in two and sent a column of smoke thousands of feet into the air. Debris was flung across the entire area and the burning ship settled on the shallow seabed, an American destroyer attempting unsuccessfully to extinguish the flames lest they provide a beacon for night bomber attacks. *Robert Rowan* continued to smoulder for several days illuminating anchored ships by night to the benefit of German and Italian aircrews who added magnesium flares to shine their cold white light over the troops below.

Perhaps the ship most fortunate to escape serious damage off Gela on 11 July was the SS *Nicholas Gilman*. During the course of the early morning it was fired on by tanks of the Hermann Göring division, wounding one of the naval Armed Guard aboard. Later, in the attack that sank *Robert Rowan*, ten bombs landed close enough to be categorised as

SS *Robert Rowan* explodes off Gela after being hit by bombs from Junkers of KG 6 and KG 54.

near misses, five more later in the afternoon, one bomb striking No 1 hatch, causing fires that were swiftly brought under control. Throughout the day and for the following week, the ship's gunners slept at their action stations and were credited with shooting down two aircraft and assisting in the destruction of a third.

Near Licata the American *LST-158* was hit at 0810hrs by a bomb from an Fw 190 that struck directly amidships. Badly damaged, the burning hulk was beached as flames eventually gutted the entire vessel. Thirty-three US Army and six US navy personnel were killed. Further tragedy followed above the American beachhead later that evening. A fresh bombing raid of Gela at 2150hrs resulted in near misses recorded by USS *Boise* and several destroyers. With minor damage from bomb fragments on both naval and merchant ships, Allied fighters joined the melee amidst an intense volume of anti-aircraft fire. As the Luftwaffe began to withdraw, into this inferno flew C-47 and C-53 transport aircraft carrying Major General Matthew B. Ridgeway's 504th Parachute Infantry Regiment, en-route to an airborne drop to reinforce elements of the 82nd Airborne already in action. The leading flight began jumping on to the Gela-Farello landing ground at 2240hrs, five minutes ahead of schedule, but the second flight was within sight of its objective when first a single machine gun, and then almost every anti-aircraft battery both afloat and ashore opened fire on the slow-moving aircraft. Despite the navy having been informed of this planned paratrooper transport lift, tense and exhausted gunners stressed by the power of the aerial bombardment had misidentified the aircraft. Eight pilots immediately aborted their mission and returned to North Africa, one later finding his aircraft to have a thousand bullet and shrapnel holes in its fuselage. Those pilots who had managed to reach land dropped paratroopers wherever they could, several landing in the sea. At his command post ashore in Scoglitti, General Bradley, the II Corps commander, watched in helpless fury as the troop carrier formation was cut to pieces.

Some paratroopers were killed while still aboard their aircraft, others hit while descending and even a small number killed after landing by Allied troops who had plainly lost control. Over 300 American paratroopers were massacred in the friendly fire incident. In the British sector, the same tragedy overtook some of the 1,856 men of the British 1st Parachute Brigade that approached Sicily later that night. Thirty-three aircraft strayed from their course and passed over an Allied convoy in the darkness, which shot down four of the transports, killing all on board.

Several sharp air raids had already been recorded on 11 July off the British landing sectors 'Acid South' and 'North' and at 1235hrs the Dutch ammunition carrier 5,481GRT SS *Baarn* lying at anchor received a near miss from a bomb dropped by an attacking Ju 88 that ignited petrol stored in No 1 hold. Flames spread rapidly and, faced with the risk of stored ammunition exploding, the Dutch freighter was quickly abandoned and scuttled in forty-two metres of water. A second ship, SS *Joseph C. Cannon* received a direct hit, the bomb exploding in No 5 hold, the hold and propeller shaft alley swiftly filling up and the ship settling heavily by the stern. Fortunately, as the hold was nearly empty there was no subsequent fire and *Joseph C. Cannon* was later repaired in Malta.

Strong fighter protection thwarted most attempted attacks over the days that followed, though the hospital ship *Dorsetshire* – clearly marked and illuminated – was attacked and suffered some structural damage and casualties from near misses on 12 July, while HMS *Eskimo*, three miles south of Cape Murro, was hit in Nos 5 and 6 fuel tanks, retreating to Malta for repair under tow by HMS *Tartar*. The freighter

SS *Ocean Peace* was attacked off 'Jig' Sector at dawn, a near miss at the fore end igniting cased petrol in No 1 hold and the ship hurriedly scuttled to prevent explosion.

With the Luftwaffe's Stuka strength in the Eastern Mediterranean, it was left to the *Regia Aeronautica*'s Ju 87s to try their hand at penetrating the defending aerial umbrella over the Sicilian beachheads.[5] Four Ju 87Ds of 207° *Squadriglia* based at Bocca di Falco airfield near Palermo, opened the Italian dive-bombing attacks on the day of the first landings. Within twenty-four hours, another Stuka unit, 121° *Gruppo*, was hurriedly formed with twelve Ju 87Rs and rushed to Gioia del Colle airfield from where seven of them began launching attacks under escort by Macchi 202 fighters. On 13 July the Liberty ship SS *Timothy Pickering* was hit by Italian Ju 87s off the landing beach of Avola, in the British sector code-named 'Acid North'. This was to be the pinnacle of their most successful raid, the freighter carrying a full cargo of war supplies and laying at anchor a mile offshore for its turn to unload. Aboard the ship were 128 men of the British 57th Anti-Tank Regiment, twenty-three naval defensive gunners and a crew of forty-three.

The weather was clear, the sea choppy, ruffled by a south-westerly breeze and the sun almost directly overhead. Other ships lay nearby also at anchor when the first dive-bombers appeared overhead. Only one hit the Liberty ship, a single 250kg bomb striking No 4 hold, penetrating the deck and exploding in the engine room and No 4 deep tank. Parts of the stored cargo blew up and fire broke out amidships, a twenty-foot hole blown in the starboard hull, and the deck lifted off above. From the destroyed cargo, fragments were propelled in all direction, showering the Liberty ship SS *O. Henry* with debris and a flying truck wheel which killed one soldier on board. All the ship's machinery was damaged except for the anchor which remained fast. *Timothy Pickering* began to immediately settle by the stern and survivors started abandoning ship, most picked up by nearby landing craft or anchored ships, but the loss of life was heavy. Of the British troops aboard there was only a single survivor, while sixteen gunners and twenty-two crewmen were also killed, the smouldering remains of the wreck later being scuttled by a Royal Navy destroyer.

Despite such events, the invasion of Sicily was never jeopardised by German or Italian air power. Now fighting a two-front war, Hitler had cancelled the remainder of Operation *Zitadelle* by 13 July after it had become bogged down. Berlin still viewed the greatest Allied

Mediterranean threat to likely be directed soon at the Balkans, or possibly southern France, the probable loss of Sicilian air bases also bringing Allied air power closer to northern Italian industrial centres and those in Romania and southern Germany. For the Italians, the matter remained clear. Mainland Italy would soon come under direct attack for which it was unprepared militarily, psychologically and politically. The fall of Tunis and then Pantelleria had already led most Italians to finally admit the war was lost, the invasion of Sicily merely confirming the fact. General Vittorio Ambrosio, Chief of Staff of the Italian Army, believed the only path left open for his country was to withdraw from the Axis and seek peace. He pressed Mussolini to tell this to Hitler face to face in a meeting scheduled to take place in a villa near the northern Italian town of Feltre but Mussolini had baulked at the chance to be so direct, overpowered by the German dictator's presence and his own inferiority. That night the Allies heavily bombed Rome for the first time and Mussolini abruptly left the meeting, much to Hitler's chagrin. Germany had lost the final vestiges of faith that it had once had in its Italian ally, aware that defence of the Italian mainland and the Balkan region would fall squarely on their shoulders.

During *Husky*'s first week, the Luftwaffe response had been fractured and of little real concern to the Allies. Though brief localised successes were experienced, most raids were little more than nuisance value, and strong anti-aircraft and fighter defences forced an over-reliance on small fighter-bomber attacks. The Luftwaffe action against invasion shipping was not strictly speaking a maritime offensive, more the use of available dive-bombers and fighter-bombers against targets of opportunity that happened to include targets on the water. Torpedo aircraft of Fink's *2.Fliegerdivision* were unable to attack inshore Allied vessels as the depth of water was thought insufficient to allow successful use of the weapon. The ironic twist to this fact was that the Luftwaffe's front-line stock of F5 *Lufttorpedo* stood at its highest-ever level. Despite the heavy construction requirements of chromium, aluminium, lead, tin and copper for each torpedo, during July production reached its pinnacle when 693 were added to those already held in stock, bringing the number held to 2,620. Of those only 95 were used in action, as opposed to 145 the previous month.

Despite inshore invasion shipping considered impossible to attack by torpedo, offshore transport convoys were targeted, but by crews that were frequently inexperienced and seemingly unable, or unwilling, to press

Junkers Ju 88s of KG 26.

home their attacks. Resulting successes were few and casualties relatively high, including the loss of *Hptm*. Hans-Detlef Spiering, *Staffelkapitän* of 7./KG 26, posted as missing in action after his Ju 88 A-4 , '1H+AR', was shot down while attacking ships between Syracuse and Catania.

It was the dive-bombing attacks of the II.*Fliegerkorps'* Ju 88s that carried the brunt of the offensive against *Husky* shipping, although several of the more experienced maritime formations had been withdrawn following grievous losses since the fall of Tunis. The aircraft of *Maj*. Wilhelm Stemmler's KG 77 were extracted from their increasingly bombed Italian airfields, I and II.*Gruppe* transferring during July to East Prussia where they were to rest and re-equip as torpedo *Gruppen*.[6] Only II.*Gruppe* remained in Italy, based at Piacenza near Milan, using Foggia and Rome-Ciampino as forward staging points. At the latter they lost five Ju 88A-4s in a severe bombing raid mounted by USAAF B-25 and B-26 bombers of the North-west Africa Airforce on 19 July. Escorted by P-38 Lightnings, the bombers wrecked buildings and aircraft facilities, heavily cratering the airfield and dispersal stations and – in addition to those aircraft lost by KG 77 – destroyed twelve Do 217 K-1s, three Do 217 E-4s, another Ju 88 A-4, one He 111 H-3, three Ju 52s and a single Fieseler Storch 156.

During August the depleted *Gruppe* departed Piacenza for Barth where they underwent training in shadowing techniques and for future use as pathfinders. *Major* Peter Schnoor's IV./KG 77 had already departed Montpelier the previous May, flying occasional anti-shipping missions over the Baltic Sea from Gross-Schiemanen airfield in East Prussia.

Of *Oblt.* Volprecht Riedesel Freiherr zu Eisenbach's KG 54, only its staff and III.*Gruppe* remained in Italy, based at Grottaglie, in the Italian heel fourteen kilometres from Taranto, which had come under repeated bombing attack since June. Both I. and II./KG 54 had departed after the fall of Tunis for refurbishment at Ingolstadt and would not return to the Mediterranean until September. To replace the Ju 88 units removed from the region had come I. and II./KG 1 from the eastern front, basing at Airasca near Turin in northern Italy, and I. and III./KG 6 from northern France to Foggia.

Three Dornier Do 217Ks of Jope's III./KG 100 attempted to use the 'Fritz-X' for the first time on the night of 20/21 July against shipping at Augusta harbour. Attacking in conjunction with Ju 88s of I. and II./KG 1 and III./KG 54, the raid marked the first operational deployment of the guided weapon, although the *Kette* that had taken off from Foggia airfield for their twilight mission were driven off by medium and light naval anti-aircraft fire as they approached from the direction of Messina. No chance presented itself for missile launch, and the aircraft returned to Foggia with weapons intact, only narrowly avoiding overshooting the runway with the increased onboard burden. This small advance *Kette* of Dorniers withdrew to Istres only ten days later to rejoin the remainder of III./KG 100, after Foggia airfield was heavily bombed on 15 July, destroying ten stationary aircraft.

Of the remaining Ju 88s involved in the attack on Augusta, two were shot down by anti-aircraft fire, but in return the 7,056GRT SS *Empire Florizel* and the 7,174GRT SS *Ocean Virtue* were sunk, though the latter remained aground on an even keel allowing cargo to be unloaded and the ship salvaged, later remodelled as a cargo liner. *Empire Florizel* had been carrying 4,000 tons of military stores, a crew of forty-eight and twenty-one gunners, as well as fourteen passengers. Of these, two crewmen, four gunners and three passengers were killed. The 7,131GRT British freighter *Fort Pelly* bearing cased petrol and 3,300 tons of military stores was also hit and caught fire, the flames causing some damage to American SS *William T. Coleman* moored to the same buoy. Attempting to escape, the Liberty ship ran aground and was endangered by the pool of burning oil spreading around the British ship whose stored ammunition cargo soon exploded, spraying debris in all directions and killing thirty-two of the forty-seven crewmen aboard and six of twenty-three gunners

In Rome, the seemingly inevitable fall of Mussolini happened on 25 July, proving a pivotal moment in the battle for Sicily. Ambrosio, frustrated at Mussolini's lack of candour with Hitler at Feltre, set in motion the coup-d'état to remove the Italian dictator; Mussolini was dismissed by King Victor Emmanuel III as head of the government and replaced by the sycophantic Marshal Pietro Badoglio. Italy's steep decline was hastened by Allied bombing, Italian forces in Sicily being on the brink of collapse, and nationwide food shortages and labour strikes for the first time since 1925. Mussolini was arrested and spirited away to incarceration at Campo Imperatore in Abruzzo. While Badoglio maintained public support for the alliance with Germany, he dissolved the Italian fascist party and initiated covert peace talks with the Allies, eventually negotiating an armistice to be linked to an Allied landing on mainland Italy.

German reinforcement of Sicily was immediately curtailed, and contingency plans prepared for evacuation from Sicily, Sardinia and Corsica. Two further operations were hurriedly prepared for potential immediate implementation: *Eiche*, the rescue of the incarcerated Mussolini by German troops, and *Student*, the planned occupation of Rome by Army Group B under the command of Erwin Rommel and restoration of Italian fascism. Badoglio's assurances of Italy's commitment to the Axis were justifiably treated with great suspicion by Hitler's government and in the event of an Italian armistice with the Allies, Operations *Achse* and *Schwarze* would also be carried out; the capture of the numerically powerful Italian Fleet by combined Kriegsmarine and Luftwaffe movements and seizure of key land-based Italian military positions respectively.

Dönitz was informed in a Berlin conference with Hitler that in the event of Rome's occupation the Kriegsmarine, with Luftwaffe support, would be responsible for the seizure of the Italian fleets in La Spezia, Taranto and Genoa as well as Italian merchantmen present in all ports. U-boats were also to be used as a cordon to destroy any Italian warships attempting to defect to the Allies, though they proved an abject failure. Dönitz and most ranking Wehrmacht officers did not believe that the fascist party would resume control of Italy regardless of Mussolini's personal situation, the dictator's resignation having been accepted by the populace without a murmur of protest. However, Hitler retained his belief that a liberated Mussolini would rally the country behind him once more as an Axis ally. Regardless, German defensive lines would be shortened if Italy collapsed entirely.

As July ended, the trickle of Allied maritime casualties to Luftwaffe attack continued, though aircraft serviceability was seriously affected by a lack of spare parts, effective airfields and the dislocation of ground staff between bases as Allied bombing continued to take its toll on regional airfields. By 19 July the serviceability of the Focke-Wulf 190 fighter-bombers in action against shipping off the beachheads had shrunk to thirty-five percent, and the Luftwaffe was left with little choice but to withdraw active units from Sicily, *Schnellkampfgeschwader* 10 relocating to Crotone in Calabria and *Schlachtgeschwader* 2 to Aquino, nine kilometres west of Cassino. On 23 July – and in raids over the course of that week – those newly-arrived Fw 190s were badly hit by bombing by NASAF B-26 Marauders, causing such destruction that many pilots of II./SChl.G. 2 were flown to Bari to pick up replacement aircraft.

With defeat in Sicily looming, in Berlin *OKW* remained firmly under the impression that the invasion of the island remained either a diversion, or a minor stepping stone before the main Allied blow would land elsewhere. On 28 July *SKL* recorded:

Intelligence Service reports, from Spanish source in Gibraltar, that the landing in Sicily is not the invasion of Europe and is regarded as of secondary importance. The main objective will rather be the Balkans, which will be approached from Turkey. More than one and a half million men and an enormous quantity of war materiel, which is still constantly being increased via the Persian Gulf and Trans-Jordan, are concentrated in Palestine, Iraq and Iran for that purpose. The first target would be the Dardanelles and Greece followed by an attack on Bulgaria and Romania both by land and from the Black Sea, with the aim of joining forces with Russia.

Besides this, another major operation is said to be planned against France, for which about 1,000,000 men, now on the North African Coast, are to be used. This operation is to be preceded by the conquest of Corsica. It is also said that naval demonstrations and landing attacks will be made on the Balkan coasts for a divisionary purpose.

Meanwhile, the evacuation of rear-echelon troops from Sicily began, full-scale evacuation only getting underway on 11 August. By skilful withdrawal of defensive lines and extremely effective Kriegsmarine transportation, the Wehrmacht extricated its troops from Sicily with minimal interference. The evacuation was completed within six days and the island fell to the Allies.

While the withdrawal was underway, both I. and III./KG 26 were ordered to renew torpedo operations against western Mediterranean convoys and forty He 111s from I./KG 26 and twenty Ju 88s (each with a single torpedo and drop tank) from III./KG 26 were readied to attack Convoy KMS21, reported at Gibraltar by German intelligence. KMS21 had left Liverpool as combined Convoy OS52/KMS21 on 19 July, splitting up nine days later as twenty-four ships arrived at Gibraltar and the remaining forty-two carried on towards various North African ports, the final ships ultimately bound for Port Said, Egypt. *Major* Klümper's *Geschwader* had been reinforced with the transfer of 1./Kü.F.Gr. 906 to III.*Gruppe*, redesignated 8./KG 26 and equipped with Ju 88A aircraft, marking the official end of *Küstenfliegergruppe* 906. While II./KG 26 remained in

A Heinkel He 111 of KG 26, the '*Löwe Geschwader*'.

Grossenbrode where they continued to re-equip with Ju 88s, Klümper's available aircraft comprised the backbone of the *Torpedofliegerverbände*. On 5 August the entire Luftwaffe torpedo force comprised:

I./Kü.Fl.Gr. 406 (twelve He 115C, ten serviceable), Sörreisa, Norway;

Stab and I./KG 26 (forty He 111C, twenty-five serviceable), Salon-de-Provence, France;

II./KG 26 (six Ju 88A, one serviceable), re-equipping in Grossenbrode, Germany;

III./KG 26 (twenty-one Ju 88A, fourteen serviceable), Montpellier, France;

Stab./KG 77 (one Ju 88A), training in Königsberg;

I./KG 77 (eleven Ju 88A, five serviceable), training and re-equipping in Grieslinen;

II./KG 77 (twelve Ju 88A, six serviceable), training and re-equipping in Wormditt.

The two KG 26 *Gruppen* stationed in the south of France were readied, carrying a total of 100 torpedoes into action against KMS21 near Alboran Island north of the Moroccan coast on 13 August. Klümper led the attack which flew in radio silence past the Balearic Islands before dividing into two waves, one for each *Gruppe*, the Heinkels of I./KG 26 opening the assault at 2054hrs.

The convoy was proceeding on a westerly course at 8 knots on a fine Mediterranean summer evening when the first wave of Heinkels struck. One slight casualty was suffered aboard the escorting Australian corvette HMAS *Gawler* after a sailor received a bullet wound in the thigh from strafing. None of the escorting ships suffered any significant damage, though there were further strafing casualties aboard several freighters. The Heinkels were first sighted in line-ahead formation, flying parallel to starboard of the convoy track at a distance estimated to be between twelve and fifteen miles. Only metres above the sea surface, they remained below radar detection height and kept barely above the visible horizon. The Heinkels then turned to attack out of the setting sun in line abreast as the escorting sloop HMS *Shoreham* opened fire on the weaving bombers at a range of 8,000 yards. The Heinkel formation broke up and attacks were made from all directions, torpedoes generally being released from between 2,000 and 3,000 yards. Several Heinkels passed between the convoy columns, turning to attack vessels on either side.

After their torpedoes had been released, the bombers dropped small bombs and opened fire with machine gun from an altitude of only 30 metres. The convoy returned fire, one Heinkel being hit and immediately disintegrating; six others seen to crash into the sea and claimed by Allied gunners, as others disengaged, trailing smoke.

Records giving the exact number of aircraft brought down appear to be contradictory, generally attributed to between six and four Ju 88A-4s of III./KG 26 and possibly nine Heinkels from I./KG 26, another ditching in the sea off Toulon after exhausting its fuel in the return flight. At least two men were fished out of the sea near the convoy and taken prisoner; *Lt.* Helmut Frommhold whose 9./KG 26 Ju 88 '1H+BT' had crashed with only Frommhold surviving, one of his dead crewmen, Walter Laterner, later washing ashore and being buried in a local cemetery on Alboran Island. *Oberfeldwebel* Heinz Jährling, of the same *Gruppe*, was also captured. *Feldwebel* Walter Kell's Ju 88 '1H+DS' of 8./KG 26 received enough damage to be forced to attempt an emergency landing at Reus Tarragona, Spain, where he and his crew were interned and later repatriated, the aircraft itself later being repaired and used by the Spanish Air Force. A second Junkers radioed that the engines had been severely hit as they began jettisoning guns, ammunition and a certain amount of fuel, but still failed to keep the aircraft airborne on an even keel. Klümper ordered the crew to head for Spanish territorial waters where it successfully ditched while his own radio operator signalled an international SOS. The German military attaché communicated the situation to the Spanish Navy who subsequently rescued the crew and, within four weeks, they too had been repatriated.

Despite the losses, there was some measure of jubilation within KG 26 as they claimed hits on at least thirty merchant ships and seven warships; an estimated 40 per cent success rate for torpedo launches made that day. Within three days of the attack, the official Wehrmacht news service broadcast the *Kampfgeschwader*'s success:

As already reported in a special announcement, during the early hours of 13 August a German torpedo *Geschwader* under the leadership of *Major* Klümper made a surprise attack on a heavily defended convoy entering the Mediterranean east of Gibraltar. In spirited attacks, or crews successfully scored torpedo hits on thirty-two ships. Two destroyers and four fully-laden merchant ships, including a tanker, sank immediately. Eight further ships were left burning and listing badly. With darkness approaching and because of heavy flak defences, the fate of the remaining torpedoed ships was, at first, unknown. However, reconnaissance later confirmed that at least 170,000GRT from the convoy was sunk or severely damaged. Seven of our own aircraft failed to return.

The reality was vastly different, extreme Luftwaffe overclaiming attributable to the fact that most crews involved were inexperienced, some only on their first combat mission. Only the American freighter SS *Francis W. Pettygrove* and the British SS *Empire Haven* had been successfully torpedoed, the latter taken in tow by the minesweepers HMS *Hythe* and *Rye* respectively and safely returned to Gibraltar. While *Empire Haven* lay there until 1946 awaiting repairs, the American Liberty ship was beached and declared a constructive total loss. Indeed, the defeat of the German attack was so complete that Admiral of the Fleet Sir Andrew Cunningham, Commander-in-Chief, Mediterranean Fleet, later signalled:

> I congratulate you, the escort force and convoy KMS 21 on your sturdy defence of convoy against heavy harassing attack. The enemy got a sore head he is likely to remember.

Justifiably satisfied with their defence against the torpedo bombers, in the Bay of Biscay the Royal Navy faced a new and intimidating threat. While in July the 'Fritz-X' had been unsuccessfully carried into action by III./KG 100 in the Mediterranean, II./KG 100 used the rocket-boosted Henschel Hs 293 for the first time off the northern tip of Spain on 25 August against Royal Navy ships engaged on Operation *Percussion*. The end of the highly successful operations *Musketry* and *Seaslug* had not indicated cessation of anti-submarine missions in Biscay. The RAF's Operation *Derange* – suspended in June and replaced by *Musketry* and *Seaslug* as U-boats gathered for mutual air defence – was briefly resumed on 2 August in the waters north-west of Cape Finisterre. However, Dönitz temporarily halted outward U-boat movements and ordered those inbound to gather and move through the 'Piening' route, including the inbound blockade breaking Japanese submarine *I8* which reached Brest at the end of August.

In an attempt to sever the 'Piening' route, the British launched the combined naval and air Operation *Percussion* on 23 August, which would last, intermittently, for five months focussing on waters off the south-west coast of France and comparatively close to the north coast of neutral Spain. The naval forces initially involved were the Royal Navy's

40th Escort Group and the Royal Canadian Navy's 5th Support Group strengthened by the light cruiser HMS *Bermuda* while, once again, the air component comprised Air Vice Marshal B.E. Baker's No 19 Group RAF Coastal Command.

Opening the operation, the 40th Escort Group – the frigates HMS *Exe*, *Moyola* and *Waveney*, and the sloops HMS *Landguard*, *Bideford* and *Hastings* – patrolled the north-west corner of Spain between Cape Ortegal and Cape Villano. As the Canadian 5th Support Group (the British frigates HMS *Nene* and *Tweed*, and the Canadian corvettes HMCS *Calgary*, *Edmundston* and *Snowberry*) arrived as relief, twelve Do 217E-5s escorted by seven V./KG 40 Ju 88C-6s were spotted approaching. Incorrectly identified as all Junkers, 40th Escort Group prepared for a level bombing attack, but were thrown off balance as the attacking aircraft turned to fly at distance on the starboard beam. Instead they braced for a possible torpedo attack as the Dorniers, led by *Hptm.* Heinz Molinnus, separated into groups of three, maintaining a range of approximately six miles. Aboard the British ships a puff of smoke was observed from the wing of one of the distant bombers, quickly developing into a streamer trailing a projectile, thought at first to be maintaining proximity to the aircraft but in fact headed on a constant bearing towards HMS *Landguard*. As it neared, the projectile was identified as a 'small aircraft' which ceased its brief smoke trail, evidently the ten-second rocket burst having exhausted the projectile's fuel. Headed directly for the ship, at about 1,200 feet distance the rocket banked abruptly to starboard, lost height and exploded 300 feet from *Landguard*'s starboard quarter. Two more were launched which similarly missed, though shrapnel sprayed the ship, and considerable damage was caused by shock waves. Aboard HMS *Bideford* the same style of attack was recorded, resulting in four near misses and one Hs 293 hitting the ship but failing to explode completely.

> The first hit the rigging, carried on and exploded on striking the water on the port side . . . The second passed across the bows and headed for the second ship (HMS *Landguard*). The third passed very close to the *Bideford*'s stem and burst on the port bow holing all forward compartments and causing casualties. Portions of filling from the bomb were recovered indicating only the type of filling . . . but partial detonation only had taken place . . . The fourth struck the water thirty yards short abreast the bridge, starboard side causing no damage.[7]

A Dornier Do 217 of KG 100.

The attack killed Able Seaman Charles W. Boardman and seriously wounded sixteen men aboard HMS *Bideford*.[8] For the Germans' part, *SKL* recorded the following result of the first Hs 293 attack:

> Owing to a number of technical failures and faulty operations only five near misses were scored on two destroyers. Most of the bombs went wide. One destroyer stopped, emitted a plume of white smoke, and blew up at 1450.[9]

Two days later a second attack on the *Percussion* ships was made by twelve Do 217s led by *Hptm*. Fritz Auffhammer, *Kommodore* of KG 100, escorted by seven 15./KG 40 Junkers Ju 88C-6 *Zerstörer*. At that time HMS *Bermuda*, departing to refuel at Plymouth, was replaced by the destroyers HMS *Grenville* and the Canadian HMCS *Athabaskan*. Lieutenant John Herbert RNVR was aboard HMS *Grenville* as the attack developed and later recounted his story to *The War Illustrated* in 1947:

> It was about 1 o'clock when the alarm sounded. Everyone in the wardroom made a dive for the door, and on reaching the bridge we found we were being attacked by around twenty Ju 88s which had come in very high but were now flying at about 3,000 feet circling around us. All ships had

broken formation and were now manoeuvring at high speed. Over towards Spain I saw a long line of splashes where a stick of bombs had fallen quite near to one of the frigates. The Captain ordered 'Open Fire', and the *Grenville* shuddered at the first salvo . . . Presently we noticed that several aircraft were flying parallel to each ship's course and not attempting to make the usual bombing attack. That was ominous, for the day before we had received a signal from another ship that had been attacked by aircraft armed with a new secret weapon.

Suddenly an object, looking rather like a paravane – a small body with short wings set in the middle – darted out from underneath the fuselage of the aircraft nearest to us. The bomb, which was emitting quantities of smoke from its tail where there seemed to be some kind of rocket propulsion, started off in the opposite direction to that in which we were going. When it was about 300 yards in front of the parent aircraft it started to turn towards us. The captain altered course and the bomb changed direction with us; it was approaching us fast now and everyone's gaze was fixed on this uncanny horror.

Lieutenant Commander Roger Percival Hill DSO, RN, ordered *Grenville* thrown hard to starboard at full speed and the incoming Hs 293 impacted in the ship's wake.[10] A second also missed as the destroyer continued to twist and turn with all guns blazing. For two other Royal Navy ships, however, the attack was far more effective. The sloop HMS *Egret* received a direct hit believed to have been launched by Auffhammer's observer *Oblt.* Otto Paulus that detonated either the magazine or stored depth charges, *Egret* exploding and rolling over to sink rapidly. Only thirty-five men were rescued, 198 going down with the ship. Among them were four RAF Y-Service electronics specialists, operating surveillance equipment installed to monitor Luftwaffe bomber communications.

Hauptmann Wolfgang Vorpahl, *Staffelkapitän* of 5./KG 100, also managed to hit HMCS *Athabaskan* squarely on the port side behind 'B' turret slightly aft of the bridge. Ironically, it appears that the Hs 293 had been set for the heavier armour of a cruiser and passed straight through the ship, exploding seven metres from her starboard side. In the path of the rocket projectile three men were killed and twelve hideously wounded by the scythe-like fins of the bomb. There was considerable damage in number one boiler room, and 'B' magazine; the provision room flooded and two fuel tanks opened to the sea. Due to its damaged hull the destroyer was only able to make a maximum of 15 knots as she limped back to Plymouth with all but one of the *Egret*'s survivors transferred aboard. The battered Canadian ship also carried fragments of the new weapon and traces of its fuel, allowing Allied Intelligence its first glimpse into this new threat.

Captain Godfrey Noel Brewer, RN, Senior Officer of 1st Support Group, immediately communicated with C-in-C Plymouth:

> From evidence of generally increased air activity and of today's attack I am convinced continuation of Spanish coast patrol will only lead to further loss of valuable ships without any compensating return of U-boats destroyed. The control of these bombs is extremely accurate and wide misses previously reported must have been due to mechanical failure.[11]

A meeting to discuss the new danger was called that same afternoon in Plymouth with representatives of the DGD (Director Gunnery Division), DTM (Division of Torpedoes and Mining) and DSD (Signals Division). Though the Hs 293 bombs were judged by the British to launch from 5,000 feet at a range of three to five miles, well beyond the range of defensive gunnery, it was considered that the shallow diving projectile could be dodged at speed and potentially exploded by Oerlikon fire.

The first attacks in the Bay of Biscay using this new weapon had been a moderate success for the Luftwaffe. While far from the onslaught envisioned by Göring against massed ships of an enemy convoy, the destruction of one destroyer and damaging of two others achieved largely what Dönitz had hoped as pressure on the 'Piening' route was eased. The appearance of this new weapon for which there was no immediate counter, the subsequent loss of HMS *Egret* and a simultaneous need to reinforce Atlantic convoy escorts led to a temporary withdrawal of *Percussion* forces from Biscay and the rerouting of Gibraltar convoys further to the west beyond Luftwaffe range.

In Italy, Allied deception operations continued to deflect German attention towards a potential invasion of the Balkans rather than the Italian mainland and their preparations continued unhindered. An initial landing across the Messina Strait by XIII Corps of the British Eighth Army – Operation *Baytown* – was planned for early September, though it was a move staunchly opposed by the Eighth Army commander General Bernard Montgomery as he believed the his troops would be better utilised in the main landing planned for the bay of Salerno – Operation

Avalanche – rather than the diversionary assault on Calabria. Nonetheless, his superior General Sir Harold Alexander believed that *Baytown* could both secure freedom of navigation through the Strait of Messina while also engaging Kesselring's troops defending southern Italy, preventing them from supporting those at Salerno. Decrypted signals intelligence had already betrayed the German decision to reinforce only the north of Italy, as well as the deeply fractured state of the Rome–Berlin Axis as Italy reached the breaking point of its unwelcome war. Their conclusion that the inevitable collapse of Italy would cause Germany to abandon its erstwhile ally and retreat to the northern border where Wehrmacht and Waffen-SS power was concentrated, erroneously led them to expect little serious defence of the Italian mainland. It was a costly mistake.

By the end of August, it had become obvious in Berlin that the quantity of Allied troops assembling in North Africa were most likely to be landed in southern Italy, far surpassing requirements necessary for operations against Sardinia or Corsica. Although an attack against Southern France had not been completely ruled out, it was considered unlikely with the distance that would be required by covering Allied aircraft, although the Balkans were still considered the ultimate objective.

German bombers directed by Peltz as *Kampffliegerführer Mittelmeer* had raided the embarkation port at Bizerte on several occasions, although its most successful attack had been the virtual destruction of Palermo's main dock on 1 August. During an early-morning raid by four waves of Do 217s (III./KG 100) and Ju 88s, the 2,708GRT British collier SS *Uskide* was destroyed and the American minesweepers USS *Strive* and *Skill* both damaged beneath the light of drifting magnesium flares. The minesweepers had only just towed the destroyer USS *Mayrant* into harbour after she had been damaged in the anchorage by Ju 88 dive-bombers. Railway cars carrying 900 tons of ammunition in the harbour area were set on fire and shell fragments from exploding ordnance rained down on ships in the harbour for hours. An LST was damaged by the bombing raid and strafing also caused casualties aboard the destroyer USS *Glennon*. Fortunately for the embarked troops of the American 9th Infantry Division, the five converted passenger liners and seven Liberty ships in which they waited offshore escaped the attention of the German bombers, disembarking their passengers later that morning in the shattered harbour following the end of a second raid. A further attack on Palermo was mounted on 4 August, met this time with fierce anti-aircraft fire after successful radar warning. USS *Shubrick* was hit amidships by a single bomb which caused flooding of two main machinery spaces and killed nine men, twenty others being wounded in the attack, eight of the latter so badly burned that they later died in hospital. During that morning, USS *Butler* sighted a drifting life raft and rescued *Fw.* Christian Köbke of 8./KG 30 who had bailed out of his Ju 88 four days previously. A third attempted raid on Palermo two days later was even less successful, the bombers driven off by Allied fighter cover.

Richthofen had become dissatisfied with Peltz's performance as *Kampffliegerführer Mittelmeer* and, despite Peltz being a favourite of Göring's, successfully replaced him during the middle of August with the experienced maritime pilot *Oberst* Walter Storp. Recently the *Kommodore* of KG 6, Storp was freshly promoted following wounds from an air raid on the KG 6 airfield at Aghero, Sardinia, on 28 June. He took control of the vacated dual post of *Kampffliegerführer Mittelmeer* and *Fernkampführer/Luftflotte* 2 on 17 August, Peltz appointed head of IX.*Fliegerkorps* based in Le Coudray-en-Thelle, near Beauvais during September.

As Allied preparations for the assault on Italy were completed, on 29 August Werner Klümper, *Kommodore* of KG 26, was decorated with the Knight's Cross. His promotion to *Oberstleutnant* would follow at the beginning of October, while in the meantime the torpedo and missile aircraft of 2.*Fliegerdivision* resumed sporadic operations. By 20 August, only five of the thirty Do 217s of Jope's III./KG 100 were operational. Nevertheless, nine days later launching an attack in the western Mediterranean. Luftwaffe reconnaissance reported a carrier force having recently departed Gibraltar, the Dorniers scrambling to intercept until the target formation reversed course and returned to harbour. Instead, the airborne bombers carrying 'Fritz-X' bombs were directed towards a potential battleship and light cruiser sailing eastwards north of Alboran. The attack was launched in the last glimmering twilight between 2105 and 2130hrs from an altitude of 6,500 metres, enemy fighters spotted 1,000 metres below but remaining oblivious to the Dorniers. Due to what was described by the German pilots as the 'remarkable breadth' of the largest vessel, she was believed to be a battleship, and a direct hit was claimed, the missile striking the ship to starboard and bringing it to a halt. Another hit was claimed on the cruiser's stern that resulted in a cloud of fire and smoke. A third missile missed the cruiser by about ten meters as the Dorniers broke away, unable to make further observations due to the onset of darkness.

The targets had actually been the fighter direction ship HMS *Ulster Queen* and the escorting 'Hunt' class destroyer HMS *Cleveland*, neither being badly damaged though *Ulster Queen*'s engines were disabled by a near miss, the ship returning to Gibraltar the following day with tug assistance. Bomb fragments found aboard betrayed the use of the 'Fritz-X', no radar contact having been made with the attacking aircraft which were not sighted although some crew members reported the faint sound of distant aircraft engines. The incoming missile was sighted at the last moment; reports of a slight green trail of light and whirring 'hiss' coming from it about two seconds before detonation, later incorrectly attributed to a rocket motor.

A conventional torpedo attack against a convoy of transports and aircraft carriers was carried out on the evening of 2 September by thirty-four combined He 111 and Ju 88 aircraft west of the Algerian port of Tenes. Eight aircraft reached their target and launched torpedoes, claiming damage to three steamers. Drifting, patchy haze limited visibility, allowing the aircraft to approach relatively close after being mistakenly identified by US Navy escorts as friendly. The first torpedoes narrowly missed USS *Tillman*, saved by rapid evasive manoeuvring, the torpedo passing slightly ahead and down the ship's port side. USS *Kendrick*, patrolling astern of the convoy at 12.5 knots, was targeted by two torpedoes launched by Lt. Karl Rath's He 111H-11 of I./KG 26 from a range of 1,500 yards on the starboard quarter. The American destroyer swung hard left to 'comb' the torpedo tracks, one missing to port while the other detonated against the trailing edge of the rudder which was in the amidships position. The rudder and steering gear were destroyed and the stern severely damaged and crumpled, part of the ship's main battery also being put out of action. Though the shafts were thrown out of alignment, both propellers remained undamaged and the engines functioned normally, one minor electrical fire being quickly extinguished. The ship did not develop any list, although a slight change in trim by the stern resulted. Two depth charges thrown off the stern detonated about 150 yards astern of *Kendrick* as her speed momentarily dipped to 10 knots immediately after impact but she returned to her original speed within two minutes.

Two of *Kendrick*'s 40mm anti-aircraft guns continued firing, one of the regular gun captains being stunned by the blast and his place taken by Alvin T. Burleigh, Gunner's Mate 3rd Class, who directed fire that successfully shot down Rath's Heinkel flying only fifty metres above the water.[12] With one man killed in the engine room by the attack, and two seriously injured, *Kendrick* initially held position astern of the convoy before being directed to Oran, steering at reduced speed using her engines. American crewmen threw life rings to Rath and his crew seen in the water where their Heinkel had gone down, their position being reported by radio although they were never recovered.[13]

On 3 September, British troops crossed the Strait of Messina and landed on the toe of Italy at Reggio Calabria, Montgomery soon proved correct in his objections. As he had expected, Kesselring declined to strongly oppose the British landings, correctly deducing it to be a diversion and the main Allied effort being likely to be directed either at Salerno or, more worryingly, closer to Rome, perhaps at Anzio. While the latter possibility presented greater peril to Kesselring, potentially cutting the Italian mainland in two and isolating southern units, it also presented greatest risk for the Allies being beyond effective fighter protection range, other than those that could be accommodated on aircraft carriers. Interestingly, even as the first British troops had come ashore in Calabria, the German naval staff remained convinced that it still did not herald an all-out attack against Italy.

Kesselring in conversation with *Maresciallo d'Italia* Ugo Cavallero, Chief of the Italian Supreme Command until January 1943. Kesselring was an avowed Italophile and initially refused to believe that the Italians would abandon the Axis.

> At the moment Naval Staff considers that this operation has been solely undertaken to gain a bridgehead and to complete the defence of the Strait of Messina. This will probably be followed by the occupation of Calabria and Apulia with a view to crossing the Adriatic to the Balkans. A campaign on the Apennine peninsula towards northern Italy seems less likely, nor would it fit in with the British temperament.[14]

Luftwaffe reconnaissance identified Allied landing craft previously assembled between Mers-el-Kebir and Tunis moving eastward and two days later it became obvious that large numbers had also departed Bizerte and entered the latitude of southern Calabria. Because of the scale of these developments, Kesselring reasoned them too large for mere tactical landings in support of the British Eighth Army, or even an attack against Sardinia, looking instead for a likely major invasion of the Italian mainland. In Calabria German troops of the 19th Panzergrenadier and 26th Panzer Divisions withdrew before the British advance, demolishing bridges and blocking roads, leaving the inhospitable terrain to take care of slowing any progress made by *Baytown* forces. Still, Kesselring was firmly opposed to the abandonment of the Puglian plains with its valuable airbases and pleaded with Hitler to release Wehrmacht or Waffen-SS units held in northern Italy to enable formation of a southern defensive line. It had been Rommel who had first proposed defending only northern Italy, an idea Hitler embraced, and he denied the request.

The Luftwaffe likewise made little effort to interfere with *Baytown*, Storp instead spending the brief respite since the fall of Sicily husbanding whatever resources he could and resting his exhausted bomber crews. Reinforcements began arriving at the beginning of September as he based seven *Kampfgruppen* in the complex of airfields around Foggia. While the torpedo aircraft of KG 26 remained in southern France, the three *Gruppen* of KG 30 brought in from Norway were split between Viterbo and Foggia. The well-established facility at Viterbo, built for the Italian Air Force in 1937, lay north-north-west of Rome and had come into major Luftwaffe use since June, becoming one of the main central Italian Luftwaffe airfields until mid-1944. Like most Italian airfields, Viterbo had been heavily bombed by B-17s on 29 July, four Ju 88A-4s of I./KG 30 and three Ju 88A-4s and A-5s from III./KG 30 destroyed. Both I. and III./KG 30 were in Viterbo while II./KG 30 remained in the forward airfield at Foggia alongside III./KG 54 and KG 76.

Richthofen was ordered by Kesselring to mount an airborne rearguard action over Calabria, but the *Luftflotte* 2 commander objected, making only limited fighter-bomber sorties in order to maintain the appearance of obedience. Minor bombing raids on shipping concentrations in North African harbours also achieved little, a number of LT 350 circling torpedoes being dropped by seventeen Ju 88s of III./KG 54 in Bizerte harbour on 6 September, yet causing no damage and a single Ju 88 being brought down by a British night fighter. Meanwhile Allied bombing of Italy intensified, as well as a raid mounted by 180 North-west African Strategic Air Force (NASAF) B-17s on 17 August against the French Istres-Le-Tubé and Salon-de-Provence airfields.

The British bombardment of the Calabrian coast brought the *Leander* class light cruiser HMS *Orion* to the Messina area, deployed alongside Monitors, gunboats, and destroyers. Patrolling with an active radio link as potential naval gunnery support north of Messina, *Orion* was attacked by III./KG 100 Dorniers with 'Fritz-X' bombs during the afternoon of 5 September, the attacking aircraft wrongly identified as a Heinkel He 111. The aircraft launched weapons at an altitude of about 4,000 metres, after making two clearly-heard runs towards the ship; the first unobserved due to cloud cover, the second momentarily glimpsed. The missile was released on the third run through a gap in the cloud, a vapour trail streaming behind it that at first was mistaken by observers below for an Allied fighter engaging the bomber. The 'Fritz-X' was observed descending in two close spirals before diving towards its target, at first thought to be a crashing aircraft before its trajectory straightened, trailing flame and smoke and narrowly missed thirty yards astern. Interference to the cruiser's Type 279 radar began approximately one minute before the missile struck the water, terminating with the explosion though the after-action report states that 'listening and jamming was started too late and blind four-inch fire withheld because of [nearby] Spitfires'. The radar receiver had been momentarily completely saturated, entirely erasing ground wave and land echoes from the screen, providing the first glimpse at a potential weakness in the German radio guidance system and hastening Allied research into swift development of electronic interference capability. Jope's *Gruppe* lost a single Dornier, *Lt.* Ernst Prollius' '6N+CD' from Stab III./KG 100, shot down by a Spitfire of 154 Squadron flown by Rhodesian Flt. Lt. William Maguire. Though the entire crew managed to parachute from their stricken aircraft, Prollius' parachute became entangled in the Dornier's radio transmission cable and he was dragged to his death with the plunging aircraft.

Operation *Avalanche* consisted of the Anglo-American US Fifth Army under Brigadier General Mark W. Clark landing in the Salerno Gulf with the objective of seizing the port of Naples and dividing Italy from the Tyrrhenian Sea to the Adriatic Sea, potentially trapping Kesselring's southern troops. While *Avalanche* unfolded, the 1st British Airborne Division would land at Taranto in Operation *Slapstick*, securing the southern arch of the Italian heel, capturing the port and nearby airfields, and acting as a diversion for Salerno. Eventually the two forces were planned to meet at Foggia, capturing its strategically important airbase.

Between 5 and 6 September, nearly 600 vessels allocated to the Task Force 80 (Western Naval Task Force) under overall command of Vice Admiral Henry Kent Hewitt, USN, departed from North Africa in sixteen different convoys sailing toward the Gulf of Salerno. The Western Naval Task Force included warships from the American, British, Dutch and Polish navies and, when combined with attendant merchant shipping, totalled around 900 vessels. This Task Force was further subdivided into the Northern and Southern Attack Forces. Due to air cover provided by land-based North-west African Coastal Air Force and Malta Air Command being at the limit of its range, additional fighters were provided by two carriers of Force V, protected by Force H of battleships and destroyers. The convoys expected harassment from the Luftwaffe, but German air attacks proved much lighter than expected, weak air raids culminating in the strongest on the eve of the landing, in the night of 8 September. That night KG 26 He 111 torpedo bombers and KG 30 Ju 88s attacked Force H between 2100hrs and 2215hrs. Red flares were dropped by a shadowing aircraft near the warships to guide the attacking torpedo bombers which approached from the north, attacking 'singly and persistently' though without success with several shot down by anti-aircraft fire and night fighters.

General Clark had taken the baffling decision not to bombard the invasion beaches despite all strategic surprise having obviously been lost. While Hewitt compiled a target list based on prisoner interrogation and intelligence sources that totalled 275 locations suitable for preliminary bombardment, Clark denied the request, citing the element of surprise and concern over potential civilian casualties and destruction of non-military structures. Hewitt vehemently disagreed, arguing that German air activity already demonstrated that strategic surprise had been

Bombardier and pilot aboard an He 111.

lost, but Clark's decision stood. However, Allied bombing of Army and Luftwaffe installations reached a fresh crescendo, an attack on Kesselring's and Richthofen's headquarters rendering it temporarily out of action to try and replicate the chaos caused by targeting II.*Fliegerkorps* headquarters during the invasion of Sicily. At 1210hrs on 8 September, 131 USAAF B-17Gs of four Bomb Groups bombed Frascati with the aim of neutralising Kesselring, Richthofen and their respective staffs.

As flak batteries opened fire at the American bombers overhead, Kesselring and his staff were in conference regarding defence of the Italian mainland. The first bombs landed near the palatial villa's veranda, others striking the ground near the air-raid shelter to which Kesselring and his men hurried. However, the raid caused less damage to the military headquarters than it did the town of Frascati, half of which was destroyed, killing 485 civilians and blocking all exits from the town with bomb craters and uprooted trees. The Luftwaffe signals unit at Frascati suffered one female auxiliary killed alongside twenty operators of the radio monitoring battalion. Virtually all communications were severed, except for a single telephone line from *General* Westphal's bedroom which remained in contact both with *OKW* and Kesselring's subordinate commands. A single B-17 was shot down, maps found aboard the aircraft by German troops showing Richthofen's and Kesselring's headquarters clearly marked, an ardent Italian Royalist attached to Kesselring's staff later being identified as a spy and shot.[15] Ultimately, the *Luftflotte 2* headquarters was only briefly out of action. The precautionary establishment of an alternative communications cable to Rome and preparation of a secondary command post in Monte Cavo reaped enormous reward as immediately following the attack, Kesselring, Richthofen and their respective staffs drove around the road blocks to Monte Cavo and were able to resume operations within one and a half hours. Though Frascati had been disabled as a communications hub, new circuits were hurriedly connected while radio communications centralised on Monte Cavo. The *Kampfgeschwader* air traffic control centre remained functional in Frascati, despite a dud American bomb being lodged in the centre of its barracks.

The Germans immediately assumed the air attack presaged an imminent Allied landing and Kesselring soon received his first intimation of the Italian surrender when Jodl telephoned from *OKW* headquarters to ask whether he was aware of the rumoured Italian capitulation. Berlin had monitored an English radio broadcast announcing Badoglio's armistice, the German Embassy in Rome receiving formal notification

Kesselring and Richthofen's headquarters that was targeted by Allied bombers; Villa Falconieri at Frascati.

from the Italian Ministry of Foreign Affairs within an hour and Kesselring issuing the code word '*Achse*' initiating occupation of Italy and Sardinia, offensive action against Italian forces and the seizure Rome as well as former Italian possessions within the Balkans and southern France.

Kesselring and Richthofen had both found themselves under considerable nervous strain in the weeks leading to Italy's surrender, the duplicity of planning for this eventuality whilst maintaining a 'friendly' working relationship with their Axis partners being difficult to maintain. While Hitler created policies predicated upon imminent Italian betrayal, Kesselring, an avowed Italophile, harboured hopes to the very last that Italian defection could be averted issuing a circular during July stating that the Italian government had firmly declared their continuation of the war giving 'no cause for special measures or for uneasiness'.[16] From the naval standpoint Admiral Raffaele De Courten, Chief of Staff of the *Regia Marina*, had as late as the evening of 7 September met with Kesselring and repeated the bluff that the Italian fleet was preparing to sail on a last suicide mission against the gathering Allied invasion traffic, as he had already promised Dönitz during the middle of August. For the Luftwaffe, Richthofen was less certain of Italy's fidelity. He had already removed the Luftwaffe liaison officer for the Italian air forces, *General der Flieger* Maximilian Ritter von Pohl (*Chef des Verbindungsstab* attached to *Italuft*) and dissolved his office. On 7 September, Richthofen had also summoned Jope from KG 100 to his headquarters, briefing him on the necessity of preparing an aerial attack on Italian capital ships anchored in La Spezia. With the armistice now revealed, the Luftwaffe activated their part of *Achse*, coordinated by IX.*Fliegerkorps* headquarters with Frascati momentarily out of action. During the following day, *OKW* Operations Staff reorganised the chains of command in Italy, including the withdrawal of *Luftflotte 2* from *Oberbefehlshaber Süd* control.

While Italy's air and ground forces were almost immediately neutralised by the announcement of the armistice, the *Regia Marina* remained a sought-after prize for both Germans and Allies, numbering 206 ships including the battleships *Roma*, *Vittorio Veneto* and *Italia* of the *Squadra Navale* (main Italian fleet) based at La Spezia. Article Four of the Armistice demanded the 'Immediate transfer of the Italian Fleet and Italian aircraft to such points as may be designated by the Allied Commander in Chief, with details of disarmament to be prescribed by him'. The Allies' primary concerns were that elements of the *Regia Marina* might fight on, loyal to the fascist cause, be scuttled or, in their worst-case scenario, be taken over by the Kriegsmarine. Correspondingly, the Italian naval units on the west coast – primarily in Genoa and La Spezia – were instructed to sail for North Africa, those in Taranto to sail directly for Malta.

At La Spezia the main part of the Italian fleet narrowly escaped German seizure. Late in the afternoon of 8 September, the battleships were being prepared for sailing when De Courten informed Admiral Carlo Bergamini, commander of the *Squadra Navale*, of the armistice. Only at that point did he order a bewildered Bergamini to sail; not to engage the Allied invasion ships as expected, but instead to make for the Sardinian naval base at La Maddalena. After conferring with his officers and convincing them of their duty to follow orders, *Roma*, *Italia* and *Vittorio Veneto* left the harbour at 0300hrs the following morning in company with the cruisers *Eugenio di Savoia*, *Raimondo Montecuccoli*, *Emanuele Filiberto*, *Duca d'Aosta* and eight destroyers, *Legionario*, *Grecale*, *Oriani*, *Velite*, *Mitragliere*, *Fuciliere*, *Artigliere* and *Carabiniere*. They were joined by the Genoa-based cruisers *Duca degli Abruzzi*, *Giuseppe Garibaldi* and *Attilio Regolo*, sailing in accord with Allied instructions off the western shore of Corsica intending to rendezvous at La Maddalena. Black flags of surrender were raised at each masthead as behind them Rommel's troops hastily occupied La Spezia.

Aboard the flagship *Roma*, Bergamini was soon informed that La Maddalena had been occupied by German troops, receiving fresh instructions to steam to Tunisia where the fleet would be surrendered to the Allies. In broad daylight, the great ships sailed within range of Jope's Do 217K-2s of III./KG 100 at Istres. During the morning, *Vizeadmiral* Wilhelm Meendsen-Bohlken, *Befehlshaber der deutsches Marinekommandos in Italien* (Commander-in-chief of the German Naval Commands in Italy), had removed all doubt as to the Italians' intentions when he signalled: 'The Italian fleet has departed during the night to surrender itself to the enemy.' Fuelled and loaded with a single light blue 'Fritz-X' beneath each of the eleven aircrafts' starboard wing, the Dorniers lifted off at 1400hrs, only two hours after Jope had received orders to attack the Italian fleet.

With dawn the Italians were joined by an escort of RAF Martin Baltimores of 52 Squadron and Martin Marauders of 14 Squadron, both experienced in maritime reconnaissance and convoy escort. However, Luftwaffe radio intelligence detected the ships at 0941hrs thirty miles west-north-west of Ajaccio headed south, reporting 'an

Italian naval force of three battleships, six cruisers and six destroyers making for Maddalena'. With the Sardinian port now occupied, the Italian ships changed course westwards when Jope's Dorniers spotted them in almost perfect visibility fourteen miles off Cape Testa in the early hours of the afternoon. Jope and his pilots flew around the Italians at an altitude of 5,000 metres, anti-aircraft shells exploding some distance below them. The Italian no doubt expected dive-bombing to follow, incorrectly identifying the aircraft as 'definitely Ju 88s' manoeuvring independently and maintaining the barrage to keep the bombers out of effective conventional bombing range. The Dorniers approached in three successive line-ahead waves, before splitting up and making individual attacks, each bombardier choosing their own target, unable to identify specific ships, merely aiming for the largest. Jope later recalled:

> I remember very well the group of around four to five battleships and, including the other smaller ones, a convoy of twenty to twenty-five ships in all. We came from the east, we had been flying for about an hour and a half. It was early afternoon when we saw them, and once we were certain it was the Italian Fleet, each one of us prepared to do what he was ordered to do. All of the aircraft were only a short distance from each other, and we flew over the target and looked for a good position from which to attack. Each pilot chose his own target, but as we had done throughout the flight, without using too much radio communications, because otherwise the enemy could intercept them, and the element of surprise would be gone. Then, the first crew that started the bombing announced to the rest that the attack was beginning, and each plane started to release their missiles, then trying to direct them with the radio control on to the chosen target.[17]

The Dorniers passed overhead, maintaining their altitude before diving at an angle of between 20 to 30 degrees immediately prior to weapon release after which they flattened out and continued a dead straight course; only a single aircraft seen to alter course after launch. The Italian flak was heavy but inaccurate as ships twisted and turned to upset the bomb aimers above. Several runs were made over the Italian ships until a perfect shot could be achieved, weapon launch only made from within an arc of 40 degrees of the fore and aft line and preferably from astern. At no point did the escorting Allied aircraft even catch sight of the attacking bombers.

The first few strikes showed a tendency to miss slightly astern, which was obviously corrected by the aircraft that followed. Italian survivors later recalled how the incoming projectile's high velocity and steadiness in flight was remarkable, taking about twenty seconds from launch to impact. Each release was marked by a puff of smoke and coloured lights visible below. The falling bomb emitted a smoke trail which ceased after a while as its trajectory steepened, terminating vertically and with no discernible course change. Despite being credited in some published works with the first hit, Jope later recalled having missed with the missile launched by his bombardier, *Uffz.* Klapproth. Instead it was the aircraft piloted by *Lt.* Klaus Deumling, his observer *Uffz.* Penz guiding the 'Fritz-X' to its target, hitting *Roma* amidships as the battleship swung under full rudder at a speed of 30 knots. The armour-piercing missile passed through 8in of steel and the 1in splinter-proof deck, eventually coming out and exploding under the keel, causing severe damage. Water immediately flooded the aft engine room and two of the ship's boiler rooms, causing the inboard propellers to stop and causing several small electrical fires. With only two functioning screws, *Roma*'s speed dropped, and the ship fell out of formation. As *Roma*'s damage control

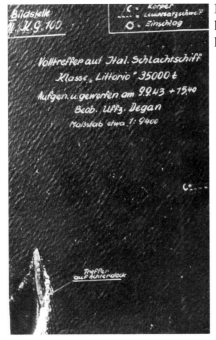

Luftwaffe photograph of *Roma*, already hit once, with a second 'Fritz-X' high-lighted inbound from right.

parties attempted to control the flooding, *Italia* was also hit on the forecastle deck, blasting a hole twenty inches in diameter, the missile passing through and exiting the ship's side where it exploded, causing enough damage for the battleship to begin taking on more than 1,000 tons of water. The cruiser *Garibaldi* experienced two near misses only twenty metres from the quarter deck and five from the forecastle, though the explosions barely jarred the ship.

At around 1602hrs, a second 'Fritz-X' believed to have been dropped by *Obfw.* Kurt Steinborn's aircraft and controlled to impact by observer *Uffz.* Eugen Degan slammed into *Roma*'s starboard side abreast of 'B' turret. Again the missile penetrated the decking, exploding in the forward engine room, causing small sympathetic detonations until a magazine explosion blew the entire gun turret over the side of the crippled battleship. A thick column of flames and smoke rose over *Roma* as the ship began to sink by the bow while the Dorniers departed, their ammunition spent. Jope recalled:

> We took another hour and a half of flying time to reach our base, and immediately some of the *Gruppe*'s aircraft, about five, left for another bombing action on the Italian Fleet. I was not with them, I only participated in the first bombing . . . The pilots dropped their bombs, one for each plane like everyone in the group, but they didn't hit any ships. When the pilots of this second group had also returned to Istres-Marseille they reported that two ships were missing from the grid, and so we knew that we had hit them; but without knowing which ships they were, and not even being sure of having sunk them.[18]

The next day, 10 September, the triumphant Jope was appointed *Kommodore* of KG 100, his place as *Gruppenkommandeur* of III.*Gruppe* taken by *Hptm.* Gerhard Döhler.

Behind them *Roma* sank within twenty minutes, listing progressively to starboard as she submerged bow-first until the hull eventually broke in two. The official inquest that followed concluded that *Roma* had a crew of 1,849 when she sailed with only 596 surviving, leaving 1,253 men going down with the ship. However, it appears that around 200 men of Bergamini's staff were also aboard *Roma*, increasing the complement to 2,021 and the number of fatalities to 1,393. Among those killed were Bergamini and *Roma*'s captain, *Capitano di Vascello* Adone del Cima. Aboard *Italia*, *Commandante* Garofalo described the attack:

The *Roma* burns before sinking.

All this took place in a few minutes but we were now a long way from the point at which the *Roma* is halted and covered in smoke. The bows are almost invisible. The last vision I have of the flagship on which the day previously I have spent many hours are three flashes – like salutes – which rise up towards the sky, exploding in three red stars. The last voice which reached us is that of a radio-operator which says 'I am in danger'. This repeats after a second or two: 'I am in danger of death.'

Of the escorting Marauders from 14 Squadron, Wing Commander Law-Wright later described the attack:

The first sign of attack we saw was when the ships opened fire. For a moment we thought they were firing at us and we took violent evasive action. Then we saw flak burst far above us, obviously aimed at highflying aircraft. We saw an enormous explosion on one of the battleships. Creamy white smoke went up to about 3,000 or 4,000 ft. The smoke on the battleship subsided and it looked as if it were getting under way again. Throughout the attack the ships had taken excellent evasive action and their anti-aircraft fire was accurate. We flew over the ships and took a look at the damaged one. We arrived just as it was sinking. Under a big column of smoke, we saw the stern under water and the bow sticking up. The ship appeared to break in two and folded up with the control tower and keel forming a 'V' as the ship slowly disappeared.

Following the sinking of *Roma*, the cruiser *Attilio Regolo*, three destroyers and an escort vessel picked up survivors before heading to Port Mahon on the island of Menorca while the remainder sailed directly for Malta. The Italian training battleship *Giulio Cesare* was also attacked by ten Ju 88s as she steamed from the southern part of the Adriatic Sea towards Strait of Otranto, but only one near miss was achieved which had no effect on the aged dreadnought.

Further disaster overtook two destroyers from Genoa, *Vivaldi* and *Da Noli*, which had sailed that day for Civitavecchia, near Rome, under orders to embark the Italian king and government and bring them to La Maddalena. With the Italian royalty and government redirected to Brindisi, the destroyers' orders were cancelled only as they approached Civitavecchia. Instead they were to rendezvous with the *Roma* group, while also engaging any German maritime traffic transferring troops from Sardinia to Corsica. As they approached *Roma*'s location the two ships were shelled by Corsican coastal artillery manned by German and Blackshirt troops, with *Da Noli* sunk and *Vivaldi* damaged. The destroyer suffered further after running on to a mine and was later scuttled fifty miles west of Asinara island.

Seenotbereichskommando XIII despatched six 3.*Seenotstaffel* Do 24s and two air-traffic control vessels from St Raphael's 13.*Seenotflotille* to take part in a large-scale rescue operation for survivors from *Roma* and the two destroyers. An escort of six Ar 196 floatplanes was short-lived due to their limited operational range, leaving the Dorniers without protection. Furthermore, one of the pilots was inexperienced and, daunted by the rough sea surface, returned without landing and a propeller on one of the two *Seenotflotille* boats was also damaged, forcing a premature return. The remaining five aircraft landed as planned and began rescuing Italians from the sea, the first load of nineteen sailors – including *Vivaldi*'s commander Captain Francesco Camicia – returning at 1230hrs on 10 September. The remaining four Dorniers were found by an American USAAF Liberator B-24D bomber of the 1st Antisubmarine Patrol that circled the scene for several minutes while ascertaining the nationality of the seaplanes, at first thought to be PBY Catalinas. The American commander then ordered all his machine guns to open fire, destroying all four stationary Dorniers as they were involved in rescuing Italians, unable to return fire due to the rough sea. Nearly eighty Italian survivors were also killed by the gunfire which wounded three German crewmen, though they all managed to successfully escape their burning and sinking aircraft. *Oberleutnant* Gerhard Kersten, the ranking German officer of the group, was aware of the planned midnight arrival time of the expected air-traffic control boats and began firing flares at 2330hrs, later picked up by *Flugbetriebsboot* 604, captained by the son of *Obstlt*. Max-Georg Fengler, commander of *Seenotbereichskommando* IV. Nineteen Luftwaffe and fifty-two Italian survivors, nine of them severely wounded, were returned aboard Fengler's boat that first night, a further eight Italians being found five days later.[19]

The seaworthiness of this class of air-traffic control boat was highly praised by Fengler, being unaffected by a strengthened armament of eight anti-aircraft guns. During the high seas of the spring mistral season, they were frequently able to operate when Dorniers were unable to land. Between November 1942 and October 1943, air and sea units of the *Seenotbereichskommando* XIII rescued 270 men, though talks were soon underway with Spanish authorities to establish a neutral air-sea rescue service for the Western Mediterranean following severe losses of Dornier aircraft. The Luftwaffe also made use of whatever captured aircraft were deemed suitable.

After the Italian surrender, veteran of the Condor Legion and former *Küstenflieger Hptm*. Wilhelm Gaul operated a small unit named *Sonderkommando Gaul* 9/XI, responsible for collecting and evaluating Italian seaplanes for possible transfer to Germany or front-line *Seenotstaffeln*. On 20 November, Gaul reported seventy-six intact floatplanes at thirteen different sites in Italy. Three of these aircraft were subsequently lost in action on 15 January 1944 against American Spitfires on 15 January 1944 during a transfer flight from Marina di Pisa to Etang de Berre near Marseilles. Spitfires of the USAAF 52nd Fighter Group's 4th Squadron intercepted them south-east of Savona, misidentifying them as He 115s, one being shot down in flames with one body recovered and two missing and the others making successful forced landings from which the crews were later recovered. As with aircraft seized from France, the infusion of Italian aircraft into the air-sea rescue service provided a welcome source of material reinforcement.

With the impending Luftwaffe defence of mainland Italy from Allied invasion, *Seenotbereichskommando* XIV was established under the command of *Maj.* Ludwig Wahl on Sardinia, with headquarters at La Maddelena and satellite bases at Elmas, on a lake north-west of Cagliari, and Olbia on Sardinia's eastern coast. In Athens, *Hptm.* William Freudenberg's *Seenotbereichskommando* XI was given independence from the control of *Obstlt.* Eduard Engelhorn's *Seenotdienstführer 2* (*Süd*) command that had been relocated to Vigna di Valle at Lake Braciano, near Rome, during August 1943 and then to Venice-Lido during November.

Operation Avalanche

Between 0750 and 0850hrs on 9 September, Luftwaffe air reconnaissance reported three heavy cruisers or battleships, about twenty transports, probably LSTs, and twenty-five landing craft in and near the Gulf of Salerno. Fifty-four bombers were immediately despatched, claiming one cruiser hit by a bomb and exploding, and direct hits on another cruiser and seven other vessels. Very heavy fighter escorts were reported over the enemy landing fleet, only HMS *Mendip* suffering damage from a near miss that caused minor leaks and machinery problems though no casualties.

At Salerno the mistake of not mounting any kind of preliminary bombardment of a landscape that clearly favoured defence was soon exposed. Despite the hasty grouping of forces allocated to *General* Heinrich von Vietinghoff's Tenth Army and its deficit of logistical cohesion and communications equipment, the likelihood of a Salerno landing had allowed time to prepare to meet the amphibious attack. Swiftly mounted and well executed German counterattacks posed a severe threat to Clark's position – even prompting the American general to consider a partial withdrawal – until naval gunnery swung the tide of battle in the Allies' favour, disrupting and destroying German armoured thrusts.

The US Navy set a new standard for naval gunfire support aided by spotters on the ground and in the air, swinging into action on the morning of the landing despite the presence of unswept mines and poor communications with troops ashore. On that day alone, gunnery support ships bombarded a minimum of 132 targets with 53 per cent accuracy, *General* Siegfried Westphal, Chief of the General Staff of the German Army Command in the West, later concluding that: 'The greatest distress suffered by the [German] troops was caused by the fire of ships' guns of heavy calibre, from which they could find no protection in the rocky soil.'

It was against these that the Luftwaffe concentrated its maritime attacks from 11 September onwards. The Focke-Wulf Fw 190A-5/U3s of II. and III./SKG 10 and Fw 190F-2s of II./SchG 2 were once again heavily involved in attacks against the beachhead, supported by Bf 109G-5/R2 fighters of IV./JG 3 that carried the underwing Wfr.Gr. 21 rocket mortars into action, originally conceived for use against the tight 'box' formations flown by USAAF bombers. The Focke-Wulf attacks on enemy shipping were timed to provide not only the chance of inflicting damage, but also as a distraction for the bombing runs made by the *Kampfgeschwader*, particularly the Do 217s of KG 100 with their 'Fritz-X' and Hs 293 weapons. Providing constant fighter cover for the fleet remained difficult. Though the Allies had captured the airfield at Montecorvino, only three miles from the coastline and recently vacated by SKG 10, their intention to immediately deploy covering fighters was foiled by German artillery fire that rendered the airfield unusable.

Allied cryptanalysts on board the fighter control ship USS *Ancon* informed *Savannah* on the morning of 11 September of an intercepted German message in which aircraft were directed against specific ships, including the cruiser. The *Brooklyn* class cruiser USS *Savannah* was a centrepiece of the US Navy fire support ships, being the first American ship to open fire against Salerno's shore defences, silencing a railway artillery battery and breaking up an armoured counterattack by Panzer IV tanks and Sturmgeschütz III assault guns of the 16th Panzer Division during the first day. On Saturday, 11 September, USS *Savannah* steamed from its offshore holding position into the swept channel within the Gulf of Salerno and reached the transport area during early morning darkness. Flares periodically dropped as Luftwaffe bombers level bombed the vicinity, the cruiser's anti-aircraft batteries opening fire at 0504hrs for seven minutes to protect transport ships. Within the hour, *Savannah* had departed through the same swept channel for the designated fire support area, all engines finally stopped at 0621hrs and the sun soon rising in the east illuminating the stationary cruiser.

The crew were moved from yellow alert to red alert at 0930hrs as twelve Fw 190 fighter-bombers of 6./SKG 10 were reported approaching at speed form the north. USS *Philadelphia* suffered a near miss from a single bomb as Allied fighters raced to intercept and

Savannah began moving to execute evasive manoeuvres. The ship had reached 20 knots as gunners scanned the skies for the expected fighter-bombers, sighting a distant Do 217E-5 two minutes later, nearly overhead on the port quarter and approaching from out of the sun. As USAAF Lockheed P-38 Lightnings frantically attempted to intercept the bomber, *Savannah*'s gunners tracked the plane that cruised at an altitude of over 4,000 metres. Seconds later, a 'Fritz-X' hurtled out of the sky and scored a direct hit on the 2in armoured roof of No 3 turret, the bomb passing through three decks into the lower ammunition-handling room, where it exploded, blowing a hole in *Savannah*'s keel and tearing a seam in the cruiser's port side. The cruiser lost electric power as secondary explosions rocked the destroyed turret. The fires under four boilers were extinguished and rudder jammed at 'left standard' as the screws continued to turn. No communication was possible with the engine rooms or aft steering except by manoeuvring telephone and fires broke out in Nos 1, 2 and 3 turrets, though a magazine explosion was prevented by rapid flooding. The central station was apparently demolished, and all electrical equipment had failed, including gyro repeaters, engine telegraph, rudder indicator and control and fathometer. The swept channel was congested with anchored and moving ships, and there were fears that the cruiser would accidentally veer out of control into some of the assembled vessels, but the ship's commander successfully established contact with the aft steering compartment and engine room using the telephone system and brought *Savannah* back under control, steam temporarily being lost until lines were repaired and boilers relit, finally clearing the swept channel in an impressive display of emergency manoeuvring.

USS *Savannah* had developed a list to port as Rear Admiral Morse, Captain Shaw and Lt. Long left the ship, the cruiser's course reversed for potential beaching if found necessary. By 1100hrs, the salvage tug USS *Hopi* had come alongside to starboard, joined minutes later by a second tug, USS *Moreno*, as guns continued to fire at sighted Luftwaffe aircraft, water pumped from the cruiser in order to return it to relative trim. By midday, USS *Savannah* was out of danger and anchored, fifteen badly wounded casualties beginning to be transferred to British hospital ship SS *Aba*, a total of 197 crewmen killed, most bodies only removed after the ship had reached Malta for repairs. In Valetta's Grand Harbour, four men who had been trapped within the watertight emergency radio room were discovered and finally freed at 2100hrs on 13 September.

USS *Savannah* after being hit by a 'Fritz-X' from KG 100 off Salerno. (NARA, US ARMY SIGNALS CORP)

During the same attack, the flagship USS *Philadelphia* was unable to use its fire-control radar due to land interference as Fw 190s streaked in to attack, missing with three bombs, though a single 'high and fast' Do 217 spotted later by binoculars was tracked by the ship's Mk 33 Director. Thirty-nine 5in rounds were fired at what at first was taken to be two aircraft, the second then seen to be trailing smoke, betraying the path of another 'Fritz-X'. Witnesses aboard *Philadelphia* later reported the bomb to have 'come hurtling down. It came down very quickly and at the end of its descent was travelling at an estimated 400 miles per hour.'[20] The bomb struck abeam to starboard, throwing both fire directors off target, the Dornier circling to a reciprocal course and vanishing from sight. One man, Seaman First Class Chester A. Stoklosa, was blown overboard from the cruiser but suffered only bruising before being recovered, and several minor casualties were caused by splinters, while aboard *Philadelphia* steering control was temporarily lost, the deck to starboard and longitudinal bulkhead frames 113 to 188 slightly buckled. A slow leak had started in the starboard shaft alley and the starboard catapult damaged. *Unteroffizier* Johann Hofstätter's 4./KG 100 Do

The glazed stepless cockpit of a
Dornier Do 217K.

217E-5 '6N+DM', equipped with the Hs 293, was the sole loss to the
Kampfgeschwader over the Gulf of Salerno, he and his crew missing in
action. At least one other II./KG 100 Dornier equipped with Hs 293s
had taken off for action against the invasion shipping, Heinz-Georg
Schöneberg's '6N+LM' leaving Istres at 1031hrs but aborting the
mission and landing again an hour after midday.

A second KG 100 attack was combined two days later with Ju 88s of
KG 54 and KG 76 which mounted a series of bombing raids on the assembled shipping, the *Gruppenkommandeur* of I./KG 76, *Hptm.* Ulrich
Roch, killed in a freak accident when his bombs exploded on take-off
from Tortorella airfield. KG 100 narrowly missed USS *Philadelphia*
with another 'Fritz-X':

1445hrs . . . Without previous warning either from air fighter circuit or
radar, a flight of six or eight Fw 190s came in from the sun in a power dive
directly over the ship. This vessel opened up with starboard batteries (AA)
as planes had come in from port and crossed ship, but guns to port could
not bear in time. Only one bomb was seen to be dropped and it landed not
far from a Liberty ship which was anchored close inshore. No planes were

seen to be hit. Planes headed in over land in the vicinity of the airfield. 1446hrs. Plane 130° (R) coming toward ship. Turned away from AA fire. 1450hrs Unidentified plane 14 miles bearing 320° (T) closing. 1455hrs Bomb landed 50 yards starboard side frame 96; Lookouts, personnel on deck and members of gun crews shouted 'Here it comes', 'Silver streak coming down'; 'Glider coming towards ship'. The member of some gun crew gave relative bearing 315° as first place of sighting. The 'glider bomb' was seen to go slightly aft after being released from its mother ship and then head horizontally for some second aft. Its first appearance seemed relatively over the bridge of this ship. The glider started its vertical dive when over No.1 stack. From the time it started down until it hit the water abeam of frame 96 only about five seconds elapsed. White smoke was seen coming from the glider during its descent, with some reports that black smoke was also seen just before it hit the water. Not more than 15 seconds passed from the time of first sighting until it hit the water.'

During the same attack, two other large ships were less fortunate. The bombarding cruiser HMS *Uganda* was hit by a glide bomb, launched from an estimated altitude of 4,000 metres and seen to turn 90 degrees through the air during the attack. The armour-piercing bomb struck aft, passing through seven decks and the keel before exploding underneath, disabling the steering gear and splitting the hull for thirty feet at the bottom of the after engine room starboard side. All boiler fires were extinguished by the concussion and sixteen men killed. Over 1,300 tons of water flooded onboard, unable to be pumped out without a patch applied to the hole. As all bulkheads adjacent to the damaged compartment were strengthened and the ship lay drawing 26 feet aft, *Uganda* was able to limp on one engine out of danger, towed by the *Navajo* class fleet tug USS *Narragansett* to Malta for temporary repairs.

The hospital ships HMHS *Leinster* and *Newfoundland* were also attacked 40nm off Salerno, the latter struck by an HS 293 launched by II./KG 100 on the boat deck behind the bridge, the first of only two confirmed successes off Salerno for this unit that operated primarily in darkness. The hospital ship, with three others, had been moved offshore after a near miss in the congested waters of the inner Gulf of Salerno. Fully illuminated, the hull fringed with green lights and with large red crosses on the sides and funnel, there was no mistaking the ship for a fighting vessel. Fortunately, *Newfoundland* was carried only two patients at the time, but the German bomb hit the doctors' quarters, killing all of the medical officers aboard and disabling the pumps. An American Army nurse, Vera Lee, later wrote to her family of her experience of the attack:

At 5:10 we heard a plane & then that bad awful whistle a bomb makes & bang! – You'll never know of the thousand things that flashed thro my mind those few seconds. I thought sure I was dying – could feel hot water falling on my face & body – Had heavy boards on my chest that had fallen from the ceiling – I shut my eyes & thought it was the end – Then the next second I thought 'What the hell, I'm not dead – get out of this place' – then I could see poor Wheeler & Waldin without a stitch of clothes on trying to find anything to put on. I couldn't see for the terrific smoke in our room – but was a mass of motion trying to find my coveralls which I had hung on the post hole the nite before. I found on the floor – all soaked with water & black with dirt – put them on & found my shoes – grabbed my helmet & water canteen & grabbed on to someone's arm & followed the light that Claudine was holding. She couldn't hardly find where the door was because the wall had all been blown out.

When we got on the deck we all had to get on one side because the bomb had torn away the other side of the ship. I'll never forget seeing this one British nurse trying to get thro the porthole but was too large to make it. She was screaming terribly because her room was all in flames. One British fellow saw that she could never get out so he knocked her in the head with his fist and shoved her back in his room – She died but it was much easier than if she had burned to death.[21]

The ship's oil tanks caught fire and despite the efforts of damage control parties assisted by volunteers from USS *Mayo* alongside, the ship was finally abandoned after thirty-six hours of attempting to control the blaze, the smouldering hulk sunk by gunfire from USS *Plunkett* the following day. Six British staff nurses had been killed along with all five medical officers, eight orderlies and nineteen crew.

The destroyers HMS *Loyal* and *Nubian* had both been narrowly missed by glide bombs, the former suffering minor damage from the blast. Losses suffered by III./KG 100 that day amounted to *Oblt*. Erwin Burghoff's Stab III./KG 100 Do 217K-2 'ZY+MA' with all crew missing in action and *Lt*. Heinz Pfitzner's 9./KG 100 Do 217K-2 '6N+WT'; Pfitzner wounded, two men killed and the last crewman safely returned to German lines. The following day, 14 September, USS *Philadelphia* was narrowly missed by a glide bomb attack yet again and the Liberty ship

SS *Bushrod Washington* was hit while laying at anchor in the transport area off Salerno. Much of its cargo of trucks, landing craft and rations had been unloaded, but large amounts of high-octane aviation spirit and explosives remained aboard. At 1322hrs one Hs 293 narrowly missed the ship while a second struck in the midship house between lifeboats 2 and 4. The missile penetrated through the crew mess room and exploded below the main deck, forcibly shunting the ship's engines to starboard causing the port boiler to explode. The engine room crew on duty at that time were among the fifteen men killed in the attack which ignited stored gasoline and started a raging inferno that soon engulfed the ship as the captain frantically ordered her abandoned. *LCT 209*, which was alongside, suffered three men wounded and also caught fire, her bridge and superstructure demolished and the hull holed aft, being beached to prevent sinking. Salvage tugs swiftly moved in toward *Bushrod Washington* in an attempt to extinguish the flames as LCTs, LCIs and LCVPs came alongside to evacuate injured survivors and pluck others from the water. The captain and four volunteers later reboarded to attempt to extinguish the flames, but it proved impossible and the ship was abandoned, exploding violently and sinking at 0355hrs the following morning after the flames reached 500lb bombs stored in the forward hold.

A second Liberty ship was seriously damaged at 0755hrs on 15 September when SS *James Marshall* was hit by an Hs 293. The ship had already survived dive-bombing two days previously when a single bomb struck a 20mm gun shield on the starboard side of the bridge, bounced off and went through the deck to explode in the master's quarters. Though the explosion caused a small fire, it was soon under control and no casualties were suffered. This time the Hs 293 penetrated the boat deck and exploded near the crew's mess and engine room. Fire immediately broke out and both the engine room and No 3 hold flooded. Two LCTs lay on the ship's port side, unloading fuel from the freighter, *LCT 19* soon engulfed in flames, towed away by an LCM and later sunk by gunfire from HMS *Hambleton*. As fire raged out of control aboard the Liberty ship, the crew were given orders to abandon ship, a pair of lifeboats and two rafts launched, while others clambered down cargo nets to waiting landing craft. The seaplane tender *Biscayne* also closed to rescue survivors, one officer, twelve men and fifty Army stevedores being killed in the attack. The flames were eventually brought under control, and at 1313hrs the following day, Brigadier General Clark ordered the Provost Marshal to apprehend all crew members of the *James Marshall* and return them to their ship. Eventually, unable to locate enough crewmembers, the master and crew of SS *Bushrod Washington* were sent aboard the abandoned ship, which was later towed by SS *Empire Perdita* to Bizerte and was eventually deliberately sunk as a breakwater off Normandy on 8 June 1944.

The depredations of the guided bomb attacks and the inability to counter the parent aircraft with anti-aircraft fire prompted a request to Major General Edwin House – in command of all tactical aviation from NATAF for *Avalanche* – for the 12th Air Support Command to provide high-altitude fighters for Salerno patrols. House had already established three layers of coverage: high cover provided by Spitfires from 16,000 to 20,000 feet, medium cover by P–38s and Seafires from 10,000 to 14,000 feet, and low cover by P–51s from 5,000 to 7,000 feet. Although the coverage was exhaustively flown, naval requests frequently complained at a lack of aerial support, urging strong fighter patrols from 20,000 to 25,000 feet to combat the Dorniers of KG 100. The reply from the headquarters of XII ASC was received at 1055hrs on 17 September:

> We fully appreciate the grave menace of rocket bombing and have disposed our forces accordingly. Any information which you can pass on enemy air activities is of great assistance to us. Similarly, we will pass to you any information on this subject which may be of value to you. Coverage does not exist to give you immunity from these attacks and have informed General Clark on this matter.

A frequently acrimonious exchange of messages between House and Admiral Hewitt continued in the days that followed, House recommending thick smokescreens as the best defensive measure, robbing the German observers of their line of sight to target. Though a high-altitude fighter patrol was established, Luftwaffe fighter-bombers also continued their fast low-level attacks on beach head shipping.

Ashore, despite fierce resistance, by 16 September von Vietinghoff reported to Kesselring that he possessed no means to counter Allied air and naval superiority which had proved decisive. With British forces approaching from Calabria, Vietinghoff recommended breaking off the battle at Salerno and withdrawing forces to the Volturno defensive line; the first of many that would bar the Allied advance to the north. While tactical bombing had been a crucial factor in the defeat of German forces

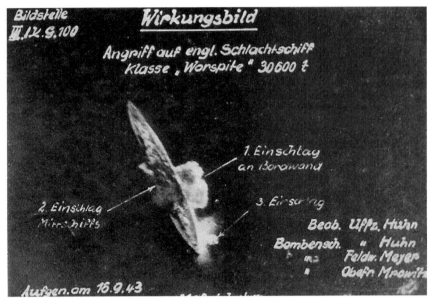

Luftwaffe photograph of HMS *Warspite* after taking damage off Salerno.

at Salerno, naval gunfire had been essential. Both the battleships HMS *Warspite* and *Valiant* conducted their final bombardment missions that day before withdrawing to Augusta, requesting night-fighter cover for the imminent passage southward. However, KG 100 continued to target the major warships even as ground forces prepared to withdraw and HMS *Warspite* was hit by a new Dornier attack as she completed her second shoot of the day on troop concentrations at Altavilla.

As *Warspite* passed at slow speed close inshore, the ship was hit by two bombs plummeting vertically, a third narrowly missing. With Fw 190 fighter-bombers launching simultaneous low-level attacks, three Do 217s of III./KG 100 were first sighted flying in formation horizontally towards the ship's beam. Each launched glide bomb appeared to follow its parent aircraft's path until vertically overhead when the missiles opened out a little and dived at great speed, converging into a very close pattern centred on *Warspite*. They were guided by *Uffz.* Huhn (from *Oblt.* Heinrich Schmetz's aircraft), *Fw.* Meyer and *Ogfr.* Mrowitzki. Despite the large number of ships present, neither the parent aircraft nor the 'Fritz-X' payloads were in sight long enough to be engaged with gunfire due to a thick heat haze that blanketed the entire area. The dive of the 'Fritz-X' missiles lasted only about two seconds in which time evasion was impossible; the first, controlled by Meyer, scoring a direct hit near the funnel on the port side of the ship, scything through six decks before hitting the double bottom and exploding, creating a twenty-foot wide hole. A second, steered by Huhn, landed alongside and ripped open the starboard torpedo bulge, while the third, controlled by Mrowitzki, landed further abeam to starboard. All engine rooms were put out of action, Nos 2, 3, 4 and 6 boiler rooms flooded, steam lost and the ship left unable to steer. Ship-wide communications were temporarily out of action and some 5,000 tons of floodwater increased *Warspite*'s draught by about five feet. The ship was left powerless and drifting, radar out of commission and unable to operate armament. Four accompanying destroyers converged on *Warspite* as mechanical steering was established, anti-aircraft cruiser HMS *Delhi* moving close to provide protection from further air attack. Despite the grievous damage, the comparatively light toll of nine men killed and fourteen injured was suffered by the crew and by early evening, *Warspite* was under tow for Malta to begin temporary repairs.

The attack had happened so quickly after the high-speed Focke-Wulf raid that many observers believed at first that the ship had been

A 'Fritz-X' mounted on its rack beneath a Dornier Do 217.

torpedoed, including New Zealander Flying Officer Alan Peart of RAF 81 Squadron who was flying one of six long range cover Spitfires over Salerno, their task facilitated by the use of drop-tanks.

> When the warship in the bay suddenly erupted in flames I immediately assumed that a submarine must have torpedoed it, however the sea was calm with no sign of the tell-tale foam trails of torpedoes, so I scanned the space around us more closely. I was astounded to see three Dornier bombers racing away to the north. It was their bombs which had hit the warship . . . Although the air was thick with Allied fighters, these three aircraft had crept in quite unnoticed. How on earth had we missed them? . . . With no hesitation we opened our throttles wide and took off after them. The three bombers had split up to make things difficult and Bill Goby, with his number two, chased one bomber whilst I with my number two, Bryan Young, and Bill Fell with his number two all found ourselves chasing another. The third escaped out attention, fortunately for him. We were soon in an attacking position with my two out to one side at a slightly higher altitude, and Fell's pair overtaking the rear Dornier at high speed. The bomber crew showed all the signs of hardened experience by weaving around as we approached and suddenly changing position as we came within firing range. The defending gunners were very accurate.

Bill Fell attacked from astern but was immediately hit in the engine by defensive gunfire, dropping out of the action and later bailing out as his wingman joined the other two focussed on the same Dornier. Peart attacked from port and hit the aircraft's wing, remaining Spitfires following but appearing to miss with their own shots as the bomber attempted to throw them off their aim and German gunnery passed uncomfortably close. Peart's next attack used cannon and machine-gun fire, a piece of the Dornier breaking off and hitting his Spitfire, forcing him to break away and assess the damage.

> The Dornier 217, for that is what it turned out to be, was losing height and it eventually crash landed on the side of a scrub-covered hill. While obviously damaged it was not on fire, and I thought that at least some of the crew might have survived. The other two Spitfire pilots were keen to strafe the downed aircraft as it had crashed in enemy territory and the crew could possibly have been rescued to fight again. On the other hand, the bravery of the crew in carrying out an operation unescorted by fighters in the face of overwhelming

odds was most impressive. They had defended themselves with great determination and skill. They deserved the chance to live so I ordered the other two off. We never did find out whether there were any survivors.[22]

The records of KG 100 list the 5./KG 100 Do 217E-5 '6N+KN' lost while engaged on a shipping attack in the Gulf of Salerno; *Lt.* Helmut Ridder and two crewmen missing in action, one other, flight engineer *Ogfr.* Hans Klein, taken prisoner.

Though undeniably effective, Jope's KG 100 had suffered heavy casualties in its attacks against the Salerno beachhead. While 8./KG 100 returned to Schwäbisch Hall to convert to He 177 aircraft on 20 September, a final successful raid on Allied shipping in Ajaccio harbour, Corsica, took place in September. There French Resistance fighters had revolted against German occupying troops and were soon engaged in heavy fighting with *Sturmbrigade* 'Reichsführer SS' and elements of the 90th Panzer Grenadier Division, supported by Italian paratroopers loyal to the fascist cause and Wehrmacht Brandenburgers. The battle continued from 9 September until the final German evacuation on 4 October. On the last day of September the French destroyer *Le Fortuné* was in liberated Ajaccio harbour and targeted by ten Do 217s of II./KG 100; nine carrying a single Hs 293 each. American Naval Intelligence officer Serge 'Peter' Karlow was present after arriving on the French destroyer, part of an advance party of OSS men.

> The morning was clear and sunny . . . I got off and was waiting for our OSS people in Corsica to meet us when suddenly an armada of German planes flew overhead. This was accompanied by sporadic anti-aircraft fire. I ducked under a balcony of a nearby building and peered out cautiously. Five or six of the planes had been shot down and were tumbling out of the sky in flames. It turned out they were new German guided glider bombs with their own motors and fiery exhaust. They headed for and hit the LST and sank it, with the much-needed anti-aircraft radar still on board.[23]

Two bombs were duds due to technical failures and two other Dorniers jettisoned theirs due to the presence of enemy fighters. A pair of Dorniers were lost over Sardinia – two prisoners later being recovered by French troops – while a third crash-landed on the beach at Istres. The Luftwaffe claimed two direct hits amidships on a 'cruiser or large destroyer', one hit on the harbour mole between vessels and another near miss. A merchant vessel in the same position was also claimed as hit directly amidships. *Gruppenkommandeur Hptm.* Heinz Molinnus, leading the attack, considered it a complete success despite accurate flak and eight defending French Spitfires which disrupted the approach of the last *Kette*, forcing them away into cloud cover 1,800 metres over the island.[24] Behind them HMS *LST-79* went down carrying radar equipment destined for installation on the island for air defence as well as HMS *LCT-2231* which was carried as cargo aboard the LST. The French destroyer suffered minor damage and an American USAAF colonel present aboard *LST-79* when it was hit was able to give the following description of the Hs 293 attack:

> Bomb was released from Dornier 217 at 9,000 feet about three miles from target which was stopped in harbour. A trail of black smoke was first seen behind Dornier, followed by a burst of flame from an object (underneath?). This was then seen to be bomb, which appeared as circular object on fire approaching target and always keeping in line with the Dornier, thus followed curved path. At last moment, before hitting, the bomb appeared to dive more steeply towards target. Wingspan of bomb appears to be half that of a Spitfire, with square tips.[25]

Proposals to find and salvage unexploded glide bombs from the ocean floor were generally deemed impractical by the British Admiralty, the difficulties in locating such a small submerged object, potentially buried in the sandy Tyrrhenian seafloor, outweighed by the resources required for the search. However, components of the two dud weapons that had landed within the confined harbour space were recovered and later despatched to Britain where fresh impetus was provided to development of jamming technology for the controlling radio signals.

In Italy, the main airfield at Foggia and its twelve valuable satellites were captured by the British Eight Army on 27 September, I./KG 76 being forced to destroy fourteen Ju 88s to prevent their capture as they abandoned the base and withdrew to France to rest and refit. Losses had also necessitated a temporary withdrawal of II./KG 76 from operations during late September, moving temporarily to Saint-Martin-de-Pallières, France, to also refit before a return to Aviano.

From Berlin came orders at the end of September to make I. and III./KG 26 and II. and III./KG 100 available from Richthofen's

Luftflotte 2 for a special mission coordinated by *Luftflotte* 3 against a major convoy sighted west of Lisbon. Orders remained in force for a single *Kette* of II./KG 100 to be held at one hour readiness – and the remainder of the *Gruppe* at three hours' readiness – from daybreak to sunset in order to counter potential Allied naval attacks against ships involved in evacuating Corsica and as events transpired, the Lisbon mission was cancelled during the afternoon of 2 October, though both *Kampfgruppen* remained subordinated to *Luftflotte* 3 until further notice.

By the beginning of October *Kampffliegerführer Mittelmeer*, *Oberst* Storp, issued orders for all bomber *Gruppen* to allocate immediate time to rest and the restoration of aircraft serviceability. By that time the dedicated maritime *Kampfflieger* within the Mediterranean theatre of action had been reduced to the following units:

Luftflotte 2, *Generalfeldmarschall* Wolfram Freiherr von Richthofen;
(*Kampffliegerführer Mittelmeer* and *Fernkampführer/Luftflotte* 2, Walter Storp)
2. *Fliegerdivision*, *Generalleutnant* Johannes Fink;

> Stab/KG 26, *Obstlt.* Werner Klümper (Salon de Provence), no aircraft;
> I./KG 26, *Hptm.* Helmut von Rabenau, (Salon de Provence), fifty-four He 111H-11s, forty of them serviceable (eight lost to enemy action in September), thirty-two crews, thirteen of which were ready for action;
> III./KG 26, *Hptm.* Klaus Nocken, (Montpellier), thirty Ju 88A-4s (four lost to enemy action and two in accidents in September), twelve ready crews.

> Stab/KG 100 *Obstlt.* Bernhard Jope (Istres), one Do 217K-1, four Do 217E-4s (one lost to enemy action in September), one Do 217E-5, three crews with two ready;
> II./KG 100, *Hptm.* Heinz Molinnus (Istres), thirty Do 217E-5s of which twelve were serviceable (four had been lost to enemy action and four to accidents in September), twenty-two crews, all but one ready;
> III./KG 100, *Hptm.* Gerhard Döhler (Istres), seven Do 217K-2s of which three were serviceable (twelve had been lost to enemy action in September), fifteen crews.[26]

The Ju 88s of II.*Fliegerkorps* – including the one-time veteran maritime specialist unit KG 30 – had become relegated mainly to night bombing missions with little to show for their efforts except a steady stream of losses. While not dedicated maritime strike units, they had been targeting the Allied shipping off the Salerno beaches and continued to do so as the *Gruppen* were gradually withdrawn to the north.

II.*Fliegerkorps*, General Alfred Bülowius;

> Stab/KG 30, *Obstlt*. Sigmund-Ulrich Freiherr von Gravenreuth (Ghedi), two Ju 88A-4s;
>
> I./KG 30, *Maj*. Freiherr von Blomberg (Ghedi), eighteen Ju 88A-4s (five lost to enemy action and three to accidents in September);
>
> II./KG 30, *Maj*. Pflüger (Villafranca), thirteen Ju 88A-4s (one lost to enemy action and two to accidents in September).[27]

> Stab/KG 54, *Obstlt*. Volprecht Riedesel Freiherr zu Eisenbach (Bergamo) one Ju 88A-4;
>
> III./KG 54, *Maj*. Franz Zauner (Bergamo) nineteen Ju88A-4s (five lost to enemy action in eptember), three Ju 88D-1s.[28]

> Stab/KG 76, *Obstlt* Rudolf Hallensleben (Aviano), two Ju 88A-4s (one lost to enemy action in September);
>
> I./KG 76, *Hptm*. Hans Coym (La Jasse), fifteen Ju 88A-4s, eight of them serviceable (eight lost to enemy action and seven to accidents in September), one Ju 88C-6, twenty-one crews, seven ready;
>
> II./KG 76, *Hptm*. Siegfried Geisler (Saint Martin), fifteen Ju 88A-4s, ten serviceable (ten lost to enemy action and three to accidents in September), twenty-four crew, eleven ready.

However, the numbers do not always indicate the paucity of serviceable machines available at any given time. Storp had requested that due to the low serviceability rate of his *Gruppen*, he be permitted the allocation of ten Italian bombers for each *Geschwader* from the number that had been seized at the Armistice. Furthermore, the use of captured communications aircraft could allow operational types to remain in the front line. His request, however, was denied, emphasis instead placed on training to improve serviceability rates.

Outside of Storp's responsibility, two *Staffeln* of Arado floatplanes remained active on the Italian mainland:

2./SAGr. 128, *Hptm.* Georg Borchert (Berre), twelve Ar 196A-3s (two lost in a mid-air collision while on ASW mission between Corsica and Elba);

2./BFl.Gr. 196, (Venice-St. Nicolo), eight Ar 196A-3s (three shot down during September), one Ar 196A-5.

The *Bordfliegerstaffel* was withdrawn from the command of *Luftflotte 2* on 2 October after two aircraft were shot down thirty kilometres east of Bastia after being attacked by twelve Spitfires while escorting a pair of Ju 52s transporting troops from Corsica to Italy. Both Arado crews were killed. With the dislocation of ground crews and supply of spare parts caused by incessant Allied bombing, by 20 October, only two of ten machines belonging to 2./Bo.Fl.Gr. 196 were listed as operational, flying ASW flights as far as La Spezia.

The two *Gruppen* of fighter-bombers from *Maj.* Heinz Schumann's *Schnellkampfgeschwader* 10 present at Salerno and two of *Maj.* Hans-Karl Stepp's *Schlachtgeschwader* 2 had also distinguished themselves as effective anti-shipping aircraft despite their small payload; their fast low-level raids not only scoring hits on enemy shipping, but sowing confusion and providing the perfect diversion for attacks to be successfully mounted using guided weapons from altitude. Losses had, however, been predictably heavy to gradually established Allied aerial superiority. The two *Gruppen* of SKG 10 had lost fifty-eight Fw 190 aircraft to enemy action over Salerno during September, a further six being written off in accidents. *Hauptmann* Werner 'Prinzchen' Dörnbrack's II./SchG 2 lost three Fw 190s to the enemy and another three to accidents.

Dörnbrack's aircraft were soon in action again against Allied landing craft after reports of Allied troops landing at the Adriatic port of Termoli. Operation *Devon* launched on 3 October; troops of No. 3 Commando, No. 40 (Royal Marine) Commando, and elements of the 2nd Special Service Brigade landed during early morning darkness, swiftly reinforced by two brigades of the 78th Infantry Division. The attack was designed to turn the left flank of the German's Volturno Line and Kesselring swiftly despatched elements of 16th Panzer Division to counterattack as II.*Fliegerkorps* threw twenty-three Fw 190s of II./SchG 2 against the landing. Their dive-bombing and strafing was 'severe' for the initial forty-eight hours, forcing supporting destroyers offshore and damaging *LCS 38*, though later repaired. However, the air attacks gradually slackened until II.*Fliegerkorps* suspended them altogether at 1800hrs on 6 October. Frantic efforts by Allied engineers had erected bridges that allowed armoured reinforcements to counter the 16th Panzer Division's thrust making headway toward Termoli. Unwilling to expend further troops, Kesselring prepared to withdraw to a second defensive position, named the Barbara Line, behind the Trigno River. The emphasis of the Fw 190 ground-attack aircraft was switched to supporting the withdrawal of ground troops, II./SKG 10 and III./SKG 10 being held at 45 minutes readiness for support missions at Guidonia and Marcigliano airfields respectively.

A reorganisation of the entire *Schlachtgruppen* arm of the Luftwaffe was at hand, all existing *Stukagruppen* and *Schnellkampfgruppen* being redesignated *Schlachtgruppen*, the ground-attack branch increasing fivefold in size on 18 October 1943. However, little changed in reality for the Focke-Wulf units that had taken part in the Salerno beachhead fighting, albeit they now operated under different designations. On 18 October, *Maj.* Wolfgang 'Bombo' Schenck's Stab/SchG 2 was redesignated Stab/SG 4 and command passed to *Hptm.* Heinrich 'Rubio' Brücker, a ground-attack expert who had begun his career in the Condor Legion. *Hauptmann* Werner Dörnbrack's II./SchG 2 was redesignated I./SG 4; in Viterbo, *Hptm.* Hanns-Jobst Hauenschild relinquished command of II./SKG 10 which was redesignated II./SG 4, command passing to *Hptm.* Gerhard Walther, while *Hptm.* Fritz Schröter's III./SKG 10 became III./SG 4 and relocated to Graz, Austria. *Major* Heinz Schumann's Stab/SKG 10 became Stab/SG 10, transferring to the Eastern front where SG 10 spent its entire war.

As the *Schlachtgruppen* were reorganised, all flying units of *Luftflotte* 2 were placed under the jurisdiction of II.*Fliegerkorps*, except the *Schlachtgruppen* whose control was exercised by *Fliegerführer Luftflotte* 2, *Obstlt.* Hubertus Hitschold, a Stuka pilot since the beginning of the war. Hitschold, who would be promoted to *General der Schlachtflieger* in November, was tasked with the close support of the 10th Army's defensive battles. At the same time, all *Luftflotte* 2 bomber units, *Aufklärungsgruppe* 122 (Ju 88 and Me 410 aircraft), 6.*Seenotsstaffel*, 2./BFl.Gr. 196 and *Minensuchstaffel* were from that point onward to be directly subordinated to II.*Fliegerkorps*; Storp's office of *Kampffliegerführer Mittelmeer* judged redundant and he later appointed temporary Chief of Staff to IV.*Fliegerkorps* on the Eastern Front.

During early October Hitler issued instructions outlining the future duties of the three Wehrmacht services in Italy. While the Army would conduct as strong a defence as possible and the Kriegsmarine was instructed to 'assist the Army in every way possible', the Luftwaffe's main task in the Italian theatre 'will still be attacks on enemy shipping' as well as ground support missions.

The inactivity that had settled over the maritime *Kampfgruppen* allowing them to rest and rebuild ended on 4 October when twenty Do 217s of II./KG 100 and thirty-seven He 111 torpedo aircraft of I./KG 26 made a low-level dusk attack on Convoy UGS 18 off Cape Tenez, Algeria, under escort by French P-39s of fighter unit GC III/6. The German bombers faced severe light calibre anti-aircraft fire and a determined defence from the French pilots, reinforced by aircraft scrambling from nearby Algerian airfields. Allied pilots claimed one German aircraft destroyed and another probable, while KG 100 gunners claimed the destruction of a Spitfire (*sic*) at 1854hrs, and a Beaufighter at 1920hrs, hit by gunners from *Ogefr*. Kurt Laufenburg's Dornier of 4./KG 100, before darkness forced the Allied pilots to disengage. The KG 100 part of the action against UGS 18 was led by *Obstlt*. Jope flying in the wireless reconnaissance aircraft that was not equipped with an Hs 293, but instead maintained the overall view. Jope later reported success:

> . . . As a result of small ships being difficult to see during the time of the attack, the main effort had to be shifted to the targets which were more easily visible. The destruction of, or at very least most severe damage to, 60,000 tons of merchant shipping can be counted on. The effect of the attacks by the missing or crashed crews (the latter with a specially well aimed bomb) are left out of account. The matter of technical failures is being followed up.

German claims far outstripped reality. The crews of II./KG 100 claimed seven hits or near misses from nineteen Hs 293s fired, one other jettisoned due to a fighter attack. Six of the fired weapons were judged to be technical failures, but the remainder included a direct hit on a transport of 10,000GRTs, a hit five metres short of a 8,000–9,000GRT transport, a direct hit amidships on a transport ship or auxiliary carrier of 10,000GRT, a hit amidships of a 12,000GRT cargo vessel, and various near misses.

Using a combination of standard torpedoes and Hs 293 guided bombs four ships were actually hit, the steamships *Hiram Maxim* and *Samite* being damaged but successfully towed to Algiers. The latter was struck in Hold No 3 by an Hs 293 – the vessel's only cargo hold not filled with explosives. SS *Selkirk* received minor damage but was able to rejoin the convoy, while the 7,130GRT SS *Fort Fitzgerald* was set ablaze by an Hs 293. Carrying 1,400 tons of volatile munitions and 5,340 tons of military supplies, the ship was abandoned and sunk by gunfire from an escort vessel. Of the attackers, I./KG 26 lost two aircraft shot down into the sea, only one survivor from both crews, *Oblt.* Fritz Laueschläger captured after '1H+PL' was shot down by naval gunners at wave-top height during his torpedo run, wounded, rescued and hospitalised in Algiers. The losses for II./KG 100 were serious; the *Staffelkapitän* 6./KG 100, *Oblt.* Wolfgang Böttger in '6N+GM', shot down in flames by French fighters and *Gruppenkommandeur Hptm.* Heinz Molinnus lost with all of his crew of '6N+CC' as the Dornier crash-landed back at Istres. Two other Dorniers crashed on landing in the dark in southern France, among them Heinz-Georg Schöneberg in his Do 217E-5 coded '6N + FM'. *Hauptmann* Heinz-Emil Middermann, German Cross-holding former *Staffelkapitän* of 6./KG 2, replaced Molinnus as *Gruppenkommandeur* II./KG 100.

A directive from Göring was received the following day concerning the operational employment of KG 100. The Luftwaffe C-in-C pointed out, once again, that such specialised aircraft were only to be used against 'worth-while targets'.

> The fundamental rule for the allocation of forces is to be that it is better to attack fewer targets of decisive importance with a large number of special aircraft as possible, rather than divide forces. Additionally, attention must be drawn to the fact that special equipment is so far only being built on to the Do 217 in small numbers. Consequently, it is particularly important for the general conduct of the war that this weapon, available in KG 100, should be conserved.[29]

The last Mediterranean convoy attack of October was carried out on 21st, when thirteen Do 217s of II./KG 100, twenty-eight He 111s of I./KG 26 and eight Ju 88s of III./KG 26 took off during mid-afternoon to intercept a large convoy sighted west of Algiers off Mostaganem being shadowed by a Ju 88D-1 of 1.(F)/33 from Istres. The attacking bombers reached their objective by early evening, the slow convoy bound for the United Kingdom, MKS 28, creating a thick smokescreen, though it appears to have been as problematic to defending gunners as the bombers.

In a twenty-minute attack, fifty-four aerial torpedoes were dropped, a total of fifteen steamers, one tanker, and a single destroyer being hit and heavily damaged, only two of them attributed to glide bombs of KG 100. American P-39D Airacobras of USAAF 345th Fighter Squadron intercepted the incoming bombers and declared four shot down, a further two credited to naval gunners. The shadowing Ju 88 was also shot down, ditching into the sea and the crew rescued by a Polish destroyer forty-eight hours later.

Two Dorniers and three Heinkels failed to return, with all crews missing in action, a fourth crashing in France killing *Fw.* Herbert Schirmann and injuring the rest. Among those lost was *Staffelkapitän* 3./KG 26, Austrian *Hptm.* Walter Hildenbrand, shot down aboard aircraft '1H+TL' only four days after being awarded the German Cross in Gold. Hildebrand, a veteran of KG 26 since the invasion of Poland, was posthumously awarded the Knight's Cross on 6 April 1944.

The convoy lost two ships; the 3,775GRT SS *Saltwick*, a British freighter travelling in ballast with 900 Red Cross parcels and probably hit by an HS 293 launched by *Fw.* Bruno Obst's 6./KG 100 aircraft, and the 4,600GRT American SS *Tivives* to a torpedo from the Ju 88s of III./KG 26. Four torpedoes were seen to miss ahead and astern before a fifth impacted behind the engine room, the ship going down in less than ten minutes, one crew member and a navy gunner killed.

The first shot fired was by the LST on our starboard side. The order had been given to open fire on any plane closer than 1,500 yards. The five planes [of the first wave] scattered, some going to starboard and some to port, strafing the decks as they went over. No torpedoes were dropped on the first run and no planes were shot down, but the whereabouts of the ship was revealed [through the smokescreen] by the intense fire of the guns as the planes went over.

The second wave came in from the port quarter and was less concentrated than the first but was longer drawn out; planes were coming in, one or two at a time and from various angles. However, it was apparent that they were concentrating their attacks on our ship. During this run, one plane coming from the starboard quarter was engaged by #7, #8 and #6 guns and was shot down. This plane exploded just before or at the same time as it hit the water about 150 yards from the ship. It broke up and its wreckage bounced along the water . . . . During this so-called wave, another plane was hit as it came in from the port bow and went off on the port quarter The tail was observed to be smoking and the plane disappeared in the smokescreen. Several torpedoes were dropped, two missing the bow. Aerial torpedoes were observed toward the beginning of this wave of attack; one glider bomb was observed which hit near the LST on our starboard side, probably exploding on contact; another came close on the port side from almost dead ahead and went off abaft the beam.[30]

The third wave of bombers attacked from all directions, aircraft barely visible through the smokescreen until they were virtually on top of the ship, and one from the port quarter hit the freighter behind its engine room, the blast of the torpedo and sympathetic detonation of a barrage balloon ordered on deck that morning by the convoy Commodore, throwing several men overboard. The ship listed heavily to starboard then rolling back to port as water rushed through the gaping hole in its hull, before rapidly sinking as the crew and gunners hurriedly abandoned ship.

It is recommended that smokescreens be discontinued. It is my opinion that they do more harm than good. We are unable to use the guns effectively because of the intense smoke which enabled the planes to know our whereabouts but made it impossible for us to see them until they were within 300 yards of us. The barrage balloon burned three men badly and they are a definite menace on deck in any locality where aircraft attack can be expected.[31]

The '*Löwe*' *Kampfgeschwader*, KG 26, had suffered badly at the hands of naval gunners, inactive until the first week of November to enable crews to rest and as many aircraft as possible be returned to fighting trim. In the meantime, on 29 October, veteran *Gruppenkommandeur* of III./KG 26, *Maj.* Klaus-Wilhelm Nocken, and *Oblt.* Heinz Jente, *Staffelkapitän* 2./KG 26, were both awarded the Knight's Cross.

Allied shipping in newly occupied Naples harbour came under repetitive bombing attack in early November, on the first evening of the month KG 54 releasing forty-four LT350 circling torpedoes. Minelayer HMS *Linnet* was hit and holed on the port side at No 2 hold by what was, at first, taken to be a mine. A repair party from USS *Extricate* was put on board to assist, the ship's pumps keeping *Linnet* afloat until it could be successfully beached. The fleet minesweeper HMS *Rhyl* was also damaged by a conventional bomb landing nearby.

Klaus-Wilhelm Nocken,
Gruppenkommandeur of III./KG 26,
awarded the Knight's Cross on 29
October 1943.

To enable torpedo missions by night, the Luftwaffe radar research establishment at Werneuchen submitted a proposal to the *RLM* on 3 November that *Luftflotte* 2 be empowered to draw on multiple units to assemble a specialist *Staffel* for the sole purpose of night attacks on enemy shipping. They would be equipped with FuG 200 '*Hohentwiel*' radar, provided and installed by engineers from the facility either on site or in Munich. Werneuchen would provide *Staffelkapitän* and instructors for a period of three months in which training could be completed. In total, the *Staffel* would comprise five Ju 88s for blind bombing, five for mine dropping, five for torpedo firing and three for flare dropping, all crews, mine and torpedo technicians being drawn from *Luftflotte* 2. Despite potential merit, available strength did not allow the formation of this specialised unit. The time in which it would be withdrawn from the front line would weaken already depleted offensive power.

That same day *General* Günther Korten, new Chief of the Luftwaffe General Staff, offered the Kriegsmarine an increase of 50 per cent in the number of '*Hohentwiel*' sets produced already assigned to it. This conciliatory move came in the wake of irritable communication between the Kriegsmarine's *Marinegruppenkommando Süd* and Richthofen at

Luftflotte 2 headquarters. *Admiral* Kurt Fricke had bluntly stated that increased Luftwaffe operations were essential to support naval warfare throughout the Black, Adriatic and Aegean Seas. Richthofen's reply was noted in the *SKL* War Diary in Berlin:

> *Luftflotte* 2 Command submitted to Operations Staff correspondence with German Naval Command, Italy in which the Luftwaffe rejects justifiable demands by the navy on the grounds of insufficient forces; *Luftflotte* 2 asks that no future demands be made that exceed the forces available – also known to the Navy – 'as these demands can be merely regarded as a contribution to the War Diary.'

To this, Korten added a more conciliatory message:

> It is true that demands have become so excessive that they can really no longer be complied with. Here also concentration points must be determined for reconnaissance, patrol, escort etc. Degrees of priority must be fixed for all sea areas, which, if possible, must be divided according to theatres of operation and in the relation of the latter to each other.

In Berlin, Dönitz and his staff were aware that it would be necessary to remind the various *Marinegruppenkommandos* that they must accommodate themselves as far as possible to the Luftwaffe's operational strength. Certain economies could be achieved by greater concentration of transports requiring escort, within the limits of naval strategy. The resultant unavoidable disadvantages would have to be weighed against the benefit of greater security as each case arose. Nonetheless, *SKL* also noted that despite the necessity of understanding from the naval point of view, 'the basic demand of the Naval Staff for adequate support of naval operations by the Luftwaffe, remained the same'.

During this period, the *Torpedoflieger* were instructed to step up operations. Reconnaissance aircraft of 2. *Fliegerdivision* were despatched to the North African coast during early November, for continuous probing for convoy traffic and on 6 November KG 26 attacked Convoy KMF 25A between Algeria and Sardinia accompanied by Do 217s of II./KG 100 and, for the first time in the Mediterranean, He 177s of KG 40, both aircraft carrying Hs 293s.[32]

The convoy had received air cover through the Strait of Gibraltar, withdrawing at sunset as the Rock faded behind. The convoy of twenty-six merchant ships reformed into three columns while passing through the swept 'Tunisian War Channel', screened by Task Group 60.2 – ten destroyers centred on the anti-aircraft cruiser HMS *Colombo* – as well as the additional escort destroyers USS *Frederick C. Davis* and *Herbert C. Jones* and two destroyers of the Royal Hellenic Navy. The two American destroyers carried prototype jamming equipment for use against frequencies used by the '*Kehlgerät*', but at that stage based on educated guesswork which later transpired to be inaccurate. A shadowing aircraft had been sighted during the afternoon, but it showed friendly 'Identification Friend or Foe' (IFF) signals. Within ten minutes of sunset, after the covering fighters had departed, destroyer USS *Laub*'s radar detected six aircraft to the north, also apparently emanating IFF signals. Its speed betrayed it as an aircraft, though the signal itself was small, similar to that received by a periscope, and periodically disappearing as the aircraft travelled at wave-top height. USS *Tillman*, on the convoy's port quarter, detected a north-westerly radar contact almost simultaneously with visual contact, identifying the aircraft as a Do 217 and opening fire, despite the great range, to warn other ships.

The Dornier 217 launched its Hs 293 at USS *Tillman* before turning away, the destroyer's port weapons pouring fire into the approaching missile which came in at a terrific speed before steeply diving only 600 yards distant and crashing into the sea. A second Do 217 released its weapon on the port beam and the American commander turned his ship bow-on, the destroyer's automatic weapons concentrating on the Hs 293 and her main batteries on the parent aircraft. The Hs 293 glided ahead of *Tillman*, turned back and splashed into the sea 150 yards on the starboard quarter as the Do 217 was hit by a full salvo of 5in shells and exploded. USS *Tillman*'s fire-control radar was disabled by the concussion of the near miss. A third Hs 293 landed 500 yards on the starboard beam.

Escort warships had been the targets of the first wave of Dorniers, attempting to disperse their firepower and pave the way for torpedo bombers approaching from the port convoy's side at wave top height. Torpedoes soon hit the water, one exploding in USS *Tillman*'s wake causing further minor damage, another hitting the passenger ship SS *Santa Elena* which carried 1,933 military personnel, 101 nurses and 133 crewmen.

USS *Beatty* on the convoy's starboard quarter detected fresh radar signals, again showing a correct IFF transponder signal, but soon visually identified as Ju 88s. As the protective screen of smoke created by the destroyers drifted over the ship, momentarily blinding its gunners, two Ju 88s appeared suddenly to starboard, being fired at by small calibre weapons before a torpedo struck the after-engine room thirty seconds later. Eleven men were killed in the initial attack, one died later of wounds and a third sailor, Radioman 3rd Class Samuel Poland, blown overboard along with a K-gun and a depth charge, which fortunately failed to explode. The ship's back was broken, all electric power lost, engine and boiler rooms flooded as damage control parties struggled to keep the listing destroyer afloat. For over four hours they attempted to save the ship before the list had reached 45 degrees and *Beatty* was abandoned, breaking in two and sinking shortly thereafter.

A third ship had also been hit; the 19,355GRT Dutch liner SS *Marnix van St. Aldegonde*, carrying 2,924 military personnel and 311 crewmen. The torpedo exploded in the engine room and, though fatally holed, there was not a single casualty aboard the liner. Both torpedoed merchant ships remained afloat and were taken in tow until progressive flooding sank both as they headed for Philippeville. It was the most successful Luftwaffe torpedo operation in the Mediterranean as far as the total tonnage sent to the bottom of the sea. However, it remained a different proposition to the claimed fourteen ships hit (totalling 149,000 BRT) and two destroyers. The Wehrmacht's announcement of the attack concluded that 'with the destroyed ships, several thousand young North American and British reinforcements found their graves beneath the waves'. Given the vessels that were hit by torpedoes, the actual death toll of sixteen was mercifully low.

For the attackers, losses were relatively high. From Klümper's KG 26 three He 111s of I./KG 26 and three Ju 88s of III./KG 26 and their crews, were lost, including *Hptm.* Eberhard Peukert, veteran of the *Küstenflieger* and *Staffelkapitän* of 8./KG 26, his aircraft colliding with another during the attack. Five days later, KG 26 was back in action, on the same day that Luftwaffe maritime forces supported the last successful offensive mounted by the Wehrmacht in the Aegean.

6

The Soft Underbelly

Battles in the Aegean and Mediterranean

The Aegean

The surrendering Italian garrison on Kos turned the island over to Allied troops. British and Greek units rushed to take control of as many Dodecanese islands as possible before German forces could react, occupying Leros and Samos by 17 September 1943, smaller islands following as part of Churchill's Balkan fixation.

Royal Air Force aircraft began operating from the airfield on Kos and German inter-island supply convoys and troop movements immediately came under attack, inadequately escorted by Arado 196 aircraft of *Seeaufklärungsgruppe* 126. Seven low-flying Beaufighters attacked a small convoy of two merchants and *UJ2014* on passage from Piraeus to Rhodes as it passed south of Naxos on 17 September. While there were casualties aboard the escorting *U-Boot Jäger*, one of two escorting Arado 196A-3s of 1./SAGr. 126 was shot down. The pilot, *Uffz.* Fritz Schaar, ditched his heavily damaged aircraft, 'D1+EH', after which he and observer *Uffz.* Herbert Schneider were rescued by *UJ2014*, the battered aircraft taken in tow but sinking as its holed floats filled with water. Expecting a second air strike, *UJ2104* radioed for urgent fighter cover as a Dornier Do 24 of 7.*Seenotstaffel* unsuccessfully tried to find the convoy and recover wounded. The convoy proceeded on its way until 2330hrs when it was attacked by the destroyers HMS *Faulknor*, *Eclipse* and HHMS *Queen Olga* near Astypalaia; both merchants were sunk and the escort *UJ2104* was severely hit and flooding, many crewmen and at least one of the Arado crew jumping overboard to escape what they believed to be a sinking ship. They later washed ashore on Astypalaia and were captured.[1]

In Berlin, *OKW* feared that British-controlled Dodecanese islands could be used as a springboard for further invasion of the Aegean islands, though they had moved fast enough to prevent Allied occupation of the biggest prize: Rhodes. The British Operation *Accolade* planned a direct attack on Rhodes and Karpathos by a total of three infantry divisions, an armoured brigade and supporting troops, the captured islands then dominating the entire Eastern Aegean. However, American refusal to take part resulted in required invasion shipping being redirected to Italy and the operation was scrubbed.

The Salerno landings had not allayed fears in Berlin that overall Allied strategy aimed at the Balkans rather than an advance along the Italian peninsula. Kriegsmarine intelligence officers lamented the lack of extensive and reliable regional Luftwaffe reconnaissance, as much due to dwindling fuel stocks as inexperienced crews, and issued 'Enemy Situation Report No. 19' on 2 October, in which they stated that:

> Inadequate air reconnaissance in the Mediterranean makes an insight into the present disposition of enemy landing craft and merchant shipping difficult. It is assumed that approximately 30 per cent of special landing craft available and approximately 20 per cent of merchant shipping in the Mediterranean is still engaged in traffic between North Africa, Sicily, and the Italian operational areas. It is expected that the focal point of future operations in the Central Mediterranean outside the Italian mainland will be the east Adriatic area (Albania/Dalmatia), while in the Eastern Mediterranean a further operation against the Aegean islands is likely.

Fiebig's *Luftwaffenkommando Südost* controlled the Luftwaffe presence throughout the Balkans independent of *Luftflotte* command, directly subordinate to the *RLM* in Berlin. Concurrently, Fiebig headed X.*Fliegerkorps* based in Athens, and issued orders in October that convoy escort within the Adriatic would be the domain of *Fliegerführer Albanien*, as insufficient forces were available in Croatia due to the ground fighting in Yugoslavia.

A First World War naval aviator, former Lufthansa pilot and Knight's Cross with Oak Leaves Stuka *Geschwader* commander, *Oberst* Walter Hagen had been appointed *Fliegerführer Albanien* in September 1943. His main offensive capability appears to have been the Bf 109s and Bf 110s of *Nahaufklärungsgruppe* 12 'Tannenburg' based at the former Italian airbase at Devoli and the *Flugbetriebsboot* 430. Both he and his northerly counterpart *Gen.Lt.* Wolfgang Erdmann, *Fliegerführer Kroatien* (which possessed no fighter units), operated aerial reconnaissance over the Adriatic, although were instructed that only shipping 'clearly recognised as a landing or commando operation' were to be attacked due to the confusion of nationalities within the region and awareness that the Allies were launching decoy operations to simulate landings along the Italian east coast. They also found losses increasing over the Adriatic as Allied fighters increased their tempo of flights in support of Tito's partisans who had launched offensives to ensure German forces remained tied down in Yugoslavia. From mid-October, maritime reconnaissance of the eastern Adriatic from Albania was limited to twenty kilometres offshore – fifty kilometres in Croatian waters – and at low level to frustrate newly-installed radar stations in captured Puglia. Radio silence was to be strictly maintained, broken only in the event of landing forces being sighted. Additionally, occasional photo-reconnaissance missions were flown over Puglia's harbours by Bf 109s.

Tito's partisans took control of much of the Croatian coastline following the Italian armistice, though the city of Split was swiftly reoccupied by the Wehrmacht and declared part of the fascist Independent State of Croatia. The task of helping supply the city with food and humanitarian materials was entrusted to 6.*Seenotstaffel* which had been forced to retreat progressively from Sicily to Taranto, Vigna di Valle (near Rome), Portofino, La Spezia-Cadimare and, finally, to German-occupied Venice in October 1943, whereafter the *Staffel* was confined to the Adriatic Sea. On 1 November two of the *Staffel*'s Do 24 flying boats were lost during such a supply mission when the city came under attack by thirty-six RAF fighter-bombers. Aircraft 'KK+LQ' was destroyed by strafing in the harbour that injured *Uffz.* Otto Zscheppank, while 'CM+IJ' was shot down. Piloted by *Unteroffizier* Paul Lösing, the latter had just lifted off with sixteen wounded men and a female nurse aboard when it was brought down with no survivors. *Luftflotte* 2 immediately suspended transport of food shipments to Split by air, the Kriegsmarine undertaking future transport missions, while 6.*Seenotstaffel* impressed some captured Cant Z.506 tri-motor floatplanes into service, also acquiring three Fw 190s for future search and escort duties.

By November 1943, with Sardinia evacuated, *Obstlt.* Eduard Engelhorn's *Seenotdienstführer* 2 (*Süd*) reported its Mediterranean sub-commands to be distributed thus:

Seenotbereichskommando X, acting commander *Maj.* Hans Haeger, at Margherita di Ligure;

Seenotflottille 10, *Hptm.* Gabbert, in Venice (later redesignated *Seenotflottille* 20 in Verona);

Seenotstaffel 6, *Hptm.* Weiss, in Venice;
Sub-bases *Seenotkommando* 15 at Savona, *Seenotkommando* 29 in
    Portofino and later La Spezia,
Seenotkommando 31 in Piombino, *Seenotkommando* 16 in Orbetello and
    Seenotkommando Pola.

The transfer of air-sea rescue boats from the Ligurian Sea to the Adriatic
was made by road from Genoa to Piacenze where they were slipped into
the Po River and travelled to Venice.

Meanwhile, on Crete, *Generalleutnant* Friedrich-Wilhelm Müller
of the 22nd Air-Landing Division, had been ordered to retake the
Dodecanese and plans were swiftly formulated for a daring amphibious
and aerial assault. Kos now hosted two Spitfire squadrons and significant
British ground forces as well as 3,500 men of the original Italian
garrison. Heavy bombardment by Ju 88s of X.*Fliegerkorps*, under Bf 109
escort, soon rendered the airfield unusable and both Spitfire squadrons
were withdrawn to Cyprus, severe casualties amongst British ground
forces resulting in one battalion being evacuated. The air raids were
subsequently widened to include Leros as, with the Spitfires gone, the

Arado Ar 196A-3 of 2./Aufkl.Gr. 125 (*See*) pictured in Crete.

Luftwaffe had achieved local air supremacy, RAF Beaufighters being at a considerable disadvantage against a reinforced presence of Bf 109 fighters. HMS *Intrepid*, the Greek destroyer RHS *Vasillisa Olga* and the Italian *MAS 534* were attacked by Ju 88 and Ju 87 aircraft of LG 1, II./KG 51, II./KG 6, and II. and III./StG 3, and sunk in Lakki harbour, Leros, on 26 September 1943. The small submarine base, naval barracks, workshops and four of the five fuel depots (all empty) were also destroyed, for the loss of seven German bombers.

The German attack on Kos – Operation *Eisbär* – began on 3 October and by dawn the following day organised resistance had ceased and the island was in German hands. An immediate attack on Leros was planned, Allied troops on Kalymnos surrendering without a fight, though destruction of a troop convoy by the Royal Navy and arrival of USAAF P-38 Lightning aircraft to the area forced postponement while the British reinforced the island, 2,500 British troops joining the 8,320 Italian soldiers and sailors on Leros.

The Royal Navy roamed the area almost unchecked with Kriegsmarine forces too light to pose a significant threat. To counteract them, between 7 and 11 November, 5./KG 100 transferred from southern France to the Aegean; twenty-two aircraft equipped with forty Hs 293s were based at Kalamaki and placed under the control of *Luftwaffenkommando Südost*. On 10 November *General* Martin Fiebig's command included the following units within the Balkans (excluding the Bf 109s of *Jagdabschnittsführer Rumänien* protecting the Ploesti oilfields):

X.*Fliegerkorps*:
SAGr. 126 *Obstlt*. H. Busch
   Stab/SAGr. 126 (Skaramanga), 4 x BV 138
   1./SAGr. 126 (Skaramanga), 12 x Ar 196A-3 and A-4
   2./SAGr. 126 (Skaramanga), 12 x Ar 196A-3 and A-4
   3./SAGr. 126 (Kos), 12 x Ar 196A-3 and A-4
   4./SAGr. 126 (Suda Bay), 12 x Ar 196A-3 and A-4 (under control of
      X.*Fliegerkorps* for the Leros attack, before transfer to Croatia)
2./SAGr. 125 (Suda Bay), 12 x Ar 196A-3
5./KG 100 (Kalamaki), 12 x Do 217E-4
3./*Nahaufklärungsgruppe* 2 (Larissa), 8 x Bf 110G-3
1.(F)/122 (Kalamaki), 12 x Ju 88A-4, C-1, D-1
2.(F)/123 (Athens/Tatoi), 12 x Ju 88 of various series and Bf 109G-6/R3s

JG 27, *Obstlt.* Gustav Rödel, (Kalamaki)
   *Stab/*JG 27 (Kalamaki), 1 x Bf 109G-6
   III./JG 27, *Hptm.* Ernst Düllberg (Kalamaki), 32 x Bf 109G-6
   IV. JG 27, *Hptm.* Joachim Kirschner (Podgorica, Montenegro), 1 x Bf
      109F4, 31 x Bf 109G-6
11./ZG 26 (Eleusis), 12 x Ju 88C-6
SG 3, *Oberst* Kurt Kuhlmey
   *Stab/*SG 3 (Eleusis), 2 x Ju 87D-3
   II./SG 3 (Marizza), 27 x Ju 87D-3/5
Lehrgeschwader 1 (Eleusis)
   *Stab/*LG 1, *Obstlt.* Rudolf Hallensleben (Eleusis), 1 x Ju 88A-4
   I./LG 1, *Maj.* Heinz Ott (Eleusis), 12 x Ju 88A-4
   III./LG 1, *Hptm.* Hans-Günther Nedden (Kastelli/Heraklion), 32 x
      Ju 88A-4
II./KG 51, *Maj.* Herbert Voss (Saloniki), 40 x Ju 88A-4.

Fliegerführer Kroatien:
Stab/Nahaufklärungsgruppe 2, Bf 109
2./Nahaufklärungsgruppe 2, Bf 109
Nahaufklärungsstaffel Kroatien, Hs 126B-1, Do 17P-2
1./Nachtschlachtgruppe 7, He 46
2./Nachtschlachtgruppe 7, Hs 126
SG 151, *Oberst* Karl Christ, Ju 87
   Stab/SG 151 (Zagreb)
   I./SG 151, *Hptm.* Karl Schrepfer (Pancevo)
   II./SG 151, *Hptm.* Heinrich Heins (Zagreb)
   III./SG 151, *Hptm.* Hanschke (Pancevo)
   13./SG 151, *Hptm.* Heinz Weitzel, 7 Ju 87D-1, 3 x Ju 87D-3 (trop).
15./KG 53, *Maj.* Gerhard Joachim, 7 x Do 17Z-3

The Royal Navy hampered initial KG 100 operations among the
Dodecanese by taking advantage of the proximity of neutral Turkey
and its three-mile territorial limit. The German Foreign Office strictly
forbade any attacks made within Turkish territorial waters, even if
missile-carrying aircraft remained outside of the three-mile exclusion
zone. Instead, reconnaissance Ju 88s of 1./(F) 122 patrolled the strips of
sea between the Dodecanese and Turkish waters.

Success for 5./KG 100 did not come until the eve of the German
attack on Leros. On 11 November, the destroyers HMS *Petard*, *Rockwood*

Upper turret diagram details from the Do 217 E-2 and E-4 handbook: Part 8A '*Schusswaffen-anlage*'.

1 Drehkranzlafette DL 131/1
2 Abwerfbare Plexiglashaube
3 Abwurfhebel für die Plexiglashaube
4 Waffenlagerung
5 Pufferung

6 MG 131
7 Schaltgriff an der Waffe
8 Reflexvisier Revi 25 B
9 Zündumformer ZUM 1
10 MG 15 der Zusatzbewaffnung rechts

Abb. 23: B-Stand, von oben gesehen

and ORP *Krakowiak* fired 1,500 4in rounds at Kalymnos' main port and a small bay to its east where German vessels were congregated for the assault on Leros. On their withdrawal, under bright moonlight, two aircraft of 5./KG 100 attacked and HMS *Rockwood* was hit by an Hs 293 at 0045hrs. The rocket bomb impacted the gear room, flooding the compartment and killing Able Seaman Clifford Lawson. Even though the Hs 293 failed to explode, the destroyer had suffered considerable damage, all lights extinguished below decks as, under continuous attack, HMS *Petard* took the damaged destroyer in tow and retreated. The Hs 293 had virtually disintegrated on impact, much of it blasting its way out of the hull, although fragments remained for intelligence officers to study later. Three destroyers also bombarding Kos were attacked that same night, but with no success. However, the minesweeper *BYMS-2072* was sighted in the darkness as it escorted landing craft near Leros' east coast, and damaged by an Hs 293 that struck forward on the port side, the resulting explosion blasting the port 20mm gun and its platform into the sea, taking along the gunner who was strapped to it and killing the remaining gun crew. In total five men died, the battered minesweeper later being captured by the Kriegsmarine.

The assault on Leros began the following morning with strong aerial support by X.*Fliegerkorps*. As the Royal Navy attempted to maintain coastal gunnery support and communication lines, an Hs 293 hit HMS *Dulverton* at 1030hrs on 13 November, blasting through the hull directly beneath the bridge and demolishing the forward superstructure completely. Only six officers and 114 crew were rescued by HMS *Belvoir*, which scuttled the battered remains of the ship with gunfire before landing many of the more seriously wounded at Bodrum in Turkey. Among the seventy-eight men killed was the ship's captain, Commander Stuart Austen Buss. Two days later HMS *Aldenham* received a near miss from another Hs 293 attack. Though sinkings may have been relatively few, the effect of constant Luftwaffe attack prompted Vice Admiral Sir Algernon Willis, C–in–C Levant, to personally message recently appointed C–in–C Mediterranean, Admiral Sir John Cunningham, and implore him to exchange his Dodecanese destroyer force for fresh ships:

> Most of mine [destroyers] have had a very bad time at the hands of the German Air Force day and night and in my opinion must have a spell at some less strenuous and hazardous work.[2]

However, the final raid had already been completed by 5./KG 100 in the Aegean as Leros fell to the Germans on 16 November. For the British the loss of the Dodecanese was a disaster. Only a tiny force left on Kastellorizo remained which, despite some isolated commando raids, the Germans were content to ignore. Nonetheless, Churchill continued to clutch at the straws of *Accolade* and an Allied assault on Rhodes. On 24 November, at the Cairo Conference, Churchill renewed his demand for the attack. Face to face with General Marshall, Churchill said: 'His Majesty's Government can't have its troops standing idle. Muskets must flame.' Marshall replied, 'Not one American soldier is going to die on [that] goddamn beach.' The subject was never raised again.

As 5./KG 100 prepared to return to southern France and the 15th USAAF Air Force bombed Athens-Eleusis with B24s, Kalamaki was also attacked by forty-four XII Air Support Command B-25 bombers.[3] Fragmentation bombs showered on the airfield and six KG 100 Do 217 E-1s, E-5s and K-3s were destroyed or damaged along with a Ju 88A-4 from 1./LG 1 and Ju 52 from I./TG 4. An aircraft hangar and fuel storage tanks were also hit and left burning. As the surviving Dorniers departed

Greece for reunification with the rest of II./KG 100 at Istres, moves were already underway to relocate all of KG 100, the French *Staffeln* having been far from idle in the interim.

The Mediterranean

On 11 November, as the battle for Leros was about to begin, a combined attack on Convoy KMS 31 (code-named 'Untrue') had been undertaken by sixteen Do 217s of II./KG 100, twenty-three He 111s of I./KG 26 and seventeen Ju 88s of III./KG 26. A reconnaissance Ju 88 picked up this eastbound convoy at 1735hrs the previous evening, reporting forty-eight ships steaming at 8 knots, forty-five miles west of Alborán Island. The next morning a single Ju 88 re-established contact and began to shadow, updating the convoy's course, composition, and local weather conditions. Through the course of the day, two other Ju 88s took part in monitoring the convoy, the last instructed at 1320hrs hours to send all future reports on radio frequencies used by combat aircraft as the attacking force had already taken off. Above the convoy pairs of P-39 fighters patrolled in three altitude brackets about three miles from the convoy, a single Walrus flying boat providing close anti-submarine cover. By night, six Beaufighters remained in the vicinity, flying ahead of KMS 31's path. As the first German bombers neared there were fifteen friendly aircraft distributed at various heights and in various positions up to fifteen miles north of the convoy, their IFF signals virtually saturating radar plots aboard escorting warships.

At 1755hrs radar traces of inbound aircraft were picked up and the convoy began making smoke, the attack unfolding within half an hour as HMS *Bicester* radioed a brief message to C-in-C Mediterranean: 'Help glider bomb attack. My position now is 36.13N. 00.11 W., course 063°, 7½ knots.'

The first Do 217s launched their Hs 293s aimed at the escort ships before the torpedo bombers that followed. Attacking from landward, eight bombers were lost in the confusing melee; six He 111H-11s of I./KG 26, two Ju 88A-4s of III./KG 26 and another Ju 88 later ditching off Barcelona after exhausting its fuel. In return, four merchant ships were destroyed. The Dornier pilots claimed three ships hit: the British 5,150GRT freighter MV *Birchbank* and the 8,587GRT MV *Indian Prince* and the Belgian 7,220GRT SS *Carlier*, while the fourth ship, the

4,760GRT French tanker *Nivôse*, was struck by a conventional torpedo, the tanker carrying 11,000 tons of heating oil and subsequently sinking after colliding with another merchant of the convoy.

Though it is difficult to determine exactly which aircraft hit which ship, both the Second Officer and Chief Engineer aboard *Birchbank* reported that they had seen the glide-bomb impact, describing it as a 'miniature fighter'. The hole blasted in the ship's hull was above the waterline with most damage internal, consistent with the effect of an Hs 293 designed to explode after penetrating the outer hull. Regardless, the ship was lost with 9,000 tons of freight, including 5,000 tons of military stores, sixty-five crew being successfully evacuated before *Birchbank* exploded. The merchant's Senior Second Engineer Officers John Grant Parkinson and gunner Able Seaman Sydney Dugdale were both killed in the attack. A single gunner was also lost from *Indian Prince*; Able Seaman Stanley Turner. Surviving crew reported their ship hit by a torpedo, but the ship's Master, Robert C. Proctor, recalled no flash or column of water which are both factors generally indicative of a torpedo strike, so she was more likely to have been hit by an Hs 293.[4] The crippled ship was taken in tow by the corvette HMS *Coltsfoot* but sank nineteen miles north-west of Mostaganem. The last of the trio claimed by KG 100 was hit by several bombs and possibly a torpedo, though it remains difficult to ascertain the truth. SS *Carlier* carried war material bound ultimately for Bombay and the Fourteenth Army in Burma, including a quantity of ammunition in two of the holds. A bomb struck the ship to starboard on the lifeboat deck, a second impacting the bridge and killing every man present. A third explosion appears to have been caused by a torpedo that impacted between the bridge and boiler room, beneath the waterline, catapulting life rafts from the forward deck overboard. A third bomb then struck Hold No 5 while simultaneously a second torpedo hits Hold No 6; both filled with ammunition and explosives. The entire stern was ripped apart in the subsequent explosion – three minutes after the first bomb hit – as the few survivors jumped overboard.

Almost miraculously, twenty-four crew survived and were rescued after two hours in the sea by USS *Trippe*. Captain Fernand Frankignoul, forty-eight crew and nineteen British military personnel were killed. The merchant ships *Takliwa* and *Josiah Parker* both reported being hit and slightly damaged in the attack, but fully capable of proceeding.

Wehrmacht communiques of the action broadcast to the German public reported four fully-laden freighters and two destroyers sunk,

Dornier Do 217E with Hs 293 mounted beneath the starboard wing, counterbalanced by a 900-litre auxiliary fuel tank beneath the port wing.

and a further eleven freighters, two destroyers and a smaller escort damaged. Within twenty-four hours, this report was updated to claim a total of twenty-three transports sunk or seriously damaged, amounting to 150,000 tons of shipping. *Hauptmann* Ewald-Günther Trost, at that time *Staffelkapitän* of the training *Staffel* 12./KG 26, was awarded the Knight's Cross on 12 November for his accumulated successes with III./KG 26.

After the return of 5./KG 100, the *Geschwader*'s two anti-shipping *Gruppen* in southern France were withdrawn from the front line during late November. Between commitment to action in July and withdrawal in November, the *Geschwader*'s staff had lost two aircraft in action, II./KG 100 six aircraft to enemy action and a further fifteen in accidents, while III./KG 100 had lost nineteen to enemy action and thirteen in accidents. While replacement aircraft could, and would, be taken on strength, the loss of valuable crew members through death or injury strained the supply of trained and experienced men.

Alongside Jope's staff flight of six aircraft, *Hptm.* Middermann took II./KG 100 inland to the Occitanie region and Toulouse-Blagnac airfield, a French factory airfield that had hosted a Luftwaffe fighter pilot school and was undergoing refurbishment into a major bomber base.[5] The surviving crews of a single *Staffel*, 4./KG 100, were despatched to Leck in northern Germany to begin conversion to the He 177. *Hauptmann* Gerhard Döhler's III./KG 100 – minus 8./KG 100 that had relocated to Fassberg on Lüneberger Heath for conversion to the He 177A on 20 September – were transferred further afield, moving to Eggebek in Schleswig-Holstein where the two *Staffeln* were held in readiness for '*Unternehmen Carmen*', a planned attack with 'Fritz-X' glide bombs on the Home Fleet in Scapa Flow, which, ultimately, never happened. Later they were also earmarked for a potential 'Fritz-X' attack to be mounted against Soviet industrial targets, though this too never got beyond theoretical consideration.

Conditions at Eggebek were less than ideal, according to III.*Gruppe*'s technical officer, Klaus Deumling. While the airfield boasted three paved runways, the aircraft were not housed in hangars, but rather in open blast pens accessible across a grass surface. The heavy aircraft frequently sank deeply into the soil while being moved to and from the runway, occasionally breaking off supporting undercarriage struts as tractors pulled them free and resulting in a relatively high rate of unserviceable aircraft. *Gruppenkommandeur Hptm.* Herbert Pfeffer frequently clashed with Deumling over the problem, the technical officer ultimately held responsible for the issue despite it being largely beyond his control. Their growing enmity would have tragic consequences.

The absence of II./KG 100 from the battlefront did not stop attacks using the Hs 293 as II./KG 40 mounted attacks using the weapon on 21 November against the combined convoys SL139, returning to Britain from Sierra Leone, and MKS30 sailing from Gibraltar. Its assembly reported to Berlin by Abwehr agents, a Ju 290 of 5.*Fernaufklärungsgruppe* flown by *Gruppenkommandeur Hptm.* Braun located them at the tail end of a sixteen-hour reconnaissance flight west of Casablanca. Braun's crew sighted sixty-seven merchant ships with seven escorts, radioing the contact to *Fliegerführer Atlantik* at 1733hrs on 15 November. Subsequent Luftwaffe reconnaissance by Ju 290s of 2./FAGr. 5, BV 222 flying boats of 1./SAGr. 129 and Fw 200s of III./KG 40 – with a noted margin of error in location reports of up to forty miles compared to later U-boat sightings – and the *B-Dienst* Radio Intelligence Service tracked them while thirty-one U-boats of the 'Schill' groups were vectored to intercept, opening torpedo attacks three days later. Forewarned by ULTRA decryption of the impending threat, escort ships destroyed four U-boats for minor damage to two merchants and by 20 November contact was lost, a shadowing Fw 200 and Ju 290 both being shot down. The latter was the first combat casualty suffered by 2./FAGr. 5; aircraft '9V+CK' flown by *Lt.* Hans Friedrich shot down by Mosquitos of RAF 157 Squadron in Biscay near Cape Ortegal.[6]

Though two U-boats had shot down enemy aircraft, *B.d.U.* was irritated by the lack of Luftwaffe support, though noting that it stemmed more from a lack of available aircraft than unwillingness. By way of redemption, SKL139/MKS30 was reacquired by *Luftflotte* 3 which had despatched five Fw 200s and three Ju 290s to reacquire the northbound merchant ships on 21 November. Located, the Luftwaffe began shadowing, though *Hptm.* Bergen's Ju 290 '9V+HK', on its maiden patrol, was attacked by aircraft from HMS *Biter* near the Portuguese coast, wounding gunner *Fw.* Walter Bauer in the leg and forcing the mission to be curtailed. Twenty-five He 177 aircraft of II./KG 40 began to take off at 1215hrs from Bordeaux-Mérignac, each carrying two Hs 293 missiles and led by *Gruppenkommandeur Maj.* Rudolf Mons. Under escort part of the way by eight Ju 88C-6s of ZG 1, five aircraft failed to contact the body of the convoy, which came under attack by the remainder during mid-afternoon. Low-lying cloud made conditions less than ideal for launching the Hs 293, visibility frequently obscured and high-altitude launch impossible, most dropped from a height above sea level of between 400 and 600 metres. Attacks against the escorting British frigates HMS *Calder* and *Drury* and the destroyers HMS *Watchman* and *Winchelsea* all failed as the missiles were outmanoeuvred, Royal Navy observers noting their red and white taillights. Most Heinkels approached from alternate beams, releasing their weapons when over the outer column of ships before tracking across the convoy body on a steady course, only two opting to run the length of the convoy body. Strafing of the ships by tail gunners was inaccurate, though so too was return fire, the Heinkels not taking, nor requiring, evasive action.

However, two straggling merchant ships were discovered and attacked, both hit by single missiles launched by *Hptm.* Alfred Nuss of 6./KG 40. The 4,405GRT freighter SS *Marsa* was found three miles astern of the convoy body, the Hs 293 striking the water between the davits of the port lifeboats, penetrating the hull and exploding in the engine room, killing ship's boy Christian Cayley as the rest of the crew abandoned ship as the engine and boiler rooms flooded and the ship lazily circled, rudder jammed hard to port by the blast. The 6,065GRT MV *Delius* received severe damage to its bridge by an Hs 293 that hit the foremast, pivoting the missile inboard and downwards whereupon it hit No 3 derrick and exploded on the port side of the hatch. The blast and flying debris killed the Master on the bridge, the lookout on the monkey island and the assistant steward in the saloon, shattering the bridge, chartroom, and wireless room. The dazed Chief Officer, Gordon Marshall, took charge as fire broke out in Nos 2 and 3 holds, though soon brought under control. Officers from the sunken *Marsa* volunteered to go aboard and help the depleted crew who buried their dead later that day and despite a strong list, no functioning compasses, no degaussing gear, faulty steering gear and two of the six engines cylinders out of commission, MV *Delius* successfully reached Greenock.

In balance, the attack by II./KG 40 failed, although differing points of view were held by *B.d.U.* and *SKL*. The latter recorded:

> The distance from [the Heinkels'] base was 1,400 km, therefore the range of 1,200 km for this type was exceeded by 200 km. The engines worked excellently. The range is now extended to 1,900 km. Weather conditions during the first attack were moderate to bad. Twenty of the twenty-five bombers reached their target, three He 177s were lost and two had engine trouble. Forty HS 293s were dropped, eleven of which did not explode . . . Luftwaffe Operations Staff attributed the poor results to insufficient training of the crews. The attacks will have surprised the enemy. It is possible that he will move his shipping route to the west out of the range of the He 177s. Operations by the formation will then be limited to the Mediterranean, but will extend there to the eastern part, thereby creating new possibilities against the Gibraltar – Suez traffic.[7]

However, as far as *B.d.U.* were concerned:

> On the whole this attack, the first to be made at such long range, may be regarded as a complete success. It is hopeful for the U-boat Arm because it may offer further possibilities of tactical cooperation against convoys.[8]

For KG 40 the results had been disappointing at best. Only a single aircraft had launched two successful shots, ultimately sinking one ship. In return, three He 177s were lost, two of them shot down by Coastal Command Liberator 'K' of 224 Squadron. Piloted by Plt Off A. Wilson, the Liberator was flying ASW cover over SL 139 and reported four separate combats with Heinkel aircraft, two of which were decisive. Wilson took his aircraft in from below and in front of the attacking Heinkels, bringing the side and rear guns to bear, though his final attack was made from above and behind, the Liberator's nose gunner silencing the Heinkel's rear turret with one burst of fire. Several aircraft were hit, three shot down and a fourth crashing some thirty-five miles from Bordeaux.

Four nights later, the depleted II./KG 40 was in action once more, this time directed against Mediterranean convoy traffic. Convoy KMF 26 (codenamed 'Annex') of twenty-four ships – including six troopships that left Oran to join the original body that had sailed from Scotland – sailed in six columns under heavy American and Royal Navy surface escort as aircraft numbers in North Africa had begun to diminish with many moved to Britain in preparation of the opening of the 'Second Front' in 1944. Among the escorts were destroyers USS *Frederick C. Davis* and *Herbert C. Jones*, equipped with their first-generation glide-bomb jamming systems. Each merchant ship, except HMT *Rohna*, streamed a barrage balloon, the convoy destined for the Middle East carrying, in large part, USAAF personnel travelling to join the 10th Air Force fighting over China, Burma and India.

At noon on 26 November, Luftwaffe reconnaissance sighted KMF 26 and an immediate attack was planned using II./KG 40, eighteen He 111s from II./KG 26 and fifteen Ju 88s of III./KG 26. The take-off of the twenty-two Heinkel He 177s from Bordeaux-Mérignac, led once more by *Gruppenkommandeur* Mons, was blighted by *Fw.* Alfred Naaf's aircraft crashing due to a broken engine crankshaft, killing four of the crew as the aircraft burned. It would be just a foretaste of the disaster to follow.

Despite the reduction in Allied North African air strength, four French Spitfires of GC 1/7, four USAAF P-39s from 347th Squadron, three Beaufighters of RAF 153 Squadron and a number from USAAF 414th Night Fighter Squadron based at Cagliari were present as the attack developed at about 1700hrs in waning light. The strong fighter defences broke up most of the attack, inflicting heavy losses; two Ju 88s, two He 111s and six He 177s in total failed to return. A seventh He 177 flown by *Hptm.* Richard Wiesner, *Staffelkapitän* of 6./KG 40, ditched off Montpellier after suffering severe battle damage that had disabled all hydraulic equipment, the rudders and landing gear operated by hand with great difficulty. Diverted to an alternate airfield, the Heinkel missed the runway and landed in darkness in a lagoon nearby, the observer drowning and one other man being injured. An eighth He 177 crashed on landing at too high a speed on the alternative airfield at Cognac, all seven crew members being killed. Among the aircraft lost over KMF 26 was 'F8+DM' of Stab II./KG 40, *Gruppenkommandeur Maj.* Rudolf Mons and his crew being posted as missing in action, and *Hptm.* Alfred Nuss of 6./KG 40, victor from five days previously, missing in action. German gunners claimed four Spitfires and two Beaufighters shot down, though only 153 Squadron's Wing Commander I.R. Stephenson's Beaufighter failed to return, a second badly damaged but reaching its home airfield.

The first wave of He 177s had once again attempted to target the escort ships and clear a path for the torpedo bombers, but every shot failed, the anti-aircraft cruiser HMS *Colombo* and the destroyer HMS *Atherstone* both evading Hs 293s aimed at them. Six were reportedly seen to be affected by jamming signals from the American destroyers, though this appears unlikely as the primitive jamming equipment in play was tuned to the wrong frequencies. The troopship HMT *Banfora* narrowly avoided an Hs 293, gunners shooting its wing off and the bomb striking the radio antenna before crashing into the sea nearby as the second wave of He 177s approached. The leading, and largest, troopship HMT *Orion* was the target of the first of *Maj.* Hans Dochtermann's Hs 293s which missed, the second, guided by *Uffz.* Hans Georg Zuther, arcing straight towards the second troopship in that column, HMT *Rohna*. The missile hit the 8,602GRT ship about five metres above the waterline on the port side at the after end of her engine room and No 6 troop deck, stopping the propeller immediately. The explosion blew through the starboard promenade deck and badly holed *Rohna*, disabling all electrical gear including pumps and setting the ship aflame as she listed to starboard. Number 4 bulkhead was demolished, and six of the twenty-two lifeboats destroyed, the remainder on the port side unable to be lowered to the water as the blast had pushed the hull plates so far out that they obstructed their fall to the water. Only eight lifeboats were launched, though nearly 100 life rafts were thrown into the sea.

A strong six-metre swell was running as the minesweeper USS *Pioneer* and the freighter SS *Clan Campbell* closed to rescue survivors, helped later by the tug *Mindful* and covered by HMS *Atherstone* which made smoke and fired her anti-aircraft weapons at milling Luftwaffe bombers until full darkness when she joined in the search for survivors. Within ninety minutes the aft bulkhead collapsed and *Rohna* settled by the stern as the Master, Captain T. J. Murphy, chief, second and third officers, senior medical officer and four US soldiers were the last to abandon ship.

The final death toll from the *Rohna* was 1,149 men, of which 1,015 were American servicemen travelling to India and China to construct airfields for B-29 bomber squadrons. Thirty-five other Americans later died of their injuries. Of the remainder of the casualties, five of *Rohna*'s officers, 117 of the 195 crew, twelve DEMS gunners and one hospital orderly went down with the ship. The sinking of HMT *Rohna* was the second worst disaster at sea for the United States, surpassed only by the sinking of USS *Arizona* at Pearl Harbor in 1941.[9]

The surviving Heinkels approached southern France, initially using music from Radio Andorra as a navigation aid until picking up Luftwaffe beacon signals. Weather over Bordeaux had deteriorated, and so most of the KG 40 Heinkels were diverted to Cognac, landing in the late evening and returning to their home field during the following day.

The fallout of the attack was profound on both sides. Dochtermann and his crew were ordered to *Generalleutnant* Fink's headquarters near Istres to deliver a first-hand account of the attack and sinking of *Rohna* in the presence of Werner Klümper and *Hptm.* Hermann Fischer, acting commander of FAGr. 5. Days later, Dochtermann was then flown to

The rear gunner climbs into position aboard his Heinkel He 177.

Schwäbisch Hall to repeat his experiences to the provisional *Kommodore* of KG 40, former naval aviator *Maj.* Rupprecht Heyn, *Oberst* Storp (*Kampffliegerführer Mittelmeer*) and *Maj.* Werner Baumbach (*Inspizient der Kampfflieger, appt General der Kampfflieger 2*). However, the meeting did not go well.

> 'We didn't exactly expect hymns of praise' from Baumbach, said Dochtermann. 'But we also hadn't expected that he would bring a message from the Reichsmarschall to shit on us.' According to Göring and Baumbach, the attack on KMF 26 and the sinking of the *Rohna* 'had been a complete failure effectively to utilize the weapon Hs 293.' After all, most of them had missed. Only one had scored. Such an 'armchair judgement' took Dochtermann's breath away. He recovered quickly, however, and recklessly suggested that 'in case the Reichsmarschall [Göring] should speak to Baumbach again on this subject, please convey to him that he ought to be proud that he still has flyers who approach the enemy with such unconditional courage, despite the strongest air defenses' against them. He considered Göring's and Baumbach's attitudes as sheer ingratitude for what he and his crew had done. It would be several years before he could reconcile himself to these criticisms.[10]

The losses to II./KG 40 were severe, nine aircraft needing major overhaul and repair of battle damage. The lost *Gruppenkommandeur* was replaced by *Maj.* Walter Rieder, a former maritime pilot with Kü.Fl.Gr. 406 and *Staffelkapitän* of 8./KG 40, who would only hold the position until February when he too was shot down and killed. The *Gruppe* was given time to rebuild and establish new tactical methods before being recommitted to action; operations now to be launched by night as the He 177 had proven vulnerable to anti-aircraft fire and enemy fighters. Each aircraft would carry sixteen 50kg flares in its internal bomb bay, a new tactic known as '*Zentrale Angriff*' requiring one *Kette* to drop flares on the convoy's beam while a second *Kette* attacked the illuminated ships from ten kilometres away.

For the Allies, hopes that six Hs 293s had been successfully jammed proved premature. However, specialist officers aboard USS *Frederick C. Davis* and *Herbert C. Jones* of the US Naval Research Laboratory (NRL) picked up and recorded multiple radio signals from the attacking aircraft while two German-speaking Army radiomen monitored inter-aircraft conversations. The missile radio direction frequencies were finally identified as 48.5, 49.0, 49.75 and 50.0 megacycles, the priceless information soon winging its way to Washington and the NRL.

Eleven days previously, amidst the wreckage left behind by the evacuating Germans at Foggia aerodrome, a Lt.Comm. Plunket reported to the British Admiralty that he had secured parts of two 'PC 500 rocket bombs', including the 49 A1 charging head fuses. The burnt-out remains of several KG 100 Dorniers were searched thoroughly, but only fragmentary evidence of '*Kehlgerät*' found. However, the 'Fritz-X' included receiver components, enough to confirm the frequencies used by the '*Kehlgerät*' and provide an approximation of the weapon's control surfaces. With the radio frequencies established, creation of an effective jamming system could finally proceed.

Very little by way of Luftwaffe maritime activity took place throughout the remainder of 1943 as the *Kampflieger* had suffered grievous casualties to Allied aerial superiority in all areas bar the Aegean for a brief window of time. The bombing of occupied Italian harbours continued sporadically, Naples, for instance, being attacked by Ju 88s four times during November, using circling torpedoes on at least one raid, though at heavy cost and for little tangible result. For example, on the night of 26 November thick smokescreens shielded Naples and bombing was scattered, its effectiveness unknown. For this meagre result, eleven aircraft were lost. However, in late November, Kesselring chaired a conference with Richthofen, Peltz, Baumbach and other senior Luftwaffe officers regarding the most effective way in which to delay the seemingly unstoppable Allied advance in Italy. Foggia's airfields in Allied use were initially considered suitable primary targets, though Richthofen successfully argued for an attack on the port at Bari instead. One of three ports through which Allied supply traffic passed – the others being Taranto and Naples – Bari was especially important to further establishing the air force units at Foggia as well as providing supplies for the British Eighth Army. Bari port hosted a major pipeline on the eastern mole for discharging tanker loads of high-octane aviation fuel into tanks outside the dockyard itself. The port area was far less well protected than Naples, though still boasting a considerable number of British and Italian anti-aircraft guns and a total of thirty-two searchlights.

However, the only aircraft nearby were USAAF bombers and RAF transport aircraft, useless as defensive aircraft, the nearest RAF fighters already being committed to escort duties elsewhere. Richthofen was aware through intelligence reports that such was the confidence of the

Allies that Bari port was unloading freighters throughout the night with all lights blazing.

With the decimation of Luftwaffe Mediterranean bomber strength, a level of complacency pervaded Allied higher command. On the afternoon of 2 December Sir Arthur Coningham, commander of the North-west African Tactical Air Force, proclaimed in a Bari press conference that the Mediterranean Luftwaffe was finished, quoted as saying: 'I would regard it as a personal affront and insult if the Luftwaffe would attempt any significant action in this area.'

That same afternoon, *Oblt.* Werner Hahn piloted his Me 410 of 2./(F)/122 on a high altitude reconnaissance mission over Bari, counting a multitude of freighters; at least thirty both docked and those awaiting their chance to unload cargo on the crowded quaysides. Armed with Hahn's fresh report, one hundred and five Ju 88s from all six *Gruppen* present in northern Italy – I. and II./KG 30, I. and II./KG 54 (both returned to Italy after periods of retraining for young and inexperienced replacement crews) and I. and II./KG 76 – took off from multiple airfields for Bari. Though seventeen were forced to abort the mission for various reasons, the remainder headed far out into the Adriatic at wavetop height in order to approach the port from an unexpected seaward southerly direction below enemy radar. A second reconnaissance sweep conducted by two Bf 109s late that afternoon had confirmed conditions and as darkness fell a small vanguard of pathfinder aircraft carrying *Düppel* – small strips of aluminium foil similar to the Allies' 'Window' for disrupting Allied radar – circled the harbour and began dropping the strips into the night air. They were also carrying flares, released east of the harbour as guiding lights though they were barely necessary as the first bombers swept over the clearly illuminated port at approximately 1930hrs, gaining height at the last moment and discharging the first bombs, some also carrying LT 350 circling torpedoes. The effect was catastrophic.

The earliest bombs overshot the harbour area and landed on Bari itself, corrected by subsequent aircraft which 'walked' their bomb loads toward the line of ships anchored at the east jetty, severing the fuel pipeline and causing the high-octane aviation fuel to ignite. The Liberty ship SS *Joseph Wheeler* took the first direct hit and burst into flames. Moments later at Pier 29 SS *John L. Motley* took a bomb on its No 5 hatch, the deck cargo catching fire and spreading not only towards its shipment of bombs and aviation fuel but also to the neighbouring ship SS *John Harvey* packed with ammunition. The subsequent explosion of

John Harvey rocked the entire port, setting four other ships on fire, one of the latter also blowing up and setting fire to the outer harbour and ships therein. The flames leapt so high that they reached within metres of the attacking Junkers. Compounding the lethal explosive effect of the raid was the release of stored cargo from within *John Harvey*'s shattered holds. Part of the cargo manifest was 540 tons of American-type M47A1 100lb mustard gas bombs, guarded by a unit of the 701st Chemical Maintenance Company. This top-secret consignment, apparently brought to Bari for potential retaliation to a feared German gas attack in Italy, did not explode, but the bomb casings cracked, and their toxic contents spilled into the harbour which was covered in burning oil. The oil proved the perfect solvent for the mustard gas, contaminating anybody encountering it and infusing clouds of smoke from the burning oil that drifted across the city. An estimated 1,000 military and merchant marine personnel were killed, and 628 military personnel hospitalised due to mustard gas poisoning, from which eighty-three died. Bari civilians who presented themselves at the military hospital were turned away from the overcrowded centres, the number of their dead unclear, but probably well over one thousand. Welsh Nurse Gwladys Rees recalled the aftermath of the bombing in the 98th British General Hospital that had been established in Bari during October:

> Only a few hours before dawn following the raid we began to realise that most of our patients had been contaminated by something beyond all imagination. I first noticed it when one or two of my patients went to the sink looking for a drink of water. This was odd because drinks had been taken round as usual and we could hardly control them. They were complaining of intense heat and began stripping off their clothes, and patients confined to bed were desperately trying to rip their dressings and bandages off. What little knowledge we had, our first thought was that these boys were suffering from mustard gas burns for there were blisters as big as balloons and heavy with fluid on these young bodies. We were not sure whether the staff was at risk as we did not know what the fluid contained. Although we tried to get tests done, we were never informed of the results. We did everything humanly possible, draining the blisters, constant intravenous and eventually mild sedatives, but it was no good. It was horrible to see these boys, so young and in such obvious pain. We could not give them stronger sedatives, since we were not quite sure how they would react with whatever had poisoned them.[11]

Bari harbour after the devastating attack of 2 December 1943.

In London the decision to evoke absolute secrecy regarding the presence of the mustard gas ammunition robbed medical professionals at the scene any chance of treating its effects. Not until decades later would the British government admit its presence, begrudgingly paying backdated military pensions to men whose lives had been all but destroyed by its lingering consequence.

Confusion over casualty numbers remains and even establishing the exact number of ships sunk or damaged yields conflicting numbers, generally some of the smaller Italian vessels not included in such previously published lists that tend to agree on seventeen ships sunk. The number is, however, much greater.

Sunk:

SS *Ardito* (Kingdom of Italy), 3,732GRT.

MV *Barletta* (Kingdom of Italy), auxiliary cruiser, 1,975GRT, empty. Forty-four crew killed. Four men from the crew killed in action and four men were wounded. The military crew had twenty-two men killed in action, fourteen missing in action and forty wounded. Raised in 1948–9 and repaired.

SS *Bollsta* (Norway), 1,832GRT, 1,427 tons of cargo still aboard. Raised in 1948, repaired and returned to service as *Stefano M.*

SS *Cassala* (Kingdom of Italy), 1,797GRT, declared a total loss, empty.

SS *Corfu* (Kingdom of Italy), 1,409GRT, declared a total loss.

MV *Devon Coast* (United Kingdom), 646GRT, 50-tons of cargo aboard.

SS *Fort Athabaska* (Canadian, operated by MoWT), 7,132GRT, forty-six men killed, still carrying 76 tons of cargo, mail and fragments of captured German rocket bombs, ready for departure.

SS *Frozinone* (Kingdom of Italy), 5,202GRT, 1,000 tons of cargo still aboard.

SS *Genespesca II* (Kingdom of Italy), 1,628GRT.

SS *Goggiam* (Kingdom of Italy), 1,934GRT, declared a total loss.

SS *Inaffondabile* (Kingdom of Italy), fishing schooner.

SS *John Bascombe* (United States), 7,176GRT, 8,344 tons of cargo, including acid and high-octane fuel still aboard. Four crewmen, ten armed guards killed.

SS *John Harvey* (United States), 7,176GRT, cargo of 5,607 tons aboard, including mustard gas bombs. Thirty-six crewmen, ten soldiers, twenty armed guards killed.

SS *John L. Motley* (United States), 7,176GRT, cargo of 5,131 tons of ammunition aboard. Thirty-six crewmen, twenty-four armed guards killed.

SS *Joseph Wheeler* (United States), 7,176GRT, cargo of 8,037 tons aboard. Twenty-six crewmen, fifteen armed guards killed.

SS *Lars Kruse* (Denmark, under MoWT control), 1,807GRT, 1,400 tons of aviation fuel aboard. Nineteen crew killed.

SS *Lom* (Norway), 1,268GRT, 906 tons of cargo aboard. Four crew killed.

SS *Luciano Orlando* (Kingdom of Italy), cargo ship.

SS *Lwów* (Poland), 1,409GRT, at anchor in the middle harbour, empty.

MB *10* (Kingdom of Italy), armed motor boat, 13GRT.

SS *Norlom* (Norway), 6,326GRT, 7,458 tons of coal, most of which was salvaged. Six crew killed. Refloated November 1946.

SS *Porto Pisano* (Kingdom of Italy), 226GRT.

SS *Puck* (Poland), 1,065GRT, 770 tons of ammunition aboard.

SS *Samuel J. Tilden* (United States), 7,176GRT, scuttled by two British torpedoes to prevent damage to other ships as it burned. 1,711 tons of cargo aboard. Ten crewmen, fourteen US soldiers, three British soldiers killed of 209 embarked troops.

SS *Testbank* (United Kingdom), 5,083GRT, empty apart from 50 tons of high-octane fuel. Seventy crew killed.

SS *Volodda* (Kingdom of Italy), 4,673GRT, scuttled at Bari, refloated and repaired, in service 1947.

Damaged:

SS *Argo* (Kingdom of Italy), 526GRT.

HMS *Bicester*, 'Hunt' class destroyer, 1,050GRT, seriously damaged. Towed by *Zetland* to Taranto.

SS *Brittany Coast* (United Kingdom), 1,389GRT, medium damage.

SS *Christa* (United Kingdom), 2,590GRT, carrying fuel, medium damage.

MV *Coxwold* (United Kingdom), slight damage.

SS *Dagö* (Latvia, under MoWT control), 1,996GRT, light damage.

SS *Director* (United Kingdom), 5,107GRT, very slight damage.

SS *Fort Lajoie* (Canadian, operated by MoWT), 7,134GRT, medium damage.

SS *Grace Abbott* (United States), 7,191GRT, slight shrapnel damage, struck by bomb that failed to explode.

SS *John M. Schofield* (United States), 7,181GRT, very slight damage.

La Drôme, French naval auxiliary tanker, 1,055GRT medium damage.

SS *Lyman Abbott* (United States), 7,176GRT, anchored in the middle harbour, one armed guard, one crewman, Army Cargo Security Officer and one passenger killed (the latter from mustard gas), heavy damage.

SS *Odysseus* (Netherlands), 1,038GRT, medium damage, but sailed from Bari.

SS *Vest* (Norway), 5,074GRT, seriously damaged, remaining half coal cargo intact.

HMS *Vienna*, Coastal Forces Depot Ship, 4,227GRT, seriously damaged. Towed to Brindisi, damaged in another raid 6 February 1944.

HMS *Zetland*, 'Hunt' class destroyer, 1,050GRT, blast and fragment damage.

In return, the Luftwaffe lost just two Ju 88A-4 aircraft. A single USAAF Beaufighter on patrol near Bari failed to contact the enemy, nor did three others that scrambled as the attack unfolded, but anti-aircraft fire accounted for aircraft '4D+IL' of 3./KG 30, shot down with *Uffz.* Karl-Heinz Hellwig (pilot), *Uffz.* Otto Schuhmacher (observer), *Uffz.*

Karl Rittner (wireless operator) and *Ogefr.* Waldemar Gebert (air gunner) listed as missing in action, and 'B3+EH' of 1./KG 54 with *Fw.* Walter Klein (pilot), *Ofw.* Hugo Hinsch (observer), *Uffz.* Julius Rübel (wireless operator) and *Gefr.* Paul Höfler (air gunner) also missing in action. Two days later one final casualty could be attributed to the after-effects of the Bari raid as Me 410 'F6+YK' of 2.(F)/122 was shot down by fighters while attempting to photograph the harbour, *Oblt.* Josef Schumm (pilot) and *Uffz.* Heinz Kummer both being posted as missing.

Somewhat ironically, given the propensity for exaggerated claims of success evidenced by crew debriefings and subsequent Wehrmacht bulletins, the Germans remained unaware of just how successful their attack had been, publicly claiming two ships sunk, two others loaded with munitions or fuel exploding and numerous others damaged. The port was a shambles, remaining closed for three weeks and seriously impacting both land and air operations in the British sector as preparations to assault the Gustav Line were underway.

No further Luftwaffe maritime operations in the Mediterranean took place in 1943 as the glide-bomb and torpedo *Staffeln* rebuilt or were redirected to the Atlantic where they would be employed in protecting the last incoming blockade-runners from the Far East. Beyond the occasional harassing bombardment there was little activity, the minor attacks contributing mainly to the steady trickle of German casualties.

7

Running the Gauntlet

Supporting Atlantic Surface Forces

O N 18 AUGUST 1943, *Generaloberst* Hans Jeschonnek, Chief of the Luftwaffe General Staff, committed suicide with a bullet to the head. The scapegoat for much of the Luftwaffe's failure and its incompetent leadership, Jeschonnek finally crumbled after a severe Allied air raid against Peenemünde. In his place came *General der Flieger* Günther Korten, a pre-war Army engineer who had transferred to the Luftwaffe in 1940, holding a variety of staff positions before taking command of *Luftflotte* 1. Korten, appointed on 25 August, brought with him fresh impetus to provide strategic direction to the Luftwaffe, including reaffirmed commitment to transform Kessler's *Fliegerführer Atlantik* into III.*Fliegerkorps* of forty-two *Staffeln*. However, it was an ideal never realised as Germany's war situation steadily deteriorated, strangling fuel supplies, depleting manpower and pushing aircraft production towards defensive fighters on Hitler's direct orders.

General der Flieger Hans Ritter, long-time Luftwaffe representative to the Commander-in-Chief Navy (*General der Luftwaffe beim Oberbefehlshaber die Kriegsmarine*), informed Naval Staff on 6 September that the Luftwaffe would discontinue production of large flying boats in favour of fighter aircraft. Korten's staff planned to reequip the flying boat formations of *Luftflotte* 3 with Ju 290s, *Luftflotte* 6 in the Black Sea with Ju 88s and Norway's *Luftflotte* 5 with a combination of both aircraft types. The Luftwaffe General Staff intended to withdraw both BV 138s and BV 222s from the Atlantic area once *Hptm.* Hermann Fischer's *Fernaufklärungsgruppe* 5 had completed formation at Achmer bomber base in Lower Saxony during mid-1943, before posting to Mont-de-Marsan.

Fischer, previously decorated for reconnaissance activity on the Eastern Front, had been appointed acting commander of FAGr. 5 at its inception, though by October 1943 his entire strength consisted of two Ju 290A-3s and a single Do 17P for *Hptm.* Josef Augustin's

General der Flieger Hans Ritter, Luftwaffe
representative to the Naval Commander-
in-Chief.

1. *Staffel*, four Ju 290A-2s for *Hptm.* Karl-Friedrich Bergen's 2.*Staffel*
and a Staff flight that did not possess any aircraft until the arrival of a
single Ju 290A-3 in November. From its inaugural combat mission on 15
November to 15 December, FAGr. 5 flew thirty reconnaissance flights
accruing 415 flying hours and covering 120,350 kilometres. However,
although the aircraft handled well in the air it lacked the necessary range
to fully engage transatlantic convoys and required increased defensive
armament. The limitations of the defensive weaponry had already been
illustrated during commitment to transport missions at both Tunisia
and Stalingrad; only one MG 151/20 fitted in the turret and an MG 131
in the rear gunner's position.

Regardless of the acquisition of Ju 290s for *Fliegerführer Atlantik*,
the Luftwaffe's proposal to remove flying boats from Biscay met strong
Kriegsmarine protest, Ritter asked to convey their reply in full to the
Luftwaffe General Staff.

As the request made for further production of BV 222 aircraft shows,
Naval Staff attaches great importance to their operations in the western
area, and indeed wishes them to start as early as possible and to continue
as long as the tactical suitability of the BV 222 Type permits. Naval Staff
considers it inadvisable to withdraw the BV 222s from the western area

after the arrival of *Fernaufklärungsgruppe* 5. Every additional long-range reconnaissance aircraft available there will be an asset to the tasks to be carried out. Even if no operations need to be undertaken for the U-boat arm at present, reconnaissance requirements for Naval Staff's measures in general are so numerous – especially when the dispatch of blockade-runners is being planned – that BV 222 aircraft will be a welcome addition to reconnaissance facilities. It should be recalled that last year not even with the forty available FW 200s was it possible fully to satisfy reconnaissance requirements. The Naval Staff specifically requested BV 222s for operations in the western area; they are being provided by Luftwaffe Operations Staff for these operations and they have been included in the planning of Commander in Chief, Luftwaffe.

Only if it should be found in the course of operations that this type of aircraft is unsuitable for the combat conditions existing in this sea area shall sufficient reason exist for transferring them to other areas. It is of the utmost importance to Naval Staff that in such an event, despite the difficulties anticipated for the ground organization, operations of the BV 222 from the Norwegian area be ensured.

Putting the BV 222 crews to a different task – with *Fernaufklärungsgruppe* 5 for instance – is only to be envisaged if for some reason the flying boats are definitely withdrawn from front line operations. In such an event, it is important that these especially well-trained crews are not lost to the transport service but are retained for long-range reconnaissance and long-range combat operations at sea.[1]

Fortunately for Dönitz, his stock remained high with his *Führer*, something of which the politically astute Göring was fully aware. Where once he would have attempted to bully and bluster Raeder if he had made such a request, instead, during a meeting between he and Dönitz and their respective Chiefs of Staff on 10 September at *Führer* Headquarters, the urgent commitment of operational BV 222 flying boats both in Travemünde and already in the West was confirmed, as was the assignment of new Ju 290 aircraft as they became available.

At the end of September *Fliegerführer Atlantik* possessed no active bomber units – the He 177s of II./KG 40 not yet being available – reconnaissance forces provided by Condors of III./KG 40, BV 222s and BV 138s of 1.(F.)/129 at Bisacrosse and Ju 88s of 3.(F)/Aufkl.Gr. 123 based at Rennes. For fighter aircraft, Kessler mustered the following:

Jagd Kommando Brest: five Fw 190A-4s;
1./SAGr. 128: seventeen Fw 190 and Ar 196s;
V./KG 40: forty-four Ju 88C-6s;
II./ZG 1: thirty-nine Bf 110G-2s:
2./KG 40: nine He 177A-5s;
7. and 9./KG 40 Fw 200s.

The withdrawal of *Obstlt*. Lothar von Janson's I./ZG 1 Bf 110s to Austria where they would experience greater success in intercepting American bombers from the south, did not mark the end of I./ZG 1 as part of *Fliegerführer Atlantik*'s command. Instead, the Bf 110-equipped I./ZG 1 was redesignated I./ZG 26, which had been temporarily disbanded during the previous April and resurrected as part of the 'Defence of the Reich' devoted to bomber interdiction. A new I./ZG 1 was created from the heavy Ju 88C fighters of V./KG 40 during October. Stab I./ZG 1 was reformed from Stab V./KG 40; 1./ZG 1 from 13./KG 40; 2./ZG 1 from 14./KG 40; 3./ZG 1 from 15./KG 40. The decision to renumber these units of V./KG 40 formally detached the Ju 88C heavy fighters from the bomber *Geschwader*, and officially reclassed them as 'heavy fighters' – *Zerstörer*.

The Me 410s of III./ZG 1 were also relocated in October, and renumerated as II./ZG 26 in Austria, while III./ZG 1 was reformed at Bordeaux-Mérignac. A new Stab III./ZG 1 and 7./ZG 1 were formed from scratch at Kerlin-Bastard, near Lorient, equipped with Ju 88C aircraft, while, during early 1944 8./ZG 1 would be created from 1./SAGr. 128 at Brest-Hourtin, and a dedicated night fighter unit 9.(Nacht)/ZG 1 from a cadre of 16./KG40 which had only formed during the previous August.

Dönitz was ready to attempt the reinvigoration of U-boat warfare assisted by improved flak weapons and the new acoustic G7es (T5) '*Zaunkönig*' torpedo. The Kriegsmarine were also on the cusp of introducing the improved D-type pressure fuse for ground mines and the A-105 acoustic fuse designed to fire at the approach of a ship, while also capable of recognising and ignoring noise-buoys, detonator sweeps and the nearby detonation of other mines. The AD-104 acoustic-pressure combination fuse unit was also ready for use, developed for the Luftwaffe by Dr. (Ing.) Rudolf Hell.

The issue of minelaying continued to be problematic between the Kriegsmarine and Luftwaffe. Their lack of cooperation remained the greatest weakness in Germany's minelaying offensives, as the Luftwaffe continued to insist upon independence of action from the Naval Mining Section despite naval insistence that every such operation was, by definition, naval. Such interservice politics had played a part in Luftwaffe development of the 'bomb mine' (BM) to be used in place of the naval *Luftmine* (LM), and allowing deploying aircraft to fly higher and faster while retaining the weapon's characteristics, merely in the shape of a conventional bomb. However, the first 'bomb mine' orders had been placed without firm understanding of the principles of aerial minelaying as the Luftwaffe, at that time, had no independent technical staff sufficiently knowledgeable in the matter.

When the Luftwaffe undertook its own minelaying experiments, available testing facilities were small and makeshift, generally utilising equipment used for torpedo testing at Travemünde. Suggestions from the Luftwaffe that trained naval officers be attached to assist in the developing programme were rejected until 1943 when the Kriegsmarine finally relented and released such an officer. Ultimately, the Luftwaffe wasted much effort designing and modifying firing systems for the 'bomb mine', for which dropping requirements proved far more restrictive than the original *Luftmine*. Furthermore, nearly all suitable

Luftwaffe parachute mine being unloaded in its carrying frame at an airfield in northern France. (Australian War Memorial)

fuse types, except the pressure unit, had already been developed for the *Luftmine*. Production of the D-type pressure fuse heralded major Luftwaffe and Kriegsmarine disagreements over core principles of use and, therefore, its final design. Both services eventually created their own models of the same thing. Even once in use, they then disagreed on which other units with which to combine the fuse; the Kriegsmarine insisting it be linked with the magnetic fuse, while the Luftwaffe preferred the acoustic one.

Despite these issues, new mines were made available and Dönitz laboured at repairing the deep rifts between the two services to obtain full Luftwaffe cooperation for minelaying. Staff officers established a fresh schedule for training Luftwaffe crews in naval reconnaissance and minelaying techniques, though ideas of sowing defensive fields in the West as a pre-emptive move against invasion remained problematic for Dönitz. Not only was there insufficient stock available for solid barrages, but they would likely impede coastal German convoys. Instead, he urged stockpiling for offensive action when appropriate. In the meantime, emphasis was again places on U-boats, with the support of *Fliegerführer Atlantik*.

On 21 November He 177s of II./KG 40 had roared into action against the combined SL139/MKS30 convoy inbound to Britain, to little effect.   The following day, combined Convoy OS59/KMS33 was located by a BV 222 of 1./SAGr. 129, clashing inconclusively with a B-24 Liberator while accurately reporting convoy composition and location. Next morning three Ju 290s of FAGr. 5 were despatched to shadow as *B.d.U.* formed a new U-boat group from the remaining '*Schill*' boats, named '*Weddigen*'. Though all three Junkers returned safely, it appears that their navigational fixes were inaccurate as the U-boats were directed west of the convoy's location, missing it entirely. Dönitz incorrectly attributed this failure to reaction to the attack on SL139/MKS30, the Admiralty pushing the convoy track west beyond bomber range. During the course of further reconnaissance, Ju 290A-4 '9V+FK' of 2./FAGr. 5, piloted by *Obfw.* Josef Mohr, crashed shortly after take-off, the aircraft climbing abruptly vertically, rolling over and diving into the ground where it exploded, killing the entire crew.

A third convoy, SL140/MKS31, was located by two Ju 290s on 26 November, being sighted by aircraft 'D' in the early evening, though altering course to the north following the aircraft's departure, placing them far to the east of the '*Weddigen*' patrol line. The next day two

III./KG 40 Condors and a single BV 222 of 1./SAGr. 129 resumed the hunt, the flying boat making contact and transmitting beacon signals reported almost simultaneously by five U-boats (*U238*, *U764*, *U262*, *U107* and *U843*), the bearings all indicating an east-north-easterly direction. The BV 222 remained with the convoy until 0130hrs and continued to transmit until forced to depart due to fuel limits. It was too late for '*Weddigen*' to hope to intercept, three U-boats lost with no successes to report. Undeterred, Dönitz drew as many positive conclusions from the attempt as possible:

1) The enemy has now resorted to the method of altering course drastically as soon as the shadowing aircraft observed by him has departed . . . It is therefore difficult to dispose the patrol line for the next day based on a single aircraft report. It is essential to have a fresh aircraft report at latest 12 hours after the convoy is first picked up, so that the U-boats' positions can be improved. A 'current' air reconnaissance of this sort depends solely on the number of reconnaissance aircraft available and cannot at present be carried out.

2) It is quite possible for an aircraft fitted with shipping detection gear to shadow the convoy by night. The transmission of beacon-signals at night gave satisfactory results.

3) The enemy is making systematic attempts to deceive the boats as to the convoy's position by means of escort vessels firing flares. It is therefore essential to provide visual aids (shadowers' signal buoys dropped by the aircraft) to make it easier for the boats to find the convoy. (Equipment of Atlantic aircraft with signal buoys is in progress). It is important to change the characteristics of the signal buoys frequently, as the enemy is likely to make attempts at deception.[2]

For the remainder of 1943, bad weather, betrayal of U-boat movements by ULTRA decryption and frequently inaccurate navigational fixes combined to render all further U-boat–Luftwaffe cooperation futile. On 15 December, Fischer, *Gruppenkommandeur* FAGr. 5, issued his own analysis of his unit's first full month of operations. He recommended that Ju 290s be given an offensive capability for use against sighted convoy traffic, rather than continuing their purely passive reconnaissance and shadowing roles, advocating '*Kehlgerät*' and either 'Fritz-X' or Hs 293 weapons. In the meantime, the *Gruppe* took delivery of new A-5 model aircraft, with enhanced armament and fuel capacity.

At his headquarters in Angers, Kessler issued a new document on 3 December entitled 'The Principles Governing the Conduct of Operations by *Fliegerführer Atlantik* and an Appreciation of the Types of Aircraft Available'. Within its pages he outlined broad tactical principles for cooperation with *B.d.U.* and *MGK West* for safeguarding German surface and U-boat forces, as well as potential operations against enemy supply shipping in the event of enemy landings.

The document advocated the concentration of 'all appropriate forces' in accordance with both *B.d.U.* requirements and independent operations. Reconnaissance was henceforth to be carried out primarily with ship locating radar, by sectors at 1,000 metres altitude, thereby not reliant on prevailing visibility. Convoy reconnaissance was to commence in the morning, repeated in late afternoon to provide as up-to-date information as possible and, in the case of supporting the formation of U-boat groups, should continue into the night, using flares and the newly developed FuG 302 '*Schwanboje*' (Swan Buoy); a VHF beacon dropped by parachute resembling a normal bomb and carried on a 250kg bomb rack. The buoy carried a telescoping frame aerial that protruded from its tail fins and transmitted for up to five hours, powered by accumulator batteries.

On the other hand, reconnaissance for *MGK West* in support of blockade-runners, auxiliary cruisers and prize vessels either entering or leaving the Biscay ports was primarily a safeguard against enemy surface ships; providing course amendments to avoid detected enemy vessels. Furthermore, defensive patrols against enemy landings on the French Atlantic coast were to be conducted in late afternoon, covering sea areas through which landing forces could have passed by night. Armed reconnaissance against single enemy ships off the Spanish and Portuguese coast by flights of two or three long range bombers were only to be undertaken based on firm intelligence reports, and by dusk or a clear night.

Attacks on enemy convoys were to be made with a mandatory minimum strength of one *Gruppe*, carried out in the evening so that returning to France would be covered by darkness. In cloudless weather, bomber units were to be escorted by twin-engine fighters. As He 177 and Fw 200 aircraft fitted with either '*Kehlgerät*' or the Lofte 7D could only mount attacks in slight, high or medium cloud and the fact that convoys frequently used bad weather as cover, *Fliegerführer Atlantik* recommended that the He 177 be modified to potentially carry torpedoes, although the He 177A-3/R7 torpedo bomber version had already been abandoned in favour of the He 177A-5 main production model, only three prototypes having been constructed.[3]

In the document, the types of aircraft available to *Fliegerführer Atlantik* were listed, along with each model's advantages and disadvantages.

I. *Reconnaissance aircraft.*
1. **FW 200** is at present available in three different models:
   a. Normal Fw 200 with a radius of 1,500km.
   b. Fw 200 fitted with auxiliary fuselage tanks (known as long-range Condor) with a radius of action of 1,750km.
   c. Fw 200 fitted with auxiliary fuselage tanks and two exterior tanks (known as maximum-range Condor) with a radius of action of 2,200km.

Only the long-range and maximum-range Condor are suitable for the present operational commitments of *Fliegerführer Atlantik*. Use of the maximum-range Condor is limited due to the difficulties involved in taking off at night due to overloading and its use can only be recommended for major operations. In view of its inadequate armament and lack of speed the Fw 200 cannot be used in areas covered by enemy twin-engine fighters. Recent encounters between Fw 200s and enemy twin-engine fighters when cloud cover has been insufficient have nearly always led to the destruction of the Fw 200.

Further development of the Fw 200 is not recommended since:
a. It has been exploited to the limit of its potentialities,
b. It is being replaced by the He 177.

2. **Ju 290**. The Ju 290 meets the present requirements as far as radius of action is concerned. Thanks to its good armament and even better armament proposed, it is also suitable for operations in areas covered by enemy twin-engine fighters. At the moment the Ju 290 is the most suitable aircraft for Atlantic reconnaissance. Its use is at present restricted to certain areas and to certain seasons of the year due to the absence of de-icing equipment . . .

3. **Ju 88D-1** or **A-4**. This aircraft does not come up to operational requirements either in range or speed. The Ju88D-1 has to be used by *Fliegerführer Atlantik* for sea reconnaissance in areas covered by British day and night fighters. Duties can only be carried out when weather conditions are particularly favourable. Requests for suitable aircraft have been made to *General der Aufklärungsflieger* [*Generalmajor* Karl Henning von Barsewisch].

4. **BV 222**. On account of its performance the BV 222 has been called upon to carry out roughly the same duties as the Ju 290. Its operational potentialities are only restricted because of:

a. Its insufficient armament and unprotected tanks,

b. Its lack of speed.

Its tactical radius of action will be increased by 300 km to 2,700 km when in, in January 1944, delivery is taken of the new V-10 and V-11 subtypes fitted with diesel engines.

5. **BV 138**. In view of its lack of speed and small radius of action, this aircraft is only suitable for defensive reconnaissance along the French coast and on anti-submarine patrols. For these purposes, however, it is very suitable.

II. *Bombers*

He 177. With a tactical radius of action of 1,500km, this aircraft cannot, by any means, be used in all the sea areas covered by *Fliegerführer Atlantik*'s reconnaissance. Its use is thus limited to the Western Atlantic and north west Biscay. The performance of the He 177 make it suitable for use with glider bombs (*Kehl*) and as a torpedo bomber. The He 177 is well armed and has no cause, particularly in formation flights, to fear any type of enemy aircraft operating over the Atlantic.

Recommendations for further development:

a. Radius of action to be increased to that of reconnaissance aircraft while retaining the same bomb capacity.

b. To be adapted for quick change over from '*Kehl*' to torpedo bomber (according to weather conditions).

c. Increase in speed to cope with expected presence of faster enemy twin-engine fighters and as a counter measure to anti-aircraft defence.

III. *Fighters and twin-engine fighters.*

1. **Ju 88**. The twin-engine fighter formations are made up of Ju 88C-6 aircraft, subtypes R2 [night fighters with BMW 801 engines], H2 [Fighter variant intended to attack Allied long-range convoy escort aircraft armed with six forward-firing MG 151/20] and G1 [BMW 801 radial engines with 1700 PS, FuG 220 '*Lichtenstein*' SN-2 radar].

The armament of the H2 and G1 meets present day requirements. The expected radius of both models of 1,600 to

KG 40 He 177 prepared for an Atlantic mission.

1,800 km is adequate for present needs, but the ultimate objective must be to increase the range up to that of the long-range bomber.

With regard to speed, the Ju 88R2, H2 and G1 which are fitted with BMW 801 engines are superior in speed to most enemy aircraft used over the Atlantic with the exception of the Mosquito which is now appearing in ever increasing numbers.

2. **Fw 190**. In areas other than the normal operational zones of RAF fighters, the Fw 190 is the most useful of the limited number of operational aircraft in use by *Fliegerführer Atlantik*. The most unsatisfactory aspect of all is that, in spite of the new developments expected in the air situation over the Atlantic, the radius of action of the Fw 190 (even with auxiliary tanks) is still too small. What is required is a fighter with at least the same armament as the Fw 190, but a greater radius of action without auxiliary fuel tanks.

3. **Ar 196**. In armament, radius of action and performance this aircraft is obsolete. The Ar 196 can only be used for reconnaissance in coastal areas and for anti-submarine patrols and escort duties.

Aerial reconnaissance on behalf of U-boat groups had comprehensively failed in December 1943, Kessler also being allocated the task of reconnoitring for incoming blockade-runners from the middle of the

Arado Ar 196 aircraft at Hourtin near Bordeaux.

month. Five heavily-laden ships had departed Batavia during October and November, the first two to approach Biscay being the 6,951GRT *Osorno* – codenamed 'Bernau' – and the 2,729GRT MV *Alsterufer* – codenamed 'Trave'. The Allies, informed by ULTRA, had instigated Operation *Stonewall* using combined air and naval units already on Biscay patrol redirected to find blockade-runners and sink them. On 18 December 1943, the outbound *Pietro Orseolo*, code-named 'Eifel', was lying at anchor in Concarneau in preparation for departure carrying a varied cargo of machine parts, diesel engines, aluminium and nickel ingots, petrol, oil, two aircraft, and three small tracked motorcycles (*Kettenkrad*). Torpedo-armed Beaufighters (Torbeau) of RAF 254 Squadron were ordered to attack, accompanied by five Beaufighters of 248 Squadron whose task was to silence harbour anti-aircraft installations with their 25lb solid-shot rockets and devastating cannon fire. Escorted by eight Typhoons of RAF 183 Squadron, the Torbeaus scored two torpedo hits and left the ship crippled and blazing, listing heavily to starboard. Two days later two tugboats from Brest began moving *Pietro Orseolo* but, in worsening weather, she became stuck on a sandbank, floating free on rising tides the next day until a bulkhead collapsed and the ship went down.

The incoming *Osorno* was sighted by Luftwaffe reconnaissance on 22 December amidst hailstorms and heavy seas, as was US Navy Task Group

TG 21.15. Centred on the escort carrier USS *Card*, the Task Group had been forced south-west by the bad weather which prevented launch of the carrier's fighters to intercept the shadowing aircraft. Six ships of 8.*Zerstörerflottille* and another six of 4.*Torpedobootflottille* departed France the next morning to rendezvous with the incoming *Osorno* while Ju 290 '9V+DK', eight Condors and a single BV 222 were directed to find and shadow the American carrier force. As the weather moderated *Card*'s aircraft had already overflown *Osorno* as the blockade-runner streamed a British flag and ran up a four-letter identification hoist which, although of a general British merchant vessel characteristic, were later found to be outdated. Fortunately for *Osorno* the American pilot made no radio report of the sighting, rather by message drop an hour later on his return to *Card*. An urgent despatch was then sent to the American liaison officer in Gibraltar for potential ship identification, the reply confirming that no British vessel was in the area. Photographs later identified the ship as *Osorno*, though by that stage the US carrier had been advised to leave the blockade-runner for RAF land-based aircraft to attack now that its position had been roughly established.

Meanwhile a strong force of II./KG 40 He 177s was readied with Hs 293 glide bombs, intended to attack the carrier. Beacon signals from a shadowing Ju 290 were transmitted to guide the bombers towards USS *Card* until the Junkers was forced to break off its contact under enemy fighter attack and the Heinkel strike was aborted. Instead, U-boats of the nearby '*Borkum*' patrol line were vectored towards the Americans, *U275* sinking the escorting destroyer USS *Leary* with a *Zaunkönig* torpedo on the morning of Christmas Eve and USS *Card* being narrowly missed by torpedoes from *U415*. HMS *Hurricane*, escorting Convoy OS62/KMS36 which '*Borkum*' had intended to intercept, was sighted that evening and sunk by a *Zaunkönig* from *U415*.

Despite cessation of the beacon, II./KG 40 despatched its six operational He 177s at 0615hrs on armed reconnaissance alongside two Condors of III./KG 40 and ten Ju 88 *Zerstörer*. This would leave no bomber forces available until 1500hrs, *MGK West* and *Fliegerführer Atlantik* gambling on the armed reconnaissance contacting enemy ships in pursuit of *Osorno*. The German destroyers were in turn being shadowed by enemy aircraft, turning briefly to a northerly course lest they lead the enemy to the blockade-runner, the six torpedo boats sailing independently towards *Osorno* undetected. Eventually, with the torpedo boat *T27* momentarily detached following severe rudder damage, and the destroyer *Z23* forced to return prematurely after heavy seas flooded compartments 13 and 14, the remaining Kriegsmarine surface ships made contact with *Osorno*, under enemy aircraft observation, and the small group suffering ineffectual air attack. Twenty-two extra Ju 88C-6s of ZG 1 were scrambled along with sixteen Fw 190s to provide protection for the naval forces but they made no contact with the enemy.

The same was not true, however, of the six Heinkel He 177s. After two hours aloft they encountered RAF Beaufighters of 143 Squadron on Biscay patrol. Squadron Leader Bill Moore led his aircraft into the attack and was immediately hit by fire from the guns aboard *Lt*. Richard Kranz's 'F8+LM' of 4./KG 40, the Beaufighter exploding in mid-air. The remaining fighters concentrated their fire on Kranz's aircraft and, with the starboard engines on fire, the Heinkel crashed into the sea and disintegrated with no survivors.

During Christmas Day, *Osorno* and her escorting ships came under repeated air attack, though with little damage inflicted as German gunners consumed large quantities of ammunition keeping the attackers at bay. Sixteen He 177s of II./KG 40 were once again despatched on armed reconnaissance to intercept vessels of Operation *Stonewall* but, despite sighting enemy warships, were foiled by low-lying cloud preventing use of the Hs 293, proof of Kessler's determination to be able to use the He 177 as a torpedo aircraft capable of wave-top attacks.

Finally, under protection of Ju 88s, destroyer and torpedo-boat gunners and shore-based anti-aircraft, *Osorno* entered the Gironde River and reached Bordeaux, though the ship was damaged within sight of her goal by striking the submerged wreck of *Sperrbrecher 21*. Run aground to prevent harm to her cargo, she was subsequently unloaded by lighter.

Aware of the strong forces arrayed against *Alsterufer* as well as the three succeeding blockade-runners *Rio Grande*, *Weserland* and *Burgenland* waiting in the South Atlantic, consideration was given to rerouting them north through the Denmark Strait rather than across Biscay. However, though *Weserland* was given the green light to make such an attempt, it was considered impractical for *Alsterufer* which was already in Biscay's western reaches. Instead the blockade-runner continued to her planned rendezvous with the same torpedo boats and destroyers as *Osorno*. *Fliegerführer Atlantik* despatched 'Hohentwiel'-equipped Condors, Ju 290s and one BV 222 to locate *Alsterufer* during 26 and 27 December, Ju 290 '9V+DK' flown by *Oblt*. Werner Nedela lost when it flew into

The blockade-runner *Alsterufer* burns after attack by a Sunderland of 311 (Czech) Squadron. Failure by *Fliegerführer Atlantik* to protect the blockade-runners contributed to the cessation of the programme.

a Spanish mountainside in bad weather while heading for Monte de Marsan at the end of its patrol.[4] However, during the morning of 27 December, as the Luftwaffe searched for the motor vessel, *Alsterufer* fought off an initial Sunderland attack before another Sunderland of 311 (Czech) Squadron located and identified the ship, attacking with rockets and bombs, destroying her wireless capability and setting her on fire. The crew subsequently abandoned ship as *Alsterufer* sank without being able to transmit news of the disaster to *MGK West*.

During the next twenty-four hours the Luftwaffe and Kriegsmarine continued to search for the missing ship as a fresh disaster unfolded when Kriegsmarine vessels encountered the *Stonewall* cruisers HMS *Glasgow* and *Enterprise*.

At 0305 Group West informed the 'Trave' [*Alsterufer*] that Fw 200, He 177, Ju 290 and Ju 88 aircraft would be despatched.

At 0945, the 8. *Zerstörerflottille* and 4. *Torpedobootflottille* united, reached the rendezvous and were detected by enemy reconnaissance.

Since 'Trave' was not encountered, the 8. *Zerstörerflottille* steered to meet the ship from BE 6672 on course 285 degrees, speed 17 knots until 1000. The 'Trave' was informed of this at 1125.

At 1208 Group West ordered 'Trave' to report her position. If no answer was received by 1400 the flotillas were to return.

Fliegerführer Atlantik's eight aircraft searched for *Alsterufer* from dawn between 43° and 49° North and as far as 16° West, reaching as far as they could into the Atlantic before turning back. Unfortunately for the Kriegsmarine, this meant that the outbound eastern portions (up to 12° West) of their sectors were crossed during hours of darkness; '*Hohentwiel*' sets being unable to distinguish friend from foe even if contact was made. Owing to the northernmost aircraft suffering mechanical problems, and not replaced until later that day, a major gap was created in the reconnaissance screen and the British cruisers remained undetected approaching from the north-east while the aircraft were outbound. They were not seen until return flights in the early afternoon by which time they had progressed unobserved for three hours towards the destroyers and torpedo boats. It proved too late to prevent them clashing with the smaller German surface ships or provide adequate aerial protection.

Marinegruppenkommando West requested that Kessler despatch all KG 40 He 177s towards their destroyers and torpedo boats for a dawn rendezvous, considered the most dangerous period when confronted with unknown enemy forces. Thereafter, the Heinkels were to cover the surface ships through much of the daylight hours. However, Kessler raised objections on account of the difficulty involved in heavily-laden He 177s taking off in darkness and successfully meeting the German task force only at first light. Additionally, a low cloud ceiling in the combat zone would render the use of '*Kehlgerät*' impossible. By way of compromise, he despatched four Condors of III./KG 40 between 0636hrs and 0800hrs, each carrying Hs 293s into action for the first time. Despite a *Schwan* transmitter buoy having been dropped, the Condors were unable to keep formation and spread some distance apart as they flew west, the requested He 177s held at one-hour's readiness and their commitment guaranteed by Kessler if needed despite the ineffectiveness of their glide bombs in such weather conditions.

Like the three other Condor crews, *Hptm.* Wilhelm Dette and his men had only recently returned from a month of training at Peenemunde in glide-bomb use. Outbound towards the enemy's last reported position they briefly encountered a Sunderland in strong winds and heavy cloud, the British flying boat banking away, seemingly unaware of their presence. Not long afterwards, a thin stream of white vapour was observed by flight engineer *Uffz*. Willi Hackler coming from the Condor's outer starboard engine, followed by a sudden and devastating engine fire as the engine was cut to conserve fuel. The Condor was forced to ditch, six survivors being rescued from their life raft four days later by the ASW trawler HMS *Lord Nuffield* after being spotted by an American aircraft. One other aircraft was forced to abort with mechanical problems, while the two remaining Condors launched an unsuccessful attack on a cruiser and 'destroyer' sighted at 1305hrs.

> At 1525 *Fliegerführer Atlantik* transmitted a preliminary, report according to which his reconnaissance reported an engagement between two cruisers and four of our destroyers. or torpedo boats in BE66. Evidently the vessels IMA and HAF located by our radio intelligence were involved. If no stronger forces than these two cruisers were involved a favourable development of the situation for our own forces could be expected. However, Trave's position became the subject of considerable anxiety. Should the order from Group West to report her position remain unanswered, a successful breakthrough could no longer be expected considering the enemy situation since the afternoon of 27 December, and certainly not should the destroyers and torpedo boats no longer be able to remain at their rendezvous position.
>
> At 1520 Group West reported that at 1458 the destroyer *Z27* was out of control in BE 6938.
>
> At 1524 the destroyer *Z23* reported: 'Am attempting to withdraw westward; am being pursued by two cruisers in BE6923.'
>
> At 1615 the Chief, Naval Staff called the *Fliegerführer Atlantik* personally and asked for every possible support for our forces in the Bay of Biscay, since the situation was grave. The *Fliegerführer* was of the same opinion and reported that sixteen He 177s with '*Kehlgerät*' had been despatched.[5]

That afternoon, the sixteen promised He 177A-3s of II./KG 40 took off to attack the enemy surface ships in very poor weather. Instead, some of the bombers ran headlong into eight Mosquito IIs of RAF 157 Squadron that shot down *Hptm*. Bernard Eidhoff's 'F8+IN' of 5./KG 40 which exploded on hitting the water. Six Heinkels never engaged the target due to poor weather, the remainder attacked with no result.

By the end of the day the Kriegsmarine had lost the destroyer *Z27* and the torpedo boats *T25* and *T26*, with heavy damage to *T22*. Of the 672 men from the three destroyed ships only 283 were rescued by U-boats, British minesweepers, an Irish freighter guided to the location of rubber rafts by Luftwaffe reconnaissance aircraft and Spanish destroyers. Among the dead was *K.z.S.* Hans Erdmenger, commander of the 8.*Zerstörerflottille*.

Osorno was the last blockade-runner to reach Europe from Japan, the three remaining ships being sunk by the US Navy during the first week of January with the aid of ULTRA intelligence and exhaustive aerial reconnaissance. Following the failure of all but one of this third wave of blockade-running, the entire programme of using large freighters was finally cancelled on 18 January 1944. From that point onward, smaller-capacity U-boats would be used.

The impotence of *Fliegerführer Atlantik* in the face of a numerically and technologically superior enemy was nowhere more manifest than the failure of the December operations which had tested it to beyond its limit. Most reconnaissance on behalf of *B.d.U.* had been curtailed by the need to commit forces to *MGK West*, and the few missions flown to locate convoys had either failed to find anything or successfully summon U-boats. A small number of damaged U-boats were effectively shepherded by ZG 1 Junkers to port, each boat flying a visible yellow flag for the benefit of identification by the escorting aircraft. Yet, by the beginning of January Kessler's command had suffered a sudden reduction in the number of planes at operational readiness.

The maritime airfields at Bordeaux-Mérignac and Cognac were repeatedly heavily bombed by the USAAF, beginning on New Year's Eve, destroying or severely damaging hangars, workshops and aircraft, as well as killing both ground and air crews. By 6 January Kessler reported that III./KG 40 was completely non-operational and would remain so for at least five weeks. All reconnaissance Condors and those equipped with 'Kehlgerät' were out of action, with no Condor expected to be operational in the immediate future. In the interim, *MGK West* requested *Luftflotte* 3 release KG 26 to bolster *Fliegerführer Atlantik*, soon impossible as fresh developments within the Mediterranean saved Richthofen the bother of having to refuse.

The Luftwaffe were very aware of shortcomings in long-range bomber forces situated in the Mediterranean and Biscay areas and did their utmost to limit operations to a minimum. By such action they hoped to raise operational efficiency of each *Geschwader* either through refitting of active units or training by each unit's own IV.*Gruppe.* Flurries of activity in Biscay were, theoretically, meant to only occupy brief periods of the winter months though continuing Allied pressure on U-boats and their harbours necessitated Luftwaffe response.

In action against enemy twin-engined fighters, the Ju 88s of ZG 1 had continued to suffer casualties, when able to fly between bouts of harsh winter weather. During December alone the *Geschwader* lost seven Ju 88C-6 with all crew killed, including *Oblt.* Hermann Horstmann, *Staffelkapitän* of 1./ZG 1, lost in action against Beaufighters when outnumbered two to one. In return, ZG 1 had destroyed three Mosquitoes and five Beaufighters during the same period, but it was an attritional rate of exchange that the Luftwaffe could not sustain. Kessler assessed the situation that *Fliegerführer Atlantik* faced at the end of 1943 as follows:

> The present situation on the Atlantic is characterized by British air supremacy. Naval command, which believed that in Biscay they had possessed the desired gateway to the Atlantic, are now as locked in Biscay by enemy air forces as the Navy had been in the North Sea during World War One. German Naval Command has swapped the blind spot of the North Sea with the dead triangle of Biscay . . . [6]

Though faced with seemingly insurmountable odds stacked against him, Kessler continued to appeal for more aircraft to be afforded to his ailing command. He listed minimum requirements as a single long-range reconnaissance *Gruppe* (50 aircraft), two long-range bomber *Geschwader* (150 aircraft) one *Zerstörer Geschwader* (150 aircraft) and one ASW seaplane *Gruppe* (64 aircraft). With this, he reasoned, he could independently sink 500,000GRT of enemy shipping within the eastern Atlantic.

In this he received Dönitz's full support, the naval leader possessing Hitler's ear and confidence to a degree that the Kriegsmarine had never had before. On 16 December, in a personal letter to the *Führer*, Dönitz explained difficulties now faced by the U-boat service, their ability to engage in surface tactics now at an end therefore rendering them even more reliant than previously on the search capacity of aircraft. The output of the most effective reconnaissance aircraft – the Ju 290 – was paltry at best, Kessler due to have only twenty machines by the end of 1944. Dönitz urged Ju 290 production be accelerated, to which Hitler agreed, forcing Göring to also acquiesce to save face. In a telephone conversation with Dönitz the *Reichsmarschall* pledged all Ju 290s being manufactured would be dedicated to air reconnaissance on behalf of *B.d.U.*, though accelerating production was impossible due to the demands of building fighters to protect the Reich and also replacing bombers wasted in retributory attacks on Great Britain as part of the disastrous Operation *Steinbock*. Although killing 1,556 British civilians over a period of four months from January 1944, *Steinbock* achieved nothing of strategic value. Demanded by Hitler as vengeance for the Allied bombing of Germany, the scale of available Luftwaffe effort of, on average, less than 200 bombers per raid, could in no way compare with the massed attacks by the RAF and USAAF. Instead, valuable aircraft and experienced crews – including the few with maritime experience from II./KG 30, I. and II./KG 40 – were lost in futile action over Britain.

In Biscay Dönitz's U-boats had been comprehensively robbed of cover. By day there were insufficient escorting aircraft to provide protection, by night the darkness provided no cover from radar and Leigh-Light equipped bombers. Consideration was even given to using the '*Wild Saue*' method of night fighter defence over Biscay in January. 'Hajo' Herrmann had pioneered this tactic by which ordinary day fighters were used in darkness to attack British bombers, illuminated by natural moonlight, searchlights, flares and the burning cites below. In this way the Luftwaffe could commit additional aircraft to night fighter tasks without the prerequisite equipment or training.

However, over Biscay, the method was unsuitable. Despite needing to combat radar-equipped U-boat hunters, such '*Wild Saue*' tactics hinged upon a chance meeting with solitary enemy aircraft, rather than the bomber streams trailing across Germany. The available Fw 190s could only carry out short flights, night flying over the sea by a single-engine aircraft equalling completely blind flying, its resultant pilot strain considered out of proportion to possible results. Similarly, using the available Ju 88C-6 *Zerstörer* of ZG 1, with no radar sets or homing receivers, depended entirely upon chance encounters on a bright night. Free-lance night fighter operations using '*Hohentwiel*' were considered theoretically possible, but inherently wasteful as aircraft could only be located using the ship-location gear at distances up to 15 kilometres. Thereafter the target had to be perceptible to the naked eye for the actual attack, rendering such missions only possible in bright moonlight. Instead, it was reasoned by *MGK West* and *Fliegerführer*

Dönitz among the Third Reich's hierarchy, including Martin Bormann, Bruno Loerzer and Göring, pictured here visiting Hitler with a visibly diminished Mussolini after the abortive bomb plot of 20 July 1944.

Atlantik that aircraft engaged on Biscay night fighter missions required either the FuG 227 '*Flensburg*' passive radar set and FuG 350 '*Naxos Z*' radar warning receiver as well as a FuG 212 '*Lichtenstein*' C-1 or wide-angle radar set.

With so few aircraft available in the west at the end of 1943 and beginning of 1944, minelaying by *Gen.Maj.* Dietrich Peltz's IX.*Fliegerkorps* was halted. Despite being requested by *MGK West*, Peltz's bombers were diverted to *Steinbock* which he had also been tasked to coordinate. Instead S-boats were intended to take charge of minelaying in British waters, using the extended hours of winter darkness as cover.

Korten, as Chief of the Luftwaffe General Staff since August, had supported naval requests for a renewed minelaying offensive. The new acoustic and magnetic/acoustic fuses were to be utilised after Hitler overruled plans to deploy pressure mines, lest the British capture one, copy it and use it within the Baltic Sea. Korten intended to expand the Luftwaffe's minelaying force to eleven *Gruppen*, equipped with He 177 and Ju 188 aircraft and with naval backing, a fresh minelaying offensive had begun with the new moon period on 15 September. However, it was brief, abandoned by 3 October after heavy bomber losses and the sowing of 600 mines. Thereafter, aircraft that Korten had earmarked for minelaying were diverted to conventional bombing and swallowed up by the demands of *Steinbock*.

Beginning on 20 January 1944, *Fliegerführer Atlantik* reckoned on only five Ju 290, two BV 222 and three Ju 88 aircraft being available for reconnaissance. This meant that for any operation lasting multiple days, only four aircraft could be employed on any given day. Heinkel He 177 and Ju 88 bombers were available, although *MGK West* advocated torpedo formations be allocated to Kessler's command, as prevailing low cloud conditions negated use of '*Kehlgerät*'. *Luftflotte* 3's request for KG 26 to be redirected to *Fliegerführer Atlantik* was unrealistic as the *Geschwader* was experiencing its own problems during January. Both I. and III./KG 26 were used in the first torpedo mission of the New Year on 10 January, attacking Convoy KMS 37N south-east of Fomentera. The twenty-six escorted eastbound freighters were the fourth convoy sighted that day by Luftwaffe reconnaissance, thirty-eight torpedo bombers despatched to attack, only eleven of which found their target. Intercepted by Beaufighters of RAF 153 Squadron, two Ju 88s were claimed shot down with a third probable. In return a single Beaufighter was hit by defensive machine-gun fire and set ablaze, exploding during its attempted return to base with both crew killed. In total KG 26 lost two Ju 88s, and two He 111H-11s, one shot down by anti-aircraft fire and the other running out of fuel off Palma de Mallorca, two crew members later being rescued from the water.

SS *Ocean Hunter* and *Daniel Webster* were both hit by torpedoes, the latter limping onwards with the convoy after being holed towards the bow. The Liberty ship's internal bulkhead proved strong enough to prevent the ship sinking and allowed her to reach Oran where she was beached and later declared a total constructive loss. The 7,173GRT *Ocean Hunter*, laden with military stores for Malta, sank soon after being hit, a single crew member being killed, the remainder rescued from the sea and taken to Algiers.

Aware of the importance of the French Mediterranean airbases to regional Luftwaffe operations, thirty-seven B-17 bombers of the USAAF 15th Air Force bombed Istres-Le-Tube and Salon-de-Provence on 21 January, causing considerable damage to buildings and runways and rendering both airfields temporarily unserviceable. The following day, Allied troops landed at Anzio.

8

Outflanked

Last Gasp in the Mediterranean

O PERATION *SHINGLE* WAS INTENDED to outflank the German defensive Gustav Line anchored on the formidable obstacle of Monte Cassino. Preceded by a six-day air offensive against German communication lines and airfields, Luftwaffe reconnaissance capability was reduced to virtually nothing, impeded at any event by seasonally bad weather. Correspondingly, the *Shingle* armada that sailed overnight from Naples and began landing troops at Anzio at 0200hrs on 22 January 1944 arrived completely undetected.

Though the landing's exact time and place surprised Kesselring and his staff, an attempted outflanking manoeuvre was considered likely despite Abwehr assurances to the contrary. The Allied ground advance had stalled before German defences; an effort to land in its rear and directly threaten Rome was considered logical by Kesselring, though he possessed scant reserves to combat such an eventuality.

Due to the gathering of landing craft in Britain preparatory to a cross-Channel invasion, the Anzio landing force was relatively small. More crucially perhaps, it was beset by confusion as to its goal. The landing was of British design, dreamt up by Churchill to capture Rome, only thirty miles distant, but commanded by US Major General John P. Lucas who had little confidence in the plan and believed its purpose to be diversion of defensive strength from the Gustav Line, rather than an independent invasion front. Initial landings were made by two infantry divisions, the British 1st and US 3rd, coordinated by the latter's senior officer Major General Lucian K. Truscott. Six miles north of the small port town, the British landed as part of 'Peter Force' supported by the light cruisers HMS *Orion* and *Spartan*, twelve destroyers, two anti-aircraft/fighter direction ships, four transports, sixty-three landing craft, gunboats, minesweepers and ancillary vessels, including four hospital ships. An American Ranger Group stormed ashore at Anzio's port from a single transport, subchaser and seven landing craft, while the 3rd US

Infantry Division landed east of Nettuno as 'X-Ray' Force, supported by the light cruisers USS *Brooklyn* and HMS *Penelope*, eleven destroyers, two destroyer escorts, 166 landing craft, minesweepers, subchasers and smaller units. The naval elements of *Shingle* were designated Task Group 81, led by Rear Admiral Frank J. Lowry, USN; the two destroyers USS *Frederick C. Davis* and *Herbert C. Jones* carrying '*Kehlgerät*' jamming equipment forming their own semi-autonomous sub-group 'Task Group 80.2' under the command of Lt.Comm Alfred W. Gardes Jr., USN. Experience already gained accompanying convoys attacked by glide bombs had refined their jamming equipment and technique, more powerful equipment installed aboard both ships in December, marking the end of what the US Navy deemed the 'investigational' [*sic*] phase and beginning of the 'protective' phase.

The initial Luftwaffe response to the surprise landing was led by Bf 109 fighters clearing a path for Fw 190 fighter-bombers of SG 4 that sank two American and a single Royal Navy landing craft, fighting both strong aerial defences and waterlogged airfields in northern Italy. The landings, despite a relative paucity of supporting forces, were remarkably successful and within the first twenty-four hours, 36,000 troops were ashore with only thirteen men killed. However, Richthofen's

Heinkel He 111s in flight.

Luftflotte 2 quickly assembled all available maritime bombers to strike offshore support by the second day of *Shingle*. *Luftflotte* 2 still controlled 2.*Fliegerdivision* and for initial Anzio operations *Generalleutnant* Fink moved his battle headquarters to Merate in northern Italy (former headquarters of II.*Fliegerkorps* which had transferred to northern Europe in expectation of anti-invasion measures). Fink mustered the following torpedo and glide-bomb units:

Stab/KG 100 (Istres), *Obstlt.* Bernhard Jope, Do 217;

II./KG 100 – minus 4./KG 100 – (Toulouse), *Hptm.* Heinz-Emil
    Middermann, Do 217;

I./KG 26 (Salon), *Hptm.* Jochen Müller, He 111;

III./KG 26 (Montpellier), *Hptm.* Klaus Nocken, Ju 88;

II./KG 40 (Bordeaux-Mérignac), *Maj.* Walter Rieder, He 177, on
    attachment from *Fliegerführer Atlantik*.

Alongside these specialists, Ju 88s of I and III./KG 1 were available for conventional bombing missions and 1.(F)/Aufkl.Gr. 33 provided reconnaissance from its airfield at St. Martin.

Tactically, the maritime attacks attempted its most successful combination of virtually simultaneous dive-bombing and low-level torpedo attacks while the stand-off aircraft launched Hs 293 glide bombs from a distance. The lack of heavy warships rendered deployment of III./KG 100 with its armour-piercing 'Fritz-Xs' redundant and they took no part in the Anzio battle despite relocating to Toulouse during February in expectation, each aircraft carrying two ground crew aboard for the low-level flight from Eggebeck while the remainder following by rail.

Most Luftwaffe attacks at Anzio were timed for dusk or later, allowing retreating bombers the relative cover of darkness to make their escape. Bright magnesium flares were dropped to illuminate targets in low light, also shielding attacking aircraft from anti-aircraft gunners below. With Toulouse at the maximum range for II./KG 100 Dorniers, they staged out of the airfield at Bergamo, each aircraft carrying a balanced load of a single Hs 293 and an auxiliary fuel tank. The He 177s from Bordeaux, capable of greater distance, were able to bring pairs of Hs 293s into action by direct flight from the French Atlantic coast. For the Junkers Ju 88s of III./KG 26, the staging airfield at Piacenza was used, although local stocks of available torpedoes soon ran out, reducing the maritime crews to attacking with fragmentation bombs for which they were ill-equipped, possessing few of the necessary bomb racks, no dive-bombing bomb sights or high-altitude oxygen equipment for level bombing.

The opening raid for Stab/KG 100 began badly when *Hptm*. Hans Eberthäuser's Do 217 '6N+CC' crashed on take-off from Toulouse, injuring the crew. However, it was the sole loss to KG 100 while KG 26 faced the brunt of the enemy's defending fighter strength. Intercepted inbound to the Anzio beachhead by Spitfires, I./KG 26 lost three He 111s and III./KG 26 six Ju 88s, 4./KG 40 also losing two He 177s. The first was flown by *Staffelkapitän Hptm*. Bernhard Kobrink, killed with his entire crew, the second shot down by a Beaufighter after passing over Corsica due to faulty navigation. *Oberleutnant* Paul Dietrich's 'F8+AM' was detected by radar and the night fighter unleashed two brief bursts of fire which ignited stored flares, the Heinkel crashing in flames. Two men were killed, the remainder bailing out and being captured as their aircraft came down on the west bank of the River Ostriconi, four miles north-east of Palasca. While most of the Heinkel disintegrated, battered remains of the '*Kehlgerät*' transmitter were recovered along with at least one almost intact Hs 293 that had buried itself in the ground on impact; recovered and shipped to Naples for examination.

Anti-aircraft fire during a Luftwaffe night attack.

In return glide bombs hit the destroyers HMS *Janus* and *Jervis* engaged in shore bombardment north of Anzio harbour. As they retired seaward, *Janus* was hit by an Hs 293, frequently claimed to have been a torpedo though the balance of evidence suggests otherwise. The ship was hit between bridge and forecastle, starting a major fire and detonating stored ammunition in 'B' magazine that broke the ship in two, sinking in twenty minutes with only eighty members of the crew saved. HMS *Jervis* was struck by an Hs 293 that blew the entire bow section off to the ninth bulkhead. Miraculously, there were no casualties and *Jervis* remained watertight and sailed to Naples.

The Luftwaffe mounted a strenuous effort against Allied ships off the Anzio beachhead over the days immediately following the landing. The operational *Gruppen* of *Obstlt.* Sigmund-Ulrich Frhr. von Gravenreuth's KG 30 (Stab, I. and II.) which had been wasting their strength and abilities as part of Operation *Steinbock* from airfields in The Netherlands, was rushed to Istres to join the intensifying battle. The Royal Navy situation report of 25 January states:

> Shipping off beaches was under attack by fighter-bombers all day yesterday, but little or no damage was sustained. At dusk a considerable raid by bombers took place and this continued intermittently throughout the night. In these attacks, two more US destroyers [USS *Plunkett* and *Mayo*] were damaged, one hospital ship sunk, one hospital ship damaged, and one hospital ship attacked but undamaged. These hospital ships were fully lighted and marked and were well out of the landing area.[1]

The sinking by an aircrew of KG 100 of the 800GRT hospital ship HMHS *St. David* on 26 January is inexplicable in relation to the international rules of war. There was no mistaking the nature of the Red Cross vessel which was clearly marked and illuminated as it sailed to an offshore position beyond the destroyer screen in company with two other hospital ships, HMHS *Leinster* and *St. Andrew*. The movement order received from Rear Admiral Lowry aboard his command ship USS *Biscayne* was for the sole purpose of safeguarding the hospital ships, but the trio came under strong bombardment by dive-bombing and Hs 293 attack during their withdrawal seaward. *Leinster* was bombed three times with conventional bombs, hit forward to starboard and set aflame, though the crew managed to extinguish the fires without assistance.

A mile offshore, and well beyond the beachhead's outer destroyer screen, a Ju 88 overflew *St. David*, crossing from starboard to port and releasing four flares. A single Ju 88 dived out of the darkness and dropped two bombs, one of which struck No 3 hold near the after end of the promenade deck. It was probably then that the Hs 293 hit the ship near No 2 hold, bringing it to a shuddering halt as all electric power failed. *St. David* began to settle by the stern with a port list, and the ship's Master, Captain Evan Owens, gave the order to abandon ship. Attempts were made to lower water ambulances, though those to starboard were soon fouled and inoperative. To port, No 2 ambulance was lowered with great difficulty into heavy swell, while Nos 4 and 6 ambulances could not be freed in the five minutes it took for the ship to sink, being taken to the seabed with *St David* and an unknown number of people trapped within.

Artist Roland Davies' impression of the unjustifiable bombing and sinking of the hospital ship HMHS *St David* off Anzio, published in *The Sphere* newspaper, Saturday 19 February 1944. (Illustrated London News Group)

Captain Owens was last seen in the water, killed along with twelve of his crew, twenty-two Royal Army Medical Corps personnel, and twenty-two wounded men.

In London, the Admiralty requested those responsible be added to the list of war criminals as the British government communicated via Switzerland with Berlin 'protesting most strongly' against the deliberate targeting of hospital ships and requesting German authorities issue categoric instructions to all naval and air forces that hospital ships secure the full immunity to which they were entitled under international law.

Subsequent Allied interrogation of a captured German officer from a downed He 177 established that Luftwaffe aircrew were expressly forbidden to attack hospital ships, the inference being that either identification had been difficult or an 'exceptional type of pilot' was guilty. As the attack had lasted for over an hour, all ships were clearly lit in good visibility and the attackers used flares, the former appears difficult to believe.

After continuous Luftwaffe attacks against the Anzio beachhead, the USAAF 15th Air Force once again concentrated attention on maritime bomber airfields on 27 January. Twenty-seven B-24s unloaded 80 tons of bombs on Istres, sixty-four B-17s dropping 186 tons on Salon and sixty-eight B-17s a further 204 tons at Montpelier. All locations suffered heavy damage to buildings, hangars and workshops, and airfield surfaces rendered temporarily unusable due to cratering.

Though the American bombing complicated *2.Fliegerdivision* operations, they persevered and by month's end the Liberty ship SS *Samuel Huntingdon* and the British *Dido* class cruiser HMS *Spartan* were both sunk by glide bombs. HMS *Spartan* was anchored at sunset on 29 January when the 'Anzio Red' warning of incoming aircraft was issued. A patchy smokescreen drifted across the anchorage, ship radar being ineffective due to strong land echoes as Do 217s of II./KG 100 attacked from landward. Six glide bombs were launched, their red taillights visible streaking towards the cluster of immobile ships. One appeared to be heading just astern of *Spartan* before a last-minute correction sent it impacting the after end of 'B' funnel casing, passing through the ship and exploding high up on the port side near 'B' boiler room. A large hole was blown in the deck as the boiler room flooded, the main mast collapsed, steam and electrical power failed throughout the ship which began to burn. The glide bomb's explosion wrecked the port torpedo tubes, some of their air lines exploding, blowing warheads aft into the recreation space between 'X' turret and the main mast. The blazing warheads started a large fire in the vicinity of the after galley and recreation space and *Spartan* listed heavily to port, settling by the stern as firefighting efforts struggled vainly. Almost an hour later, after the list had become so pronounced that loose gear from the upper deck was sliding into the sea, the cruiser was abandoned and turned over ten minutes later in shallow water. Five officers and forty-one crew were lost, another forty-two injured.

As HMS *Spartan* burned, the Liberty ship SS *Samuel Huntingdon* was also hit by an Hs 293, which penetrated the boiler room and exploded, killing four men. Two cargo hatches were blown off by the blast that hurled a stored jeep into the flying bridge. Power failed and the ship's Master ordered the crew overboard as flames spread toward the 7,296 tons of cargo that included ammunition, gasoline and TNT. Fifteen minutes after the last lifeboat had pulled away, explosions battered the ship which settled on the bottom, only a metre beneath its keel. US Navy salvage craft USS *Weight* attempted to combat the blaze, but by early the following morning had admitted defeat, the Liberty ship's gasoline cargo finally igniting and blowing the *Samuel Huntingdon* into pieces that rained down on other ships within the Anzio anchorage.

Spartan's loss depleted an already small number of anti-aircraft defence and fire-support warships. Other vessels had been destroyed by mines and damaged by strafing and after the sinking of HMS *Janus* the Royal Navy had already requested their cruisers return to Naples rather than remain on station and by the end of the month they did so, sailing at dusk to Naples on the proviso of being available for fire support at five hours' notice. In reality the Anzio landings had thus far achieved little, though this was due to Allied caution rather than staunch German defence. Major General Lucas, instead of striking aggressively toward Rome, chose to consolidate his beachhead, allowing the energetic Kesselring time to reinforce previously scant defences.

Despite the relative success of the Wehrmacht at Anzio, losses to the Luftwaffe maritime bombers had been severe. Night fighters regularly intercepted incoming raids and the battered He 177s of II./KG 40 were withdrawn and redirected to convoy interception once more after losing seven aircraft with no confirmed victories.

Kesselring planned a vigorous counterattack for the beginning of February, codenamed '*Fischfang*' (fish trap). It finally opened on the 16th, a four-day battle that failed to destroy the beachhead but presaged a continual series of counterattacks. Initially, maritime bombers were to target Allied warships on the eve of the attack, though Allied air superiority promised little chance of success and potentially heavy losses. Instead, Richthofen's fighter-bomber strength was boosted while heavy ground artillery and railway guns would engage bombarding warships.

Yet Luftwaffe reinforcement of fighter-bombers for potential maritime strikes was somewhat illusory as many were diverted to support the Cassino battles. Everywhere within the Mediterranean, the declining power of the Luftwaffe was evident. While long-range bombers regrouped in northern Italy and southern France and dive-bombers moved to the Eastern Front and the defences of the northern Balkan area, Luftwaffe operations within the eastern Mediterranean had become negligible. Only routine convoy escort, reconnaissance and ASW patrols were remotely possible. The Ju 88s of both the Staff flight and I.*Gruppe* of *Oberst* Joachim Helbig's LG 1 moved urgently from Athens to Aviano in north-eastern Italy, at the Anzio landings, III./LG 1 transferring shortly thereafter from its Cretan base at Heraklion also to Aviano. The airfield had previously been an advanced training base for the *Regia Aeronautica*, its levelled grass surface having good drainage and generally avoiding waterlogging by winter rains. On 28 January it was bombarded by sixty-four USAAF B-17s, fragmentation bombs destroying buildings and hangars and rendering the runway surface temporarily out of commission.

Heavy losses of Ju 88s committed against Anzio supply shipping led to solitary night harassment missions against the beachhead itself being made instead. A small number of U-boats of the 29th U-Flotilla – deemed 'the only effective weapon against the landing fleet' by *SKL* on 31 January – had been tasked with attacking Anzio shipping from seaward while air attacks became solely the domain of glide-bombers and torpedo-bombers and, during February, Fw 190 fighter-bombers. Increasingly reduced numbers of aircraft mounted first and last-light missions during the first two weeks of February, hindered by bad weather but also redirection of bomber effort back against convoy traffic near the North African coast, now with additional fighter escort.

During January a number of aircraft and crews from III./ZG 1 had transferred from Bordeaux to Istres in order to protect anti-shipping bomber operations in the western Mediterranean. The transfer itself was not without incident; a bus carrying men of the *Zerstörer Gruppe* by road on 16 January was ambushed by French Maquis fighters who had stepped up their clandestine operations against German road and rail links during the month. In the firefight that followed, *Gruppenkommandeur Hptm.* Horst Grahl was lightly wounded while pilot *Oblt.* Herbert Hintze was hit in the leg by bullets thought to be 'dum-dums' – expanding bullets prohibited under the Hague Convention – and seriously injured. Hintze, who had led the attack that downed Leslie Howard's DC-3 aircraft, never flew operationally again, remaining hospitalised for the remainder of the war.

The *Zerstörer* flew their opening Mediterranean mission from Istres on 1 February, escorting a mixed bomber formation of He 177s of II./KG 100 and II./KG 40, and Ju 88s and He 111s of KG 26 against Convoy UGS 30 (code-named 'Tropical'). Sighted near Oran late on the previous day, the convoy was initially protected by bad weather, though the first day of February dawned relatively clear and the attack launched. Six RAF Beaufighters of 39 Squadron led by Flying Officer Neil Cox intercepted the bombers while still inbound at 1800hrs. The Beaufighters were based at Reghaia, Algeria, preparing to move to a new station on Sardinia but on call as part of Operation *Hamper*: defence against enemy aircraft attacking or reconnoitring convoys near the North African coast. The Beaufighters had scrambled upon reports of German reconnaissance aircraft but detected nothing in their assigned patrol area, turning for base when the two large formations of bombers were spotted just before dusk.

In the melee that followed *Lt.* Robert Baumann's ZG 1 Ju 88C-6 '2N+Pl' was shot down in a head-on attack by F/S Freddie Cooper, whose Beaufighter also caught fire and was forced to ditch. Baumann was the sole survivor of his Junkers, rescued the following day by an RAF launch that also picked up Cooper and his navigator F/S Brindle. A second ZG 1 Junkers was shot down in the air battle, *Uffz.* Helfried Schlegel and his two crewmen killed. A second group of Beaufighters of RAF 153 Squadron scrambled for freelance patrols over UGS 30 and succeeded in breaking up the body of bombers, only seven eventually contacting the convoy. *Unteroffizier* Paul Moller's 3./KG 26 He 111H-11 was among the seven brought down by flak with only Moller surviving to become a prisoner. A second He 111H-11 of 2./KG 26 later ran out of fuel and crash-landed south of Barcelona, while three Ju 88 torpedo bombers were lost; one to flak, another to a Beaufighter and the third running out of fuel near the Balearic Islands and crashing, leaving a single wounded survivor. *Oberfeldwebel* Oskar Adam's He 177A-3 of

4./KG 40 was also brought down during the attack. In return, as well as damage inflicted on a second Beaufighter, the Liberty ship SS *Edward Bates* was torpedoed on its port side with one man badly wounded. Taken in tow, the burning ship eventually sank.

The final casualty of a disastrous day for the Luftwaffe was the Do 24T-3 flying boat 'KO+JA' of 6.*Seenotstaffel*, shot down over La Spezia during a rescue flight by a Spitfire of the 52nd Fighter Group, pilot *Uffz.* Heinrich Ellenberg and three of his crew killed, the flight engineer and medical officer wounded but later recovered.

Within days, II./KG 100 had returned to operations against Anzio supply shipping, as the Allies edged closer to an effective counter to the '*Kehlgerät*'. During a January glide-bomb attack, a single example of the weapon had either been jettisoned or failed to explode and was later recovered from the shallow seabed relatively intact; the explosive nose, tail section with fin and majority of its electrical components – including the *Strassburg* receiver whose demolition charge had failed to ignite – recovered and shipped to Naples for examination. There, radar specialists Lieutenants R.G.R. Haggard and John C.G. Field of the Royal Navy Volunteer Reserve examined the material before it was shipped to the Royal Aircraft Establishment, Farnborough.

Junkers Ju 88T-1 of 2.(F)/Aufkl.Gr. 123 with 900-litre auxiliary fuel tanks, Italy 1944.

By the beginning of February, Task Group 80.2 had recorded about sixty glide-bomb signals intercepted during four attacks on Anzio shipping. They identified specific wavebands of the majority as well as five other suspiciously different transmission wavebands. During the most recent attacks more signals had been detected than there were bombs at any given time, an apparent attempt to mask actual control signals and deflect jamming attempts. A 'barrage jammer' was required to cover the entire bandwidth in order to combat this camouflage tactic, though a cautionary note was sounded that jamming control signals may not be the most effective protective measure if a formation of closely-packed ships was targeted, as diverting the Hs 293 from its point of aim could simply result in it hitting a different ship.

Attempted attacks on Anzio shipping in the first half of February achieved little except a steady stream of Luftwaffe casualties, including the *Staffelkapitän* of 2./KG 26, *Hptm.* August Leicht, hit by flak over Nettuno on 12 February and crashing on Corsica. Despite occasional claims to the contrary, not until 15 February did the Luftwaffe definitely sink anything off Anzio, the Liberty ship SS *Elihu Yale* being hit while discharging her cargo. An Hs 293 struck in aft No 4 hold, the only one empty apart from sand ballast, but caused raging fires amidships in the engine room, fuel tanks and living spaces to port. Twelve men were killed and the remainder abandoned ship, apart from one severely wounded man later found lying on top of boxes of ammunition, as tug USS *Hopi* pulled alongside to pick up survivors and land a fire control party. Hold No 1 was still packed with ammunition, No 2 with stored gasoline and No 3 provisions and No 5 ammunition. *Hopi*'s damage control team found John McKena in the latter, pinned under debris that had fallen on him during the initial explosion. His skull was fractured and he had internal chest injuries and a broken leg. He was evacuated as *Elihu Yale* took a heavy list to port and began sinking by the stern, though intact bulkheads kept the ship afloat long enough for *Hopi*'s men to extinguish the flames and the wrecked Liberty ship run aground the next day in an attempt to save the forepart.

LCT-35 had been tied up alongside *Elihu Yale*'s port side when the Hs 293 struck. Its crew unloading ammunition boxes from Hold No 5 onto their landing craft's tank deck, piled high with stored shells and hand grenades, when the bomb struck. The ammunition cases exploded setting the LCT's stern 20mm magazines and crew quarters on fire, skipper Lt (j.g.) Robert Esbensen immediately ordered his surviving crew to abandon ship as *LCT-35* went to the bottom.

A third ship was also damaged by the attack. The destroyer USS *Herbert C. Jones* – which had arrived back at Anzio from Capri three days previously to relieve USS *Frederick C. Davis* – was patrolling the Anzio anchorage area when it received two near misses by glide bombs launched by *Lt.* Werner Kirstenpfad's aircraft, causing slight structural hull damage and temporarily putting its onboard jamming gear out of action.

An undoubted success for II./KG 100, the *Gruppe* lost only a single aircraft, *Gruppenkommandeur Hptm.* Heinz-Emil Middermann suffering an engine fire only half an hour into its return flight to France from Bergamo the following morning, crashing near Gambolo and all aboard killed. Alongside Middermann was *Oblt.* Werner Eckert, the *Gruppen* staff Navigation Officer, *Oblt.* Dietrich Schreiber, Middermann's Operations Officer, *Ofw.* Johannes Krehn, *Ofw.* Alfred Finaske and *Fw.* Fritz Scauenberg. Jope – who received the Oak Leaves to his Knight's Cross on 24 March 1944 – temporarily took command of II./KG 100 until *Maj.* Bodo Meyerhofer was appointed to the post on 5 May.

Few raids took place during the days that followed, with the loss of two more Dorniers and no confirmed successes until dusk on 25 February when HMS *Inglefield* was hit amidships by an Hs 293. Eric Alley was a crewman aboard the 'I' class destroyer:

> As we destroyers had to act as artillery support we needed plenty of ammunition, so on 15 February, Commander [Bill] Churchill took *Inglefield* back down to Naples and on this trip we carried the remains of one of the new German glider bombs, which had been recovered almost intact from the beachhead. It was something of an omen for what was to happen ten days later. We returned to Anzio as escort for an ammunition ship. Another trip down to Naples enabled us to restock our own dwindling supply of ammunition, and return for a further spell, off the beaches – and our finale!
>
> The Germans were not unaware of the effective destroyer artillery support of the ground troops, so with determined and ingenious use of air support they made life very difficult for us offshore boats . . . The attacks came every night just on dusk and on 25 February *Inglefield* was hit just three miles off Anzio lighthouse. There was an extremely strong sirocco wind blowing at the time with a very heavy sea. We abandoned ship into

these extreme conditions and of the ship's company of 192, 35 shipmates were lost that night. Minesweepers and other destroyers rescued many of our survivors, and in particular the American USS *LCI-12*, equipped as a salvage vessel managed to pull 23 of us from the water.[2]

The attack had been made in conjunction with torpedo bombers of KG 26, a single torpedo launched at USS *Herbert C. Jones* passing down the ship's port side. HMS *Inglefield* was the last ship sunk by air attack off Anzio as the Luftwaffe pulled its bomber forces away.

Kesselring's spirited counterattacks had failed during February and a stalemate reached in the winter mud around the Anzio salient. Not until May, months after Lucas' replacement by Major General Truscott, did Allied forces finally break out, linking up with troops pushing forward from Cassino that had finally fallen. The Gustav Line battles had claimed 55,000 Allied casualties. Brigadier General Clark's monumental ego redirected Allied troops to the liberation of Rome rather than conforming to his superior General Alexander's strategic plan, the Italian capital already abandoned by German forces that retreated in good order; an act of foolhardy vanity that significantly extended the war in Italy.

For the third time, Luftwaffe maritime forces had failed to appreciably inhibit a major Allied seaborne invasion. Though undoubtedly intimidating to men within the invasion area, and causing localised casualties, their strategic effect remained minimal as the Luftwaffe suffered under the weight of Allied material and technological supremacy. Mussolini's fascist *Repubblica Sociale Italiana* had organised its own air force from Italian units that chose to fight on alongside Germany. The *Aeronautica Repubblicana* (renamed *Aeronautica Nazionale Repubblicana* on 29 June 1944) included fifteen S79 torpedo bombers of 1° *Gruppo Aerosiluranti 'Buscaglia'* that mounted ineffectual raids against Anzio shipping between 10 March and 10 April, decimated in their efforts.

With the battle off Anzio all but over, Luftwaffe maritime bombers returned to convoy interception in the Mediterranean and western Atlantic, seeking to obliterate troops and supplies shuttling from Britain and the United States to the Italian front. A shortage of torpedoes hamstrung many operations, despite a glut of available weapons at depots within Germany as rail and road supply networks suffered mounting pressure from both air and local guerrilla attacks.

Generalmajor Hans Korte had replaced Fink as head of 2.*Fliegerdivision* after the latter's transfer to control Luftwaffe forces in

Greece. With failure at Anzio, Korte's diminished *Fliegerdivision* was moved from Richthofen's *Luftflotte* 2 to Sperrle's *Luftflotte* 3 for action in the western Mediterranean and Atlantic. At the beginning of March, *Hptm*. Wolfgang Vorpahl's 5./KG 100 was transferred from France to Aalborg for conversion from Do 217 to He 177A-5 aircraft, reunited with 4./KG 100 that moved from Leck. Only 6./KG 100 remained in Toulouse alongside *Hptm*. Herbert Pfeffer's III./KG 100 which had remained uncommitted to action at Anzio. A detachment of He 111s from *Hptm*. Jochen Müller's I./KG 26 that had been temporarily posted to Piacenza to combat the Anzio landings was returned to Salon de Provence during February, as was a similar detachment of Ju 88s from *Maj*. Ernst Thomsen's III./KG 26, Thomsen having replaced Klaus Nocken who had been appointed *Gruppenkommandeur* of the training IV./KG 26. The Heinkel He 111s of I./KG 26 were clearly obsolete by April 1944 and the surviving twelve crews were taken out of the line at the beginning of April and transferred to Grove where they began conversion to the Junkers Ju 88A-17, itself now an aircraft design that had seen the limit of its updating and conversion potential.

All three *Gruppen* of KG 30 had been withdrawn entirely, while the freshly trained torpedo pilots of III./KG 76 remained at Salon de Provence until March when it relocated to Orange-Caritat, north-west of Marseilles. There it joined *Kommodore Maj*. Wilhelm Stemmler's Staff and *Maj*. Willi Sölter's I./KG 76 and 6./KG 76, the remainder of II.*Gruppe* being posted to East Prussia. Likewise I. and III./KG 77, recently retrained as torpedo crews, arrived in Orange-Caritat from Germany on 10 March, ready for Mediterranean operations.

Over the expanse of the western Mediterranean, torpedo-bombers were instructed to undertake solitary 'armed reconnaissance' carrying torpedoes on the offchance of finding the enemy. Results were poor while casualties among the designated aircraft were heavy. On 8 March *Obfw*. Hermann Fink's Ju 88 was shot down, though the location of Convoy KMS-43, code-named 'Hannah' was confirmed and subsequently attacked by thirty-four bombers – torpedo carriers from III./KG 26 and Hs 293-equipped II./KG 100 Do 217s – under escort by twenty-two Ju 88C-6 *Zerstörer* of ZG 1. Royal Air Force 153 Squadron Beaufighters from Algeria broke up the attack, only ten bombers reaching the convoy and mistakenly reporting hits on two transports and three freighters; the Admiralty recorded no such results. During the day two bombers and two *Zerstörer* were lost, a third colliding during its return with a crane at Marseilles.

The use of KG 26 bombers as reconnaissance aircraft prompted a furious despatch from Thomsen, *Gruppenkommandeur* of III./KG 26, to II.*Fliegerkorps* headquarters in which he detailed that:

On 8.3.1944 the reconnaissance plane was lost once again, while all allocated torpedo aircraft returned after damaging 52,000 tons of merchant shipping. Intelligence provided by the *Gruppe*'s reconnaissance has never produced a result that assisted in decision made by the unit leader, but several crews ordered on reconnaissance have been lost.

The *Gruppe* has reported several times that reconnaissance flights so far bring only losses, but no worthwhile results, because:

1. The torpedo crews are trained for formation combat.
2. Reconnaissance over the sea requires intensive training and great experience.
3. The armament of the Ju 88A-4 torpedo bomber is insufficient for solo flight during the day.
4. The aircraft have no GM-1 addition [nitrous oxide injector into the engines which improved high-altitude performance]
5. Since no crew has received '*Hohentwiel*' training, searching is done by eyesight, carried out in heavily defended areas.[3]

Thomsen insisted that once convoy traffic had been reported near the North African coast, educated guesswork on its location and direction were more use than a lack of messages from a reconnaissance aircraft likely to have been destroyed.

Brief celebration took place when Thomsen's recommendation of the Knight's Cross for his Chief of Staff *Oblt.* Josef Richard Peters was approved and the award presented on 6 April. A former Kriegsmarine officer and observer in Kü.Fl.Gr. 506, Peters, who held the German Cross in Gold from October 1943, was decorated in his role as an observer of 12./KG 26 having flown 100 combat missions. Shortly thereafter, he volunteered for pilot training, though it was never completed and, with the final deterioration of the war situation, he was transferred to the ground troops of 1.*Fallschirmjäger Korps* on the Italian front during March 1945.[4]

Twice more during March combined glide-bomb and torpedo attacks were mounted against North African coastal convoys, but with no success despite German claims to the contrary. On 19 March I. and III./KG 26 attacked Convoy KMS 44, code-named 'Illicit', and lost three Junkers, ...n days later II./KG 100 lost three aircraft and III./KG 26 a single Junkers during another unsuccessful convoy attack on KMS 35, code-named 'Thumbs Up'. Not until 1 April did any torpedo strike home, the 7,180GRT SS *Jared Ingersoll* from Convoy UGS 36 being hit and severely damaged. The raid was mounted by torpedo bombers of both KG 26 and the freshly-trained KG 77, beginning with flares dropped near the convoy body at 0406hrs. The night was dark, a half-moon having already set and a haze hanging on the horizon limiting visibility to approximately five miles. As the bombers approached, radar-directed fire was opened, targets being only occasionally glimpsed by gunners, flying at wave-top height.

A single torpedo hit *Jared Ingersoll*'s No 1 hold starting fierce fires while the crew hastily abandoned ship. The escorting destroyer USS *Mills* came close alongside and placed a firefighting crew aboard the stricken freighter, bringing flames under control and allowing the merchant crew to reboard at 0615hrs, HMT *Mindful* taking the ship in tow toward shore. Despite sporadic fires aboard and flooding settling the ship low in the water, it was successfully beached at Algiers. For the Luftwaffe, on the other hand, the raid was little short of disastrous, 9./KG 26 losing two Junkers to anti-aircraft fire, and a third crashing through fuel starvation, and a total of six KG 77 Junkers shot down.

The following convoy, UGS 37, was also attacked on the night of 11 April, flares dropped at 2320hrs by pathfinders from KG 76 opening the battle, radar soon detecting approaching aircraft and escorts ordered to make smoke. The escort destroyer USS *Holder* had just begun to activate smoke generators when a torpedo bomber was sighted to port, launching its weapon at less than 400 yards range. The torpedo wake was visible arcing toward the American's hull, propellers plainly audible within the destroyer's sound room. It impacted amidships below the waterline, eyewitnesses recalling two explosions a fraction of a second apart accompanied by a bright yellow flash. The destroyer suffered sixteen men killed or missing, including the Engineering Officer, and began to settle, taking a 4-degree list to starboard as all lights went out and ship-wide communications failed. USS *Forster* came alongside the drifting ship to remove twelve badly wounded men, and at 0203hrs HMT *Mindful* took the destroyer under tow to Algiers where subsequent inspection resulted in the ship being declared a constructive total loss, towed to New York and scrapped. Once again, Luftwaffe casualties were fearful, KG 77 losing seven Ju 88A-17s in the action to a combination of anti-aircraft fire and scrambled Beaufighters, an eighth to crash-landing at Salon and 5./KG 100 a single Do 217E-5 to F/Sgt B.H.M. Smith's 153 Squadron Beaufighter.

Though the maritime squadrons were being bled dry, they continued to fly against convoys near North Africa. Eastbound Convoy UGS 38, code-named 'Whoopee', was sighted near Algiers, on 20 April shadowed by a relay of aircraft that circled to landward where radar was of little use to the ships below, though one shadowing Me 410 was intercepted and shot down by French Spitfires. A combined force of nearly forty bombers from III./KG 26, II./KG 77 and II./KG 100 took off, aiming to intercept UGS 38 at twilight, escorted by Ju 88C-6s of ZG 1. While en-route at 2040hrs and still 105 miles from target, a second smaller group of three troopships escorted by the French destroyer *Tigre* and the torpedo boats *Tempête* and *Forbin*, was sighted sailing from Corsica to Algiers; Convoy CAF-31, code-named 'Donaghue'. Several Ju 88 and Do 217 bombers split away from the main formation and in an onslaught lasting twenty minutes CAF-31 was attacked. A single torpedo hit the 4,680GRT French MV *El Biar* killing one anti-aircraft gunner, the remaining 280 passengers and crew being evacuated before the ship sank bow first. Although no glide bombs hit, parts of them rained as shrapnel from near misses on to the decks of several ships, while three aircraft were claimed destroyed by French anti-aircraft fire.

The remaining bombers continued towards UGS 38, comprised of eighty-five merchant vessels arrayed in ten columns, and shepherded by twenty-one escort ships including the Dutch light cruiser HNMS *Jacob van Heemskerck* acting as fighter-direction and advanced air-warning ship, the minesweepers USS *Sustain* and *Speed* and the destroyer USS *Lansdale*, all carrying missile-jamming gear. The bombers approached from the east about thirty-five minutes after sunset, flying low with no flares dropped but using the distant shoreline as a dark background. USS *Sustain* had intercepted '*Kehlgerät*' transmissions during their approach, providing warning of impending attack. The first bombers showed up on the destroyer escort USS *Lowe*'s radar as it sailed in the vanguard within fifteen minutes of *Sustain*'s notification, multiple contacts detected ahead and on the convoy beam, as the first terrific explosion echoed from the convoy's port side and anti-aircraft guns began firing.

Aboard USS *Lowe*, a second wave of aircraft approaching low to the water from the direction of the high coastal cliffs to starboard was detected by radar, the ship narrowly combing torpedo tracks launched by five incoming Ju 88 aircraft. The Liberty ship SS *Paul Hamilton* had already been struck by a torpedo which instantly detonated her cargo of high explosives and bombs. The ship exploded and 580 men aboard – including 154 officers and men of the 831st Bombardment Squadron and 317 officers and men of the 32nd Photo Reconnaissance Squadron – were all killed, only a single body ever being recovered. USS *Lansdale* had also been hit by a torpedo in the forward fire room, breaking the ship's keel. With all power lost the destroyer was abandoned, breaking up and sinking within fifteen minutes of being hit as 235 survivors were picked up by USS *Menges* and *Newell*, a total of 47 men missing. Three other vessels had been damaged; the British 7,900GRT freighter SS *Royal Star*, SS *Samite* and the American Liberty ship SS *Stephen F. Austin*. *Royal Star* had been hit by a torpedo aft, its Master initially convinced his ship could be saved with timely tug assistance. However, despite efforts at towing the ship to shore, it gradually sank with one man missing and the remainder rescued. Both *Samite* and *Stephen F. Austin* had been hit by torpedoes in their bows, but both subsequently towed to Algiers for repair.

SS *Paul Hamilton* of Convoy UGS 38 explodes after a KG 26 torpedo hit, killing all 580 men aboard, 20 April 1944. The photograph was taken by US Coast Guard Combat Photographer Art Green.

Despite being the second-best result for a Mediterranean torpedo mission, and well planned and executed using twilight and covering land features to the fullest advantage, the casualties were yet again severe. Four escorting Junkers *Zerstörer* had been lost in combat with enemy fighters, though these had been tardy in reaching UGS 38. Of the bombers, 8./KG 26 had lost one, 6./KG 100 a single Do 217E-5 shot down by Beaufighter and a second crash-landing at Istres, and KG 77 four Junkers. Two prisoners were taken aboard destroyer USS *Menges*, observer *Ofw.* Peter Gerlich and wireless operator *Uffz.* Arndt Feddersen of 2./KG 77, their Ju 88A-17 '3Z+EK' hit by anti-aircraft fire with *Lt.* Viktor Kopp (pilot) and gunner *Ogefr.* Rolf Spranger killed. Both men were slightly injured, found as *Menges* recovered survivors from *Lansdale* after the German aviators activated a red flare from their life raft. Taken aboard, the two were stripped and given dry clothes, later described in the *Menges* after action report as 'very meek' in captivity and claiming – possibly for their own good – to have been shot down before launching torpedoes.

During this period, *Oblt.* Reimar Voss' 1./KG 26 had been directed from the Mediterranean to Romania to provide torpedo bomber protection for German troops withdrawing from the Crimea before the inexorable Soviet advance. Voss was ordered to fly first to Flensburg where his *Staffel* would be equipped with torpedoes by a specialist torpedo mechanic company. Upon arrival at Flensburg-Weich airfield Voss discovered no torpedoes, no torpedo mechanics and little protected space for his aircraft. After consulting *Geschwader Kommodore* Klümper, there resulted an enforced three-day delay as mechanics and equipment was transferred from Grossenbrode. Finally, by 15 April, the Heinkels were fuelled and loaded with torpedoes when synchronicity brought American fighter aircraft on a free-roving attack after their bomber escort mission had been completed. In several low-level strafing runs over the airfield, nine of Voss' Heinkels standing at the fringe of the dispersal area were destroyed.

Voss faced a court-martial for the disaster though he was, justifiably, fully acquitted. In place of his devastated 1. *Staffel*, the fifteen crews of *Hptm.* Rudi Schmidt's 4./KG 26, its Ju 88s already in Grossenbrode and including three equipped with '*Hohentwiel*', were despatched to Romania. They landed at Focşani-Süd, a relatively rough grass-surfaced airstrip north-east of Bucharest used by various Luftwaffe units, including *Küstenfliegerstaffel Krim* which had slowly replaced its Fw 58 aircraft with Bf 110 *Zerstörer*.

USAAF gun camera footage from Hubert Zemke's P-47 Thunderbolt attacking *Oblt.* Reimar Voss' 1./KG 26 Heinkels parked at Flensburg-Weich airfield.

Before the Soviet offensive into the Crimea, the small *Küstenfliegerstaffel Krim* had also received He 111s, several with *'Hohentwiel'*, and became tasked with myriad duties, including convoy escort, night reconnaissance, bombing of Soviet ports and interdiction of Soviet naval activity in the Black Sea. On 11 January 1944, *Küstenfliegerstaffel Krim* completed its 2,000th sortie. Still under the command of *Hptm.* Hans Klimmer, the *Staffel* had suffered heavy losses in Bf 110s during the fighting over the Taman Peninsula, several shot down by Soviet Airacobras.

On 8 April 1944, the Soviet invasion of the Crimea began. Huge numbers of Soviet troops crossed the Kerch Strait, battled through the Crimea and threatened Sevastopol with capture by the month's end. Well over 200,000 German and Romanian troops had become stranded in the Crimea and, alongside transport aircraft, a substantial fleet of borrowed Do 24s was assembled; creating *Sonderstaffel Mamaia* under the command of *Hptm.* Heinrich Guthoff. By 9 May, over 130,000 able-bodied soldiers had reached Romania from the Crimea, a staggering 17,000 by Do 24 flights alone. That same day, Sevastopol fell and the

Küstenfliegerstaffel Krim celebrate their 2,000th mission on 11 January 1944.

final German pockets of resistance on the Crimea surrendered, the costly seaborne evacuation having resulted in thousands of casualties from the sinking of overcrowded troop transports. *Küstenfliegerstaffel Krim* had been engaged in convoy escort, losing two He 111H-16s and a Bf 110, the latter shot down by land-based anti-aircraft guns near Sevastopol. Evacuating from the Crimea, Klimmer established a new base at Ziliştea, in east-central Romania. Meanwhile, *Sonderstaffel Mamaia* disbanded a month later, the Dorniers returned from whence they had originated or passed over to 7.*Seenotstaffel* in the Aegean.

With the loss of the Crimea, the need for Luftwaffe coastal reconnaissance diminished and Klimmer led the Bf 110Gs of *Küstenfliegerstaffel Krim* to Gossen where they were redesignated 12./ZG 26. His remaining Heinkels, under the command of *Hptm.* Rathgeber (designated *Staffelführer Aufklarüngsstaffel (F) Krim*), continued occasional armed reconnaissance missions until 29 May 1944 when the aircraft were folded into I./KG 4 as a *Sonderschwarm*, though before they could be committed to action after relocating to their new Hungarian base at Debrecen, they were destroyed by strafing American P-51 fighters. Between June 1943 and April 1944 *Küstenfliegerstaffel Krim* had lost at least seventeen aircraft, another five damaged. Approximately forty flight crew were killed or posted as missing in action, a further eleven wounded.

The Do 217s of III./KG 100 were finally committed to action during April, but not for Mediterranean operations with the 'Fritz-X' but rather against shipping in Plymouth harbour as an extension of the '*Steinbock*' campaign.[5] On 30 April III./KG 100 joined the multi-unit raid on Plymouth, *Oblt.* Klaus Deumling being shocked and dismayed to be relegated from command of his aircraft '6N+AD' to tower control duties as *Gruppenkommandeur* Herbert Pfeffer commandeered his aircraft. The mission for the 'Fritz-X' aircraft was the destruction of battleships reported in Plymouth harbour, though it was an abject failure. Guided by '*Knickbein II*' navigational aids, heavy flak and searchlights buffeted the bombers at 7,000 metres altitude as a smokescreen across the harbour basin completely obscured the target area. KG 100 crews attempted firing blind in the hope of hitting something but from fourteen 'Fritz-X' bombs launched only the hard standing at Barnpool was hit and its surface damaged, no other naval property being harmed. A few landed on Plymouth city, causing ten serious casualties before the raid ended, the last suffered by Plymouth during the war. Four aircraft were lost that night to Mosquito night fighters, two from KG 100. One was the relatively new Do 217K-3 '6N+IT' of 9./KG 100 that crashed at Pasture Farm near Blackawton, Devon, with its *Kehlgerät* relatively intact and immediately seized by Allied intelligence officers. The other bomber lost was Pfeffer's. Pfeffer and all but *Uffz.* Friedrich Wilhelm

Dornier Do 217K readied for take-off.

were killed, Wilhelm surviving to be captured. Pfeffer had unwittingly probably saved Deumling's life.

> Pfeffer's decision to keep me away from the mission that I wanted to take part in was the result of our early differences. He, ironically, had wanted to punish me with this measure. Since I will never know whether I would have survived the mission, I can only be happy for myself about this decision, but it took me a long time to get over this heavy loss. For a year, my men and I had been together almost every day, sharing all the good and difficult hours, overcoming all the efforts and dangers together. I found the loss of such close irreplaceable comrades very painful. Of course, you do not wish anyone dead, but what a tremendous tragedy, that the single man that I did not want to be around flew the people closest to me in the Luftwaffe to their deaths.[6]

While Pfeffer was not replaced by *Maj.* Wolfgang Vorpahl until 12 June, *Maj.* Bodo Meyerhofer took command of II./KG 100 at the beginning of May as the *Gruppe* trained in Denmark, converting from the Do 217 to the He 177. However, Meyerhofer's tenure was unexpectedly brief, he and his entire crew being killed when his He 177A-5 crashed and exploded for unknown reasons soon after take-off at Fassberg only nine days after assuming command. His place was subsequently taken by *Hptm.* Hans Molly who held the post until February 1945.

Though diminished, the Luftwaffe doggedly attempted further Mediterranean torpedo missions. An *OKW* communique issued on 12 May reported a supply convoy attacked east of Algiers and seven freighters, totalling 49,000GRT, and a destroyer sunk, with damage to twelve more merchant ships. The mistruth was profound as not a single ship had been hit from UGS 40. The convoy – code-named 'Element' – consisted of sixty-five merchant ships in eight columns, escorted by Task Force 61, and had been shadowed throughout the previous day, before a twilight attack by sixty torpedo bombers of KG 26 and KG 77, escorted by twenty-four Ju 88C-6 *Zerstörer* of ZG 1.[7] Initial plans for a night attack using flares were frustrated by low-lying cloud, and the alternative of a dusk attack with heavy fighter protection chosen instead. With that number of aircraft in the air, two rendezvous points south of the French coast were created, twenty kilometres apart, the aircraft grouping in two formation as they headed south. Sighted only three and a half miles from its estimated position, the convoy was found simultaneously by both formations and they attacked in three closely grouped waves against prepared anti-aircraft defences and RAF Beaufighters and Mosquitoes of 153 and 256 Squadrons respectively. It was a disaster.

The sheer number of attacking aircraft limited manoeuvring room while the convoy used effective smokescreening and thoroughly rehearsed anti-aircraft doctrine. In combination with the RAF fighters a total of fourteen torpedo bombers were brought down over the convoy; five of the seven crews lost by III./KG 26 flying their first combat mission and only *Lt.* Gerhard Haseney of 9./KG 26 surviving, his aircraft shot down by Beaufighter and Haseney captured. Despite launching ninety-one torpedoes, not a single hit was scored. One 256 Squadron Mosquito was damaged by return fire from a Junkers, crashing on landing as both wheels had been punctured but Squadron Leader D.R. West and his navigator Fl/Off J.H. Smithers were unhurt.

Learning the harsh lesson, the following torpedo attack on 30 May against Convoy KMS 51 was made in darkness. Approximately thirty KG 26 and KG 77 torpedo bombers attacked the merchants, homing on flares dropped by pathfinders from II./KG 76. The 2,870GRT British freighter SS *Nordeflinge*, loaded with coal, was torpedoed and sunk with eleven crewmen killed, a second ship slightly damaged by conventional bombs. But in return three Ju 88A-17s of KG 77 were shot down, a fourth crashing near Istres after aborting with engine trouble and torpedoes intact. *Oberfeldwebel* Kurt Springer, his observer *Uffz.* Siegfried Penzel and wireless operator *Fw.* Willi Breitenfeld were slightly injured in the accident but gunner *Uffz.* Josef Erbel seriously hurt, later dying from his wounds. A single returning pathfinder of 6./KG 76, 'F1+AP', was also shot down by an RAF 108 Squadron night fighter during its approach to the airfield at St. Martin de Crau. Flight Lieutenant Harry Smith sighted the Junkers and surprised it with a burst of fire that hit the fuselage from directly behind, putting the Junkers into a steep dive as a second attack set its starboard engine on fire. The Junkers crashed heavily, swinging to port and bursting into flames, the Knight's Cross-holding *Staffelkapitän* of 6./KG 76 *Oblt.* Hans Ebersbach and his crew killed in the crash.

Though they could not know it at the time, SS *Nordeflinge* had the dubious distinction of being the last ship sunk by German torpedo bombers in the Mediterranean Sea. Within days, as the battered *Kampfgeschwader* braced themselves for an inevitable next attempt on a North African convoy, Allied troops landed in Normandy and the 'Second Front' was opened on 6 June 1944.

9

Retreat
The Western Front

URING FEBRUARY 1944, *GENERAL der Flieger* Günther Korten and his Chief of Operations Staff, *General der Flieger* Karl Koller, attempted to pare away elements of the unnecessarily cumbersome Luftwaffe command structure. Mirroring its commander-in-chief, the *RLM* had become bloated and unwieldy, overseeing as it did all civil and military flying activities in Germany. On 5 February Korten established an equivalent office to that employed by the army and navy with the creation of the *Oberkommando der Luftwaffe* (*OKL*) position directly subordinate to Göring and encompassing the General and Operations Staff, weapons inspectorates, quartermaster branch and signals. Other components Korten considered unnecessary for combat operations such as training (a somewhat dubious choice), administrative duties, civil defence and technical development remained separate under the umbrella of the *RLM*.[1]

Among the first decisions taken by the newly-established *OKL* was the dissolution of *Fliegerführer Atlantik*, taken on 7 February but, bizarrely, not actually communicated to Kessler until the month's end when *Generalleutnant* Alexander Holle arrived mid-conference to inform Kessler that his post no longer existed. Startled but courteous, Kessler requested clarification from Berlin, receiving the news officially by teleprinter within a few hours. Kessler had apparently complained once too often about the starvation of resources for his *Fliegerführer Atlantik*, justifiably blaming this factor above all others for its lack of reconnaissance success. In place of the *Fliegerführer* office, Holle's former command, X.*Fliegerkorps* moved from the Mediterranean and assumed responsibility for Kessler's now defunct post. Part of X.*Fliegerkorps'* staff was used to form Fink's new command, *Kommandierende General der Deutschen Luftwaffe in Griechenland*, while the remainder moved to western France, *General der Flieger* Martin Fiebig establishing his headquarters at Château de la Violette, already in use as station headquarters for Angers airfield.

Noted for his sense of humour and cynicism towards his Berlin masters, Ulrich Kessler poses for an American cameraman after his capture in 1945 aboard *U234*.

Kessler in fact continued to operate as *Fliegerführer Atlantik* until 15 March when he was appointed Chief of the Luftwaffe Liaison Staff in Tokyo and, in January 1945, selected to be Air Attaché at the German Embassy.[2] Hard working, though perhaps too pragmatic for his career's good, Kessler was rewarded for his diligence as *Fliegerführer* with the award of the German Cross in Gold on 3 April and the Knight's Cross five days later. Nevertheless, the first three months of 1944 had continued to frustrate and disappoint both Kessler and Dönitz since aerial reconnaissance in support of U-boat convoy operations, though not a comprehensive failure, was frequently thwarted by bad weather, bad navigation, equipment failure and occasional lapses in operating procedures. More than once aircrews reported convoy sightings only after landing back at base, generally due to a failure of wireless equipment. Regardless, the time elapsed between sighting and report virtually guaranteed failure at directing U-boats to intercept.

On 28 January Kessler's headquarters notified *B.d.U.* of '200–300 landing craft' sighted by patrolling aircraft. Though considered unlikely by *B.d.U.* due to no preceding air attacks on western France and the unlikely landing of troops during the early afternoon, five outbound

U-boats as well as groups '*Hinein*' and '*Stuermer*' were ordered to proceed towards the area at high speed, regardless of the risk from enemy aircraft. The 'invasion fleet' was discovered to be a flotilla of Spanish trawlers.

However, *B.d.U.*'s surprisingly conciliatory War Diary entry of 19 February clearly shows that at U-boat headquarters at least, they understood the problems faced by *Fliegerführer Atlantik*:

Use of reconnaissance aircraft for operation against ONS 29 from 13 Feb. to 18 Feb 44. Aircraft available for reconnaissance: eleven Ju 290s, of which five were operationally effective; four Ju 88s for very long range, all operationally effective; two BV 222s, neither serviceable. One aircraft expected to be ready by 13th or 14th.
Number of sorties:

Two by Ju 88 – seventeen Ju 290 – three FW 200 – two BV 222 of which the following turned back:
a)   four Ju 290 and one BV 222, because of engine trouble.
b)   two Ju 290: because radio and radar broke down.
c)   two Ju 290: because of compass trouble.
d)   one FW 200 for other reasons.
Three Ju 290 are overdue, two probably shot down by carrier-borne aircraft, one by Mosquitoes in the Biscay (according to English broadcast).[3]

Conclusions:
The defects which arise particularly at the end of a reconnaissance are due to overworking the available aircraft so that thorough maintenance is not possible. The reconnaissance could only be flown at all because twice the necessary number of machines were used at each sortie plus a reserve. The sorties could only be flown, especially last night, thanks to great efforts made by ground staff. The essential and only remedy for the difficulties which have arisen is to get more aircraft.

Offensive Atlantic missions flown by KG 40 had also proved disastrous for Kessler's command. On 12 February combined Convoy OS67/ KMS41, being shadowed by a Ju 290 of FAGr. 5, was attacked at dusk by II. and III./KG 40, the latter attempting to engage with five Condors equipped with Hs 293s. One aircraft – flown by officer-cadet *Fw*. Karl-Heinz Schairer – was shot down while outbound by RAF 157 Squadron Mosquitoes on an 'Instep' patrol, exploding as it hit the sea.

The three remaining Condors suffered minor damage and ultimately failed to make contact.

Seven He 177A-3s of II./KG 40, also carrying Hs 293s, were left to mount the final attack, the aircraft piloted by *Oblt*. Heinz Ewers shot down while taking off by a RCAF 418 Squadron Mosquito VI on an intruder mission.

> At Mérignac airfield sighted an He 177 with wheels down on circuit. Turned in behind and fired two second burst from 150 to 100 yards below astern, and shells exploded in area of cockpit. As Mosquito undershot, Heinkel appeared to try and ram it but missed and went into ground between airfield and town.[4]

The Heinkel came down at Pessac, killing two of the crew.

As the remaining bombers neared the convoy, four Martlets of 881 Naval Air Squadron were scrambled from HMS *Pursuer*, part of 16th Escort Group, and intercepted the inbound bombers. *Gruppenkommandeur Maj*. Walter Rieder, a former pilot from Kü.Fl.Gr. 406, was shot down in flames five miles off the convoy beam, he and his crew all being killed. His place as *Gruppenkommandeur* was subsequently passed to *Hptm*. Hans Joachim Dochtermann (*Staffelkapitän* 5./KG 40). Though some Hs 293s were launched, none came near their targets

Combat cameraman in the dorsal gunner position of an He 111.

and, under constant attack by the Martlet fighters and facing heavy anti-aircraft fire, the remaining Heinkels broke off and headed back to base.

For the remainder of February, the Ju 290s of FAGr. 5 would remain on the tarmac at Mont de Marsan as weather conditions were frequently unfavourable and, even if they had flown, Dönitz had suspended Atlantic U-boat operations after severe losses, expecting to resume in September. Within most of the maritime units there began a manpower reshuffle, some experienced ground and flight personnel transferred to ground units of the Wehrmacht as *OKW* combed every available means by which to replenish the depleted ranks on the Eastern Front and in Italy.

Gruppenkommandeur Hermann Fischer took the opportunity to travel to Berlin where he met with *Generalfeldmarschall* Milch and *Generalmajor* von Barsewisch, *General der Aufklärungsflieger*, to confer about his battered *Gruppe* as it fought increasingly overwhelming odds. He proposed to use the time before the resumed U-boat offensive in September to undertake intensive training of new and existing crews, an expected fourteen fresh aircraft being scheduled to arrive. With more aircraft, several could be used on each patrol, providing mutual gunnery defence against inevitable Allied fighter interception. However, Fischer also bluntly asked questions of his superiors.

Why is Atlantic reconnaissance being conducted with substantial losses if a) the U-boats cannot sail and b) the Condors of KG 40 at Bordeaux, with bombs, cannot get far enough out to sea to attack? Are our losses not too high already, just to find out about convoys in the Atlantic? These will, if reconnaissance is to continue to be flown up to September 1944, when the U-boats are expected to be operationally ready once more, make maritime reconnaissance for the U-boat arm impossible! Is it not more appropriate, to familiarize the crews more thoroughly with the Ju 290, its armament and the '*Hohentwiel*' equipment, so that by September the maximum level of training can be achieved?[5]

In an unexpected response Barsewisch informed the assembled officers of the *Gruppe* days later at an after-dinner occasion in Mont de Marsan that he would not hear the concerns of the *Gruppe* any longer, expecting 'ruthless' commitment on all further operations as the eyes of the *OKL* were fastened on their results. Nevertheless, by virtue of their redundancy, FAGr. 5 did not resume reconnaissance operations over Biscay until 17 May. The next casualty was *Oblt.* Hans-Georg Bretnütz's

Ju 290A-7 '9V+FK', shot down on 26 May by a Sea Hurricane IIc from HMS *Nairana* as three Junkers attempted to shadow Convoy SL158/ MKS49. All eleven men aboard the Ju 290 were lost, as was Flight Lieutenant Charles Richardson, whose Hurricane was hit by defensive fire. Two more Ju 290s were scrambled, and a second, '9V+GK' flown by first pilot *Hptm.* Kurt Nonnenberg, was also shot down with five men killed and the remainder rescued from the sea as prisoners of war.

Since the beginning of 1944, the *Zerstörer* of *Obstlt.* Lothar von Janson's ZG 1 had suffered three aircraft shot down over the Atlantic as well as the heavy losses to those on detachment to Mediterranean torpedo operations. In March the inbound Japanese submarine blockade-runner *I29* – code-named '*Kiefer*' – had reached Biscay in its journey to Lorient and *X.Fliegerkorps* devoted considerable numbers of aircraft to escort the vessel safely through what had virtually become Allied air space. A pair of torpedo boats and destroyers made rendezvous with the Japanese submarine, coming under attack by four RAF 248 Squadron Mosquito fighters and two 248 Squadron 'Tse Tse' Mosquitos armed with 57mm cannon. Eight escorting Junkers Ju 88C-6s circled the German vessels and a confusing series of dogfights followed in which *Fw.* Karl Bauer's 7./ZG 1 Junkers was shot down and the crew killed, though the surface ships and *I29* escaped unscathed.

As the battle ended and all aircraft withdrew, fresh Ju 88s arrived as protective escort, led by Janson. A veteran of the 'Condor Legion', he apparently disengaged from this uneventful escort mission to refuel and was surprised by Mosquitoes on an 'Instep' patrol and shot down in flames, no survivors or bodies observed in the water. During the remainder of March three more aircraft were lost to accidents, two with all men killed, another on 5 April after '2N+FK' taxied into a bomb crater after landing at Vannes and rolled over, injuring all three men aboard. The frequency of Allied airfield bombing had increased, causing further hardship to maritime squadrons and casualties amongst the hard-pressed ground crews.

On 11 April as I./ZG 1 attempted to shield the damaged *U255* returning to France from a failed attempt to breach the Strait of Gibraltar, they clashed with Mosquitoes from RAF 248 and 151 Squadrons. In the melee that followed ZG 1 lost seven aircraft and two damaged with five crewmen injured and fifteen killed, including the experienced *Staffelkapitän* of 1./ZG 1, *Hptm.* Günther Moltrecht.

Combined with the severe casualty rate suffered in the Mediterranean, *Zerstörergeschwader* 1 was being ground down to nothing.

A likely Allied assault on western France was now evident to all, and ZG 1 was given the task of reconnoitring towards the western British ports searching for signs of invasion shipping. However, though expected, the Luftwaffe was now less prepared to counter any such invasion than it had been against Salerno landings of 1943. Sperrle's *Luftflotte* 3 was badly fragmented under various sub-commands throughout France and lacked strength and resources due to the exigencies of other fronts. The anti-shipping torpedo and glide-bomber units (KG 26, KG 77 and III./KG 100) were gathered under command of Korte's 2.*Fliegerdivision* in southern France, although I. and III./ZG 1, KG 40 and the U-boats' reconnaissance aircraft of FAGr. 5 remained under Fiebig's X.*Fliegerkorps*, the former *Fliegerführer Atlantik* headquarters and staff remaining almost identical to that which had been under Kessler's control. Peltz's IX.*Fliegerkorps* controlled two *Kampfgruppen* of long-range bombers and a *Schlachtgruppe* of Fw 190 fighter-bombers, while fighters, night fighters and *Zerstörer* were grouped under a variety of local commands, dispersed not only to cover vast tracts of occupied land but also to ensure their survival against increasingly bold and frequent Allied fighter sweeps.

Göring considered his glide-bomb units the 'cutting edge' of his anti-invasion forces, although actual availability of both the Hs 293 and 'Fritz-X' had become increasingly problematic, mired in *RLM* chaos.

The wildest confusion prevailed in the production of the guided missile. In the spring of 1943, the output of He 293s was to be raised from 300 to 950 a month within a few months. Hertel, the Engineer General responsible, reported that from April onwards 750 Hs 293 and 750 FXs would be produced monthly and an increase to 1,200 was possible. At the same time, Staff Engineer Bree, the technical expert in the manufacture of guided missiles, told us that production, especially in the case of the FX, was in a very bad way, mainly because of a lack of factory space. We had a fully developed weapon but could not produce it in quantity and employ it. When Sauer took over the Fighter Staff one of his first steps was to order the immediate transfer to fighter construction of the technical personnel engaged in guided missile production. That was the end of the new weapon.

Once again – and it is significant of the internal stresses at the time – the technical experts battled with the stupidity and short-sightedness

Airfields in Italy and France had come under increasing pressure from late
1943; here an Allied photograph of the bombing of Kerlin-Bastard, near
Lorient, on 23 September 1943.

of the military and political leaders to secure the necessary recognition and exploitation in the national interest of the weapon they had brought into being.[6]

In laboratories in Germany, some effort had been made to update both the 'Fritz-X' and Hs 293. These included larger warheads, more aerodynamic control surfaces and even a remote television guidance system for the Hs 293 to be used to provide the operator greater certainty of a hit. More importantly, conversion from radio to wire guidance was being explored for both missiles, bobbins of thin wire stretching up to eight kilometres from the launching aircraft, carrying control signals and thereby impervious to Allied jamming. However, efforts in this direction were somewhat lacklustre as the Luftwaffe failed to comprehend the extent to which Allied scientists had succeeded in developing jamming systems, soon to be used at Normandy.

Combined with the recovery of several pieces of *Kehlgerät* from crashed bombers and information from shipborne jamming operators, coded messages between the Japanese Naval Attaché in Berlin, Rear Admiral Kojima Hideo, and Tokyo provided vital knowledge on the operation of the Hs 293. Having been shown the weapon as part of information exchange between the Axis partners, Hideo's technical description for his superiors was transmitted via a diplomatic code that had been broken by Allied cryptographers. The blanks in Allied comprehension of the operation of both glide-bomb models were no more.

Of the Luftwaffe's glide-bomb units, II./KG 100 remained in training in Aalborg and would play no part in the battle that followed. *Hauptmann* Wolfgang Vorpahl's III./KG 100 was capable now of using either the 'Fritz-X' or the Hs 293. The Do 217 E-5 bombers of the newly formed 8./KG 100 (formerly 6./KG 100, but swapping designations with the original 8.*Staffel* undergoing conversion training to the He 177 at Fassberg) would use Hs 293 missiles while the surviving Do 217K-2 bombers used the 'Fritz-X' bombs. New upgraded Dornier variants were capable of deploying either weapon: the Do 217K-3, fitted with improved FuG 203-series '*Kehlgerät*' for either 'Fritz-X' or Hs 293 control, and the Do 217M-11, fitted with FuG 203d '*Kehl IV*' guidance transmitter and rack for a single 'Fritz-X' or Hs 293 beneath the fuselage. However, replacements for Do 217 losses would be limited in the future as the production line for such aircraft had been closed during September 1943 although aircraft were still being delivered as late as May 1944.

Junkers Ju 88 being readied for a mission, the *Balkenkreuz* blacked out for operations during the hours of darkness.

Major Karl Henkelmann's I./KG 40 at Toulouse and *Maj.* Hans Dochtermann's II./KG 40 at Bordeaux-Merginac were both equipped with the He 177A-5, many replacement crews undertrained and untried in combat, five serviceable He 177s equipped with '*Kehlgerät*' flown to Bordeaux-Mérignac for Dochtermann's *Gruppe*. Meanwhile, III./KG 40 was ordered back from Baltic exercises to Cognac on 26 May. Tension within France was perceptibly high, Allied bombing and French partisan activity increasing in the lead-up to invasion and at the beginning of June Henkelmann's communications system was suddenly disabled by the complete destruction of the Orléans signals installation.

Normandy

On the morning of 6 June mass landings in Normandy, Operation *Overlord*, began, the naval component being code-named Operation *Neptune*. Luftwaffe reaction was laboriously slow, though what few fighters were available within the area bravely took to skies dominated by Allied air power, achieving little against the beachhead. On that crucial first day in which the Allied foothold on the Continent was established,

Luftwaffe maritime bombers were entirely absent, having stood no chance whatsoever of approaching the beaches in daylight. Night operations would be obligatory over Normandy.

While I./KG 26 was not yet operational – still training on Ju 88A-17s in Grove – the forty operational crews of II./KG 26 were rushed from Grossenbrode and Eichwalde to Valence, south of Lyon in the Auvergne-Rhône-Alpes region, a single *Staffel*, 6./KG 26, moving to the small airfield at Montélimar. Rapidly prepared for action the first anti-shipping operations were mounted later that night, aircraft from III./KG 26 and I. and III./KG 77 targeting accumulated vessels near the Cherbourg Peninsula. Refuelling at Saumur, one KG 77 aircraft, '3Z+CL' flown by *Ofw*. Anton Günther, was lost to jittery anti-aircraft gunners of 12 SS-Panzer Division near Angers, while glide-bomb attacks were also launched by I./KG 40 from Orleans-Bricy and II./KG 40 departing from Bordeaux-Mérignac.

The combined effort resulted in abject failure. Allied reports of all Luftwaffe anti-shipping night operations against the invasion fleet all feature the same word: 'negligible.' Attacks mounted on *Overlord* the night of 6 June achieved nothing in the face of extremely effective Allied night fighters. A smattering of torpedo hits were claimed by KG 26, but none were recorded by the Allies. Though KG 26 escaped casualties that first night, the same was not true of the KG 40 Heinkels that attempted to penetrate the Normandy anchorages. Of twenty-six He 177s that flew into action, thirteen were lost, several to Mosquito XVII night fighters of RAAF 456 Squadron. The following night, as all remaining Heinkels were thrown once again into the arena, seven more were shot down and six damaged. In July after six such operations, during which II./KG 40 over-optimistically claimed the sinking of 67,000GRT of enemy shipping and several warships, the *Gruppe* was withdrawn to re-equip at Gardermoen near Oslo, joining Stab./KG 40 which had also transferred from western France.

The reality of the Luftwaffe's maritime operations against *Overlord* is that the battle had already been lost during 1943 when the back of such air units had been broken in the Mediterranean. Anzio had merely sealed their fate. Between 6 June and the first day of July, 384 torpedo bomber sorties – including Ju 88s of KG 6 and KG 54, the latter using LT350 circling torpedoes – were flown by the Luftwaffe against *Neptune* shipping, more concentrated on ships trailing back to the United Kingdom than over French air space. In general, each *Gruppe* flew only a single torpedo mission weekly, hindered by weapon and fuel shortages and fighting overwhelming enemy air superiority. Both KG 40 and KG 100 deployed glide bombs but only five ships were sunk during June.

On 8 June a Lend-Lease escort destroyer (transformed into a 'Captain' class frigate) HMS *Lawford*, serving as the embedded command post of Assault Group J.1 for Juno Beach, was hit by an Hs 293 launched by III./KG 100 Dorniers embarked on their first mission against the beachhead, the frigate sinking in twenty-one metres of water with thirty-seven men killed.

The following night USS *Meredith*, already damaged by either striking a submerged contact mine or being hit by a II./KG 40 glide bomb in the early hours of 8 June, was sunk by the effect of a conventional bomb. The original damage had been caused by an explosion deep down on the port side, causing *Meredith* to lose all power, the listing destroyer in grave danger of drifting ashore in German held territory. Its captain transferred all but essential personnel to other ships while *Meredith* settled deeper in the water and repair parties shored up damage. Awaiting the arrival of salvage tugs, secret documents and radar components were destroyed in case the destroyer was captured.

Fortunately, *Meredith* was successfully taken under tow away from the enemy shoreline, instructed by the Assistant Salvage Officer to be taken out of the transport area towards the naval gunfire support area. It was here between 0030hrs and 0200hrs on 9 June that Ju 88s made a low-level bombing attack using 1,000kg bombs. Several were dropped, one landing 800 yards off the port bow and causing destroyer's stern to move and whip sideways, opening seams shored along the superstructure deck. Thereafter the stern visibly worked back and forth against the forepart though the sea was calm and wind slight until at 1010hrs, without any warning, USS *Meredith* broke in two and went down amidships, the men aboard swiftly abandoning ship.

On 10 June, the Liberty ship SS *Charles Morgan* was sunk, probably by an Hs 293 delivered by III./KG 40 in early morning darkness off Utah Beach. The bomb dropped straight into cargo hold No 4, unloaded that day by stevedores of the 304th Port Company. The explosion blew the hull sides out and the Liberty ship settled stern down on the shallow seabed, four men of the 304th killed and six injured.

On the night of 13 June in which Luftwaffe activity had appreciably increased, glide-bomb attacks were reported north-west of Cape Barfleur and south of Portland. The Luftwaffe had returned to its method of combining glide-bomb and torpedo strikes and at 0445hrs

The Liberty ship SS *Charles Morgan* sunk in shallow water on 10 June by III./ KG 40 off Utah Beach.

HMS *Boadicea*, escorting merchant ships to France, was hit by an Hs 293 launched by III./KG 100 south of Portland Bill. Hit in the forward magazine, the destroyer exploded and sank in three minutes, only two officers and ten enlisted men surviving to be rescued by HMS *Vanquisher*.

The final confirmed sinking for June took place on the 18th when KG 26 Junkers attacked Convoy EBC-14 bound for Normandy. Twenty miles south-west of The Needles, the 1,764GRT Canadian merchant ship SS *Albert C. Field* was hit by a torpedo and sank within three minutes, taking 2,500 tons of ammunition, 1,300 sacks of post and four crewmen to the bottom.

By contrast to the effect of torpedo and glide-bomb attacks, the Luftwaffe had resumed dropping mines in the Baie de la Seine, flying 954 minelaying sorties during June depositing 1,906 mines to augment those left by covert S-boat sorties. Mines sank nine warships and seventeen merchants that month, including the 10,200GRT troopship MV *Derrycunihy* on 24 June off Sword Beach. The mine exploded beneath the keel, breaking the ship in two and causing severe casualties to 43rd (Wessex) Reconnaissance Regiment, many of its men being asleep in the after part. A 3-ton ammunition truck also caught fire, igniting oil floating on the water and causing further losses. Twenty-five of the ship's crew and 183 men of the regiment were killed and about 120 others evacuated wounded in the worst single loss of life off the Normandy beaches.

The Normandy battle also brought a Luftwaffe oddity into action for the first time; the '*Mistel*' (Mistletoe). A composite aircraft of fighter controller mounted above a bomber airframe, the concept originated in 1941 as a way to constructively use older Ju 88 airframes by filling them with explosives, flying them to a target and 'crashing' them into it, released from the fighter and guided by remote control. The explosive warhead comprised a shaped charge mounted in the Junkers nose around a core of copper or aluminium that, when the explosive detonated, would behave as a liquid, capable of penetrating up to seven metres of armour and making the '*Mistel*' a potential battleship-killer of far greater destructive power than a glide bomb.

The first successful '*Mistel*' test flight was completed in July 1943 and, with fifteen combinations ordered from Junkers, in April 1944 the small unit 2./KG101 was created, under the command of *Hptm*. Horst Rudat. Training in the Baltic was completed with ambitions to raid the Home Fleet at Scapa Flow. The Normandy landings, however, took immediate precedence and the combinations, which had been moved to

The rather bizarre '*Mistel*' ship-killer concept that made its debut at Normandy to little effect.

Grove, Denmark, in preparation for the Scapa operation, were hurriedly relocated to Saint Dizier. From there twelve '*Mistels*' took off under cover of darkness on 24 June to attack shipping in the Baie de la Seine. One was shot down by a Mosquito night-fighter, the Bf 109 fighter lost as the Ju 88 frame crashed into the sea, a second pilot jettisoning his Ju 88 after a mechanical failure, the pilotless bomber crashing ashore in Devon. Four reported hitting shipping targets, though it appears that they probably had hit the hulk of the decommissioned French battleship *Courbet*, sunk as part of the Mulberry harbour at Arromanches and dressed as a decoy by the Allies, complete with oversized tricolour flag. Their baptism of fire was over, with no success, and the potential raid on Scapa Flow never came to pass, the remaining '*Mistels*' later used against industrial targets and bridges.

E.R. Hooten's authoritative book *The Luftwaffe: A Study in Air Power* lists the Luftwaffe effort against the invasion shipping in July as amounting to 1,837 bomber sorties over the sea, of which 1,357 were for the purpose of laying 2,683 mines. Actual torpedo and glide-bomb sorties amounted to 480, expending 171 torpedoes, 64 He 293s and 14 'Fritz-Xs'. From these latter missions, excluding several unverified claims, only one ship was confirmed sunk. On 7 July No. 216 Fighter Direction Tender – HMS *FDT 216*, a converted Mark 2 LST and one of three operating off Normandy – was torpedoed and sunk off Barfleur. The ship, which was providing fighter control over the western invasion beaches, was hit by a single torpedo on the port side just astern of the bow doors, taking on a severe list which increased as 300 tons of pig iron ballast on the upper deck began to shift. The crew abandoned ship and were rescued by HMS *Burdock*, before *FDT 216* turned over completely, later being deliberately sunk so as to not to endanger shipping. Five members of the crew were listed as missing in action and never found.

The anti-submarine trawler HMT *Lord Wakefield,* also operating in the Western Task Force area off Omaha Beach, was hit by conventional bombs at 0125hrs on 29 July while lying at anchor in the convoy assembly area. Only eight survivors of her crew were rescued by HMT *Northern Sun*, transferred to *LST 498* for return to the United Kingdom.

Though the losses inflicted by Luftwaffe anti-shipping units on the D-Day armada were indeed negligible and had no appreciable effect on *Overlord*, the *Kampfgeschwader* were decimated in return. Most German casualties had been caused by night fighters, assisted by extremely effective direction from ground and ship-based control centres. Anti-

No. 216 Fighter Direction Tender (HMS *FDT 216*, a converted Mark 2 LST) which was torpedoed and sunk off Barfleur on 7 July.

aircraft fire was also formidable, and shipboard fire discipline extremely efficient during the initial assault on Normandy, though as it morphed to the build-up of supporting merchant ships it deteriorated rapidly. Naval commanders complained that if one gunner opened fire at night, others followed suit irrespective of whether aircraft had been seen or heard, a danger to Allied night fighters and any potential paratroop reinforcement. Eventually, merchant ship gunners were restricted from firing at any time during darkness and small naval ships likewise prohibited unless directly attacked.

Rarely able to field ten serviceable Ju 88s, both I. and II./KG 30 were moved into Belgium, the former to Le Chulot east of Brussels, the latter to Chièvres to the south-west. After a series of costly and unsuccessful night bombing attacks, both *Gruppen* were withdrawn from the front line. By November the surviving pilots considered most experienced began retraining on single-engine fighters, equipped with the Bf 109G and redesignated KG(J) 30 marking the end of the bomber '*Adler Geschwader*.[7]

Major Wilhelm Stremmler's KG 77 had been so devastated by its attacks against Normandy shipping that it was officially disbanded during July, surviving aircraft transferred to the depleted ranks of KG 26, although remnants of II./KG 77 were still mounting pathfinder operations in the English Channel until August. All elements of I./KG 77 were renumerated KG 26 on 20 July. The veteran Stremmler was awarded the Knight's Cross on 6 October 1944 for his leadership of KG 77, five days after promotion to *Oberstleutnant* and the award of the German Cross in Gold. The following month he would replace Werner Klümper as *Kommodore* of KG 26.

Klümper's KG 26 had also suffered tremendous casualties; at least sixty-seven men either confirmed killed or missing in action, and thirteen others shot down and captured. Among those lost were Ernst-August Wulff, *Staffelkapitän* of 6./KG 26, who flew into powerlines near Paris, his replacement *Oblt.* Rudolf Bott missing in action over the sea only four days later on 26 July, and *Oblt.* Ernst Roll, *Staffelkapitän* of 9./KG 26 being lost over the Seine estuary also in July.

Major Georg Teske, *Gruppenkommandeur* of II./KG 26 (for which service he was awarded the Knight's Cross on 31 October), was hurt during the course of bombing missions mounted at the behest of *Luftflotte* 3 against partisans, suffering a spinal injury on 10 August which resulted

Junkers Ju 88 of KG 77. The *Geschwader* was so badly mauled over Normandy that it disbanded in July.

in hospitalisation and rehabilitation in Germany until October. As D-Day approached, French Maquis activity heightened considerably, engaging in open warfare against German installations and occupation forces after invasion forces landed. By this stage many Maquis bands had begun to organise to a level thus far not achieved, transforming into the paramilitary *Forces Françaises de l'Intérieur* (FFI). Several Luftwaffe maritime units became embroiled in fighting these units, both in the air and on the ground, including the unsuitable Ju 290s of FAGr. 5, Ju 88s of ZG 1, II./KG 26 and III./KG 100. The latter two *Gruppen* mounted raids on Maquis positions using fragmentation bombs, their lack of appropriate bombsights no real handicap when bombing from such low altitude, their enemy possessing no accurate anti-aircraft weapons. Teske led Ju 88 missions from Valence against Maquis groups on the nearby Vercors Plateau, coordinating attacks with ground assault by SS units, *Fallschirmjäger* and Cossacks. Intelligence for raids by III./KG 100 was provided by the SD, the Do 217s dropping SC50 bombs and incendiaries on nominated targets, strafing the ground with the bombers' defensive machine guns.

As well as using conventional bombs, *Hauptmann* Wolf Vorpahl's II.*Gruppe* was directed to use its glide bombs against land targets at the beginning of August, Do 217s attacking the bridge at Pontaubault, that traversed the Sélune River, and near Pontorson, over the Cousenon River. Despite repeated attempts to destroy the spans, the Luftwaffe were frustrated by heavy flak and night fighters and Patton's troops crossed successfully as part of Operation *Cobra* and the breakout from the Normandy beachhead.

Kampfgeschwader 40 was battered by the Normandy mission. During June and July, I.*Gruppe* had lost fourteen aircraft in action, II.*Gruppe* twenty-three to enemy action and two to accidents. Of the III.*Gruppe* Condors, one had been lost in action over Biscay during the same period, and a staggering fifteen to other causes. On 4 July one final mission was mounted over Biscay by KG 40 against combined Convoy SL162/MKS53, but the bombers failed to make contact. After this ignoble end, the surviving Condors of III./KG 40 and He 177s of I./KG 40 relocated to Trondheim, while He 177s of II./KG 40 as well as *Oberst* Rupprecht Heyn's staff flight moved to Gardermoen near Oslo. The aircraft of KG 40 would never operate with glide bombs again. Other Luftwaffe maritime assets had also already begun relocating from France; during June the twenty-one Ju 52 minesweeping aircraft of 5./*Minensuchgruppe* 1 that had operated from Cognac, flying to Værløse, Denmark.

Losses to KG 100 dramatically affected III.*Gruppe*, which lost twenty-four aircraft to enemy action and nine to accidents during the same period, leading to the disbanding of 9.*Staffel* and redistribution of its surviving crews and aircraft between *Gruppe*'s remaining *Staffeln*. They mounted occasional glide-bomb attacks against Allied ships blockading the Breton U-boat ports and on 11 June *Fw.* Max Brandenburg of 5./KG 100 was awarded the Knight's Cross. Surviving U-boats had already begun evacuating to Norway as Brest and Lorient came under threat from predominantly American ground forces. Brest would be the scene of a devastating and prolonged battle that dragged into September and cost thousands of casualties on both sides, while the remaining ports designated 'fortresses', except Bordeaux, were under siege until the end of the war.

Despite several near misses against warships in Biscay during July and August, only HMCS *Matane* was hit by an Hs 293 late in the evening of 20 July as the frigate sailed as part of Escort Group 9 hunting straggling U-boats off Brest. A single Hs 293 exploded close alongside the hull, staving in her side and flooding the engine room, though bulkheads held the water back from the rest of the ship and she was towed to Plymouth by HMCS *Meon* under escort by HMS *Swansea* and *Stormont*. It was a rare success for the glide-bombers at that stage of the war, but not their final victory. Meanwhile, as the Wehrmacht in France faced possible annihilation, *Luftflotte* 3 was downgraded to the post of *Luftwaffenkommando West* on 26 September. Hugo Sperrle, Göring's scapegoat for the skeletal Luftwaffe's failure to contain the Normandy beachhead, had been dismissed, first briefly replaced by *Generaloberst* Otto Dessloch and then *Generalleutnant* Alexander Holle.

The French Riviera

Before its dissolution, and with Sperrle still at the helm, *Luftflotte* 3 issued orders on 8 August that in the event of any Allied landing on the French Mediterranean coast, Stab and III./KG 100 were to be immediately subordinated to 2.*Fliegerdivision*, which would then revert to *Luftflotte* 2 control. In response, *Generalmajor* Korte requested the transfer as early as 12 August, perhaps indicating that a potential Allied assault was imminent. Aircraft torpedoes were ordered shipped by rail from Germany, now an arduous process with the bombing of German and French rail infrastructure.

On 15 August the hammer finally fell on the French Riviera when Operation *Dragoon* commenced with the main landing force of three infantry divisions of US VI Corps led by Major General Lucian Truscott. The 3rd Infantry Division landed on the western end of the invasion front at Cavalaire-sur-Mer (Alpha Beach), the 45th Infantry Division in the centre at Le Muy, Saint-Tropez (Delta Beach) with 36th Infantry Division on the eastern flank at Saint-Raphaël (Camel Beach). That morning 2.*Fliegerdivision* ordered maximum effort by KG 26 and KG 100 against the invasion area.

Dragoon's ground forces were primarily American, with a large commitment of French troops alongside smaller components from Canada and Britain. Churchill had vehemently argued against the operation, wanting its resources thrown instead into the grinding war in Italy or for his cherished dream of an invasion of the Balkans to threaten the Romanian oilfields and provide a future bulwark against the communist forces of the Soviet Union. However, American planners would not budge, the chief objective of *Dragoon* being the capture of the ports of Marseille and Toulon to bolster supply of Allied forces in France.

Facing the new invasion front was *Generaloberst* Johannes Blaskowitz's Army Group G, a thinly spread, under-equipped formation that had been plundered of nearly all its best troops and material for reinforcement of the Normandy battle. Coastal defences were meagre by comparison to those of the Atlantic Wall, only having been seized by the Wehrmacht after the occupation of Vichy late in 1942 and never receiving the prioritisation of north-western France. Furthermore, Blaskowitz possessed hardly any air support, although it was into this maelstrom that KG 26 and III./KG 100 flew on the first night of the landings.

Nine KG 100 Do 217 aircraft took off from Toulouse-Blagnac with a mixed payload of available Fritz-Xs (two) and Hs 293s (seven), though one bomber aborted with mechanical problems and two others were lost before being able to attack; 8./KG 100 Do 217M-11 commanded by *Ofw.* Rudolf Blab posted as missing in action and *Ofw.* Rudolf Freiberg of 7./KG 100 shot down by anti-aircraft fire from warships supporting *Dragoon* and crashing into the sea.[8] The remaining six aircraft approached the beachhead from landward, thereby putting their transport targets between themselves and the supporting warships of Vice Admiral Henry Kent Hewitt's Western Naval Task Force. They arrived over the battlefield at 1838hrs, four aircraft being sighted in the distance by Allied observers, while two remained far overhead, probably those equipped with 'Fritz-Xs' which relied on gravitational velocity for the greatest effect.

The organisation of *Dragoon* had more in common with Operation *Neptune* than either of the previous Mediterranean landings, the Western Naval Task Force including sixty warships equipped with jamming equipment. These reported approximately seventeen radio bomb control signals logged during last light on each day between 15 and 18 August; all jammed by at least one, and frequently as many as twenty different operators. However, this very confluence of jamming ships caused its own problem, when aboard USS *Bayfield* (flagship of Rear Admiral Spencer S. Lewis' Task Force 87), jamming operators detected the signal of an Hs 293 launch, but were never given permission to commence jamming as there was some suspicion that multiple ships equipped with the same apparatus could be jamming each other. It was a fatal mistake.

Hans E. Bergner was a young officer aboard American *LST 282*, which had taken part in the build-up of troops at Utah Beach in Normandy and was awaiting its turn to unload troops in the area monitored by USS *Bayfield* as the Luftwaffe mounted its first attack:

After Normandy, we went to the Mediterranean so the ship could take part in the invasion of southern France. We knew that this time we would be beaching on D-Day itself. When we were loading north of Naples, I talked to my close friend and roommate who was the ship's gunnery officer, Peter Hughes. I said, 'Pete, I feel quite different about this one. I'm not as concerned.'

He turned to me and said, 'You know, it's strange you should say that. I really wasn't so afraid in Normandy, but this time I have a bad feeling.'

It appeared that we would have an easy day of it on 15 August. We waited offshore after watching the H-hour bombing of the beach and saw our LCVPs return safely after landing assault forces on Green Beach. We saw no enemy planes. With our binoculars we could see resort homes and the hills behind them . . . Our turn came late because there was no immediate requirement for the primary cargo we were carrying: 155-millimetre Long Tom artillery pieces of the 36th Infantry Division. The main deck and tank deck of the *LST-282* was jam-packed with those guns and their trailers full of ammunition.

We didn't get the word to the beach until about nine o'clock in the evening, after the sun had gone down. We were about three-quarters of a mile from Green Beach. I was on the forecastle, standing on a raised gun tub. My duty was to handle the sound-powered telephones on the forward battery of 20-millimetre and 40-millimetre anti-aircraft guns. Hughes, on the conning tower, was on the other end of the phones.

We spotted two planes coming in from over the land, far away off the starboard bow. We were talking back and forth about what the planes might be. Suddenly, there were three planes instead of two, and the third one appeared smaller and, we assumed, farther away . . . It headed initially toward the transport area, then turned at a right angle and dived right onto the *LST-282*. We got a few shots off with the ship's guns, but they were well astern of this bomb that was probably moving at several hundred miles an hour.

It hit right in front of our ship's wheelhouse and went into the main engine room, where it exploded. Pete was killed instantly, blown from the conn down onto the main deck. My own first conscious memory is of being on the main deck rather than on the elevated gun tubs. Whether I was knocked down by the concussion or jumped because of fear, I don't really know. I looked back at the conn and could see that it was all crumpled. There was no sign of life. Flames were starting u. The next 10 to 20 minutes were terrible. The Long Tom artillery ammunition began cooking off and exploding, as did the ammunition in the ship's own magazines.

There never was any formal order to abandon ship, but people saw the obvious and jumped overboard. I tried to warn some soldiers to stay on board, because we had been taught in midshipman school not to leave the ship until directed because conditions might be even worse in the water. But soldiers get nervous on board ship, where there are no foxholes, so they said to me, 'F___ you', and off they went.

The First Lieutenant had the bow doors halfway open when the bomb hit and all power failed. The bow ramp was still closed, and all the troops manning their vehicles on the tank deck would have been trapped. The rear cables of a large cargo elevator on the main deck were parted, however, causing the rear portion of the elevator to fall onto trucks in the tank deck. That formed a ramp from the tank deck to the main deck. Many injured soldiers, some with their uniforms on fire, scrambled up that ramp to safety. It was similar to the way red ants escape from an ant hole when someone pours in gasoline.

By now the ship had moved to within about half a mile of the beach. Lieutenant [Lawrence E.] Gilbert, the skipper, got the Navy Cross for his actions that night, and he deserved it. He ordered hard left rudder, which kept the exploding *LST-282* from moving in among the LSTs already lined up on the beach. As it was, we careened off the port, and eventually ran aground on some rocks in front of a beautiful resort home.

In addition to his ship handling, the skipper rescued a signalman, George Heckman, who had a badly broken leg. He carried Heckman down three flights from the bridge to the water's edge, and there someone else took over and began pulling him ashore. Then the captain went back and got the engineer officer, Edward Durkee, who was unconscious and had a back full of shrapnel. The captain secured him by his life belt to the rudder post. Both were later recovered in an unconscious condition by rescue craft. The skipper himself had been wounded severely in one arm, so he did those rescues with one arm.[9]

Eleven bodies were recovered from the wreckage of *LST 282*, thirty-nine others being posted as missing in action.[10] German claims for the KG 100 raid indicate *LST 312*, *LST 384* and the destroyer USS *Le Long* heavily damaged, *LST 282* and a 7,000-ton freighter sunk. In reality, the two supposedly damaged LSTs were never part of the invasion, no such destroyer as USS *Le Long* existed, and the 7,000-ton freighter sunk was probably a near miss on USS *Bayfield*. Though there was damage inflicted on other landing vessels by shellfire and mines, *LST 282* remains the sole success of the day for the Luftwaffe.

The burnt-out hulk of *LST 282*, sunk on the opening day of Operation *Dragoon*. The Luftwaffe response to the invasion was patchy and largely ineffective, though fifty men were killed aboard this American vessel.

Major Sölter's I./KG 26 carried out a torpedo attack in the Mediterranean at St Raphael, while Ju 88s of II./KG 26 attempted to bomb Cap Nègre where French commandoes had come ashore to support the main landings. Neither attack was a success against heavy anti-aircraft fire and difficult twilight visibility. KG 26 undertook further conventional bombing with canisters of fragmentation bombs, attacking troop concentrations ashore, both KG 100 and KG 26 repeating their attacks on the *Dragoon* beachhead over the following two nights, but with no success and further casualties.

Air attacks had done nothing to impede a rapid Allied advance ashore as Blaskowitz initiated a fighting retreat to the north. Luftwaffe presence over the landing area had been considered so slight that aircraft of the Carrier Task Force 88, commanded by Rear Admiral T.H. Troubridge RN, were most frequently engaged in offensive fighter-bomber missions, possessing greater penetration range than Corsican-based fighter-bombers. On Friday 18 August, *2.Fliegerdivision* was subordinated to *Luftflotte* 2, its staff transferring to Bergamo and ordered to prepare all flying units for immediate transfer away from airfields threatened by Allied troops and FFI attacks. *Hauptmann* Heinrich Schmetz's III./KG 100 was ordered to evacuate its base at Toulouse and transfer to Valence where both Stab and II./KG 26 were located. Valence came under strafing attack by P-51 Mustangs that day, though I./KG 26 was ordered to carry out a dusk torpedo attack against shipping south of St. Raphael while II./KG 26 would repeat its effort with fragmentation bombs. The Do 217s of III./KG 100 had already been loaded with ordnance by the time that the transfer orders arrived, and so they completed their planned sortie before complying. A single KG 26 Ju 88 attempted to torpedo *FDT 13* off St Tropez, but the torpedo exploded 250 yards short of target. However, USS *Catoctin* – flagship of the Amphibious Force – was straddled with fragmentation bombs only moments after Vice Admiral Hewitt, Lieutenant General Ira C. Eaker (commander-in-chief of the Mediterranean Allied Air Forces) and Lieutenant General Jacob L. Devers (Deputy Supreme Allied Commander, Mediterranean Theatre) had come aboard from *PT 208* to confer with the Admiral. The Ju 88 was spotted approaching from the port side at 15,000 feet, one bomb hitting the after well deck and killing two enlisted men and seriously injuring three others, two of who subsequently died of their wounds. Three officers and twenty-nine men, as well as four on *PT 208*, received less serious injuries.

On 19 August, *Maj.* Willi Sölter, *Gruppenkommandeur* of I./KG 26, was awarded the Knight's Cross. Sölter, who had started the war with 2./KG 77, had completed 270 operational missions and been shot down five times. It was he who would coordinate his *Gruppe*'s hasty departure from southern France as the Luftwaffe joined the general retreat. That morning, I./KG 26's aircraft had transferred to Lyon-Bron, a nearby chateau requisitioned for Sölter and his staff, as they reported to 2.*Fliegerdivision* that there was no possibility of further torpedo operations, as the airfield possessed no assisted take-off gear or torpedoes. Klümper's *Geschwader* had now been ordered to Memmingen, aircraft in repair to be handed over to ground personnel to attempt restoration as long as possible before evacuation. Later that month, III./KG 26 was to return to Germany for conversion from the Ju 88 to the Ju 188A-3, its existing aircraft being passed on to restore numbers of the other two depleted *Gruppen*. By late August I./KG 26 was in Leck, operationally ready and equipped with Ju 88s; II./KG 26 at Memmingen, later moved to Grossenbrode and then Trondheim; and III./KG 26 also at Leck ready to receive Ju 188s. The training IV.*Gruppe* remained at Lübeck-Blankensee.

The Arado 196s of 2./SAGr. 128 were ordered to depart Berre and transfer 'with all its elements' to Friedrichshafen; the aircraft and crews by air via Lyon, ground staff by road. The Dornier floatplanes of 1.*Seenotstaffel* also ordered to undertake the same journey.

For III./KG 100 the new *Gruppenkommandeur Hptm.* Schmetz received fresh orders to relocate to Giebelstadt airfield near Würzburg, northern Bavaria. The aircraft completed the journey without major incident, flying during early morning hours to avoid roving Allied fighter patrols. The ground staff, on the other hand, faced a journey fraught with danger as FFI units rose in open combat against retreating German troops. Schmetz opted to remain with the ground column and led them in action at St. Hippolyte du Fort north of Montpelier, where they came under sustained attack on 25 August by the FFI, with over 300 men killed, missing or captured during the savage fighting. Not until mid-September did the survivors finally reach Giebelstadt.

However, on 20 August *OKL* ordered KG 100 disbanded and Schmetz's III./KG 100 officially ceased to exist on 7 September 1944, Schmetz being awarded the Knight's Cross on 29 October. *Hauptmann* Hans Molly's II./KG 100 remained on its conversion course to the He 177 in Aalborg until February 1945, until it too was disbanded, never having flown the aircraft in combat. The Heinkels were destroyed and all personnel transferred to ground forces. *Oberstleutnant* Bernhard Jope, somewhat of a pioneering Luftwaffe naval aviator, was appointed *Kommodore* to KG 30, including its transition to KG(J) 30 until he transferred once again to the staff of IX.*Fliegerkorps*. On 19 March 1945 he would be transferred to the *NS-Führungsstab* of *Luftkommando Reich*, the political officers maintaining National Socialist ideals in the Luftwaffe's home-defence fighter formations.

The other glide-bomb formations, I. and II./KG 40, had already relinquished their He 177 aircraft during October as pilots began retraining to fly the Me 262. Both *Gruppen* were officially disbanded on 2 February 1945, some aircraft kept at readiness into 1945, until eventually cannibalised for engines and spare parts. For the Condors of III./KG 40, their pilots had also been scheduled to begin conversion to Me 262 fighters during September, while the few remaining Condors were grouped in 8./KG40, becoming '*Transport Staffel Condor*' and returning the delicate aircraft to its original purpose by the war's end. *Major* Dr. Lambert von Konschegg's III./KG 40 was disbanded on 2 February 1945.

Bernhard Jope, pictured here while in KG 40. He ended the war as a political officer of the *NS-Führungsstab* of *Luftkommando Reich*.

Arado crews of *Seeaufklärungsgruppe* 126 taken ashore in an Aegean anchorage. They frequently escorted Ju 52 aircraft during the evacuation of Greece, such as the Ju 52 floatplane in the background.

In the 'backwater' of the eastern Mediterranean and the Aegean Sea, the aircraft of *Seeaufklärungsgruppe* 126 had remained in action as reconnaissance and convoy escort throughout the events of Operation *Dragoon*, *Maj.* Hans Nebelin taking command of the *Gruppe* from *Obstlt.* Hermann Busch during June. However, by the middle of 1944 the advance of Soviet forces into south-eastern Europe and Bulgaria's withdrawal from the Axis had threatened to cut off the troops in Greece and Hitler granted Löhr's Army Group F permission to withdraw from mainland Greece and the islands within the Ionian and Aegean Seas. On 27 August the evacuation of the Aegean islands was ordered, air transport missions beginning within three days using 106 Ju52 transports and evacuating 30,740 soldiers in 2,050 separate flights. The eight surviving Ju 52/MS minesweeping aircraft of 4./*Minensuchgruppe* 1 that had operated from Saloniki, flew to Dresden, having lost eight aircraft to enemy fighters during the previous month. Though the Arado Ar 196 fighters flew valuable escorts to many such flights, their combat power against British fighters was negligible. Stab. 1. and 2.*Staffeln* were still based in Skaramanga, 3./SAGr. 126 on the islands of Valos and Leros and 4./SAGr. 126 had been in Suda Bay on Crete, until it was disbanded

Such transport flights were highly vulnerable to British fighters and casualties were heavy.

during September. The remaining twenty-six Ar 196 aircraft were ordered to evacuate and return to Lochstädt, a seaplane anchorage in East Prussia near Pillau. They spent the remainder of the war in the Baltic Sea until the final German collapse.

On 27 September 1944, *Generalfeldmarschall* Wolfram Freiherr von Richthofen' *Luftflotte* 2 was disbanded after having been withdrawn from Italy to Vienna, replaced by the post of *Kommandierende General der Deutschen Luftwaffe in Italien.* Its mercurial commander was on sick leave with repetitive and excruciating headaches. Diagnosed with a brain tumour, an operation undertaken was deemed only a partial success, as the tumour's growth had merely been slowed and offered no hope of removal. A patient of the Luftwaffe hospital for neurological injuries at Bad Ischl in Austria, Richthofen was captured by US troops at the end of the war and died on 12 July 1945.

Biscay

During July 1944, the decision had been made to transfer three of FAGr. 5's Ju 290s to KG 200 – the Luftwaffe's 'special forces' *Geschwader.* The aircraft had already been placed on standby to operate under KG 200 control for potential flights to Japan via the polar route as an extension of the blockade-running operations, but the plan never reached fruition.[11] They were, however, used for agent delivery in North Africa, until the *Gruppe* began its withdrawal from France on 16 August. Aircraft were loaded to their maximum capacities before taking off for Mühldorf, Bavaria. The ground personnel faced an uncertain journey back to Germany through FFI-infested France, several skirmishes resulting in dead and wounded as the Luftwaffe men fought alongside briefly attached army and SS units. *Gruppenkommandeur Maj.* Fischer had attended a conference in Berlin on 7 September with *Hptm.* (rating as General) Karl Kähler, Chief of Staff and permanent representative of the *Gen.d.Aufklärungsflieger* (General Commanding Reconnaissance Aircraft) in which a somewhat overly-optimistic future plan involving his shattered unit and new aircraft had been revealed.

Representatives of the Luftwaffe directed attention to existing doubts regarding the technical construction of the Me 264 and its action as reconnaissance plane for the submarine warfare. After the Atlantic Coast has been lost and the enemy air defence has been consolidated with fighter planes and anti-aircraft weapons in the presently occupied area of the West, the flying performance of this type seems to be not sufficient anymore.

According to [Kähler's] statement, however, it would be possible with minor expenses to construct in time a reconnaissance plane of the Dornier Company; this type would not only meet the requirements of the submarine warfare regarding the speed and range, but also the necessity of the present and future situation in the aerial warfare. U-boat warfare will be started again on a large scale in April 1945, due to the rather unfavourable surface qualities of the new submarine Type XXI, the reconnaissance action will be even more important than it has been so far. [Kähler] promised with great certainty that the required number of planes would be made available in due time for the re-opening of the submarine warfare.

After the report, [Dönitz] agreed upon the alteration of the plane type for U-boat reconnaissance and stressed expressly that he never had asked for a special plane type but had always stated that merely the performance of the planes could be decisive for the choice.

Since the plane type Do 335 that has been offered now by the Luftwaffe meets all requirements to be made for the submarine reconnaissance and flying performance, and can be made available in due time, the Naval Staff asks to support its output in the most possible extent.[12]

The idea that failing German aircraft output could provide brand-new designs for field use at this stage of the war – when there was little fuel for operational flying, let alone testing programmes – was absurd.

Nonetheless, Fischer returned to FAGr. 5 and once reunited in Germany, and now bereft of aircraft, awaited instructions to begin conversion to the Dornier Do 335 or Ar 234, but neither happened – the former turbojet aircraft not even reaching prototype stage – and to all intents and purposes FAGr. 5 was disbanded in February 1945. Men were posted to the *Fallschirmjäger* or other Luftwaffe combat units, though a small number of flying elements appear to have remained active until the war's end, utilised in a bewildering array of minor operations amidst the confusion of the Third Reich's death throes.

Of the two BV 222s still present in Western France by the time of Operation *Overlord*, 'X4+EH' (S2) transferred from Biscarosse to Billefjord, Norway, during the course of two days starting on 4 July, 'X4+DH' (S4) following two days later to Oslo. The French 1. (F) SAGr. 129 was officially disbanded on 16 August, its BV 222s divided between 1./SAGr. 130 in Tromsø and 2./SAGr. 131 in Stavanger as BV 222C-12 'X4+CH', which had been damaged by a fire in its port engine during early June, also made the transfer flight from Biscarosse as planned. Once in Norway, they were joined by three other surviving BV 222s from Germany. One final French mission had been suggested for a single BV 222 during September as plans were made to fly *General der Fallschirmtruppe* Hermann Ramcke, commander of the Brest Fortress, back to Germany on 19 September. A message despatched that day by *MGK West* to Ramcke reads:

> Flying boat can carry forty people. By order of the Supreme Command of the Navy ten members of the Navy, including officers who are suitable for reporting to C-in-C of the Navy, are to be brought along.

It was, however, a forlorn hope. Following an epic street battle in Brest and then along the Crozon Peninsula, Ramcke and his final strongpoints had surrendered that day, maritime air units having long departed from northern Brittany by then. Of *Seeaufklärungsgruppe* 128, the Bf 109 and Fw 190 fighters of 1./SAGr. 128 had disbanded during January and been redistributed, while twelve Ar 196A-3s of 2./SAGr. 128 were returned to Germany and spread among Norwegian-based reconnaissance units as the *Gruppe* was finally disbanded during August.

The heavy fighters of I. and III./ZG 1 had suffered their final casualty on 28 June when a Mosquito Mark XII intercepted and shot down *Uffz.* Werner Migge's 9.(*Nacht*)/ZG 1 Ju 88C-6 near Chateaudun in early morning darkness. The retreat of the U-boats to Norway had robbed the depleted *Zerstörergeschwader* of its purpose and on 5 August it was officially disbanded; trained night fighter crews being transferred to other night fighter units while the remaining pilots were generally retrained for single engine fighters, in which their casualties were extreme.

With the withdrawal of all Biscay Luftwaffe maritime forces, and the placing under siege of the Atlantic ports, the X.*Fliegerkorps* command was made redundant and *General der Flieger* Martin Fiebig's post dissolved shortly thereafter during September.[13]

The Eastern Front

The surviving aircraft of *Oberst* Hellmut Schalke's *Seeaufklärungsgruppe* 125 had been on constant patrol over the Black Sea until August 1944, though 2./SAGr. 125 had been disbanded at the beginning of June and its seven remaining Ar 196A–3s reallocated to other units. The two last casualties suffered by 1./SAGr. 125 in the Black Sea were both forced down on 21 August by Soviet fighters. *Leutnant* Wolfgang von Zworowski later recalled:

> That day I had started around 0500hrs with two other machines to patrol as an air-sea rescue mission for a BV 138C-1 of the same *Staffel* [flown by *Lt.* Fritz Koch which had not returned and was never found]. I kept the plane to port in my sight until the return flight when I lost it. Later, I thought that I could recognise it. But then I saw many black dots around it: the plane is being attacked by Soviet fighters! Wanting to help the crew, I flew in that direction before I discovered the truth. It is not a BV 138, but a Catalina used by the Soviets as a sea rescue aircraft. It is with six fighters and I understand that they were waiting to escort a bomber formation that was incoming to attack Constanța.[14]

The Airacobra fighters immediately attacked Zworowski, wounding him and another crewman and killing wireless operator *Uffz.* Hans Neumann before the BV 138 crash-landed, being strafed as the survivors abandoned the aircraft and leapt into the water, their life raft destroyed. A second

BV 138 from the same patrol was also shot down, flight engineer *Uffz.* Horst Uhlein being killed before survivors of both aircraft were rescued by a Do 24 of 8.*Seenotstaffel* escorted by two Romanian Bf 109s, their final rescue mission in the Black Sea.

On 23 August, *Vizeadmiral* Helmuth Brinkmann (*Admiral Schwarzes Meer*) arrived at *Generaloberst* Johannes Friessner's headquarters of Army Group South Ukraine for a situation conference. That day, as the Red Army pierced the Moldavian front, King Michael I of Romania mounted a successful coup deposing the Antonescu dictatorship and effectively taking Romania out of the Axis. Romanian authorities offered German forces an unobstructed withdrawal from their country. Hitler, however, was certain that the coup could be reversed, and the regional Wehrmacht and Waffen-SS troops were immediately placed on alert to obstruct Soviet advances and Romanian 'unrest'. At 0255hrs on 24 August Brinkmann was ordered to take and hold Constanța, urgently meeting with *Oberst* Schalke, *Seefliegerführer Schwarzes Meer*, to discuss the impossible order.

It was a ridiculous notion as locally Brinkmann lacked the manpower to take and hold the Romanian port city and he informed Berlin that with his limited resources and Soviet troops only 90 kilometres away

Gunner aboard a BV 138. The BV 138s of 1. and 3./SAGr. 125 were amongst the last Luftwaffe units to leave the Black Sea.

and advancing unopposed, it was impossible to comply. Nonetheless, the order stood. On 25 August, after two nights during which Luftwaffe aircraft had bombed Bucharest and other provincial towns in a misguided show of strength, Romania declared war on Germany.

Wireless communication was lost with *Luftwaffenkommando* 4 and I.*Fliegerkorps* and confusion reigned in Constanța and Mamaia as German and Romanian troops faced each other, neither sure exactly what to do. *Seenotbereichskommando* XII, responsible for the Black Sea region, seized the initiative and organised a transport column bound for Bulgaria, 12.*Seenotflotille* vessels sailing to Varna and being handed over to the Bulgarian Navy while all serviceable aircraft lifted off for the port city. From there, three Do 24s were returned to Germany, while the remainder transferred to Athens to reinforce 7.*Seenotstaffel*. On 26 August Schalke led the BV 138s of 1. and 3./SAGr. 125 from their base at Mamaia to Saloniki in the Aegean, before returning to Germany and service within the Baltic. The Luftwaffe maritime presence over the Black Sea was ended.

There remained little Luftwaffe presence in southern European latitudes. By the autumn of 1944, German air-sea rescue ships that still plied the Adriatic were constrained to night operations as Allied aircraft from occupied Italian airfields established complete aerial superiority. During August 1944, *Obstlt.* Eduard Engelhorn's *Seenotdienstführer* 2 (*Süd*) post was disbanded as part of the reduction of air-sea rescue forces, Engelhorn transferred to pilot school (*Flugzeugführerschule*, FFS) A/B 5 at Gablingen. *Major* Hans Haeger had already passed command of *Seenotbereichskommando* X to *Maj.* Ludwig Wahl, though this post was also dissolved during August. While Wahl was posted to command the police unit *Wehrmachtsstreifendienst-Gruppe z.b.V. beim AOK 7*, Haeger was transferred as an air-sea rescue staff officer to *Gen.* Maximilian Ritter von Pohl's *Kommandierende General der Deutschen Luftwaffe in Italien*. *Hauptmann* Braue, commander of 20.*Seenotgruppe*, formed in Verona that month, was given command of all *Seenot* forces within the Italian theatre of operations. With devastating enemy air power now an undisputed fact, Braue made use of a search *Staffel* of Fw 190 fighters under the command of *Oblt.* Heinz Langer, comprising part of 80.*Seenotgruppe*.[15] By April 1945 all air-sea search and rescue operations in the Italian theatre had ceased and the remaining *Flugbetriebsboote* were handed over to the Kriegsmarine who used them as small combat units alongside S-boats and other patrol craft.

10

Epitaph

The Final Struggle in Norway

LUFTWAFFE TORPEDO OPERATIONS IN southern latitudes drew most available aircraft away from Norway during the first half of 1944. However, regional U-boat strength had only increased with withdrawal from the Atlantic, coinciding with the resumption of Arctic convoys. Unfortunately for German ambitions, Allied naval and air operations around the Norwegian coast had also improved and intensified. Royal Air Force anti-shipping strikes had begun to truly bite from the very beginning of 1944, long-range Mosquito fighters escorting Coastal Command strike aircraft in what were known as 'Outstep' patrols, the twin-engined fighters acting as 'outriders', free-ranging fighters looking for enemy aircraft or targets of opportunity. On 19 January, RAF 307 Squadron Mosquito IIs claimed three BV 138s either destroyed or probably destroyed on one such sweep over Stavanger, and a Junkers Ju 34 shot down while in the air. Mosquitos were also used on solitary reconnaissance missions over the Norwegian coast. On 21 January aircraft 'K' of RAF 333 Squadron was over the Norwegian coast in mid-afternoon.

> In position 61 17 N, 04 40E sighted one BV 138 on port quarter flying north at 500 feet. K/333 at 200 feet . . . turned to port and coming up behind enemy aircraft, which turned to 270 from 500 yards and 300 ft. Fired one burst which set two outer engines of enemy aircraft on fire. Enemy aircraft altered course to starboard and flying south extinguished fires. Fired another burst, set same two engines afire which spread to whole of port wing. 'K' closed to 200 yards and fired third burst. Enemy aircraft crashed into sea, sank at once, only debris being seen. No return of fire. Light seen during whole of action from tail of fuselage of enemy aircraft.[1]

The flying boat belonged to 3./SAGr. 130 and *Oblt.z.S* Gerhard Saatz, his crew of four and two passengers aboard were all posted as missing in action.

Blohm & Voss BV 138s continued to serve as coastal escorts and reconnaissance aircraft in Norway until the final days of the war.

The Norwegian squadron claimed the first loss suffered by the remnants of the *Küstenflieger* on 6 February when 1./Kü.Fl.Gr. 406 He 115B 1 'K6+OH' flown by *Ofw.* Hermann Borgards was shot down while travelling from Stavanger to Trondheim escorting a convoy of ten small merchants. Mosquito 'P' of 333 Squadron scored several hits, causing one of the Heinkel's engines to burst into flames as gunner *Uffz.* Konrad Esser briefly, and inaccurately, returned fire. In front of onlookers ashore, the blazing Heinkel crashed into the sea, sinking to the bottom upside down with no survivors.

The Arctic convoys of 1944 began with JW 56A in January which remained undetected by Luftwaffe aircraft in appalling visibility but lost three ships to U-boats. JW 56B that followed at the month's end lost the destroyer HMS *Hardy*, hit by a U-boat's acoustic torpedo. The February Convoy JW 57 was the first to be sighted by a reconnaissance Condor, but Wildcat (previously known as Martlet) fighters from HMS *Chaser* soon forced the shadowing aircraft away, a subsequent U-boat attack sinking the escort destroyer HMS *Mahratta*. However, the subsequent attempt at intercepting Convoy JW 58 bound for Murmansk was disastrous. Included in its covering force were two escort carriers – HMS *Tracker* and *Activity* – and on the final day of March a reconnaissance Ju 88D-1 of 1.(F)/Aufkl.Gr. 22 was detected by radar and shot down by a Wildcat fighter, hitting the sea almost vertically, leaving no survivors.

Nonetheless, the forty-seven merchant ships had been reported. Condors replaced the lost Junkers as shadowing aircraft, but over the hours that followed hours three Condors of 3./KG 40 were shot down, with the loss of all twenty crew members. The following day a BV 138C-1 of 3./SAGr. 130 was also brought down, *Oblt* Kurt Kannengiesser and his five men listed as missing in action. The final Luftwaffe casualty was a second Ju 88D-1 of 1 (F)/Aufkl.Gr. 22 and by the time the convoy reached the Soviet Union without loss, three U-boats and six aircraft had been destroyed. The Condors shot down were the last in the Norwegian theatre, soon being withdrawn from front-line service and KG 40 finally being disbanded in November 1944.

After returning Convoy RA59 departed the Soviet Union in late May, Arctic traffic was suspended in deference to requirements for Operation *Overlord*. Not until 15 August did Convoy JW 59 sail from Liverpool towards the Kola Inlet. In the interim, from April 1944 until the end of the war the Royal Navy increased the intensity of carrier aircraft attacks against Norwegian coastal shipping and military installations. Of more than thirty operations, four were made with large fleet carriers, but the majority were handled by smaller escort carriers. Combined with direct attack, the aircraft also laid extensive minefields, clogging the coastal convoy routes and sinking near 200,000GRT of shipping.

On 8 May 1944, Wildcats of 898 Naval Air Squadron had shot down two BV 138C-1 aircraft of 2./SAGr. 130 during one such operation codenamed *Hoops* directed at harassment of coastal shipping. HMS *Searcher* provided the escorting Wildcats for bomb-carrying Hellcats from HMS *Emperor* that attacked merchant ships south-west of Kristiansand, oil tanks at Kjen and a fish oil factory at Fosnavaag.

Three carrier operations were also mounted against *Tirpitz* in her anchorage at Kaafjord. The first, Operation *Tungsten*, took place in April, achieving complete surprise and causing enough damage to incapacitate the battleship for three months. The ship's four Ar 196A-5 aircraft were destroyed, wounding three men and killing the crew of 'T3+BH'; pilot *Ofw*. Günter Behrendt and observer *Oblt.z.S.* Ekkehard Doerstling. A number of further strikes on *Tirpitz* were cancelled in April and May, including *Brawn* which was aborted in mid-May despite the carriers being in position on account of adverse weather conditions, while a diversionary operation, *Pot Luck*, resulted in probable damage to one and possible

An Arado belonging to *Tirpitz* is recovered from the sea. The *Tirpitz* remained the sole surface threat in the Arctic until her disabling during October 1944 and destruction the following month. (James Payne)

damage to three large merchant ships and confirmed bomb hits on two *Vorpostenboote* and a fish oil factory. Additionally five He 115 floatplanes of 1./Kü.Fl.Gr. 406 were destroyed on the water at Rørvik, three from the *Staffel* reserve, strafed and bombed by Hellcats from HMS *Emperor*.

In August Operation *Goodwood* was a final unsuccessful series of carrier attacks on *Tirpitz*, bombs failing to hit the battleship though two of its replacement Arado floatplanes were destroyed in Bukta harbour. As a diversionary raid, eight Seafires from HMS *Indefatigable* attacked the seaplane station at Billjefjord, destroying four BV 138s of SAGr. 130 and a single He 115 from 1./Kü.Fl.Gr. 406. By chance *U354* sighted the escort carriers HMS *Nabob* and *Trumpeter* accompanied by the cruiser HMS *Kent* and several frigates. Reporting contact, *Kaptlt*. Hans-Jürgen Stahmer fired a spread of FAT torpedoes at close range, observing a single hit and 'cloud amidships and slight list to starboard' on one carrier. HMS *Nabob* was hit in the starboard stern, badly holed and soon dead in the water. Over 300 men were evacuated while the remainder struggled to bring the carrier back under control before Stahmer fired a coup de grâce *Zaunkönig* that actually hit the frigate HMS *Bickerton*, killing thirty-eight men, the frigate being abandoned and scuttled by a torpedo from HMS *Vigilant*. Following Stahmer's attack, *Seeaufklärungsgruppe* 130

345

One of a remarkable set of photographs belonging to the observer of this aircraft aboard *Tirpitz*, helping, at far left, to return the aircraft to the battleship's port hangar.

launched a pair of BV 138C-1 aircraft to find and shadow the retreating Royal Navy forces, but both were shot down by Seafires of 894 Naval Air Squadron with all crew lost. The British continued attacks against *Tirpitz* over the following days, destroying her last Arado 196 while stationary on the water, but failing to significantly damage the battleship. *Luftflotte* 5 was requested to urgently increase fighter cover in the region, but with aircraft needed on all parts of the front, the request was denied.

Though intensely damaging to *Küstenfliegergruppe* 406 and *Seeaufklärungsgruppe* 130, *Goodwood* had decisively failed in its attempt to destroy or disable *Tirpitz*. The Fairey Barracuda bombers used were simply not up to the task, being slow, lumbering aircraft with a relatively small payload. Not until November 1944 would *Tirpitz* be finally neutralised by Tallboy bombs delivered by Avro Lancasters of RAF 617 and 9 Squadrons, hitting the battleship and causing her to capsize at her anchorage near the Norwegian town of Tromsø.

The last year of the war saw a seemingly interminable change in the command structure of the Luftwaffe, with posts renamed and higher echelon officers shuffled from place to place. In Norway the forces of *General der Flieger* Josef Kammhuber's *Luftflotte* 5 were no exception and the following three redesignated sub-commands were formed in June 1944:

Fliegerführer 3 in Kirkenes from *Fliegerführer Eismeer*, commanded by *Oberst* Hermann Busch and disbanded during late December after the retreat from Finnmark;
Fliegerführer 4, formed in Kjeller from *Fliegerführer Nord (West)*;
Fliegerführer 5, formed in Trondheim with *Gen.Maj.* Ernst-August Roth in command from *Fliegerführer Lofoten*.

On 16 September, *Luftflotte* 5 itself was disbanded, the post renamed *Kommandierende General der Deutschen Luftwaffe in Norwegen* with Kammhuber still at the helm for little over a month. He was succeeded by *Gen.Maj.* Eduard Ritter von Schleich, who in turn, on 15 November, was replaced by *Gen.Maj.* Roth.

During October *Küstenfliegergruppe* 406 lost two more Heinkels to low-flying enemy aircraft strafing their Hommelvik anchorage, reducing its available number of aircraft to eight. With a dwindling manpower pool and the obsolete Heinkel He 115 barely viable as convoy protection, this final *Küstenflieger* unit was disbanded during October 1944. Its aircraft were redistributed, some to the *Transportstaffel (See)* in Kiel and small *Ergänzungs-Küstenfliegerstaffel (Fern)* that formed in Copenhagen, operating within the Baltic Sea. At least one of them, He 115 B-2/C 'GA+MC' was severely damaged by flak from Allied forces besieging La Rochelle on 27 December as the aircraft attempted to carry supplies to the port city's trapped garrison. Those men of the *Küstenfliegergruppe* no longer required for aircraft duty were transferred to ground forces, many finding themselves involved in the upcoming Ardennes offensive. The last whisper of Raeder's original master plan for an independent naval air arm was finally silenced.

Though the battle lines in Finnmark had barely shifted in three years of war, an exhausted Finland finally agreed armistice terms with the Soviet Union, effective on 19 September. The expulsion of all German troops from Finland was a primary condition and thus began the 'Lapland War'. As Wehrmacht troops prepared to evacuate their positions in Finnmark, skirmishes with Finnish troops were initially minor until increasing pressure on the retreating Wehrmacht led to the eruption of intensive fighting. The Germans mounted a 'scorched earth' retreat that left a trail of blazing destruction in its wake. Anything deemed potentially useful to the Red Army was destroyed, from livestock to houses to telegraph poles. Soviet troops captured Petsamo after German troops had sabotaged the mines on 15 October and Kirkenes was demolished and abandoned ten days later. A new defensive line was established at Lyngenfjord using the mountain range's natural barrier east of Tromsø and constructing a line of fortified bunkers by use of forced labour by Soviet prisoners. The German retreat had been skilfully conducted and Soviet forces were unable to inflict significant casualties, while Finnish troops were unwilling to advance beyond their own border. To the chagrin of the Kriegsmarine, the BV 138 and BV 222 aircraft of SAGr. 130 in Tromsø were briefly removed from all reconnaissance duties during mid-October, operationally subordinated, to *General der Flieger* Willi Harmjanz, *Kommandierende General der Deutschen Luftwaffe in Finnland*, for the 'transport of important goods'.[2] That same day *Marinekommando Ost* issued an urgent request to the Luftwaffe:

> The Naval Command, East requests that the 'Buschmann *Gruppe*' consisting of AR 95 aircraft and at present situated in Pillau be put into action for U-boat escort of the 2nd Task Force. However, Naval Staff has learned from the Chief, General Staff, Luftwaffe that this *Gruppe* will be disbanded as it is manned for the most part by absolutely unreliable Latvian personnel having partly deserted to the enemy. A new echelon will be organized with the aircraft.

The 'Buschmann *Gruppe*' was the namesake of *Hptm.* Gerhard Buschmann, a former Abwehr officer and civilian pilot. Buschmann was *Volksdeutch*, born in Tallinn, Estonia, and strongly desired to assist an independent Estonian military. After the 'liberation' of Estonia from Soviet occupation in 1941, Buschmann took the germ of 'Aero Club Estonia' and its five aircraft and proposed the formation of an Estonian *Staffel* with supported from *General der Flieger* Alfred Keller of *Luftflotte* 1 who desired the *Staffel* for coastal patrols and intelligence gathering. Ironically, initial approval was forthcoming from neither the Luftwaffe nor Kriegsmarine High Commands, and Buschmann obtained official permission from the *Reichsführer*-SS and Estonian police service, his 'Security *Staffel*' to be recognised as an auxiliary police unit.

Hauptmann Gerhard Buschmann of the Estonian 'Buschmann *Gruppe*' that metamorphosed into *Seeaufklärungsgruppe* 127.

Assigned duty by the Kriegsmarine, aircraft, fuel and spare parts by the Luftwaffe and provisions and financing from the SS, '*Sonderstaffel Buschmann*' was officially activated on 12 February, 1942, with four Estonian PTO-4 two-seat, low-winged monoplane training aircraft that had survived the Soviet occupation. Originally operating over the Gulf of Finland, the aircraft were unarmed, their crew wearing a mixture of Luftwaffe and Estonian uniforms and civilian clothes. Several other near-obsolete trainers were accumulated until Buschmann acquired Arado Ar 65 biplanes originally intended for export to Chile.

Unfortunately, the sensitivities of the Finnish High Command were upset by the arming of Estonian pilots by the Luftwaffe and Hitler ordered *Sonderstaffel Buschmann* disbanded late in 1942, though he was only partially obeyed. Instead, in July 1942 the *Staffel* was officially drawn into the Luftwaffe as 15./Aufkl.Gr. 27 (*See*). Within a year Buschmann's unit had expanded to *Auflklärungsgruppe* 127 (*See*), based at Lake Ülemiste near Tallin, the Estonian volunteer numbers bolstered by conscription both in Estonia and Latvia. A year later it was renamed *Seeaufklarungsgruppe* 127, engaged in patrolling the Baltic Sea for Soviet submarines.

However, by mid-September 1944 the Wehrmacht began to retreat from Estonia, *Seeaufklarungsgruppe* 127 relocating to Latvia from where several crews deserted by flying to Sweden for internment. *Generalmajor* Klaus Siegfried Uebe, commander of *Luftflotte* 1, ordered an immediate ban on Estonian aviation units, terminating their fuel allowance, and requesting the unit's dissolution, suggesting some of the most 'reliable' Estonian volunteers be retained while the remainder be transferred to the SS or auxiliary forces. Subsequently, on 1 October, the Luftwaffe Quartermaster General issued Order No. 13215/44, disbanding all Estonian and Latvian aviation units. Buschmann was subsequently wounded on the Leningrad front but survived the war, emigrating to the United States where he died on 13 March 1981.

As part of the withdrawal from Finland and the northern Norwegian lines II./KG 26 relocated from Banak to Trondheim, operationally ready by November at which point *Maj.* Otto Werner departed as *Gruppenkommandeur* to be replaced by *Hptm.* Rudi Schmidt. Werner, a pre-war Kriegsmarine officer and former *Küstenflieger*, became Chief of Staff to *Generalleutnant* Alexander Holle in his new role as *Kommandieren der General der Luftwaffe in Dänemark. Oberstleutnant* Werner Klümper also left command of KG 26 in November, to be replaced by *Obstlt.* Wilhelm Stemmler. Klümper, one of the pioneers of German maritime

Junkers Ju 88s of KG 26 photographed in Bardufoss, Norway, 1945.

air warfare and leading expert in aerial torpedoes moved to the post of a regional airfield commander in which he ended the war.

On 31 October, former *Gruppenkommandeur* II./KG 26 *Maj.* Georg Teske received the Knight's Cross for his *Gruppe* leadership. Still recovering from his spinal injury, he had volunteered for fighters, briefly being posted to a school for *Generals der Jagdflieger*, before fighter training. However, in February 1945 he would return to KG 26, this time to become the final *Geschwaderkommodore* as Stemmler departed. *Oberfeldwebel* Herbert Kunze, an observer with 8./KG 26, was also decorated with the Knight's Cross on 9 November. By this time, III./KG 26 had completed re-equipping with the Ju 188 and moved to Trondheim, I./KG 26 relocated to Bardufoss, seventy kilometres south of Tromsø. Fresh prioritised targets were decreed by Göring who demanded the sinking of aircraft carriers escorting the Arctic convoys to protect U-boats from air attack. However, the *Geschwader* was on temporary suspension from flying, enforced by the dire fuel situation. Fears of an Allied lading at Narvik had again dominated Hitler's Norwegian thinking, perceived slackening of Soviet pressure in Finnmark leading to the mistaken belief that it presaged an Anglo-American assault from the west; either one of design or an opportunistic lunge to thwart further Soviet domination of the Arctic region. The *Führer* demanded strengthened aerial reconnaissance over northern waters.

Fuel supplies had, however, become critical. Kammhuber was informed that although the order to increase reconnaissance activity had originated from the *Führer*, it would be possible only at the expense of bomber activity. There was no fuel available except in the event of a 'threatening danger North' invasion alarm, whereby defensive measures were to be taken regardless of fuel stocks.

With the collapsing front in Prussia and reconnaissance reporting up to twenty-five Soviet submarines now preparing for action in the Baltic, *SKL* requested *Seeaufklarungsgruppe* 126, recently transferred from the Aegean, be given responsibility for ASW work within the Baltic. Its available *Staffeln* were transferred to bases on and near Rugen Island under the control of *Fliegerführer* 6 at Kamp. Furthermore, in Berlin, *OKL* informed the Kriegsmarine that the Arados of 1./BFl.Gr. 196 in Pillau and Stab and 2./Bo.Fl.Gr. 196 in Aalborg were to be subordinated to *Generalmajor* Andreas Nielsen, *Luftflotte Reich*, in all respects. The floatplanes were to be employed as escort aircraft as well as reconnaissance and ASW patrols over the central Baltic under close cooperation with local Kriegsmarine operational headquarters. A special allocation of aircraft-fuel for their purpose could, however, not be made.

By December 1944, Norway's maritime aircraft had been distributed between three separate regional *Fliegerführer* commands:

Fliegerführer 3: Bardufoss.
   1.(F)/124, Ju 88/Ju 188 (Bardufoss);
   1./*Aufklärungsgruppe* 32, Fw 189 (Bardufoss);
   Stab/S.A.Gr. 130, 3 x BV 222 (Tromsø);
   3.(F)/S.A.Gr. 130, 7 x BV 138 (Tromsø).

Fliegerführer 5: Trondheim
   Stab/KG 26, Ju 88 (Trondheim-Vaernes);
   I/KG 26, Ju 88 (Bardufoss);
   II/KG 26, Ju 88 (Trondheim - Vaernes);
   III./KG 26, Ju 188 (Trondheim-Vaernes);
      1.(F)/SAGr. 130, 7x BV 138 (Trondheim);
   Arado-*Kette*, 5 x Ar 196 (Hommelvik);
   51.*Seenotstaffel*, Do 24 (Tromsø)

Fliegerführer 4: Kjeller
   2.(F)/S.A.Gr. 131, 13 x Ar 196, (Sola);
   1 (F)/120, Ju 88/Ju 188 (Eggemoen):
   1.(F)/22, Ju 88 (Kjevik)

   50.*Seenotstaffel*, Ar 196 (Sola)

   Transporfliegerstaffel 'Condor', Fw 200 (Vaaler)

   Jagdfliegerfuhrer Norwegen Forus
   ZG 26, JG 5 and *Nachtjägerstaffel Norwegen*.

New Year 1945 brought with it fresh British attacks on German convoy traffic plying the Norwegian coastal route; Operation *Spellbinder* launched by the escort carriers HMS *Premier* and *Trumpeter*, the cruiser minelayer *Apollo*, the heavy cruiser *Norfolk*, the light cruisers *Bellona* and *Dido*, and nine destroyers of the 17th Destroyer Flotilla. On 11 January they attacked a German convoy off Egersund, sinking a minesweeper and causing two merchant ships to be abandoned with heavy damage.

In retaliation, II./KG 26 mounted an attack on the carriers, but were driven away by covering naval fighters, though without loss.

The following month saw a return to attacks on the Arctic convoys, JW 64 of twenty six merchants under heavy escort – including two carriers – being detected by Luftwaffe reconnaissance and shadowed by Junkers of 1.(F)/Aufkl.Gr. 124. Initial attacks by U-boats achieved nothing and on 7 February, twenty-five Ju 88s of II./KG 26 took off with strict instructions via teleprinter from Göring to attack the carriers. Over the next three days, reinforced by III./KG 26, the torpedo bombers repeatedly attempted to batter their way through heavy anti-aircraft fire and carrier fighters to attack the convoy, the carriers themselves never seen. The corvette HMS *Denbigh Castle* was the sole casualty from JW64, torpedoed by *U992*. Bosun's Mate John Johnson was aboard the corvette:

Joining the convoy we were placed on the port side, outer ring. The weather got rougher and colder. At sea we were in two watches – four hours on and four hours off. Even when off-watch we had work to do e.g.; getting up to put out new foxing gear, or daytime the ship still had to be under normal working.

A few days out the convoy was attacked by 50 Junkers 88, mainly carrying torpedoes. I was on look-out on the port side of the bridge. I jumped on to the port bridge Oerlikon and fired at the nearest planes, which made them gain height and fly away over the other side of the convoy. The Germans lost six planes from guns and escort carrier fighters.

Two days after, a Junkers 88 came astern of us and dropped a torpedo which porpoised along our starboard side, coming over our bridge and one of our twin Oerlikons opened up, hitting the plane which caught fire and swerved away and crashed into the sea about half a mile away. I watched for some time. Nobody got out.[3]

During the disastrous battle and because of accidents in appalling visibility, KG 26 lost twenty-one men confirmed killed and forty-five missing, including *Oblt*. Rudolf Rögner, *Staffelkapitän* of 6./KG 26. Surviving crews claimed a freighter and destroyer sunk and damage to three warships and a merchant. Their inexperience, intermittent visibility and smoke and flame from crashing aircraft all probably influenced such wishful thinking as not a single hit had been made. Some Junkers only narrowly survived the battle, *Lt*. Hans-Werner Grosse's '1H+NL' of 3./KG 26 almost being lost while taking evasive action from heavy flak at wave-top height, the aircraft's starboard propeller blades striking the sea surface and shearing a considerable amount off each blade. He nursed his badly vibrating aircraft back to Bardufoss. However, despite the exorbitant claims, Göring, furious at the lack of success against the carriers, angrily teletyped his displeasure to the *Geschwader* headquarters.

By this stage KG 26 had been reduced to two *Gruppen*, I./KG 26 disbanding in January and most pilots and crews sent to II.*Gruppe*, though at least one officer, and the *Gruppe* staff posted to single-engine fighter units in Germany. The ground crew were dispatched to Denmark and enlisted into the ranks of a Luftwaffe field division, expecting to see action soon against British ground forces.

On 17 February Convoy RA64 of thirty-three merchants departed Kola Inlet for Great Britain in bitter winter conditions of gales and exceptionally poor visibility. The convoy was involved in 'Operation Open Door' in which 525 Norwegian civilians were evacuated from the island of Sørøya by British and Canadian destroyers at the request of the Norwegian government following fighting between German troops and Norwegian resistance. Deposited in Murmansk, they were then distributed among the merchant ships returning to Britain. Despite the severe weather, U-boats torpedoed three ships from RA64 before the weather ominously moderated. KG 26 then attempted to attack on 20 February, RA64 only just having managed to reform after being scattered by the storms. In the face of relentless anti-aircraft fire the torpedo-carrying Ju 88s failed to score a single strike on the main body of the convoy or four stragglers nearby, while losing six aircraft to Wildcat fighters from HMS *Nairana*. Unfortunately, in a crass overstating of the facts, probably exaggerating already inflated claims by the torpedo crews, *OKW* issued a communique through its daily reports in which it stated that:

> As already announced on 20 February, torpedo aircraft units under the command of *Obstlt*. Stemmler in stormy seas and difficult weather conditions attacked a convoy travelling from Murmansk to England, sinking two light cruisers, including one of the Leander Class, two destroyers and eight merchant ships totalling 57,000GRT. Three other merchants of 19,000GRT were so badly damaged by torpedoes that their loss is certain. Our units lost only two aircraft despite heavy defences.

Junkers Ju 88A-17 of 3.KG 26 ready for take-off from Bardufoss.

The days following yielded no KG 26 success as both *Gruppen* mustered every serviceable aircraft to attack RA64 again, losing three aircraft and incorrectly claiming two freighters. Not until 23 February, the final attempts against RA64, did a torpedo actually strike home. During the previous day one of the worst storms encountered in the Barents Sea had struck, Force 12 easterly gales scattering the convoy once more, intensifying yet further after nightfall as temperatures plunged to 40° below zero. The 14,245GRT freighter SS *Henry Bacon* suffered damage to her steering gear, causing her to drop out of station for repair, when it was sighted by the bombers 47 miles from the main body of the convoy. Gunners opened fire at the attacking Ju 88 and Ju 188 aircraft, claiming five shot down before a torpedo struck the starboard side of No. 5 hold, causing the aft ammunition magazine to explode. Badly holed and with steering gear and propeller destroyed, the ship sank by the stern and was gone within an hour. A lack of undamaged lifeboats left several crew members stranded on the sinking ship, Chief Engineer Donald Haviland relinquishing his place to a younger crew member and subsequently dying with his ship. His selfless courage was posthumously rewarded with the Distinguished Service Medal. The ship's Bosun created a makeshift raft for six gunners and five stranded crewmen, saving their lives, while he stayed with Haviland, posthumously awarded the Meritorious Service

Medal. Three destroyers were despatched to rescue survivors from the freezing water, arriving on the scene to find people barely conscious and unable to move, Royal Navy men jumping into the sea with ropes fastened to them to assist survivors. While twenty-two crew members – including Captain Alfred Carini – and seven members of the US Navy Armed Guard were killed, the remaining crew and every one of the Norwegian refugees aboard were saved.

Ironically, the unexpectedly tough resistance from *Henry Bacon* led to KG 26's premature disengagement, many aircraft now low on fuel or suffering damage from the anti-aircraft fire. The remainder of RA64 remained unmolested and SS *Henry Bacon* was the last ship to be sunk by Luftwaffe torpedoes.

Few operations were flown by KG 26 until April, although several Ju 88s and Ju 188s attempted to attack a convoy near Iceland on 30 March, failing to locate their target but suffering casualties nonetheless. Low on fuel, one Ju 188A-3 of III./KG 26 crashed at Høknesvatnet Namsos, the crew successfully bailing out. A second Ju 188 crashed further to the south on Rostu mountain in Sunndal, the crew also bailing out and landing in the area of Hoddøy/Spillum where one man drowned. A Ju 88A-17 made a forced landing at Ellingsråsa, Utvorda, low on fuel while a fourth aircraft, another Ju 188, was reported missing at sea, west of Trondheim.

As the Wehrmacht faced destruction, men were still recognised for their service and during March *Oblt*. Reimer Voss, *Staffelkapitän* of 4./KG 26, and *Hptm*. Rudolf Schmidt, *Gruppenkommandeur* of II./KG 26, were both awarded the Knight's Cross.

The lull in operations ended on 12 April when orders were received from Oslo that both *Gruppen* would embark on an 'armed reconnaissance' of Britain's north-east coast to attack presumed shipping concentrations. For this poorly conceived mission, ten crews of II./KG 26 led by *Oblt*. Fritz Dombrowski, *Staffelkapitän* 6./KG 26, and eight of III./KG 26 under the command of *Hptm*. Fritz Gehring, *Staffelkapitän* 7./KG 26, were made ready to cover the area between the Orkneys and Firth of Forth; both *Gruppen* planning landfall at Petershead, Dombrowski then turning north, Gehring to the south.

Almost predictably, once over the North Sea, the outbound Ju 88A-17s and Ju 188s were intercepted by thirty-seven RAF Mosquitos, escorted by twenty-four P-51 Mustangs, returning from shipping attacks in the Skagerrak. The battle that followed resulted in KG 26 jettisoning its torpedoes, losing six aircraft and all of their crews from II./KG 26

The '*Hohentwiel*'-equipped Ju 188A-3 of 9./KG 26 flown from Trondheim to RAF Fraserburgh, Aberdeenshire, Scotland, on 2 May 1945 by *Oblt.* Rolf Kunze.

including Dombrowski and *Oblt.* Friedrich Ebert the *Staffelkapitän* of 6./KG 26, and a single aircraft from III./KG 26, all four men killed including observer Knight's Cross holder *Ofw.* Herbert Kunze.

At the end of April radio monitoring detected traces of convoy traffic near Murmansk, which was confirmed by aerial reconnaissance, and all airworthy aircraft of KG 26 were readied for yet another attempted attack. Crews were briefed, aircraft armed, and engines preheated before ignition as KG 26 prepared for action despite the odds against success. Fortunately for them, news of Adolf Hitler's death in Berlin forestalled any such attack, cancelled as the aircraft made ready to take off. The end of the Third Reich was evident to even the most ardent believers and 22-year-old *Oblt.* Rolf Kunze of 9./KG 26 flew his '*Hohentwiel*'-equipped Ju 188A-3 from Trondheim to RAF Fraserburgh in Aberdeenshire, Scotland, on 2 May to surrender. Aboard his aircraft, ironically, he had the *Gruppe*'s NSFO – *Nationalsozialistische Führungsoffiziere* – the officer charged with ensuring his unit adhered to the ideals of Nazi Germany, a position created in the Wehrmacht following the 20 July attempt on Hitler's life. That same day Knight's Cross holder *Hptm.* Fritz Gehring, *Staffelkapitän* of 7./KG 26, and his crew were killed in an accident when his Ju 188 A-3 crashed at Lavangsfjorden, north of Narvik, during a ferry flight to the south.

The observer officer from *Tirpitz*'s Arado complement, at left, held in French captivity at Mulsanne Officers' Camp from May 1945 to July 1947. As yet not firmly identified, he began his career in the Kriegsmarine and here stands in illustrious company alongside a naval medical officer and U-boat commanders *Kaptlt.* Horst von Schroeter, *Kaptlt.* Karl-Heinz Marbach, *Kaptlt.* Alfred Eick, and an unidentified Army *Oberleutnant.* (James Payne)

Kampfgeschwader 26 – the '*Löwe Geschwader*' – had been the Luftwaffe's first dedicated torpedo bomber unit, following the lead established by the *Küstenflieger*, and it remained its last. On the final day of the war aircraft of the *Geschwader* were involved in the evacuation of wounded troops from Kurland who faced, at best, certain Soviet imprisonment. Each aircraft flew with only pilot and wireless operator, leaving room for up to eight men to be taken aboard. They joined the efforts of *Seenotstaffel* flying boats and surface craft and *Seeaufklärungsgruppe* 126 that had been shuttling thousands of retreating troops and civilians as part of an air bridge from the island of Rugen to the west. Several aircraft were shot down including one Do 24 brought down by Soviet tank fire and crashing into the Kamper See killing the crew and at least seventy-five refugee children passengers shortly before the final collapse and surrender, effective as of midnight, 8 May 1945.

Appendix

Aircraft Introduced into the Luftwaffe Maritime Forces 1942–1945

Blohm & Voss BV 222 'Wiking' (Viking)

Ordered initially by Deutsches Lufthansa, following initial trials it was modified for Luftwaffe transport purposes, eventually finding its way to long-range reconnaissance. Though underpowered, it was robust and popular to fly.

General characteristics
Crew: Eleven–fourteen
Length: 37m
Wingspan: 46m
Height: 10.9m
Empty weight: 30,650kg
Powerplant:
(V1-V6 and V8): Six Bramo 323 R (from 1842 R-2) 9-cylinder petrol engines
A series (V7, C-series): Six Junkers Jumo 207C 6-cyl. liquid-cooled opposed piston 2-stroke diesel engines

Performance
Maximum speed: 330km/h @ 46,000kg @ sea level
Cruising speed: 300km/h @ sea level, 344km/h @ 5,550m
Range: 6,100km (4,067nm) at 245km/h
Endurance: 28 hours at 245km/h
Service ceiling: 7,300m

Armament
Three 20mm MG 151/20 cannon (one each in forward turret and two wing turrets, upper surfaces behind outer nacelles)
Five 13 mm MG 131 machine guns (one in nose and four in beam positions)

Dornier Do 217

The Do 217 was a successful design able to carry a greater bomb load than both the Ju 88 and the He 111 at high speed. Until the introduction of the He 177 it was the Luftwaffe's largest bomber. However, it was plagued with issues of poor stability in flight, and underpowered engines for an aircraft of its size.

General characteristics
  Crew: Four (E, K, and M bomber models)
  Length: 17.3m
  Wingspan: 19m
  Height: 5m
  Empty weight: 8,850kg
  Powerplant:
    (E-2, J-2) Two BMW 801A or 801M 18-cylinder two-row radial engines
    (K-2) Two BMW 801D 18-cylinder two-row radial engines
    (M-1) Two Daimler-Benz DB 603A V-12 inverted liquid-cooled piston
    engines
Performance
  Maximum speed: 475km/h @ sea level, 560km/h @ 5,700m
  Cruising speed: 400km/h @ optimum altitude
  Range: 2,180km (1,178nm) with maximum internal fuel
  Service ceiling: 9,500m without bomb load, 7,370m with maximum internal
    bomb load
Armament
  E-2:
  One fixed 15mm MG 151/15 in the nose
  One 13mm MG 131 in dorsal turret
  One 13mm MG 131 in lower rear gondola
  Three 7.92mm MG 15 in nose and beam windows
  K-2:
  As above plus four 7.92mm MG 81 fixed rearward-firing in tail, plus optional
    pair in fixed rearward facing nacelles operated by pilot
  M-1:
  As E-2 plus MG 15s replaced by MG 81s
  Bomb load: Maximum bomb load 4,000kg internally, or (E-2) two FX 1400
    glide bombs or (K-3) two Hs 293 guided missiles

Heinkel He 177

The only operational long-range bomber of the Luftwaffe, it was plagued with
design problems and faults. A four-engined aircraft, it outwardly appeared twin-
engined with two occupying each nacelle. Among the many faults was a badly design
oil pump hindered engine lubrication, causing myriad problems within the tightly
packed engine area that could lead to fire so much so common that it gained the
nickname *das Reichs fliegende feuerzeug* (the Reich's flying lighter) from airmen. An
insistence that it be capable of dive-bombing, led to ludicrous delays in reaching
a viable production model, and was never highly regarded for its airworthiness
though it was capable of high speeds if handled well.

General characteristics
  Crew: Six
  Length: 22m
  Wingspan: 31.44m
  Height: 6.67m
  Empty weight: 16,800kg
  Powerplant: Two Daimler-Benz DB 610 24-cylinder liquid-cooled piston
    engines 2,900 PS (2,860hp; 2,133 kW) (paired DB 605 V-12 engines)
Performance
  Maximum speed: 565km/h @ 6,000m
  Combat range: 1,540km (832nm)
  Service ceiling: 8,000m
Armament
  One 7.92mm MG 81 machine gun in glazed nose
  One 20mm MG 151 cannon in forward ventral Bola gondola position
  One 13mm MG 131 machine gun in rear ventral Bola gondola position
  Two 13mm MG 131 machine guns in *Fernbedienbare Drehlafette* FDL 131Z
    remotely-operated forward dorsal turret, full 360° traverse
  One 13mm MG 131 machine gun in manned *Hydraulische Drehlafette* HDL
    131/1 aft dorsal turret
  One 20mm MG 151/20 cannon in tail position.
  Bomb load: Up to 7,000kg internally, up to 2,500kg externally on each ETC
    2000 underwing rack, or up to three FX 1400 glide bombs or Hs 293 guided
    missiles (with FuG 203 *Kehl*)
  MCLOS transmitter installed) externally, or two LT 50 torpedoes under the
    wing

Junkers Ju 188

A development of the versatile Ju 88, the 188 possessed a larger, yet more streamlined
crew and extensively glazed compartment, more aerodynamically efficient pointed
wings and a larger, squared tail. The crews fortunate enough to be assigned to the
aircraft held it in high regard, although it was never produced in sufficient quantity
to have any real effect on the war.

General characteristics
  Crew: Four
  Length: 14.948m
  Wingspan: 22m
  Height: 4.45m
  Empty weight: 9,900kg
  Powerplant: Two BMW 801D-2 14-cylinder air-cooled radial piston engines

Performance

Maximum speed: 499km/h @ 6,000m
Cruising speed: 375km/h @ 5,000m
Combat range: 2,190km (1,460nm)
Service ceiling: 9,347m with 2,000kg bomb load

Armament

One 20 mm MG 151/20 cannon in nose
Three 13mm MG 131 machine guns (dorsal turret, rear dorsal, rear ventral)
Bomb load: 3,000kg internally, or two torpedoes under inner wings

Junkers Ju 290

Like many heavy Luftwaffe aircraft, the Ju 290 originated as a civil Lufthansa design. Capable of long distances – three A-5s made a round trip to Manchuria in 1944 – once equipped with heavy armament, thicker armour and extended fuel capacity (able to be jettisoned) it became an effective maritime reconnaissance aircraft though too few were ever produced and too late in the war.

General characteristics

Crew: Nine
Length: 28.64m
Wingspan: 42m
Height: 6.83m
Empty weight: 24,000kg
Powerplant: Four BMW 801D 14-cylinder air-cooled radial piston engines

Performance

Maximum speed: 439km/h @ 5,800m
Cruising speed: 360.5km/h @ 5,800m
Range: 6,148km (4,099nm)
Service ceiling: 6,000m

Armament

Two 20mm MG 151/20 cannon in dorsal turrets
Two 20mm MG 151/20 in tail
Two 20mm MG 151/20s at waist
One 20mm MG 151/20 in gondola
Two 13mm (MG 131 machine guns in gondola
Bomb load: Up to 3,000kg or up to three FX 1400 glide bombs or Hs 293 guided missiles.

Notes

Chapter 1

1 *General der Flieger* Ulrich Kessler, Report of Interrogation #5779, 20 September 1945, interviewing officer Captain Halle.
2 SKL KTB 19 March 1942.
3 SKL KTB 14 April 1942.
4 SKL KTB 9 June 1942.
5 SKL KTB 28 March 1942.
6 The FF suffix denoted '*Flügel Fest*' (fixed-mount) while the M related to the '*Minengeschoss*' (explosive shell) moulded with thinner walls allowing an increased explosive charge. Being lighter it possessed a high muzzle velocity with less recoil than earlier projectiles.
7 SKL KTB 26 June 1942.
8 *B.d.U.* KTB 11 June 1942.
9 The commander of HMS *Wild Swan*, Lieutenant Commander Claude Sclater, was awarded the DSO for the action. The sinking of the Spanish trawlers was not officially recognised by Franco's government until 1947 and no official complaint lodged.
10 On Hitler's insistence Udet had been appointed to this position, for which he was completely unsuitable. Udet, a First World War Ace of Richthofen's 'Flying Circus', was obsessed with dive-bombing, but unable to see clearly where it was an unsuitable concept such as the He 177. Unable to cope with the bureaucracy and intricacies of his position, blamed for many of its disastrous decisions by Milch and Göring, not all of which he had a hand in, he committed suicide on 17 November 1941.
11 Quoted in David Irving, *The Rise and Fall of the Luftwaffe*, p.190.
12 Stenogram of Göring conference, Göring conf, 13 September 1942, quoted by Irving, *The Rise and Fall of the Luftwaffe*, p.192.
13 David Irving, *Göring*, p.562.
14 Leopold Wenger's letters from France, February – July 1942, http://carolyn yeager.net/leopold-wengers-letters-france-february-july-1942. Though I completely disagree with Ms Yeager's politics and historical viewpoint, Poldi's letters are fascinating.
15 Frank Liesendahl was posthumously awarded the Knight's Cross on 4 September 1942, credited with 142 combat missions.
16 Admiralty War Diary, 17 July 1942.

17 Schröter was awarded the German Cross in Gold on 21 August and later, on 24 September, the Knight's Cross for the accumulated tally of two small warships and 20,000 tons of merchant shipping destroyed.

18 Dennis Richards and Hilary St. George Saunders, *Royal Air Force 1939-1945, Volume II, The Fight Avails*, HMSO, 1954, p.108.

19 Mallmann Showell (ed.), *Führer Conferences on Naval Affairs*, p.280.

20 SKL KTB, 30 May 1942.

21 Mallmann Showell (ed.), *Führer Conferences on Naval Affairs*, p.283.

Chapter 2

1 Hajo Hermann, *Eagle's Wings*, p.145.

2 Baumbach, *The Life and Death of the Luftwaffe*, pp.157–8.

3 Efficient Allied intelligence was a prerequisite for the success of *Torch*. Combined with ULTRA and battlefield listening posts, the Allies had also consistently broken the Abwehr and *Sicherheitsdienst* (SD) ciphers, gleaning information on the effectiveness of deception operations, intended countermoves to the invasion and Vichy French and Spanish reactions to the initial landings.

4 On 5 November 1942, the incoming Convoy KMF1 divided west of Gibraltar into KMF1 (A) (Fast) (Algiers, Algeria) and KMF1 (O) (Fast) (Oran, Algeria). The second major Convoy KMS1 (Slow) divided into KMS1 (A) (Slow) (Algiers, Algeria) and KMS1 (O) (Slow) (Oran, Algeria).

5 After Action Report, 12 November 1942, NARA NND735017.

6 Kretschmar was promoted, ending the war a *Major* and *Staka* of 4. *Seenotstaffel*. Account cited in *Major* W. Kretschmar, *Der Aufbau des Seenotdienstes an der Lybischen Kueste*. Kretschmar's unpublished study was prepared for the United States Air Force and in turn used as source material for Oberstleutnant Carl Hess' *The Air Sea Rescue Service of the Luftwaffe in World War II*, unpublished manuscript held by USAF Air University.

7 Martlet was the initial British designation for Grumman Wildcat fighters, though by early 1944 they were reverted to the name Wildcat to eliminate confusion with American suppliers.

8 S.D. Felkin, 'Radio Controlled Bombs,' ADI(K) Report No. 465A/1943, 14 November 1943, UK National Archives, Air Ministry Directorate of Intelligence: Intelligence Reports and Papers, Assistant Director of Intelligence, AIR 40/2876.

9 Baumbach, *The Life and Death of the Luftwaffe*, p.105.

10 Ibid, pp.155–6

11 Interrogation of *Reichsmarschall* Hermann Göring, Ritter Schule, Augsburg, 10 May 1945.

12 Admiralty War Diary 31 December 1942.

13 Graber and his remaining crew – *Uffz.* Rudolf Gerlach, Co-pilot; *Ogefr.* Karl Heinz Graebig, Obs; *Ofw.* Walter Jüttner, R/O 1; *Uffz.* Xaver Rappl, R/O 2; and *Uffz.* Heinz Fröhling, Gnr, were all subsequently posted as missing in action.

14 *Luftwaffenkommando Südost* became an independent command from 10 March 1943, answering directly to the Luftwaffe Operational Staff. Von Waldau was killed in an air crash near Petric on 17 May 1943, after which Göring ordered 'the

use of Storch aircraft for flights to the front is forbidden. Only twin-engine or multiple-engine aircraft are allowed.'

15 Rudi Schmidt, *Achtung – Torpedos Los!*, pp.166–7.

16 *Fort Babine* would later be sunk by Luftwaffe aircraft in September 1943 in the Atlantic.

17 The attack on Gonnosfanadiga remains a subject of some controversy in Sardinia where eyewitnesses contest to this day the USAAF account of poor visibility over the town itself. By their recollections it was a bright sunny day, and the bombers were preceded by P-38 escort fighters before beginning to unload their bombs over the town centre itself.

18 Koch was attached for temporary duty to III./KG 40 until June 1943.

19 Kesselring maintained his new command's headquarters at Frascati, alongside Richthofen.

20 Schröter, *Erinnerungen aus meinem Leben*, pp.215, 218, unpublished autobiography, quoted in Morten Jessen and Andrew Arthy, *Focke-Wulf Fw 190 in the Battle for Sicily*.

Chapter 3

1 Buccholz had been superseded in November 1941 by *Oblt.* Walter Bestehorn, formerly a pilot with 2./Kü.Fl.Gr. 506, and rated as an 'active and excellent squadron leader'. Bestehorn was removed as *Staka* on 29 May 1942 during an investigation into the accidental deaths of *Ob.Gefr.* Karl-Heinz Schwidrowski (pilot), *Uffz.* Günther Bruhns (observer) and Erhard Jürgensen (engineer) after their He 59 'NE+TF' crashed after take-off. Apparently due to ground crew negligence, one of the aircraft's wings had not been secured following repairs and detached shortly after take-off. Bestehorn, as *Staka*, was held ultimately responsible as he had given permission for the test flight to be made. On 6 August 1942 he was transferred to 3./Aufkl.Gr. 125 and named provisional *Staka* of the redesignated 3./SAGr. 125 on 29 June 1943.

2 *Major* Walter Gladigau, *Der Seenotdienst der Luftwaffe im Schwarzen Meer.* Gladigau's unpublished study was prepared for the United States Air Force and in turn used as source material for Oberstleutnant Carl Hess' *The Air Sea Rescue Service of the Luftwaffe in World War II*, unpublished manuscript held by USAF Air University.

3 The Ju 90 had, in turn, been inspired by the long-distance Ju 89 'Ural bomber' requested by the far-sighted *Generalleutnant* Walther Wever and cancelled following his death as the Luftwaffe concentrated on tactical bombers and ground support aircraft instead.

4 J.L. Roba, and C. Craciunoiu, *Seaplanes Over the Black Sea*, pp.57–8.

5 Though 132 U-boat commanders were awarded the German Cross in Gold, only four had received the decoration for service in the Luftwaffe: Jürgen Ebert (*U927*) awarded 25 November 1942 when *Staka* 10./KG 77; Ralf Jürs (*U778*) awarded 24 June 1943 while on Stab/*Aufklärungs-Führer Schwarzes Meer West*; Helmut Knollmann (*U1273*) awarded on 31 August 1943 while in Stab II./KG 26; and Rolf Thomsen (*U1202*) awarded 14 October 1943 while in KG 26.

6 On 9 July, while establishing a small weather station on the north coast of Bear Island near Gravodde, a shore party from *U629* found the Ju 88. The U-boat men saw damage to the undercarriage while the middle of the fuselage was burnt out. Emergency rations inside the aircraft were intact and a rubber dinghy was found on the beach. The U-boat men blew up the stranded Junkers before returning to *U629*. The pilot, *Oberfeldwebel* Otto Schenk, and his crew were later lost after transfer to the Mediterranean when their 4./KG 30 aircraft '4D+MM' was shot down near Djidjelli on 22 November 1942.

7 SKL KTB 29 April 1942

8 Aircraft HE 115B1/C 'SD+XP' transferred to 1./Kü.Fl.Gr. 906 and was shot down by flak on 13 September 1942; He 115 B2/C 'CA+BW' transferred to 1./Kü.Fl.Gr. 406 and was subsequently lost to storm damage on 26 January 1943; He 115C 'K6+LH' transferred to 1./Kü.Fl.Gr. 906.

9 David B. Craig, *The Story of the SS Dover Hill in Russia, 1943*. World War 2: People's War; http://www.bbc.co.uk/history/ww2peopleswar/stories/36/a5268936.sHptml.

10 Ibid. Captain Wilfred Geoffrey Perrin (Master) and four of his officers were awarded the OBE, while the remaining fourteen men – including Craig – were awarded the King's Commendation for Brave Conduct.

11 Zezschwitz was former the *Staka* of 2./Kü.Fl.Gr. 506, commander of elements of Kü.Fl.Gr. 706 based in southern Norway before appointed Chief of Staff *Luftflotte* 5.

12 SKL KTB 28 July 1943.

13 Both Canadians were later killed in a crash south-west of Launceston in Cornwall, on 28 June 1944.

14 The remainder of the crew were taken prisoner. Hubert Both died on 7 September 1943 in a prisoner of war camp in Astrakhan. Paul Claas had flown at least 350 combat missions, winning the Knight's Cross on 14 March 1943 by which time he had already carried out 311 such flights, 208 of them on the Eastern Front.

Chapter 4

1 On the morning of 12 December 1942 limpet mine explosions damaged the blockade-runners *Dresden* and *Tannenfels*, and the merchant ships *Portland* and *Alabama*; a result of Operation *Frankton* in which ten Royal Marines, launched in five kayaks from the submarine HMS *Tuna*, had penetrated Bordeaux Harbour basin along the Gironde River. Six of the British commandos were captured and executed, two died of hypothermia and only two survived.

2 Hiroshi Yasunaga, *Shito no Suiteitai*, Asahi Sonorama, 1994. Selected text quoted on www.j-aircraft.com/research/stories/yasunaga1.html. One of the Arados was eventually burnt out and replaced by a bartered Japanese Reishi floatplane. Horn's command departed Penang in November 1944 under increasing Allied pressure and relocated to Surabaya, handing over its aircraft to the Imperial Japanese Navy at Germany's surrender.

3 SKL KTB 1 March 1943.

4 Necesany was appointed Chief of Staff of I./ZG 1 in November 1943 and killed in action in February 1944 over Biscay, his Ju 88C-6 hit by gunfire from a

PB4Y-1 of VB 103. He was posthumously awarded the *Ehrenpokal*, credited with six victories.

5   Sönke Nietzel, *Der Einsatz der Deutschen Luftwaffe über dem Atlantik und der Nordsee*, Bernard & Graefe, 1995, p.194.

6   Mallmann Showell (ed.), *Führer Conferences on Naval Affairs*, p.333.

7   Ibid, p.334

8   Chris Goss, *Bloody Biscay*, pp.72–3.

9   Sönke Neitzel, *Soldaten – On Fighting, Killing and Dying: The Secret Second World War Tapes of German POWs*, Simon & Schuster UK, 2012, Kindle Edition Location 1287.

10 02.06.1943 No 461 Squadron Short Sunderland GR3 EJ134 N F/Lt Colin Braidwood Walker, http://aircrewremembered.com/walker-colin.html

11 SKL KTB 10 June 1943.

12 *264 Squadron News*, January 2017, Issue 1/17, 'My Time with 264 Squadron, by Harry Reed', p.10.

13 (B) *Obltn.d.R.* Karl-Heinz Jammers, (FF) *Fw*. Fritz Raßge, (Bf) *Uffz*. Ralf Hansen, (Bs) *Ogefr*. Kurt Riedel, (Bm) *Ogefr*. Rudolf Mischek. It was the second BV 138 lost by Aufkl.St. (DSee) in as many days, 'KI+MQ' being shot down near the Spanish coast during reconnaissance mission with the entire crew also posted as missing in action: (B) *Lt*. Hans Spanniel, (FF) *Fw*. Willi Seidelmann, (Bf) *Uffz*. Heinz Scholz, (Bm) *Uffz*. Alfred Krata, (Bs) *Uffz*. Werner Halwas.

14 SKL KTB 21 June 1943.

15 'X4+FH' (the first prototype of 'C-series', involved in Baltic trials) and 'X4+GH' were also allocated on that date though still in trials and never actually deployed to the Atlantic, instead entering August service as transport aircraft in Norway.

16 Baumbach, *The Life and Death of the Luftwaffe*, pp.119–20.

17 Matern was posthumously awarded the Knight's Cross the following day.

18 *Major* Helmut Liman – *Staka* 7./KG 40 – who led the attack on the 'Faith' convoy was later killed on 27 September 1944 while engaged on a passenger service flight from Germany to France. His Fw 200 was shot down and crashed at St Nicolas-les-Citeaux, Cote d'Or, killing all on board after being attacked by a Beaufighter of USAAF 415th Night Fighter Squadron, piloted by Capt. Harold F. Augsburger. *Oberleutnant* Egon Scherret and his crew were taken prisoner on 13 December 1943 after their aircraft force-landed near Ballydrennan Village, NW of Nenagh, County Tipperary, Ireland, two engines failing due to anti-aircraft fire from Convoy ON 214. *Hauptmann* Ludwig Progner was awarded the German Cross in Gold on 17 October 1943 and rose to be *Staka* 12./KG 40 at the beginning of November. He ended the war as *Staka* Verb.St. Norwegen.

19 Chris Goss, *Fw 200 Condor Units of World War 2*, Bloomsbury Publishing, 2016, Kindle Edition Locations 1118–1119.

20 Rich Tuttle, 'The War's Oddest Dogfight', *Air & Space Magazine*, May 2015. https://www.airspacemag.com/military-aviation/wars-oddest-dogfight-180954663/#RmoIeQVGPcfgA8g2.9

21 Ibid.

22 SKL KTB 22 August 1943.

Chapter 5

1 Bülowius later relocated his headquarters to Sala Consilina on the Italian mainland.

2 SKL KTB 9 July 1943.

3 War Damage Rep #46 – LST Rep of Torpedo, Projectile, Bomb & Fire Damage Including Losses in Action to 12/7/43, Bureau of Ships, 9/1/1944. NARA, Record Group 38, Roll 1252.

4 'History of the Naval Armed Guard Afloat – World War II, Office of Naval Operations, USN Administration in WWII', OP-414, p.135. The US Naval Armed Guard was a service branch responsible for defending US and Allied merchant ships from attack by enemy aircraft, submarines and surface ships, its men serving primarily as gunners, signalmen and radio operators on cargo ships, tankers, troopships and other merchant vessels.

5 The *Regia Aeronautica* had operated its own procured Ju 87s since 1940 after the first team of Italian pilots and groundcrew completed a conversion training course at Graz, Austria, in August 1940.

6 Stemmler had had a remarkable war thus far. Having fought with the Condor Legion's bomber unit K/88, he had been appointed *Staka* of 4./KG 51 in September 1940, moved to 4./KG 51 for Operation *Barbarossa* where he was shot down behind Soviet lines near Ternopol and burned on his face and hands. For fourteen days he was hidden by sympathetic Ukrainians before the German lines advanced and he was able to re-join his unit. In December 1942 he was made *Gruppenkommandeur* II./KG 77, rising to provisional *Kommodore* by February 1943.

7 'HS and FX bombs: technical information', September 1943, Air Ministry, UK National Archives, file AIR 14-3611.

8 Molinnus was later made *Gruppenkommandeur* on 10 September but was killed in an accident aboard Do 217E-5 '6N+CC' at Istres on 4 October.

9 SKL KTB 25 August 1943.

10 Lt. Comm. Hill subsequently rightly reckoned that radical evasive manoeuvring by a ship under attack could turn inside the turning circle of an Hs 293 which would stall and fall into the sea if the operator attempted to follow it closely.

11 Admiralty War Diary, 27 August 1943.

12 Burleigh was awarded the Silver Star for his actions.

13 USS *Kendrick* was later towed to the shipyards in Norfolk, Virginia, and repaired, re-entering service by December 1943 with a rebuilt stern.

14 SKL KTB 5 September 1943.

15 With many survivors of the Frascati bombing fleeing into the countryside, the Wehrmacht at first considered razing the ruins with flamethrowers lest disease spread from the hundreds of unburied corpses. However, local townspeople, with Wehrmacht assistance, eventually recovered the dead and buried them. After the destruction of Frascati, Richthofen moved his *Luftflotte* 2 headquarters to Malcesine on Lake Garda, while Kesselring relocated to a location in the Sabine Hills north-east of Rome, that included a labyrinthine bunker complex stretching

nearly four kilometres constructed originally on Mussolini's orders at Monte Soratte.

16 National Archives DEFE 3/573.

17 Italian campaign and WWII history. https://digilander.libero.it/historia militaria3/bombafritz-jope.htm

18 https://digilander.libero.it/historiamilitaria3/bombafritz-jope.htm

19 Fl.B. 604 survived the war and was taken as a prize by the US Navy and initially used as a Rhine River patrol boat, before it was returned to the Bundesmarine in 1956.

20 USS *Philadelphia* War Diary, Sept. 11 1943, https://www.fold3.com/image/ 1/270249585

21 https://www.historynet.com/an-army-nurse-describes-a-deadly-attack-on-a-hospital-ship.htm

22 Alan Peart, *From North Africa to the Arakan: The Engrossing Memoir of WWII Spitfire Ace Alan McGregor Peart DFC, RNZAF*, Grub Street, 2008 Kindle Edition Location 142.

23 Peter Karlow *Targeted by the CIA: An Intelligence Professional Speaks Out on the Scandal That Turned the CIA Upside Down*, Turner Publishing Company, 2001, p.62.

24 Jope urgently requested the use of bombers against Allied airfields on Corsica and Sardinia in order to preserve the possibility of further daylight raids by KG 100, but the resources available to the exhausted Luftwaffe bomber units of *Luftflotte* 2 would not allow it.

25 Admiralty War Diary, 1 October 1943. NARA, Roll 2172, Microfilm K-18-D

26 On 20 September 8.*Staffel* had been ordered to depart Istres for Schwäbisch Hall to begin conversion to the Heinkel He 177, later moving to Fassberg. II./KG 26, *Maj*. Georg Teske, was undergoing conversion to Ju 88A-4 in Grossenbrode at that time; I./KG 100, *Maj*. Hansgeorg Bätcher, was attached to I.*Fliegerkorps* at Kirovograd with a strength of four He 111H-11s and a single He 177A-3.

27 III./KG 30, *Maj*. Helmut Störchel, was in Leck, northern Germany, transferred from Viterbo during September with no aircraft on strength; nine lost to enemy action in September, six to accidents and the remaining seven machines transferred to other units as III.*Gruppe* moved to Germany to refit.

28 I./KG 54, *Hptm*. Gerhard Molkentin, had moved to Ingolstadt to rebuild on 6 June after serious losses in North Africa, and did not return to Italy until 7 October, while II./KG 54, *Maj*. Horst Bressel, had been in Vienna since May, returning to Bergamo on 9 October.

29 National Archives, DEFE-3-883

30 *Report on Attack by Enemy Aircraft on SS Tivives*, Lieutenant P.L. Geddes, USNR Armed Guard Officer aboard SS *Tivives*. NARA, Record Group 38, Roll 0627.

31 Ibid.

32 The Heinkel 177s were normally based at Bordeaux but moved to the forward airfield at Montpellier for that attack.

Chapter 6

1 This was not Schaar's first crash-landing: a ruptured fuel line forced him to crash-land 'D1 + KH' on 23 August, the aircraft being written off and the crew rescued by the *Seenotdienst*.

2 Admiralty War Diary, C-in-C Levant to C-in-C Mediterranean, 15 November 1943.

3 *Hauptmann* Karl August von der Fecht, commander of the *Einsatzstaffel*/KG 100 – an operational training *Staffel* of the training unit of instructors and trainees that could act as a de-facto combat unit – was wounded in the attack on Eleusis. The *Einsatzstaffel* had been formed there in April 1943 from twenty-one He 111H aircraft from II./KG100, and was disbanded in November.

4 Second Engineer Officer William White later died on 26 January 1945 as a result of wounds sustained in the attack.

5 Toulouse also hosted Louis Bréguet's aviation factory which had manufactured seaplanes and floats. Following the German occupation of Vichy it became a major centre for the repair of damaged Junkers and Heinkel aircraft.

6 Friedrich, and his crew of *Lt.* Gottfried Sachse (co-pilot), *Lt.* Heinz Arnold (observer), *Uffz.* Wilhelm Schief (wireless operator), *Fw.* Friedrich Gerschwitz (flight engineer), *Fw.* Adolf Martens (gunner), *Obgef.* Horst Bentke (gunner) and *Gef.* Heinz Engelleitner (gunner) were all posted as missing in action, the *Gruppe*'s first combat casualties. A second Ju 290 that took off loaded with life rafts to search for survivors found no trace. Finally, Schief's body was recovered by a Spanish fishing vessel near La Coruña on 15 December, the decomposed body identified by its identity disc.

7 SKL KTB 21 November 1943.

8 *B.d.U.* KTB 21 November 1943.

9 It is frequently written that the sinking was kept secret from the American public, though this is only partially correct. Many survivors were ordered not to mention the sinking in personal letters, but the loss of over 1,000 men on a troopship was officially acknowledged by February 1944, though the specifics of the enemy's use of remote-controlled missiles were omitted, the sinking originally being attributed to a U-boat. Controversy continues to this day regarding blame for the high casualty rates, frequently attributed by American sources to inept British control of the vessel and handling of the convoy as well as the cowardice of the Lascar crew. British sources refute this.

10 *Allied Secret: The Sinking of HMT Rohna*, pp.131–2. Prepared with an unpublished account written by Hans Dochtermann, *Angriff auf den US Geleitzug KMF26 vor der Bucht von Bougie,* 14 July 1992, and held by the University of Kentucky.

11 George Southern, *Poisonous Inferno. World War II tragedy at Bari Harbour*, first published by Airlife, 2005, Kindle Edition 2012, Locations 1491–1504.

Chapter 7

1 SKL KTB 6 September 1943.

2 *B.d.U.* KTB 28 November 1943.

3 The He 177A-3/R7 carried four LT 5 750kg torpedoes, two beneath the fuselage and two outboard of each engine.

4   The bodies of the entire crew were later recovered by men from FAGr. 5 Staff Company and returned to France where they were buried in the airfield's military cemetery.

5   SKL KTB 28 December 1943.

6   *Fliegerführer Atlantik* Br. Nr.1814/43 g.Kdos. vom 24.12.1943.

Chapter 8

1   Admiralty War Diary. III./KG 30 remained refitting at Leck where it had been since September.

2   Eric Edward Alley, *WW2 People's War*, https://www.bbc.co.uk/history/ww2peopleswar/stories/43/a4015243.shtml

3   Rudi Schmidt, *Achtung – Torpedos Los!*, p.187.

4   Peters survived the war and died in Essen in December 2004.

5   Also over England was *Oblt*. Kurt Maier's I./KG 100 which had returned from the Eastern Front the previous October, converted to He 177 bombers and begun flying from Chateaudun on conventional bombing missions, losing four aircraft thus far during April.

6   Deumling, *41 Sekunden bis zum Einschlag*, p.85.

7   Eyewitnesses also reported two Hs 293s seen, one jamming vessel also reporting a single signal detected and interfered with. However, it is unclear whether KG 100 took part in the attack.

Chapter 9

1   *General der Flieger* Günther Korten was severely injured by the bomb planted by Claus von Stauffenberg on 20 July in his attempt on Hitler's life. Two days later he died in hospital, being succeeded by *General der Flieger* Werner Kreipe until October and then Koller until May 1945.

2   Kessler surrendered to the Allies as a passenger aboard the U-boat *U234* when it surrendered at Portsmouth, New Hampshire on 19 May 1945, while en-route to Japan.

3   *Hauptmann* Karl-Friedrich Bergen, *Staka* 2.(F)/FAGr. 5, was killed aboard Ju 290 A-5 '9V+DK' shot down by 811 FAA Squadron fighters from HMS *Biter* while shadowing a convoy off Ireland.

4   After Action Report, Pilot 1.Lt. J.F. Luma (USAAF), Observer F/O C.G. Finlayson, 418 Squadron, NA AIR 27/1821/4.

5   Robert Forsyth, *Shadow Over the Atlantic*, p.161.

6   Baumbach, *The Life and Death of the Luftwaffe*, p.106.

7   It was a similar fate for many of the *Kampfgeschwader*, including KG 6 redesignated KG(J) 6 in November 1944 and deploying Bf 109 fighters, and KG 54, redesignated KG(J) 54 and trained on Me 262 fighters. All personnel not required for the new *Staffeln* were distributed amongst the Wehrmacht's ground forces.

8   The crew – *Fhr.* Oskar Grüner, observer; *Uffz.* Ernst Herbert Huber, wireless operator; *Uffz.* Helmut Ende, gunner and *Ogefr.* Hans Wassermann, flight engineer – were rescued by Spanish fishermen and interned in Spain. Wassermann was the only crewmember reportedly repatriated to Germany.

9   Paul Stillwell, *Assault on Normandy*, p.5.

10   During salvage operations, the US Navy recovered human remains which were interred as 'Unknown Soldiers' in the US Military Cemetery at Draguignan on the evening of 22 August 1944.

11   KG 200 was commanded by *Obstlt.* Werner Baumbach between 15 November 1944 and April 1945. *Major* Adolf Koch – formerly of '*Sonderkommando Koch*' within the Mediterranean – was *Gruppenkommandeur* of I./KG 200 between 19 April 1944 to April 1945, including the operation of a small number of seaplanes for the dropping of Abwehr and SD agents behind enemy lines in Finland. In April 1944, 2./KG 200 operated, amongst other aircraft, three Ar 196s, two He 115s and a pair of He 59s, while 3 (Erg.)/KG 200 operated three captured French LeO 246 flying boats and two Ar 196s. However, by the beginning of September 1944, operations by the KG 200 *Seeflieger* had virtually ended with the imminent defection of Finland from the Axis.

12   SKL KTB 5 October 1944.

13   Fiebig was placed in OKL reserve until February 1945 when he was appointed commander of II.*Fliegerkorps*. He was arrested after the war and sentenced to death for alleged war crimes in Yugoslavia related to the bombing of Belgrade in April 1941 and executed on 24 October 1947. Alexander Holle, promoted to *Generalleutnant*, was appointed temporary commander of *Luftflotte* 4 before ending the war as *Kommandierende General der Deutschen Luftwaffe in Dänemark*.

14   Roba and Craciunoiu, *Seaplanes Over the Black Sea*, pp.79–80.

15   Langer was posted as missing in action on 16 February 1945 after his Fw 190A-8 was shot down by P-51D Mustangs of USAAF 318th Fighter Squadron south of Gado. He had been credited with three aerial victories.

Chapter 10

1   National Archives, AIR 27/1731/18, *Squadron Number: 333 Records of Events: January 1944*. A mixed Mosquito and Catalina squadron of Norwegian pilots and crew, it had originally been created as a detachment (No. 1477 (Norwegian) Flight) of RAF 210 Squadron.

2   SKL KTB 19 October 1944.

3   John Johnson, *The Last Voyage of HMS Denbigh Castle*, Castle Class Corvette Association, Ships Logs' Association Publication, Summer 2009.

Bibliography

Books

The Rise and Fall of the German Air Force, The National Archives, 2001.

Balke, Ulf, *Kampfgeschwader 100 'Wiking'*, Motobuch Verlag, Stuttgart, 1981.

Barnett, Correlli, *Engage the Enemy More Closely*, Hodder & Stoughton, 1991.

Baumbach, Werner, *The Life and Death of the Luftwaffe*, Ballantine Books, 1960.

Bollinger, Martin, *Warriors and Wizards*, Naval Institute Press, 2010.

Dabrowski, H.P., *Heinkel He 115*, Schiffer Publishing Ltd, 1994.

Deumling, Klaus, *41 Sekunden bis zum Einschlag*, H.E.K. Creatv Verlag, 2008.

Dönitz, Karl, *Memoirs*, Weidenfeld & Nicolson, 1959.

Fontenoy, Paul E., *Aircraft Carriers: An Illustrated History of Their Impact*, ABC-CLIO, 2006.

Forsyth, Robert, *Shadow over the Atlantic: The Luftwaffe and the U-boats: 1943–45*, Osprey Publishing, 2017.

Goss, Chris, *Bloody Biscay*, Crécy Publishing, 2013.

Goss, Chris, *Fw 200 Condor Units of World War 2*, Osprey Publishing, 2016.

Griehl, Manfred, *Torpedo Fluzgeuge der Luftwaffe 1939-1945*, Podzin-Pallas Verlag, 2000.

Hayward, Joel S.A., *Stopped at Stalingrad*, University Press of Kansas, 1998.

Heinkel, Ernst, *He 1000*, Hutchinson, London, 1956.

Hermann, Hajo, *Eagle's Wings,* Guild Publishing, 1991.

Hooten, E.R., *The Luftwaffe, A Study in Air Power 1933-1945*, Classic Publications, 2010.

Hümmelchen, Gerhard, *Die Deutschen Seeflieger 1935-1945*, J.F. Lehmanns Verlag, 1976.

Irving, David, *Göring*, William Morrow & Co, 1989.

Irving, David, *The Rise and Fall of the Luftwaffe*, Electronic version copyright © 2002 by Parforce UK Ltd.

Isby, David, *The Luftwaffe and the War at Sea*, Chatham Publishing, 2005.

Jessen, Morten and Arthy, Andrew, *Focke-Wulf Fw 190 in the Battle for Sicily*, Air War Publications, 2015.

Jung, Dieter, Wenzel, Berndt and Abendroth, Arno, *Die Schiffe und Boote der Deutschen Seeflieger 1912-1976*, Motorbuch Verlag, 1995.

Kemp, Paul, *Convoy!*, Arms and Armour Press, 1993.

Kemp, Paul, *Friend or Foe: Friendly Fire at Sea 1939-1945*, Pen and Sword, 1993.

König, Christian, *Erste am Feind: Bordflugzeug und Küstenaufklärer Heinkel He 60*, Helios Verlag, 2017.

Krug, Hans-Joachim, Hirama Yōichi, Sander-Nagashima, Berthold and Niestlé, Axel, *Reluctant Allies*, Naval Institute Press, 2001.

Mallmann Showell, Jak. P. (ed), *Führer Conferences on Naval Affairs*, Greenhill Books, 1990.

Marriott, Leo, *Catapult Aircraft: Seaplanes That Flew From Ships Without Flight Decks*, Pen and Sword, 2007.

Massimello, Giovanni, Shores, Christopher, Guest, Russell and Olynyk, Fran, *History of the Mediterranean Air War, 1940–1945: Tunisia and the End in Africa, November 1942–1943*, Grub Street Publishing, 2018.

Müller, Wolfgang and Kramer, Reinhard, *Gesunken und Verschollen*, Koehlers Verlag, 1994.

Murray, Williamson, *Strategy For Defeat, The Luftwaffe 1933-1945*, Qintet Publishing 1986.

Neitzel, Sönke, *Der Einsatz der Deutschen Luftwaffe über dem Atlantik unde der Nordsee 1939-1945*, Bernard & Graefe Verlag, 1995.

Norman, Bill, *Luftwaffe Losses over Northumberland and Durham: 1939-1945*, Pen & Sword, 2002.

O'Hara, Vincent P. and Worth, Richard, *To Crown the Waves: The Great Navies of the First World War*, Naval Institute Press, 2013.

O'Hara, Vincent, Dickson, David W. and Worth, Richard, *On Seas Contested: The Seven Great Navies of the Second World War*, Naval Institute Press, 2014.

Otter, Ken, *HMS Gloucester, The Untold Story*, Pen & Sword, 2017.

Raeder, Erich, *Grand Admiral*, Da Capo Press, 2001.

Roba, J.L. and Craciunoiu, C., *Seaplanes Over The Black Sea*, Editura Modelism, Bucharest, 1995.

Schmidt, Rudi, *Achtung – Torpedos Los!*, Bernard & Graefe Verlag, Koblenz, 1991.

Spang, Christian W. and Wippich, Rolf-Harald, *Japanese-German Relations, 1895-1945: War, Diplomacy and Public Opinion*, Routledge, 2006.

Stillwell, Paul, *Assault on Normandy: First-Person Accounts from the Sea Services*, Naval Institute Press, 1994.

Thiele, Harold, *Luftwaffe Aerial Torpedo Aircraft and Operations*, Hikoki Publications, 2004.

Thompson, Adam, *Küstenflieger*, Fonthill Media, 2014.

Tomblin, Barbara, *With Utmost Spirit: Allied Naval Operations in the Mediterranean, 1942-1945*, The University Press of Kentucky, 2004.

Vajda, Ferenc A. and Dancey, Peter, *German Aircraft Industry and Production, 1933-1945*, Airlife Publishing, 1998.

Wolf, William, *German Guided Missiles: Henschel Hs 293 and Ruhrstahl SD 1400X*, CreateSpace Independent Publishing Platform; 5 edition, 2012.

Zöller, Paul, *Die letzten Junkers-Flugzeuge I: Frühe Junkers-Entwicklungen von der Junkers J1 bis zur Junkers A50*, Books on Demand, 2017.

Articles and Reports

Elefteriu, Gabriel, *Air and Naval Power in the Black Sea, 1941-1944* (essay), 26 June 2016. Written in March 2011 at the War Studies Department, King's College London (National Security Research Fellow at a Westminster policy think tank).

Gould, Major Winston A. USAF, *Luftwaffe Maritime Operations in World War II: Thought, Organization and Technology*. Research Report, Maxwell Airbase, Alabama, 2005.

Hayward, Joel S.A., *Seeking The Philosopher's Stone, Luftwaffe Operations during Hitler's Drive to the South-East, 1942-1943*, Dissertation University of Canterbury, 1996.

Jucker, Hans H., *Early German Airborne Radar Transmitter Technology*, Tube Collector Association Bulletin, Medford, OR, U.S.A. October 2002.

Plocher, *Generalleutnant* Hermann, '*The German Air Force Versus Russia*', USAF Historical Division Aerospace Studies Institute, 1958.

Reed, Harry, *264 Squadron News*, January 2017, Issue 1/17, '*My Time with 264 Squadron*'.

Stoll, Hans G. Lt. Col., USAF, *Luftwaffe Doctrine and Air Superiority Through World War Two*. Research report submitted to the Faculty, Maxwell Air Force Base, Alabama, April 1994.

Tavoy, Tal (Ph.D.), *1930s German Doctrine: A Manifestation of Operational Art*, May-June 2015, Military Review pG 56-64.

Web Resources

Axis History Forum – www.axishistory.com

Das Archiv der Deutschen Luftwaffe – www.luftarchiv.de

German Luftwaffe – www.germanluftwaffe.com

Lexicon der Wehrmacht – www.lexikon-der-wehrmacht.de

Luftwaffe der See – www.luftwaffe-zur-see.de

The Luftwaffe 1933-1945 – www.ww2.dk

The Luftwaffe Blog – http://falkeeins.blogspot.it

Warbirds Resource Group – www.warbirdsresourcegroup.org

Resource for various Allied War Diaries – www.fold3.com

Index

Page numbers in *italics* refer to captions.

People

Luftwaffe units

Ships (naval)